HANUKKAH IN AMERICA

Hanukkah in America

A History

Dianne Ashton

NEW YORK UNIVERSITY PRESS
New York and London

NEW YORK UNIVERSITY PRESS
New York and London
www.nyupress.org

References to Internet websites (URLs) were accurate at the time of writing.
Neither the author nor New York University Press is responsible for URLs
that may have expired or changed since the manuscript was prepared.

Library of Congress Cataloging-in-Publication Data
Ashton, Dianne.
Hanukkah in America : a history / Dianne Ashton.
pages   cm. — (The Goldstein-Goren series in American Jewish history)
Includes bibliographical references and index.
ISBN 978-0-8147-0739-5 (cloth : alk. paper)
1. Hanukkah—United States. 2. Judaism—United States—History—
21st century.   I. Title.
BM695.H3A84 2013
296.4'350973—dc23   2013014009

New York University Press books are printed on acid-free paper,
and their binding materials are chosen for strength and durability.
We strive to use environmentally responsible suppliers and materials
to the greatest extent possible in publishing our books.

Manufactured in the United States of America

10 9 8 7 6 5 4 3 2 1

Also available as an ebook

For Evan, Leah, and Lexi

CONTENTS

Introduction

One December evening when I was five years old, my mother helped me dress for a special occasion. She chose my turquoise satin blouse and black felt skirt decorated with big turquoise cabbage roses. It was the fifties. Mom smiled as I traded my play clothes for the outfit she had laid out, but, curiously, she remained in the same blouse and slacks she had worn all day. I alone prepared to be the center of attention. Suitably dressed and coiffed, I went off to—our living room!

There, my father had set up a tripod—huge, it seemed to me—with four blinding flood lights focused on the area in front of our fireplace. He waited for me to enter the scene before beginning to film. With mom nearby but out of range of the camera's lens, I sang the three Hanukkah candle blessings in Hebrew. As tradition mandates, they praise God first for commanding us to kindle the Hanukkah lights, second, for performing a miracle for our forefathers long ago at this season, and third, for sustaining us in life to reach this occasion. With the helper candle my mother had already lighted for me to use, I lighted the holiday candle that had already been placed in the special Hanuk-kah candelabra—called a Hanukkah menorah. Thus we marked the holiday's first evening. After the brief ceremony concluded, I opened a lovely wrapped gift (a sweater—it was Buffalo), smiled, and waved at my dad behind the camera. If my parents coached me from off screen, we will never know. While the Kodachrome eight-millimeter film dad used made the evening's movements and colorful images almost indel-ible, the camera could not preserve sounds. But it did preserve a signifi-cant turn in religious observances common in American Jewish homes in that era.

The change became apparent two nights later when my father's cousin Albert joined me in the ceremony and on camera. I recited the blessings with him, but then Albert, without a second thought, struck the box of matches and lighted both the helper candle and the first of that evening's three candles in the menorah himself. I burst into tears. Although Jewish law requires that children must be taught to light the Hanukkah candles, the tradition among most Jews who traced their heritage to eastern Europe—like my family—prefers that men light them. Albert believed he acted appropriately and never considered doing otherwise. Startled and surprised, he turned to my father for guidance. Behind the camera, my father must have instructed Albert, because he handed the lighting job over to me. Despite Jewish custom, for many mid-twentieth-century American Jewish families like mine, Hanukkah's significance lay in its ability to create memorable religious experiences for their children. The holiday that had for two millennia thanked God for preserving Judaism in the past had become a means to try to ensure the American Jewish future by impressing youngsters of its importance.[1]

The seeds of my interest in writing this book may have been planted during that confused Hanukkah evening. Clearly, it seemed to me, ordinary Jews like my family felt quite at ease in adapting and modify-ing the religious customs they practiced. In particular, those rites and customs enacted at home, without rabbinic supervision, could easily be reshaped to better express their own values. My parents' Hanukkah became a vehicle for featuring their child in a Jewish domestic frame. What other changes had American Jews made to it, and why? I won-dered. How have the experiences of other Jews in America changed the way we celebrate the holiday? The answer, I have learned, involves almost two hundred years of Jewish history in the United States. Without government support for religious institutions or clergy, Americans —Jews and non-Jews alike—must take much of religious life into their own hands. Thus, American Jews can reshape, support, aggrandize, or neglect religious practices as they see fit. Forming new congregations, they institutionalize their choices. Clergy, for their part, find it essential to persuade and educate, to inspire and motivate their coreligionists to follow approved paths. As Jews participated in American society and learned its cultural values, their religious lives reflected their encounter with that broader world. In the past and today, each person, young or old, makes a choice. Whether drawing a sharp boundary between themselves and American society or cultivating a way to navigate being Jewish while fully participating in the larger society, American Jews create their religious lives.[2] Hanukkah itself raises questions about religious boundaries and, not surprisingly, became a key occasion for thinking about the complex issues that boundaries raise.

The religious lives that American Jews create sometimes reach deep into the Jewish past and emerge with elements that are crafted into new traditions that speak to Jews' American experience. But Jews have created continuity despite historical changes before. Historians Albert I. Baumgarten and Marina Rustow explain that at many points in Jews' long history, they have "papered over" changes in their religious practices with strong appeals to older traditions, sometimes inventing new rituals that are legitimated by their aura of historicity. Baumgarten and Rustow argue that "appeals to continuity became the means by which Judaism either absorbed and legitimated innovations or sacralized ancient practices."[3] For example, two thousand years ago, the early rabbis pointed to understandings about biblical law that seemed to have descended from Moses, down the generations, in an oral tradition, to legitimate their own work on adapting biblical laws to the new circumstances of a diaspora existence. With that authority, their rabbinic teachings about ways to apply biblical law became normative for Judaism. Their creative use of the past should not surprise us. Jewish studies scholar and educator Yehuda Kurtzer points out that "memory becomes more magical, fantastical, and commanding in the hands of those who are less bound by what actually transpired and more inspired by what they might learn from it."[4] Over centuries, Jewish religious rites and traditional customs developed in a rich array, often by claiming continuity with the ancient past. Through religious recitations and rites that brought selected elements and understandings of past events into contemporary view, says professor of Jewish history and culture Yosef Hayim Yerushalmi, Jews created a distinctive historical memory linked to religious practice.[5] Their American experience posed new challenges to Jews whose previous diaspora experiences set them apart from gentile populations in varying ways, including—but not limited to —legal, political, and labor restrictions as wells as limiting where they could reside. Few of those limits described most Jews' American lives. In the United States, Hanukkah's recitations and rites were augmented, reshaped, and redefined to create memories and occasions more meaningful to American Jews.

Hanukkah's strongest American advocates seem to have been those who felt the complexities of American Jewish life most acutely. A dynamic alliance of rabbis and women became the most effective force advocating enhancing the holiday's importance. Liberal rabbis, whose congregants tended to follow few of Judaism's dictates, especially urged Jews to be more like the loyalist heroes of Hanukkah's story and to resist assimilation to American culture so influenced by Christianity. Yet liberal rabbis themselves owed their authority as much to American conditions that gave free rein to religious variety as to Judaism's teachings. Before the latter decades of the twentieth century, American Jewish women, for their part, were denied an education in Judaism's authoritative religious law and so carried little authority in religious matters. They, like most American Jews, lived in the broad and wide borderland where Jewish and American cultures coexist. For them, Hanukkah's timing in the midst of the Christmas season offered a way to perform their Jewish commitment through the holiday's rite and, for a moment, to resolve the ambiguity of being an American Jew. The holiday's story about the triumph of ancient religious loyalists in their battle to control Judaism's most sacred locale, the Temple in Jerusalem, encouraged them in their effort to remain Jews. Hanukkah's domestic focus enabled them to vivify their familial bonds, and its joyousness helped them to be happy to be Jews at a time when, in the American cultural calendar, they are most conscious of their minority status.

The eight days of Hanukkah are marked with special hymns in synagogues, but its real celebration is the domestic candle-lighting rite.
Parents recently surveyed about Hanukkah reported their most vivid
Hanukkah memory to be, as Philadelphian Philip Steel put it, "seeing
our children and grandchildren's eyes."[6] Many Jewish parents give their
children gifts at Hanukkah, sometimes on each night of the holiday.
In addition, the Hebrew words for Hanukkah and for education share
a common root, and thus custom encourages donations to charities,
especially to support Jewish educational institutions.

Gifts can strengthen both family and social relationships, and Hanukkah gifts have become especially popular over the past century in
America as parents created a Jewish alternative to Santa Claus. Their
Hanukkah gift giving reinforced the bond between parents and children as family but also as members of the larger Jewish world.[7] Jews
rarely constituted more than three percent of the population of the
United States, and many parents worried that their children might
feel left out of the national festivities surrounding Christmas without
a comparable celebration of their own. Even worse, that feeling might
lead them to dislike being Jewish. Bostonian Carol Kur explained, "We
count on those eight little candles to outshine the splendor of trees, tin-
sel, . . . [and to stand up to the] sparkling electricity of sight and sound,
so dazzlingly packaged by Madison Avenue's best, it's simply too much
to ask. Even the Maccabees [heroes of Hanukkah's origin] did not face
such overwhelming odds."[8] Hanukkah brought Jews closer to each
other and made them more visible to their communities. Some Jews living in areas without a sizeable Jewish population make a special effort
to create memorable Hanukkah experiences for their children. Anne
Bayme, who raised her children in the small town of Vidalia, Georgia,
in the 1970s, recalled, "We always got our family with grandparents
together. We also got together with friends." The Baymes also attended
their synagogue's Hanukkah Family Night, and Anne made educational
presentations in her children's school, hoping to help her children "not
to feel invisible" in December.[9] But Jews in big cities often also share
Anne's concern.

American manufacturers look to the purchasing power of Jewish
families such as the Steels and the Baymes and market their December goods for Hanukkah as well as Christmas. Publishers use National

Jewish Book Month each autumn to promote books of Jewish interest for purchase as Hanukkah gifts. In 2007, Hallmark's website offered seven different Hanukkah cards, all in a color scheme of blue and white or silver, reminiscent of Jewish prayer shawls (Hebrew: *tallitot*) and the Israeli flag. By then, those colors had become the standardized color scheme that helped customers find Hanukkah cards in stores near the red-and-green Christmas goods.[10] The American marketplace offered Jews the opportunity to express and reaffirm their Jewish identity by purchasing items to use as ritual objects that might also be displayed in their homes and to exchange as gifts on Hanukkah.[11] In the twentieth century, concerns about both children and profits, in other words, helped to lift Hanukkah to prominence.

Yet many Jews have opposed those trends. Jewish law rates Hanukkah only a minor festival, one of the two least important festivals in the Jewish religious calendar. The other is a winter festival called Purim, which, like Hanukkah, also commemorates an occasion of rescue, but that of Jews rather than Judaism, as Hanukkah does. Rules for both holidays allow Jews to work as they would on any ordinary day, unlike on the Sabbath or on an important holiday. At Hanukkah, work is banned only while the candles remain lighted. Except for the Sabbath that occurs during the week of Hanukkah, Jews are free to travel to visit each other and to attend special events. Throughout the nineteenth and twentieth centuries, those who felt Jewish life ought to be guided by rabbinic standards of religious law—often called "tradition"—resisted the power of the American holiday calendar to reshape Judaism. At least one rabbi felt it "distorted" Hanukkah, and he challenged synagogues that regularly publish the Hanukkah blessings for their members' use to also publish other blessings, such as those used on Shabbat, on Sukkot, and during morning prayers.[12] Other rabbis insisted that families who fully observed Judaism's yearlong ritual calendar kept their children sufficiently engaged in Jewish life to resist the lure of the American Christmas season and did not need a unique American-style Hanukkah.[13] Gertrude Braun Migler, whose father served Pittsburgh's Jews as a kosher butcher and maintained an Orthodox home, recalled Hanukkahs of her childhood in the 1940s that meant nothing more than lighting the candles—fat, orange-colored items.[14]

Forty years later, sisters raised in a highly traditionally observant home recalled that their religious day school in Dallas, Texas, which also served many students from minimally observant families, made Hanukkah decorations at school and at home, sang holiday songs, and read and discussed the special Hanukkah issue of the Jewish children's newspaper, *Olomeinu* (Our World). Their religious schools' lessons for Hanukkah turned on the "dangers of assimilation and acculturation." Yet, when the family relocated to Baltimore, the more observant school they attended "just didn't talk much about it in any formal sense." Religious knowledge and loyalty were "assumed."[15] In a similar way, the women's organization of the Conservative movement recently argued that "any child who has built a *sukkah* [booth constructed for prayers and meals during the autumn holiday of Sukkot] will not feel deprived of trimming a [Christmas] tree."[16] In their view, those children would not need Hanukkah to be any more elaborate than rabbinic standards made it. During the 1990s, scholars who studied attitudes about Hanukkah among a group of Jews who regularly celebrated the festival found that it "elicited no strong emotions" and was largely performed "for children."[17]

Some American Jews have felt that the commercialism demeaned Hanukkah. In 1915, a Yiddish newspaper admonished its immigrant readers to resist advertisers because "we do not want death from pleasure."[18] From that perspective, the scarcity and want that many Jewish immigrants had known in Europe lent their religious holidays, each with its own particular material goods and ritual practices, an aura of distinction and an emotional power. It made religious life more magical than the day-to-day existence. Without that contrast between the loveliness of religion and the harshness of daily life, the writer thought, Jewish life might wither and die. By the last decades of the twentieth century, when one catalog of Judaica offered fifty-three different Hanukkah menorahs with designs featuring artistic invention and whimsy, sports, family photos, or Mickey Mouse, others argued that the welter of goods specially marketed for Hanukkah had buried the holiday's religious meaning under crass commercialism.[19]

But a parade of parents, rabbis, teachers, journalists, playwrights, poets, authors, song writers, hippies, mystics, members of various men's and women's clubs, Zionists, restauranteurs, merchants, and choreographers who, since early in the nineteenth century, have exalted

Hanukkah with new hymns, songs, concerts, stories, ceremonies, lessons, customs, pageants, crafts, and foods hoped to reach the many, many other Jews among whom "the practice of religious ceremonials and rituals [was] rapidly declining."[20] Applying their many different talents to the task, Hanukkah's advocates promoted its significance in schools, clubs, and synagogues, in public squares, in their businesses, and in American Jewish homes. They turned the national seasonal celebration for domestic religion, although based in Christianity, into a festive occasion for the country's Jews, often hoping to inspire a Jewish religious renewal. Their efforts produced a religiously informed American Jewish culture that took shape each year at Hanukkah.

Rituals are "prominent in all areas of uncertainty, anxiety, impotence, and disorder," argued anthropologist Barbara Meyerhoff, and Hanukkah's rituals have long shined a bright light on the difficulties of Jews' December religious decisions, dubbed the "December dilemma."[21] Contemporary historians of religion point out that rituals are "fluid and multidimensional, capable of adapting to the changing circumstances of community life and capable of deploying meanings on several planes: for the individual, for the local community, for the (implied) universal membership. . . . [Ritual] accordingly both conserves tradition and enlarges it as it orders the practical activity of worship."[22] Because the Hanukkah culture that has been annually created and re-created is so fluid, it has been uniquely able to reflect Jews' attitudes about Jewish life in America as it has changed with new historical circumstances. Another popular Jewish holiday, the spring event called Passover, carries extensive and elaborate rules that limit creativity—although, because it, like Hanukkah, is also a domestic occasion created by families, it has also seen new American rewrites that modify its historical meaning. By contrast, the important autumn holidays of Rosh Hashanah and Yom Kippur are synagogue events under the control of clergy and so are not amenable to the creation of a holiday culture that could significantly modify their meanings. While Passover, Rosh Hashanah, and Yom Kippur hold far more important places in the Jewish religious calendar than does Hanukkah, no occasions in the fall or spring American calendars provoke the December conundrums for American Jews that Hanukkah has been able to address through its holiday culture.

Those myriad Hanukkah cultural creations largely consist of ways either to supplement the brief Hanukkah rite, to reinterpret its meaning, or to change its cultural significance by changing its performers. They have been created by both clergy and laity whose attitudes about both Judaism and America have varied across a wide spectrum of approaches, from wholehearted embraces to wary suspicions about both the authority of religious tradition, on one hand, and the power and allure of American cultural standards, on the other. Those approaches themselves have responded to changing historical circumstances that American Jews have faced over almost two hundred years.

Holidays are often complex events, bringing together—not always harmoniously—stories and practices, communities and objects, traditions and inventions. This is certainly the case with Hanukkah celebrations. Starting in the 1840s, a wide swath of Jewish interest groups took hold of the occasion and shaped it into something that held importance for them and for the particular, often widely divergent goals they hoped to achieve. Beginning with members in a Charleston, South Carolina, congregation who voiced a new meaning for the holiday in order to make it resonate within their local Jewish community as well as their Protestant religious environment, and continuing with rabbinic debates about how Judaism could survive in the progressive mood of nineteenth-century America, Hanukkah found advocates who insisted it held greater importance for modern Jews than tradition acknowledged. A new regard for the heroes of Hanukkah's origin, the Maccabees who led a revolt against a foreign conqueror of ancient Judea and then reinstated Jewish worship in the Jerusalem Temple, signaled that Hanukkah itself held a new significance for Jews in America. Over the course of nearly two centuries, various Jews have added their own creations and arguments to make sure the festival would not be overlooked or ignored. By the opening years of the twenty-first century, it has become a broadly known, public, Jewish American event.

American Jews stand in a long line of people who have fashioned special Hanukkah customs. The biblical reading for Sabbath Hanukkah from the prophet Zechariah instructs Jews to "sing and rejoice," encouraging them to create jovial festivities. Rejoicing can take many forms, and for this largely domestic occasion on cold winter evenings, mental gymnastics became common. In many eras of the Jewish past, riddles, acrostics, and arithmetical puzzles in which the answer is always forty-four (the total number of lights burned on Hanukkah) became widespread. By the fifteenth century, card games surpassed puzzles in popularity. In warmer climates, Hanukkah pleasures moved outdoors. In the Middle Ages, Jews in Venice rowed gondolas through their district, "greeting each illuminated house with a benediction and a merry Hebrew chorus." The dreidel, a small top carved with four letters that is used for one of the simplest and most enduring of Hanukkah games, has enjoyed widespread popularity, especially among children, across historical eras and climates alike.[23] By the eighteenth century, some Jewish communities made donations to educational institutions, teachers, and impoverished students on Hanukkah.

Many Jews have made Hanukkah a specially pleasurable time for children and adults. In nineteenth-century Europe, children often received Hanukkah *gelt* (German and Yiddish: coins), often with the expectation that they would give some of it to their teachers. Rabbis approved gambling only on Hanukkah, and in Alsace, in that era, people expected to "have a good time and, above all, to play games" while enjoying pickled meats.[24] Poor children in Persia visited neighbors' homes on Hanukkah, offering to protect households from the Evil Eye by burning special grasses in return for gifts. Mothers in Yemen gave children coins for purchasing sugar powder and red dye—ingredients for a sweet Hanukkah beverage. In eastern Europe, folk songs in Yiddish, the everyday language of those Jews, augmented Hanukkah's repertoire of religious tunes in Hebrew. Synagogues often hosted concerts with instrumental accompaniment, something normally banned at worship. Music, therefore, also became especially associated with Hanukkah festivities.[25]

Judaism takes food seriously. Leviticus set down rules on animals that could not be eaten (pigs and other animals that do not chew their cud or have a cloven hoof; animals that swarm, such as bugs or, among sea creatures, shellfish; and animals that die of natural causes). It also banned cooking a calf in its mother's milk.[26] Rabbinic rules extended and modified those rules, for example, banning the consuming of meat and milk in the same meal and identifying special symbolic foods to be eaten at the Passover seder. But ordinary Jews also elaborated food customs for other holidays, creating customs that symbolized each distinctive occasion. At Hanukkah, foods cooked in oil or a dairy dish that recalled elements of Hanukkah's origin stories became customary. In addition to foods that carried symbolic meaning, Jews distinguished the holiday with particular foods. Wealthier Jews might feast on roast duck, while poorer folk ate pancakes. In the twentieth century, in Jewish settlements in the future state of Israel, some Jewish children in families from the Levant visited their neighbors demanding foods for a Hanukkah feast; others serenaded householders with Ladino songs.[27] Today's Israelis eat jelly doughnuts on Hanukkah. Whatever the locale, whatever the age, Jews have deemed Hanukkah ripe for embellishment with foods, songs, charity, and games.

Yet all those embellishments, across the world and across a millennium, did not lift Hanukkah to the prominence in the Jewish calendar that it achieved in the United States in the twentieth century. Choreographed pageants in music halls, specially crafted synagogue festivals, amateur theatricals, decorations for the home, commercial greeting cards and distinctive gift items, restaurant dinner specials, crafts, holiday programming in museums and Jewish community centers, and public menorah lightings have elaborated on the simple rite to create something far more grand. I began my investigation into the holiday's popularity with one simple assumption: few people choose to do things that hold no meaning for them. If contemporary surveys show Hanukkah to be one of the two holidays American Jews celebrate most often (the other is Passover), then these Jews must have reasons for doing so. A vast sea of historical data, including private letters, articles in Yiddish-language newspapers and newsletters of congregations and women's associations, hymnals, pageant programs, and original plays and holiday manuals, suggests that four foundational conditions allowed Hanukkah to become so popular in America.

First, Hanukkah lent itself to reshaping as a significant American Jewish event because its rite is so simple. Taking only a few minutes to complete, it can be embellished with ease. Enacted in the privacy of the home, without supervision by a religious authority, modifications and adornments can be determined according to the performers' tastes. It is easy to mold.

Second, Hanukkah had the good fortune to occur in the midst of a holiday season when American culture encourages people to celebrate something that, like Christmas, brings families together and indulges children. Hanukkah enabled Jews to accept that invitation to celebrate a sanctified family life in December. Jewish children never, it emerged, begged to be taken to church. Rather, they begged for decorated trees and Santa Claus. Jews replied with Hanukkah.

Third, Hanukkah's story depicted an ancient conflict that could be retold in ways that highlighted American Jews' own dilemmas. At the holiday's origin, Jews differed, disagreed, and ultimately fought about the degree to which they should embrace Hellenic culture and customs. In America, the diverse ways Jews modified their religious practices reflected their accommodation to American culture. Through lay-run congregations, the rise of Jewish denominations, and modifications to the liturgy, they have continually transformed Judaism. In the process, endless conflicts have emerged between Jews over the proper balance between modernity and tradition. Changing trends in American cultural values also encouraged new religious adaptations, especially expanding women's roles and opportunities. Hanukkah gave American Jews an annual occasion to ponder the demands of Jewish loyalty, the dangers of dissension among Jews, and the courage they would need to remain faithful Jews while living as a small minority—something they are most aware of during December, when their minority status becomes most vivid.

Finally, Hanukkah provided an occasion to ponder God's presence and intervention in Jewish history. While every Jewish holiday directs worship to the divine, Hanukkah's story also focused attention on a crisis in the ancient Jewish past when Jews achieved something extraordinary—defeating a conqueror who had banned Judaism and regaining their religious and political independence. Different interpretations judged it either as accomplished through Jews' own devotion and bravery or as the result of divine rescue. The upheavals and terrors that modern Jews experienced in the nineteenth and twentieth centuries lent that Hanukkah story special significance. Hanukkah helped them assess the dimensions of their freedom and safety in the United States.

Today, public and private Hanukkah activities in homes, synagogues, museums, community centers, restaurants, and public squares, in media and on the web, provide American Jews with a holiday that is rich in activities for both children and adults and that appeals to the senses, the emotions, and the intellect. Hanukkah in its season looms large in the American Jewish psyche.

Many Jews argue that Hanukkah became important in the United States only as a Jewish foil to Christmas's cultural dominance in December. As such, they say, Hanukkah synthesized Jewish and American cultures. Yet what did that mean? Was the common wisdom correct? The ways in which Jewry developed Hanukkah, the meanings it selected and the activities it created, show that while it embraced some elements of American culture, it redefined or resisted others. Jews themselves often disagreed about how to understand Christmas, asking, for example, if a decorated fir tree is a sacred Christian item or not. Not only did Jews differ on how—and whether—to modify Hanukkah, but the holiday itself became a vehicle by which they commented on their differences and contested over them. But most agreed that Jewishness, with or without religious content, deserved its own cultural space.

Jews even disagreed about how to spell *Hanukkah*. American advertising, English translations of Jewish literature, and religious documents spell it in myriad ways. Because it is a Hebrew word whose first letter has no equivalent sound in English, American Jews tend to write it in ways that mimic their own pronunciation. In the 1970s, one writer concluded that the best spelling is "Chanukah"; the "Ch" signals people in the know to use the back-of-the-throat sound of the Hebrew letter *het*. But that spelling led everyone else to mispronunciations sounding like the "ch" in *chair*. Some publishers placed a dot under the *H* at the beginning of *Hanukkah* to indicate the Hebrew pronunciation, but that, too, seemed to signal correct pronunciation only to those who already knew it but left others with a simple "H" and bewilderment. Contemporary scholars of the European Jewish language, Yiddish, often spell it "Khanike," which comes closer to that language's pronunciation. In 1889, the *New York Times* wrote "Hanukkah" in its condensed version of an article that originally appeared in the *Jewish Messenger*, a local Jewish newspaper. The *Times* has spelled it that way ever since. That spelling is now itself an American Jewish tradition.[28]

Hanukkah, therefore, holds a complex relationship to American culture. In magnifying the simple holiday, Jews acted on their desire to be part of the larger society's winter festival season. In creating and revising new holiday songs and stories, they inscribed American values into Hanukkah's meaning. At the same time, though, they used their expanded Hanukkah festival to resist the lure of Christianity. By making

Hanukkah an important part of their Jewish lives, they enlivened a Jewish religious and cultural tradition. Celebrating Hanukkah each year, Jews acknowledge boundaries between themselves and Christian society. But by touting Hanukkah's "fit" with the values of the Christmas season and of American culture, they insist on their right to be different, because, "underneath," people are all the same. Moreover, by elaborating on their own religious festival that commemorates a miracle, Jews also refute secular trends in America that diminish religion's importance. So while it appears at first glance that Hanukkah elaborations are all about Jews fitting into America, closer analysis suggests that Hanukkah is the vehicle through which Jews draw distinctions between themselves and the majority society while asserting their common humanity.

Christmas may have prompted many Jews to take a new look at Hanukkah's relevance, but what they found in Hanukkah held little link to Christianity. Completely apart from Christmas's culture, American Jews used Hanukkah's story to understand the changes in their own religious condition. They retold its dramatic account of oppressors, traitors, loyalists, and faithful followers in myriad ways as diverse elements of American Jewish society faced off over questions about Judaism's survival in the modern world. The ways in which they understood God's role in Hanukkah's story, and the likelihood of divine rescue as Jews withstood the terrors of the twentieth century, defined them to each other. As they retold the holiday's story each year, it became a narrative that reminded them of ancestors who might be models for their own lives. It also made their contemporary challenges less novel. Contemporary American experience is not so different, Hanukkah's story suggested. Jews have faced this disarray before. The holiday's homey traditions and inspiring messages consoled and comforted adults who, through their celebrations, made sure it cheered both their children and themselves. Those who advocated for Hanukkah's increased importance assured their coreligionists that they could, indeed, live joyous Jewish lives in America despite the challenges they faced as a religious minority whose own diversity fragmented their religious communities. In this season that brought their differences from American society and from each other into sharpest focus, Hanukkah arrived to tell a Jewish story of a time when unity, power, and divine favor emerged to overcome disarray, weakness, and religious confusion.

1

What Is Hanukkah?

Hanukkah has always had something of a protean character. It emerged in the ancient world in a conflict between Judeans and one of their conquerors (except for roughly eighty years between 142 and 63 B.C.E., foreign powers controlled Judea from 586 B.C.E. through 70 C.E.), as well as among Jews themselves. The primary documents that tell us about Hanukkah's origin were written perhaps generations after the event, and "legends seem to be inextricably interwoven with historical traditions."[1] They also reflect the interests of their different, anonymous, authors. One document, written about 100 B.C.E., describes Hanukkah originating amid the rebuilding and rededicating of the Jerusalem Temple in 164 B.C.E. during the war against a particularly nasty conqueror, Antiochus IV, who had forbidden Jewish religious practices. A second text, written about twenty-four years earlier, explains it as part of a late celebration of the autumn festival, Sukkot, that had been delayed because of wartime disruptions.[2] Historian Lee I. Levine wondered why one year's delayed Sukkot celebration would initiate an annual Hanukkah celebration and suggested two contributing factors. First, those who cleaned and dedicated the Temple undoubtedly knew about previous occasions when the Temple was rededicated, notably, King Hezekiah's centuries-earlier purification of the Temple in a ceremony lasting eight days. Hezekiah's effort is described in the biblical book Chronicles, written in the fourth or third century B.C.E. They may also have been influenced by a popular pagan winter-solstice festival of lights that also lasted eight days.[3] Each of those factors may have contributed to the initial creation of Hanukkah celebrations.

Yet the rules and norms for celebrating the holiday that have been practiced for the past millennium became institutionalized hundreds of years after the Temple's rededication, among a very different group of Jewish religious leaders working in Babylonia, who reshaped the holiday to reflect their own perspectives. Rhetorically asking "What is Hanukkah?" their reply defined the way the holiday came to be understood for future Jews. They focused the holiday on the kindling of lights in memory of divine deliverance, which is how they viewed the victory against Antiochus IV. Yet their Hanukkah creation, too, came to be elaborated in later texts and practices written by medieval and early modern religious leaders who thought about lessons to be learned from Hanukkah. All those creations and modifications occurred long before American Jews entered the scene.

Like most Jewish holidays, Hanukkah commemorates ancient events. For this one, the Temple in Jerusalem proved pivotal. From 536 through 332 B.C.E., Judea (then called Yehud) existed as one of many different temple-states, each worshiping its own god, that dotted the eastern Mediterranean and lived under Persian rule.[4] Judea's political identification with the Temple continued for the next four hundred years, until the Temple's destruction in 70 C.E. Believed to house "the Living God, [the Temple] radiated its holiness over Jerusalem" and served as the "central religious institution" for Jews in both Judea and the diaspora.[5] First built by King Solomon in the tenth century B.C.E., it stood for more than four hundred years before being destroyed in 586 B.C.E. by Babylonia during that country's conquest of Jerusalem. Rebuilt around 515 B.C.E. after Persia conquered Babylonia, the Second Temple dominated Jerusalem for another 585 years.

The Temple's specific location in the Judean hills has been identified as both Mt. Zion and Mt. Moriah (where Abraham promised to sacrifice his son, Isaac).[6] "Defended by a stone wall . . . on the northern summit of the eastern ridge" of the Judean hills, it dominated the city.[7] Its design expanded on the instructions for a house for God described in Exodus and featured outer and inner courts where Jews gathered. Within those stood the House of the Lord, a small building set on an east-west axis, with gold ornamentation and a curtain covering its entrance. Most likely, this structure was divided into three parts, a Vestibule, the Holy Place, and the Holy of Holies.[8] More sacred than anything else in the Jewish realm, the Holy of Holies was the most religiously important spot in Jerusalem. Only once each year, on the day of fasting and repentance called Yom Kippur, did the high priest enter it. Priests stood outside that inner room within the Temple to conduct daily sacred sacrifices to God. A seven-branched candelabra —called a menorah—burned throughout each night. The sixth-century B.C.E. prophet Zechariah said that the menorah symbolized the divine presence and called its lights the eyes of God.[9] Each morning, priests cleaned it and prepared it for the upcoming evening.[10]

Priests also maintained strict rules for their own ritual purity in order to be fit to enter the Temple, and they performed their duties according to rules set down in Leviticus (1–9).[11] Each morning and afternoon, they performed incense offerings before the Holy of Holies. Twice each day, they sacrificed a lamb and sprinkled its blood on the Temple's altar. Outside, in the Temple's courtyard, priests sacrificed animals selected from among ten different species, as well as grains. In addition to those daily acts, priests conducted special sacrifices each Sabbath meant to assure the divine connection to the Jewish people.[12] Public monies stored in the Temple purchased the items to be sacrificed on these occasions and also provided charity to widows and orphans.

The lives of ordinary Jews were also linked to the Temple. On three festivals each year, Passover in early spring, Shavuot (Weeks) in early summer, and Sukkot (Tabernacles) in autumn, Jews traveled to Jerusalem to offer their own sacrifices to ensure God's protection over their households. Yet concerns about maintaining the Temple's ritual purity limited those pilgrims to the Temple's courtyards only. Non-Jews could not enter the Temple precincts at all. Through these many rules and rituals, Jews believed they maintained the Temple's ritual purity, assured the nation's continuing link to God, and contributed to the people's material well-being.[13]

When Alexander the Great won control of Judea from the Persians in 332 B.C.E., he strengthened the power of the high priest, largely because he generally distrusted the secular rulers whom he conquered. Religious leaders became the spokesmen for conquered peoples and often enjoyed honors and riches.[14] Yet, at the same time, Hellenic culture became more influential, especially in urban areas near the coast. Even before Alexander's conquest, Jews used objects that reflected Greek culture and style, such as Greek imported tableware, painted vases, and sculptures. Greek fashions in clothing became popular, as did Greek names, too, lending a cultural tone to an economic and somewhat geographic divide.[15] Some Jews participated in athletic contests in which the norm of performing in the nude offended the historical Jewish sensibility almost as much as did the participation in activities that were sometimes dedicated to a foreign god. Other Jews studied Greek literature, sparking new ideas and new literary styles.[16] For example, scholars argue that the biblical book Qoheleth (Ecclesiastes) reveals a Hellenic attitude about the meaning of life quite different from earlier biblical texts, evidence of growing Jewish engagement with Greek culture in the two centuries before Jesus.[17] Its assertion that human striving is futile —because God knows and determines everything in advance—offers a fatalistic philosophy of life at odds with the instructions to obey God's rules in order to earn a divine reward in this life and in the world to come, instructions that fill much of the Pentateuch.

In many areas under Alexander's rule, he founded new Greek cities and settled them with his military veterans and other migrants, leaving local peasants of the conquered territory to farm the land. Those locales invariably became prestigious and prosperous, and their success enticed residents of other towns and cities to transform their own places into Greek cities, even though they lacked a population that could claim Greek ancestry.[18] Yet, while Greek values, styles, and politics influenced much of Judea, the Temple underwent little change. After expanding the power of the high priest, Alexander did not interfere with the Temple, and the daily and Sabbath Temple rites continued.

That situation changed after Alexander's death in 323 B.C.E., when his four generals divided his kingdom, and Judea ultimately came under the control of Seleucus of Syria. Judea spanned a mere eight hundred square miles, but its location near the Mediterranean plain made it attractive to larger nations from the east, north, and southwest whose armies traversed the area and competed for power.[19] Seleucus's large territory underwent sweeping administrative reforms that strengthened Seleucid power throughout the Middle East. Greek customs remained preeminent over indigenous cultures. Especially in urban areas, a Greek-speaking class dominated the Seleucid state.[20] Despite those changes, the Temple still remained relatively free of foreign influence. "The pagan world was known for its tolerance," Levine explains, "a characteristic that flowed, inter alia, from the recognition that there were many deities and temples in the world, and honor was due them all."[21]

Although the Seleucid king Antiochus III displayed goodwill toward Jerusalem and Judea, not so his son, Antiochus IV, who came to power in 176 B.C.E. In Judea, different attitudes toward Hellenic culture and religion soon exacerbated the hardening political divisions. Since the Syrian wars of the previous century, Judea's population remained divided by family feuds, political disagreements, and diverse foreign-policy connections.[22] These divisions contributed to ongoing unrest which ultimately reached the Temple itself. We can see traces of those differences in the different accounts of the events that occurred. One account chronicles the actions of armies, kings, and priests, while others recount Seleucid cruelties and Jewish martyrdoms that might promote faith and loyalty in their listeners and readers and harden their opposition to the Seleucids.[23]

Events that led to Hanukkah seem to have been set in motion with particularly corrupt individuals claiming the powerful and remunerative office of the Temple's high priest. A year after the new Seleucid king (Antiochus IV) took the throne, Jason, the brother of Judea's ruler, Onias III, purchased the office of the high priest for himself. Within Jason's first year, he encouraged worship dedicated to Greek gods in the Temple, to be conducted by Jewish priests in Greek garb. He sent Jewish emissaries to festivals dedicated to foreign gods in order to represent Jerusalem on the international stage. In 172, a priest named Meneleus wrested the office of the high priest away from Jason by offering bribes to Seleucid officials, and then he arranged to have Onias III murdered.

These actions, along with Greek worship in the Temple, outraged some Jews. Rioting erupted near the Temple, and three members of the Jerusalem Council of Elders were murdered. To quell the violence, Antiochus took military control of the city in 169 B.C.E., killing resisters, men, women, and children. He drove out Jason and his followers. Documents of the period suggest that contrary to historical custom that respected local temples, Antiochus then entered the Temple and took the gold ritual items—the menorah and the table for the showbread, along with libation jars, bowls, ladles, gold cornices, coins, and other precious articles—and carried them back to Antioch. His general, Apollonius, created a new fortified area around the Temple called the Akra. Some of its original residents fled the city, and new settlers sympathetic to Antiochus came to the fortified area. In that way, Antiochus established an area of Jerusalem loyal to the Seleucids. He left the rest of the city undefended, however, and Jerusalem refugees fleeing the area may have spread unrest to other parts of Judea.[24]

Meneleus and Antiochus replaced some Jewish religious practices with Hellenic rites and allowed acts that were seen by some Jews to further defile the Temple. Documents from the period differ regarding exactly how these events occurred. Some versions describe Temple entry by ritually impure Seleucids, the king, his emissaries, and nonbelievers, with Meneleus leading them. Most documents list the robbing of the Temple treasury, the erecting of a statue representing Zeus Olympus–Baal Shamaim (the god identified as protecting the Hellenic and Syrian conquerors), and the lodging of Antiochus's troops within its precincts—each act an affront to Judea.[25] Worship of the Greek and Syrian deity erected in the Temple included the sacrifice of pigs, animals deemed unclean and forbidden to Jews by biblical law. Pious Jews saw each of those acts as polluting the Temple. Just as importantly, the money stolen from the Temple treasury depleted funds for the daily and Sabbath sacrifices and for charity.[26] No open rebellion occurred, but resentment brewed.

The changes made during Antiochus's rule turned the Temple into a place where Jews could be forced to worship a deity other than the God of the Bible, which according to Judaism is the most terrible of sins.[27] If priests still performed the daily sacrifices, pious Jews may have considered them ineffective in a Temple now polluted by idol worship. In addition, by outlawing study of Torah and possession of Torah scrolls, Antiochus demanded that Jews stop promulgating their own culture and religion.[28] He also forbade rites central to Judaism, including observance of the Sabbath, a time for worship and rest, and circumcision, which Jews considered the sign of their covenant with God.[29] Thus, Antiochus IV prohibited core Jewish religious practices: Temple worship in its purity, Torah study, Sabbath observance, and circumcision. Contemporary scholars continue to debate why he broke longstanding custom and tried to quash Judea's religious life.[30]

Accounts of Antiochus's brutality in enforcing his decrees appear in several sources, attesting to death sentences carried out against resisters.[31] In vivid images, and following the Greek pathos literary style, some of them describe mothers who had circumcised their babies being killed with their infants "at their neck."[32] Some historians doubt Antiochus's mental stability, while others suggest that military threats from Egypt compelled Antiochus to strengthen his kingdom by unifying it under common worship. He may have thought that by making Judea and Jerusalem fully Greek, its wealth would increase and the likelihood of rebellion would diminish. With Judea calmed, he could deploy all his forces against outside threats to his kingdom. Thus, tight control of Judea may have been part of Antiochus's larger plan to unify his territories and to concentrate his armies against an external enemy that enjoyed significant military and political power.[33] Whatever his reason, he made it nearly impossible for Jews to live "according to their ancestral laws."[34]

Jews responded to the new repression of their religion in different ways. Menelaus and others living in the Akra supported Antiochus's policies. Elsewhere, while some Jews resisted nonviolently, others took up arms.[35] The revolt against Antiochus IV and the Jerusalem priesthood erupted in 164 B.C.E. in Modein, a small town northwest of Jerusalem, away from the seat of Hellenic power, home to a family of priests called Hashmon/Hasmoneus. The First Book of Maccabees, written about 100 B.C.E., roughly two generations after the actual revolt, is one of our earliest accounts of events. (It seems likely that the original Hebrew version was soon lost and the Greek version became standard.) In it, Mattathias, the family's father, says, "We see the temple, which is our splendor and glory, laid waste and desecrated. Why should we go on living?" He and his five sons tear their garments, put on sackcloth, and "mourn loud and long."[36] Soon after, one of Antiochus's officers comes to Modein to enforce the new Hellenic sacrifices. Antiochus's emissaries built statues of Greek divinities in several Judean towns. When Mattathias sees an Israelite participate in the rite, he rushes forward and "cut[s] him down on the . . . altar." He then kills the officer sent to enforce the new worship and "demolishe[s] the pagan altar." We do not know the name of the author of First Maccabees, but we can guess that he or she knew the Bible, because this book hints of more sacred writings. Mattathias turns to the crowd and says, "Follow me, all who are zealous for the law and stand by the covenant!" echoing Moses's call to followers after the debacle of the golden calf described in the biblical book Exodus.[37] In weaving this account into Judaism's memory of its most revered leader, Moses, the writer lent some of Moses's authority to Mattathias. Or, read another way, Mattathias signaled his own loyalty to biblical tradition by invoking Moses's words. Thus, the revolt against Antiochus IV also resembled a civil war pitting biblical loyalists against those willing to accommodate a foreign religion.

Rebellion against Antiochus's army began before the Hasmoneans, the family that ultimately led the revolt, took up arms.[38] But the rebellion soon came under the leadership of Mattathias's five sons, Judah, Jonathan, Simon, John, and Eleazar. Judah, and later Jonathan, led the military actions. Together, the band came to be known as the Maccabees. Maccabeus might have been a nickname for Judah, the brother famous for his physical strength, because it is similar to the Hebrew word *makevet*, meaning "hammer," but another source speculates that it may mean "designated by God."[39] First Maccabees says Mattathias led his sons and other followers into the hills to begin a guerrilla war against Antiochus's forces, and many culturally Hellenized Jews fought alongside them to retake the Temple.[40] Mattathias soon died and left his son Judah in charge of the army.[41] Another account of events emerged from Jews in Egypt, who seem to have been the first to use the term "Hellenism" as a reproach, contrasting it with the "Judaism" of faithful Judeans.[42] Mosaic allusions are missing from their text, and they focus on Judah's leadership and military prowess. Yet their account also admits that adoption of some Greek customs was "important to function effectively in a Greek world."[43] Even this triumphant account of the Maccabean revolt reveals ambivalence toward Hellenic culture that had long permeated the Near East.

Victory

Scholars suggest that the Judean revolt against Antiochus IV succeeded because it coincided with an uprising in Antioch that weakened his hold on Judea.[44] The uprising took place largely in the countryside, although the city of Jerusalem remained the ultimate target. The goal of retaking, cleansing, and rededicating the Temple motivated the fighters and defined, for them, their purpose. They were usually sharply outnumbered. Yet, after several battles, in 164 B.C.E., Jews retook the Temple, rededicated it, and restored the Jewish Temple cult.[45]

The Hebrew word *Hanukkah* means "dedication," and the holiday of Hanukkah commemorates that rededication of the Temple. Judah, his brothers, and the men with them decreed a celebration of the Temple's rededication annually on the twenty-fifth of the Hebrew month of Kislev, to be marked with eight days of "gladness and joy." Today, Jews who learn about this dedication ceremony talk about the lack of pure oil with which to relight the menorah, and a tiny drop that miraculously burned for eight days until more could be made. But that story does not appear in the early documents about the event. In those first accounts, the Maccabees' own celebration began with hymns of thanksgiving accompanied by harps, lutes, and cymbals in the Temple, after they had rebuilt the stone altar. They rejoiced for eight days with various offerings to God. The "garland[s] . . . and flowering branches . . . [and] palm fronds" in their celebration mirrored the autumn festival of Sukkot, which the fighters were not able to celebrate because war raged and the Temple remained in Antiochus's hands.[46] Sukkot celebrations, in turn, built on traditions of earlier Temple dedications. Specifically, the holiday, along with recalling the temporary shelters built by the Israelites in the wilderness noted in Leviticus, recalled the celebration undertaken by King Solomon in dedicating the First Temple in the tenth century B.C.E.[47] Thus, Hanukkah underscores dedication in Jewish literature and history. Its creation marked a successful effort to restore Jewish practices, an innovation that signaled devotion to religious continuity.

The war to overthrow Antiochus IV did not conclude with the retaking of the Temple. Judah died in battle in 161 B.C.E., and Antiochus IV himself died, seemingly of natural causes, a year later. But ultimately, the revolt succeeded under Jonathan's leadership, and the Hasmonean family claimed leadership of Judea's government. First under Jonathan and then under Simon, the Hasmoneans rebuilt walls and buildings in Jerusalem and extended the country's borders to include the adjacent areas of Idumea, Galilee, and Peraea. Jonathan had initially claimed power through favorable treaties with the new Seleucid rulers, and the family remained in power for several generations through alliances with various larger nations. With their rule, the image of the Torah (the five books of Moses in the form of a scroll) and that of the Temple became widespread sacred symbols of the realm, replacing imagery of Hellenic kings and gods on coins and reinforcing Judea's Jewish identity.[48]

. . . And Loss

Yet the successful revolt to preserve the Temple ultimately carried within it the seeds for even greater destruction. Ironically, by installing both king and high priest from the same family, the Hasmoneans reshaped Judea to look more like a Greek city-state. The ceremony installing the first Hasmonean king drew on Greek customs.[49] The Hasmoneans also soon angered the same traditionalists who had supported their revolt. Judah's brother Jonathan became high priest—and another brother, Simon, followed suit after Jonathan—despite the fact that their family did not claim descent from Zadok (which legitimated each new high priest).[50] Ultimately, the Hasmoneans' foreign alliances linked Judea to Rome and extended Rome's control of the territory. Judeans eventually lost confidence in the Hasmoneans, and Herod, the ruthless ruler later appointed by Rome, ousted every Hasmonean from public office. By 63 C.E., Judea was effectively a Roman province. Rome even appointed the Temple's high priest. For reasons still debated, but probably a combination of unjust taxes and religious insults, Jews in Galilee and Judea revolted against Rome, winning an initial battle. Rome quickly regrouped and, after a protracted war, destroyed the Temple in 70 C.E. and took many Judeans to Rome as slaves. The Jewish polity in

Judea failed, the priesthood lost the power to lead, and Temple-centered Judaism shattered forever.[51]

One man who experienced that final war, Yoseph ben Mattithias (37– c. 100 C.E.), commanded a Jewish army in a first-century battle against Rome and experienced terrible troop losses, before he fled to Rome and took a Roman name. Known to us more commonly as Flavius Josephus, the historian's many works defended Judean religion and culture. In his *Antiquities of the Jews*, a twenty-volume work completed circa 93 or 94 C.E., he explains why Jews colloquially called Hanukkah the Festival of Lights: "I think, from the fact that the right to worship appeared to us at a time when we hardly dared hope for it."[52] This term suggests that lights customarily were lighted on the holiday. Hope for a leader who would free Jews from Rome's grasp spread, and some Jews supported a rebellion in 135 C.E. Its failure resulted in the deaths of over one hundred thousand Jews and a calamity for Jewish society. Rome tightened its grip on Judea. With Jews having lost both the Temple and political independence, Jewish religious life took a different direction.

The Holiday Takes Shape

Until the new commemorative days of Yom Hashoah (Holocaust Remembrance Day) and Yom Ha-Atzmaut (Israel Independence Day) became established in the twentieth century, Hanukkah was the last holiday to have been added to the Jewish calendar. Created by a new set of religious leaders who reshaped Judaism in the wake of the devastation wrought by Rome, these men (and they were all men) became the key authorities over Jewish religious life. They codified the holiday's rite in their extensive writings, collectively called the Talmud, that adapted religious rules for Jewish life to new circumstances. They located and prescribed Jewish worship in homes, in synagogues, and in the religious structure of daily life. Known as *rabbis*, Hebrew for "my teachers," these men declared the Hebrew Bible complete around 90 C.E. Its shape and contents then is still the form we recognize today. Perhaps because they retained the biblical structure largely as it had been accepted by Jews for three hundred years, or because they were disenchanted with Hasmonean rule that had become corrupt, or because they thought it politically unwise to sanctify accounts of military revolt against a foreign power, they excluded accounts of the Maccabean revolt from the Hebrew Bible.

As the rabbis reshaped Judaism to accommodate Jewish life in diaspora, they established a new Hanukkah celebration. They explained the successful Maccabean revolt as an instance of divine intervention that removed a foreign threat to Jewish religious life. As Hanukkah was a joyous occasion, the rabbis forbade fasting during it.[53] They also designated Hanukkah to be a minor festival. Unlike major festivals of the Jewish calendar—Passover, Sukkot, and Shavuot—they banned work on Hanukkah only for the time that the candles remain lighted, rather than for the entire first or last day of the holiday. The sages who compiled the Talmud (the 5,894 folio pages that record their discussions in Aramaic about biblical laws) in the six centuries after 70 C.E. embedded their discussion of Hanukkah within another about the much more important occasion of Shabbat. The day of rest that occurs each week in the Jewish calendar from sundown on Friday to sundown on Saturday, Shabbat is the most common occasion when candles are lighted. As the rabbis shaped worship for a post-Temple Jewish life, they established rites to be performed at domestic tables that recalled Temple practices. Thus, on Shabbat, there is the kindling of lights and the blessing of wine and food. As such, their thoughts on the holiday about rededicating the Temple, Hanukkah, fit well into their discussions about Shabbat. The sages therefore used this weekly occasion as a frame for discussing the yearly celebration of Hanukkah. In this section, probably completed in the sixth century C.E., they explained the Maccabean victory as evidence of God's continuing protection of Jews. Although Rome had fallen by then, Jews did not regain Judea but remained a minority population in Europe, the Middle East, and North Africa and continued to follow rabbinic guidelines.

The rabbis designed Hanukkah recitations to focus on God's power. In the daily prayers said each night at home during Hanukkah, as well as in daily and Sabbath prayers in the synagogue during the holiday and in grace after meals, Jews today thank God, just as they have for almost two millennia, for delivering "the strong into the hands of the weak." Psalms 113–118, which praise God, are recited in synagogues, where, in the *Amida* (Standing) prayer, God is also thanked for miracles.[54] The phrase "strong into the hands of the weak" echoed the author of the

First Book of Maccabees, who recounts a stirring speech by Judah Maccabee, who rallies his small army by telling them not to be afraid of fighting the much larger Seleucid force because "victory in war does not depend upon the size of the force, but strength comes from heaven."[55] A special reading from the prophet Zechariah, including the phrase "not by might, nor by power, but by my spirit, saith the Lord," is recited after the Torah portion. Those prayers and readings credit God with the Maccabean victory, creating a powerful image of transcendent power and of God's willingness to come to the aid of Jews.

Those sages were not interested in the political gains the Hasmoneans achieved for Judea, a country which no longer existed by the time they wrote.[56] The Talmud suggests that God chose to rescue Jews in the Maccabean era because of some Jews who chose death rather than disobey divine law, as ordered by Antiochus, not because of Maccabean bravery in fighting the king's army. Rabbis included the story of the unnamed mother that appears in the Second Book of Maccabees, written in Greek circa 124 B.C.E., and in the Fourth Book of Maccabees, written between the first century B.C.E. and the first century C.E., possibly during the persecution of Jews by Caligula and before the fall of the Temple in 70 C.E. The mother watches her seven sons tortured and murdered for refusing to eat food forbidden by Jewish law and encourages them in their bravery: she kills herself to join them in the afterlife.[57] Devotion like hers, rabbis said, determined the successful outcome of the Maccabean revolt because it convinced God to intervene. They sometimes refer to her as Hannah, like the mother of the prophet Samuel, who was a model of religious devotion. Rabbinic Hanukkah narratives elaborate Jewish religious devotion for which God's miracles reward Jews.

The Talmud tractate Shabbat (21b) contains instructions for performing the holiday's rites, as well as the story of the holiday's miracle. The tractate says that when Jewish forces retook the Temple, only one small flask of the holy olive oil prepared by the priests for use in lighting the Temple's candelabra, whose flames indicated God's presence, remained unspoiled. Yet that small amount lasted for eight days until more could be prepared. Through that miracle, God conveyed to Judah and his men that divine power caused their victory. That event is original with the Talmud and does not appear in earlier sources. Yet, to this day, the eight-branched Hanukkah menorah (sometimes called a *hanukiyyah*), with its ninth branch for the helper candle, reminds Jews of the seven-branched menorah that stood in the Jerusalem Temple, its added light reminding them of the eight-day miracle of the sacred oil. The rabbis' ceremony also drew on lore about the rites Nehemiah presumably performed centuries earlier at the Temple's rededication in 432 B.C.E.[58] One of the early documents about the Maccabees' Temple dedication indicates that some sort of miracle involving fire happened, but it does not explain exactly what. It simply suggests that fire "had descended from heaven at the dedication of the altar in the days of Moses and at the sanctification of the Temple of Solomon; at the consecration of the altar in the time of Nehemiah [dedication of the Second Temple] there was also a miracle of fire, and so in the days of Judah Maccabee."[59] Miraculous fires flared at each dedication, and fires became key to Hanukkah's rite.[60]

For eight days beginning on the twenty-fifth day of the Hebrew month Kislev, Jews kindle small lights in the evening. They use a helper candle called the Shamash to light the candles, and an additional candle is added each night. Hanukkah candles are also lighted in the synagogue each day of the holiday. While lighting the growing number of candles each night, Jews recite two or three short blessings. First, they acknowledge that they are fulfilling one of God's commandments. They then thank God for performing a miracle for them ages ago "at this season." On the first night only, they also thank God for sustaining them in life and bringing them to this season.[61] The lights commemorate the miracle which the rabbis described that occurred after the Temple's cleansing from Antiochus's defilement. The rite focuses Hanukkah squarely on God and the Temple, not the Maccabean victory.[62]

The rabbis also enhanced memory of the religious loyalty of the Temple's priesthood by boosting the Hasmonean family's lineage. Although Mattathias was only a rural priest and not a member of the clan that historically provided priests for the Jerusalem Temple, the Talmud calls him a high priest.[63] Indirectly, that change lent an aura of historical continuity to a time of religious dissension and political upheaval. With the rabbinic holiday rite, Hanukkah's branch on the tree of Jewish tradition grew in a new direction.

The Hanukkah celebration, just like most Jewish holidays, at its heart embodies the essential project of the rabbis: with the Temple destroyed, they aimed to make it possible for Jews to extend the spirituality of the

Temple into their everyday lives and to maintain biblical law despite living under new circumstances.[64] The Hanukkah rite that they created and described in the Talmud is evidence that two millennia ago Jews were already concerned about how to retain religious observance.

Those rabbis touted an entirely different way of dealing with domination by foreign powers than the armed revolt conducted against Antiochus IV. Rabbinic scholar Daniel Boyarin suggests that the "earliest [rabbinic] Jewish texts" of the Roman era "present a culture of men who are resisting, renouncing, and disowning" the Roman ideal of manliness that was identified through the assertion of male physical power and status. "None of the rabbis were pacifists," Boyarin tells us, but they asserted an attitude that is probably best expressed in the phrase "Where there is life, there is hope," or "Where there is life, there is Torah."[65] Rather than being quick to take up arms against an oppressor and endorsing the supposed "manly" arts associated with violent resistance, rabbis advocated creating a tactical relationship to the larger power that allowed for survival.

Most Jewish historians, however, suggest a different explanation for the rabbinic reluctance to laud Maccabean militarism. First, the rabbis wrote after Hasmonean leaders had led Judea into Rome's grip and so may not have wanted to offer the family much praise. Second, they clearly wanted to promote a sense of dependence on God, urging Jews to look toward the divine for protection. They likely feared inciting Jews to another revolt that might end in disaster, like the 135 C.E. experience.

For much of the history of Jewish communities in the millennia since the fall of Judea, they looked to the highest governing authorities to protect them from violence at the hands of local mobs or petty officials. Historian Yosef Hayim Yerushalmi describes the situation as one in which "the practice of the Jewish religion and the vital substructure of Jewish civilization all depended on as much stability and continuity in the rule of law as possible, and on the establishment of a mutuality of interest with those ruling powers most capable of providing it. Jews, in other words, sought direct vertical alliances, even if at times this meant alienating lesser jurisdictions, and seemed to be forged at the expense of horizontal alliances."[66] Even when rulers failed to protect them, this "royal alliance," as historian Salo Baron termed it, endured as a cultural myth among Jews.[67] Furthermore, at least since the Middle

Ages, many European Jews supported their own local separate government with an array of functionaries and officials that formed the *kahal,*
or Jewish communal structure. Those offices included a *shtatdlan,* or
diplomat, whose special duties aimed to seek attitudes and laws favorable to Jews' welfare in the ruling gentile courts and who acted on Jews'
expectation that protection would more likely be found in the highest
levels of government.[68] Those enduring attitudes may have influenced
rabbinic writers of an earlier era to dampen Jews' regard for the Maccabean military prowess.

Or perhaps the rabbis' attitudes reflected something far simpler.
The Maccabean account of overthrowing foreign rulers just may have
seemed miraculous to them. Instead of praising the revolt in their Hanukkah celebration, they wrote that Hanukkah's candle lighting commemorated the miracle of the Temple oil, by which God conveyed to
Jews that divine power had led them to victory.

Anthropologist Catherine Bell tells us that rituals usually convey
their meanings in multiple and redundant ways, and this is true of
Hanukkah.[69] Its ritual primarily recalls the miracle of the oil, which
only indirectly recalls the Maccabean victory. Recalling the miracle
wrought "in those days, at this season," the blessings evoke a sense that
the past is what one scholar calls "a living force" affecting Jews' lives
in every age.[70] Each Hanukkah evening, an additional candle is placed
in the lamp. Added from right to left, the candles are lighted from left
to right. Unlike most holiday rites in Judaism, both men and women
must participate in Hanukkah's celebration. Women took it upon themselves to observe Hanukkah more stringently than men did, the Talmud
says, because the ancient Greeks forced sexual immorality on them.[71]
The miracle, as the Talmud calls the Maccabean victory, rescued those
women. That conclusion rests on an allusion in First Maccabees. Despite Hanukkah's domestic rite, families must display their correctly
lighted menorah before passersby. Only under circumstances of danger
or persecution may the lighted menorah be displayed only within the
home. Thus, the rite is repeated by all adults in the household for eight
nights, taught to the children, and displayed to the public.

Hanukkah lamps themselves sometimes reinforced key elements of
the holiday. In antiquity, Jews would create an array of small oil lamps
or use a special Hanukkah oil lamp with eight wicks arranged around

its edge. By the Middle Ages, however, designs carved into or embossed on Hanukkah lamps themselves also displayed key elements of the story; illustrated manuscripts from that era also show specially crafted Hanukkah menorahs of stone. Star-shaped or triangular oil receptacles for Hanukkah were in use from the Middle Ages through the sixteenth century. Historians date the first image of a standing menorah with eight candles to 1470 in Italy. A century later, the familiar menorah shape with arms projecting from a base appeared in Padua. By the late seventeenth century, small Hanukkah menorahs in that shape appeared for home use in Frankfurt. That standing menorah took as its model the large, seven-branch menorah that stood in the Jerusalem Temple but modified it for use during the eight days of Hanukkah.

Over many centuries, rabbis urged Jews to use beautiful Hanukkah menorahs to make the rite as magnificent as possible. Those who lived near communities with access to silver, such as Germany, Austria, and eastern Europe, recommended silver menorahs. As early as the fifteenth century, decorative elements such as scroll work or imagery such as flowers, animals, or humans, or architectural elements such as columns, adorned the menorahs, whether on back plates, stands, or arms. Despite Judaism's proscription against graven images, that of Judith—a heroine in some Hanukkah stories from the late Medieval era—appeared on some Hanukkah menorahs in Italy, Germany, and the Netherlands during the eighteenth century. Images representing Judah Maccabee rarely appeared before the twentieth century. The most common image was that of the Temple menorah.[72]

Although rabbis referred to the Maccabean revolt only in their Talmudic discussions and omitted accounts of it from the much more widely read Bible, they did not erase it from Jewish memory. In the tenth century, Saadyeh Ben Joseph (892–942), influential leader of the rabbinic academy at Sura in Babylonia, translated a text usually called the Scroll of Antiochus, from Aramaic into Arabic. That original probably was written in the seventh or eighth century, and probably in Babylonia, as it refers to Antioch as a coastal city. Ancient prayer books following the Yemenite custom included the scroll, and by the thirteenth century, it was publicly read in Italian synagogues on Hanukkah.[73] In the nineteenth century, Rabbi Isaac ben Aryeh Joseph Dov redacted a version of the Scroll of Antiochus, translated into Hebrew, which was included in a prayer book used by Jews in central and eastern Europe as the Scroll of the Hasmoneans.[74] Yiddish versions circulated among Jews in central and eastern Europe.

Despite the emergence of the Scroll of Antiochus, the dominant view that Hanukkah commemorated a miracle wrought by God to rescue Jews continued into the next millennium. In the twelfth century, Moses Ben Maimon (Maimonides), perhaps the most influential figure in Jewish rabbinic history, explained first that the Jews of the Maccabean era suffered greatly "until God had mercy upon them." Second, he mentioned that the "sons of the Hasmoneans . . . saved the Jews." Later rabbis concluded that the concept mentioned first was most important, the second, less so. Those understandings of Hanukkah remained authoritative for many centuries. In 1950, American Orthodox rabbi Eliyahu Touger explained the time-honored perspective this way: by "calling attention to the Divine origin of the Jews' victory before mentioning the Hasmoneans [Maimonides] emphasizes the miraculous and spiritual nature of the miracle."[75] Other Talmudic scholars interpreted Hanukkah similarly. In the sixteenth century, Joseph Caro compiled a guide to rabbinic law based on the Talmud's by then twenty-three large folio volumes, which, with an adaptation by Moses Isserles, quickly became the standard guide for Jewish observance. Called the *Shulchan Aruch* (Set Table), its rules regarding the placement and lighting of the Hanukkah candelabra reasserted the holiday's central meaning as commemorating the miracle of the oil.[76] Jews eat foods fried in oil on Hanukkah as another reminder of the miracle of the Temple oil. The focus on Temple miracles expressed in the Talmud and the *Shulchan Aruch* harmonized with the belief in miracles common among Jews' gentile neighbors especially during the medieval period.[77] Thus, for rabbis who reshaped ancient Judea's Temple-based religion into a body of experiences that could inspire a diaspora people, Hanukkah's importance lay in offering an episode in which God effected a miracle.

Maccabees and Miracles in Popular Memory

While rabbinic discussions set the rules for Hanukkah rites, ordinary Jews have expressed their own ideas about the holiday in far greater variety. Although Hanukkah's rites pay scant attention to the Maccabees, popular Jewish memory recalled both Maccabees and miracles alike. In tenth-century Italy, a new popular Jewish history called the *Yosippon* (loosely based on Josephus's writings) included an account of the Maccabean revolt and stirred widespread interest, as it liberally mixed folklore with history. A Hebrew edition was published in Mantua in 1476. A 1558 English translation roused curiosity about Jews among Christians in England. By 1661, an illustrated version appeared in Yiddish, then the daily language of most Jews throughout central and eastern Europe. These various editions kept the exploits of the Hasmonean family alive in Jewish memory.

The idea of miraculous rescues also inspired new Hanukkah poetry and songs. A thirteenth-century Jewish poet penned a five-stanza poem, "Maoz Tsur" (Hebrew: Sheltering Rock), recounting numerous instances of divine deliverance. By the sixteenth century, Jews in central and eastern Europe put those lyrics to a popular melody that drew on two German folk tunes. It became the customary finale to Hanukkah's candle-lighting ceremony among Jews living there.[78] In that era, a time of persecutions and expulsions, an unknown poet added a sixth stanza —rarely sung—that asks God to avenge Jews' sufferings and to swiftly return them to their homeland. "Maoz Tsur" became a standard addition to the Hanukkah ritual in central and eastern Europe as families sang it after lighting and blessing the holiday candles.

New customs for celebrating Hanukkah also developed. Because Hanukkah lights commemorate a miracle, rabbis discouraged using them for practical purposes. It has long been customary for no work to be done while the slender Hanukkah candles burn and for that time to be spent with feasting and festivities. Games, as mentioned previously, have long been part and parcel of Hanukkah. While spinning tops had been used for gambling in the ancient world, today's Hanukkah game developed in central Europe in the 1500s. Adapted from a widely enjoyed game of chance, the Hanukkah top, a *dreidel* (Yiddish: spinner) or a *sevivon* (Hebrew), has letters inscribed on its four sides indicating the game's rules. But Jews also interpreted them to mean "A Great Miracle Happened There" (in Israel, dreidels say "Here" instead of "There"). Games of chance seem to underscore Hanukkah's message that threats to Jewish life can be overturned. Through dreidel games commonly played by children, fortune is changed again and again in concrete actions that seem to make miraculous rescues plausible. Anthropologists view occasions such as the time marked by the lit Hanukkah candles as outside ordinary, everyday time.[79] These moments offer a threshold to new possibilities that can be felt during the ritual. Judaism's holidays often separate sacred time from ordinary time to create occasions for imagining events in Jews' ancient past, for experiencing a more united community, and for contacting the divine. For centuries, Hanukkah's candles, its message of God's protection, and its games provided an occasion when Jews might hope for a world where misfortune could become fortune. The luck of a game could underscore the dramatic changes that a miracle, such as that of Hanukkah, might make real.

During the eighteenth century, eastern and western European Jewish communities experienced different religious trends which influenced their views of Hanukkah. In the east, where Jews still felt the effects of the hostility that generated seventeenth-century massacres and a spreading impoverishment, mystical approaches to Judaism became popular. In the area of Podolia and Volhynia in Ukraine, a healer and wonder worker named Rabbi Israel ben Eliezer gathered followers to learn his mystical approach to worship and to understanding the Talmud. Called the Baal Shem Tov, or Master of the Good Name, he "inspired fervent and joyous fulfillment of the law." His disciples attracted followers and the movement spread rapidly.[80] For them, even more so than for the less mystical rabbis who sometimes opposed them, Hanukkah provided an occasion for religious devotion to a God who sheltered them. Hanukkah's numerous iterations and manifestations reveal both the flexibility of the holiday itself and the profound role of ordinary Jews in redirecting the dictates of rabbis, as well as the role of later rabbis who in turn recrafted the holiday initiated by the Maccabees.

Hanukkah in the Modern West

Prior to the eighteenth century, Jews in most parts of Europe lived as a people apart from the majority Christian society. Neither political nor legal authorities recognized Jews as individuals. Jews were expected to form their own communities which would oversee matters of personal life such as marriage, divorce, and inheritance, explained historian Jacob Katz. In most places, marriage contracts also required special permission from the state because they provided an important key to population control. Jews dealt with these matters by turning to their own religious laws laid out in the Talmud. European Jews also needed to obtain permission to reside where they wished. Often, higher political authorities might grant a general permission, but the local village or town also needed to agree to allow Jews to settle in their precincts. To grant that right, a special tax was levied on the community as a whole. "As late as 1777," famed philosopher Moses Mendelssohn "intervened in favor of Dresden's Jews," Katz pointed out. Hundreds of that city's Jews "faced expulsion for failing to remit the annual head tax." Moreover, settlement rights were granted to specific families, not to Jews as a group. Many other Jews who were denied that right lived "an insecure existence," either serving in the households of privileged families, traveling from community to community, or living on charity. "The Jew was utterly dependent on authority for the right to reside anywhere," Katz concluded.[81]

Under those circumstances, "Jews lived out their lives in the Jewish community." Where communities were large enough, the community maintained a synagogue and a house of study and supported a rabbi, a teacher, a kosher butcher, a burial society, and various charities. Social status recognized mainly "two criteria: wealth and Talmudic learning." Katz summed up the lives of those Jews by describing them as "thoroughly embedded in [their] own tradition[s]" and as feeling "clearly separated from Christian society."[82]

As central and western Europe modernized, its Jews faced new circumstances, and new interpretations of Hanukkah emerged among them. Beginning in the late eighteenth century, following political revolutions driven by Enlightenment values, western European Jews slowly integrated into predominantly Christian societies. In France, Jews became citizens of the state. Napoleon's conquest of Germanic lands in 1807 offered Jews there civil rights, but after his defeat in 1815, Jewish emancipation in Europe required different laws than Napoleon had promulgated. As Christian Europeans debated those laws, they voiced old prejudices and uncertainties, which sparked new anti-Jewish violence. For some Jews, emancipation's early days did little to change their appreciation for Hanukkah. For nineteenth-century Jews in small towns in Alsace, for example, Hanukkah meant visiting one another's homes for holiday meals, games, and private entertainments.[83] Socializing, like celebrating, meant being with other Jews.

On the face of it, the nineteenth century seemed to be good for Jews of the West. Late eighteenth-century political revolutions in France and the United States had proclaimed the dawn of a new age and promoted liberty in England and Germany. The era's industrial growth seemed to further define the modern era as an age of progress. Some leading American Protestants concluded that providence advanced material conditions to bring the kingdom of God.[84] The leading American minister, Henry Ward Beecher, confidently told an 1876 audience, "The Revolutionary generation built a great nation, but we are building a greater one."[85]

Yet, in the United States, clergy of many denominations worried about their own weakening influence. In both western Europe and North America, governments restricted religion's legal reach and curtailed or eliminated its governmental supports. Religions could neither obtain support from public coffers nor call on public officials to enforce religious rules. Complicating matters, "faith in individual autonomy . . . [was] a central tenet of the modern world view."[86] The modern world encouraged individual Jews to solve their religious confusions for themselves, if only with the guidance of a religious leader of their own choosing.

Ironically, Jews' encounter with modern Western culture ultimately expanded their own knowledge of Maccabean history. The few European Jews who obtained a classical education read works by Josephus, whose *Antiquities of the Jews* described the revolt against Antiochus IV. In North America, where Jews never lived in ghettos and commonly attended schools with non-Jews, a Philadelphia publisher reprinted an English translation of Josephus's work in 1775, making it available to colleges, clergy, and private scholars alike.[87] Historical perspectives on religion enjoyed wide popularity in largely Protestant countries such as the United States, England, and Germany, and publishers provided readers with such works by ancient and modern authors.

Some Western Jews, reading in classrooms or on their own, learned the Christian traditions that had preserved ancient accounts of Maccabean exploits. The First and Second Books of Maccabees passed into Roman Catholic Bible compilations. Roman Catholic tradition identifies all Jews who protested Antiochus's rule as Maccabees and frames their revolt as a type of martyrdom. The idea of martyrdom played an important role in Christianity's early understanding of the religious life. In Paul's letters to the Galatians, he describes Jesus's crucifixion in phrases that echo accounts of the deaths of Jews killed for resisting Antiochus's orders.[88] Christianity similarly incorporated their deaths into its calendar of martyrs.[89]

Rabbis had long forbidden Jews from reading Christian sacred texts, but as modernity weakened clerical power, more liberal rabbis culled these widely available Maccabee stories and Josephus's account of the Maccabean revolt for their own Hanukkah sermons and inspirational, instructional fiction. In nineteenth-century Europe, liberal-minded, university-trained rabbis urged Jews to study the Maccabean history for its own worth, rather than solely to understand God's message, and penned new works to aid them. Those works also interested American rabbis. When liberal German rabbi Abraham Geiger published his lectures on Jewish history in 1864, a New York publisher reprinted them the following year.[90] Geiger believed that if Jews knew how Judaism had changed in the past, they would accept contemporary changes he proposed. He hoped that his changes would keep Western Jews from converting to Christianity, which seemed to some a better fit with modern life.[91] Liberal rabbis in Germanic lands, who gathered in 1869 to harmonize the new religious changes, recommended that Hanukkah festivities be made both more elaborate and more solemn.[92] Later in that century, university-trained German-Jewish historian Heinrich Graetz compiled an eleven-volume history of the Jews that incorporated Maccabean exploits into a modern history of Jewish life. By the end of that century, a hefty six-volume version of Graetz's work had been reprinted in English in Philadelphia.[93] On both sides of the Atlantic, Jews reading this historical approach to their past learned more about the Hasmonean family and its military exploits than their religious tradition previously had offered. That expanded knowledge sometimes seemed to justify American Jews' own novel Hanukkah activities and creations that emerged over two centuries and expressed their particular religious experiences.

The story of how and why American Jews transformed Hanukkah into something grand reveals a mix of hope and anxiety in their experience in America. At different times in history and in different locations, Jews fared differently. Yet, in the United States, as one scholar explained, "any barrier dividing [Jews] from their neighbors eventually became so easy to surmount that it was sometimes difficult even to notice."[94] Jews who enhanced Hanukkah's importance told a Maccabean story about the appeal of foreign cultures and the oppression of foreign tyrants, the traitors who betrayed Judaism and the martyrs and loyalists who defended Judaism against them. The story was an easy sell: dramatic action and vivid imagery pervaded it, and divine rescue capped it off. The story condensed historical events into a mythic structure that lent it a timeless quality. Drawn from both ancient texts from the Middle East and authoritative Talmudic discussions by Judaism's founding rabbis, it seemed to exemplify the idea that Jewish tradition was eternally true and meaningful. In that form, it became useful to American Jews seeking to understand the complexities of their own religious lives in an open society. By 1972, one rabbi called Hanukkah "one of the most relevant of Jewish holidays."[95] As American Jews retold that story in hymns and dramas, embodied it in pageants and children's assemblies, sang it in ditties, constructed new and artistic ritual objects for its enactment and argued its lessons before the U.S. Supreme Court, they enlarged the Hanukkah branch of the tree of Jewish tradition to uniquely impressive proportions.

2

Modern Maccabees

Sometime in the middle of the nineteenth century, Hanukkah began to evolve from an often neglected occasion in the Jewish calendar to one deemed particularly relevant for American Jews. Surprisingly, it did not begin with a new emphasis on actually celebrating the holiday but with new interest in the Maccabees themselves. Their image became a recurring trope in heated debates about how Jewish life could thrive in the new land. Competing factions vied for religious leadership of the country's Jews, and each sought the legitimacy of the past by claiming the mantle of the Maccabees, whose powerful family, the Hasmoneans, had achieved military, religious, and political leadership in ancient Judea. Those ancient heroes offered an authentically Jewish model that inspired and, each side hoped, legitimated its own bid to lead. Hoping to win over the Jewish masses, each faction argued its case in the English-language Jewish press. As they did so, they also impressed on American Jews the important role that the Maccabees had played in ancient Jewry's survival.[1]

Yet Maccabees seldom appear in the letters or diaries of earlier nineteenth-century American Jews. For example, Philadelphia's Jewish educator and philanthropist Rebecca Gratz, who lived from the middle of the American Revolution to just after the Civil War, wrote hundreds of letters to her scattered family and friends during her eighty-eight years, and she often noted Sabbaths, the holy fast day of Yom Kippur, family seders at Passover, and booths built at the fall holiday of Sukkot but not Hanukkah or its heroes, the Maccabees.[2] Even New York journalist Robert Lyon's tellingly named newspaper, *The Asmonean*, seldom noted the Maccabees. Published between 1849 and 1858, before the religious debates over leadership turned rancorous, British-born Lyon thought the best route to solving the religious differences dividing American Jews would be the establishment of a centralized religious authority, such as a *beth din* (religious court) that "would standardize religious law and practice." He preferred only to report on the early debates between reformers and traditionalists and to lay the various positions before his readers. Hazan Isaac Leeser's *Occident and American Jewish Advocate* mentioned the Maccabees only five times in nearly a decade. Two of those items simply reprinted speeches given at the anniversary dinners of charitable societies, and another noted that the Jews of China owned two books of the Maccabees. A Hanukkah sermon by Rabbi Max Lilienthal urged Jewish parents to provide Jewish educations for their children, and Isaac M. Wise, who came to lead the century's Reform movement, was of two minds about the holiday.[3] As a reformer, Wise believed Judaism's strength to be in its ethics and its devotion to God, and its weakness to lie in its less rational elements such as the tales of miracles, better suited for enchanting children than inspiring adults. He also opposed the incipient nationalism that Hanukkah's story suggested. As late as 1865, he even suggested abolishing the rite of lighting Hanukkah lights.[4] Yet, four years earlier, he had penned a fictionalized retelling of the Maccabean story and featured it in his national magazine in serialized form for over thirty-nine weeks. Many other Jewish leaders also turned to the Maccabees in the second half of the century.

For most of the nineteenth century, though, American Jewish life struggled along on the distant periphery of the Jewish world, an ocean away from the great centers of Jewish learning and the leadership they provided to Jews abroad. At the time of the American Revolution, the

Jews of the United States numbered no more than twenty-five hundred individuals scattered in a handful of communities along the eastern seaboard and constituted less than one-tenth of one percent of the general population. American laws granted the country's individual Jews—who numbered roughly one million by 1900—religious freedom but banned governmental support or funding to Jewish religious authorities. With the ratification of the U.S. Constitution in 1789, the federal government could neither support religion nor prohibit its "free exercise." Yet, even before the Constitution had been ratified, the rhetoric and values of the Revolution had begun to stir a revolution in congregational life. In 1785, the leaders of Philadelphia's oldest synagogue complained about their inability to compel their congregants to obey both religious laws and the synagogue's rules of orderly behavior because "under the laws of the country it is impossible to enjoin them from" flouting the synagogue's authority.[5] One event that epitomized the leaders' powerlessness occurred in Philadelphia in 1782 when one Jacob I. Cohen determined to marry Esther Mordecai, a widow who had converted to Judaism before marrying her now-deceased husband, a marriage prohibited by the congregational leaders because Jewish law prohibits a priest (*cohen* in Hebrew) from marrying a convert. Yet the couple soon wed, because three prominent synagogue members conducted, witnessed, and signed the marriage contract despite—and in full knowledge of—the prohibition. Jacob, Esther, and the witnesses each "placed personal liberty above" the dictates of both religious law and congregational authority.[6] Thirteen years after Jacob and Esther's wedding, a group of members asked the congregation for, and won, permission to form a separate prayer group that could pray according to the customs common among Jews who, like themselves, knew the traditions of central and eastern Europe, which differed in hymn selections, melodies, and pronunciation of Hebrew from the Sephardi traditions that prevailed at the synagogue. Within a decade, that group had broken away to form a separate congregation, Rodeph Shalom (Seekers of Peace). "Congregational autonomy became the rule," explains historian Jonathan Sarna; and congregations proliferated as immigrants added to the Jewish population and as "dissatisfied" members created new congregations. A similar process led to a second Jewish congregation in New York City twenty years later. The proliferation "changed the balance of power" in favor of the laity, who now had choices among various congregations, and Jewish clergy, like Protestant clergy, felt called on to persuade their congregants to observe religious precepts and to support religious institutions.[7] In creating the most persuasive arguments, lectures, and stories, rabbis elaborated on and enlivened the available stock of religious lore. The Maccabees provided them with exceptional models of religious dedication.

American society itself tended to discourage Jewish religious observance. Its six-day workweek and long workdays wreaked havoc with Judaism's holiday schedule and especially its Saturday Sabbath. Nineteenth-century Americans themselves overwhelmingly practiced varieties of Protestant Christianity, and many Protestants also supported various efforts to convert Jews to their faith. Leading Americans such as John Quincy Adams, future president of the United States, and the heads of Yale, Princeton, and Rutgers Universities, as well as evangelical women, financed missions to convert American Jews to Christianity.[8]

Taken as a whole, this situation posed a novel challenge to Jews. Rarely in their history had they lived for so long with so few boundaries between themselves and non-Jews. Rarely had the gentile world offered so many opportunities. Yet rarely had their own religious leaders so lacked the authority to guide them in devising an effective response.

Throughout the nineteenth century, some Jews tried various ways to adapt Judaism to American life. As they began looking for images to help understand and explain what a proper response to American challenges might be, Hanukkah became ripe for reinvention. In Charleston, South Carolina, one group of Jews made Hanukkah into a time for serious religious reflection that responded to their evangelical, Protestant milieu. At midcentury, a heated debate about the future of Judaism itself erupted among American rabbis, some of whom claimed to be Maccabees for the modern world. Later, young laymen championing new Jewish institutions to promote religious and cultural life emerged, similarly drawing on the Maccabees to claim authority for themselves and to justify their own youthful leadership. In the century's last years, the movement to resettle Jews in their ancient homeland near the Mediterranean Sea likened its effort to that of the Maccabees. Each of those very different projects aimed to help Judaism thrive under challenging new conditions, and each drew on a strong appeal to the Maccabees to justify its novel work.

Religious divisions in Congregation Beth Elohim in Charleston, South Carolina, early in the century prompted a revised understanding of Hanukkah and proved that American Jews would take religious matters into their own hands when rabbinic leadership did not address their needs. A group of congregants petitioned the synagogue for reforms to the worship. Admitting that few of them understood Hebrew, they asked that each Sabbath worship service include an English discourse on principles of Jewish moral law to follow the weekly reading of the Hebrew Pentateuch and that repetitions of Hebrew prayers be eliminated, thus shortening the service. They also asked for a more dignified service that matched the standards for seriousness and decorum which their Protestant neighbors boasted for their own religious worship. Beth Elohim refused.

The petitioners broke away from the congregation in 1824 and named themselves the Reformed Society of Israelites. Sixteen years later, Beth Elohim accommodated their requests, and a new hymnal in English— mostly written by a member of the Reformed Society, Penina Moise, a famed poet whom Charleston called its poet laureate—was produced for the newly reunited congregation.[9] It also agreed to bring an organ into the synagogue to supplement worship, a move contrary to both rabbinic law and historical custom.[10] Moise's Hanukkah hymn reveals the particular challenges to Jewish life in her community and is the earliest attempt to refashion the Jewish holiday into something especially meaningful to American Jews.

Moise, like some others in her congregation, considered herself a Sephardi Jew who traced her ancestry to Iberia and the Mediterranean area. Sephardi Jews customarily sang Psalm 30 at Hanukkah; Psalm 30 is noted in the Hebrew Bible as a song "for the dedication of the house" (the word Hanukkah means "dedication"). Its four stanzas begin, "I extol you, O Lord, for you have lifted me up, and not let my enemies rejoice over me." It thanks God for being merciful and promises to praise God forever.[11] Sephardi traditions aimed to keep liturgy and its music unchanging so that, as a member of New York city's Sephardi congregation explained, "any of us, arriving from almost any part of the world" would feel immediately at home in the synagogue.[12] Yet, in Charleston, traditions underwent change. Other Beth Elohim congregants claimed Ashkenazi descent from central or eastern Europe, where at Hanukkah

Jews often sang "Maoz Tsur," a six-stanza song that recounted various episodes in which God rescued Jews from calamities. But neither the biblical psalm nor the European song sufficed.

Faced with the opportunity to write hymns that more clearly expressed the sentiments of the Charleston group, Moise wrote a song that voiced a new approach to the holiday by blending Jewish and American religious viewpoints and modified a customary Hanukkah perspective. First, unlike both Psalm 30 and "Maoz Tsur," her song is intended specifically for Hanukkah, suggesting that her congregation felt the need to sing something special for that holiday. Borrowing her Protestant neighbors' terminology for religious songs, she titled her work "Hanucca Hymn." Yet its opening line affirms her belief in Judaism's God. "Great arbiter of human fate! Whose glory ne'er decays, To Thee alone we dedicate, the song and soul of praise," it begins and in those words counters the evangelical assertion that Jesus is the deity to whom prayers ought now to be offered. The rest of the hymn supports this opening assertion by briefly recounting the Hanukkah story by which God provided the "power . . . Which . . . to triumph led."

Second, Moise's hymn mines the Hanukkah story for ways to describe an individual's spiritual crisis. When Antiochus installed Greek worship in the ancient Temple in Jerusalem, he deprived Jews of the best place to obtain forgiveness for their sins. Moise's hymn imagines the personal anguish of ancient Jews whose sacred Temple had been desecrated, asserting that "in bitterness of soul they wept." After describing the Temple restored and the "priests of God his robe resumed," she concludes by using the defiled Temple as a metaphor for a contemporary "blemished heart" needing cleansing. "Oh! Thus shall mercy's hand delight, To cleanse the blemished heart; Rekindle virtue's waning light, And peace and truth impart." The hymn speaks of virtue, whose guiding light may be waning, and addresses the inner turmoil that results from such a spiritual crisis. It asks not for an end to exile, as does "Maoz Tsur," but for a comforting personal salvation that soothes religious anguish. Jews might sing it during synagogue worship or at home during candle-lighting ceremonies. Although Moise, like most rabbis in her century and centuries earlier, believed that God guided the Maccabean victory, her hymn turns the familiar story in a different direction. Throughout, she elaborates the personal anguish of

Feast of Lights
209
Great Arbiter of Human Fate

Penina Moise
f Moderato

Edward Samuel

1. Great Ar - bi - ter of hu - man fate, Whose glo - ry ne'er de - cays,
2. A - mid the ru - ins of their land; (In Sa - lem's sad de - cline.)
3. Not long to vain re - grets they yield, But for their cher - ished fane,
4. 'Twas Thine, O ev - er - last - ing King And u - ni - ver - sal Lord!

To Thee a - lone we ded - i - cate The song and soul of praise.
Stood forth a brave but scant - y band To bat - tle for their shrine,
Nerved by true faith, they take the field, And vic - to - ry ob - tain.
Whose won - ders still Thy ser - vants sing, Whose mercies they re - cord.

Thy pres - ence Ju - dah's host in - spired, On dan - ger's post to rush;
In bit - ter - ness of soul they wept, With - out the Temple wall,
But whose the pow - er, whose the hand, Which thus to tri - umph led
Oh! thus shall Mer - cy's hand de - light To cleanse the blemished heart,

By Thee the Mac - ca - bee was fired, I - dol - a - try to crush.
For weeds a - round its court had crept, And foes its priests en - thrall.
The slend - er but he - ro - ic band, From which blasphem - ers fled?
Re - kind - le vir - tue's wan - ing light, And truth and peace im - part.

Penina Moise's Hanukkah hymn from the 1820s praised the divine power that not only led the Maccabees but also could rekindle virtue among contemporary Jews. Here it is reprinted as "Feast of Lights." (Courtesy *Southern Jewish History*)

ancient Jews whose sacred temple had been desecrated, and she assures readers that just as God ultimately purified that temple, He could lead nineteenth-century Jews to their own pure spiritual lives. Her poem gave Hanukkah a place in the emerging religious style of American culture that was dominated by the language of individualism and personal conscience derived from both Protestantism and the Enlightenment. However, neither the Talmud nor the *Shulchan Aruch* identifies Hanukkah as a special occasion to ask for the forgiveness of sins. So why is Moise focusing on sin?

Moise's hymn shares a particular religious discourse that reigned in her area of the country. Born in 1797, Moise lived in a South dominated by a Protestantism that emphasized the anguish suffered by individuals who were unsure of Jesus's mercy. Half a century before her birth, evangelicals spilled into the South from the Mid-Atlantic region and began transforming the established Anglican order. Presbyterians, Baptists, and Methodists challenged the religious status quo by reaching out to women, workers, and slaves. After the American Revolution dismantled legal and tax support for Anglicanism—now called Episcopalianism—these evangelicals expanded their influence. By the time Moise wrote, southern women evangelicals were helping their family, friends, and neighbors to find salvation in Jesus.[13] The procedure would be the same—convince neighbors of their deep unhappiness and fear because their sins would provoke God's vengeance, then offer salvation through accepting Christ as God. Moise's Hanukkah hymn suggests that she had heard these arguments. She offers American Jews a way to speak of their own personal religious confusions or turmoil using Jewish images and provides a well-formed Jewish plea for God's reassurance at a particular time in the Jewish religious calendar. She provides an individual voice for prayer and an expression of inner need for God, and she ties those elements to Hanukkah's story through its imagery. Finally, by not mentioning exile, Moise suggests that Jews are satisfied with life in America, an idea we find expressed in letters written by American Jews since the mid 1700s.[14] The hymn proved so popular that it was reprinted many times, as late as 1959, in songbooks used by both Reform and Conservative Jews.

Moise's personalized Hanukkah hymn suited the personalized religious style of American Jews. Her work for her volatile congregation demonstrated some American Jews' desire to remake Jewish practice into something more meaningful to them in their new cultural environment and signaled their power to do so. In the United States, Jews learned, religious institutions need to accommodate their members if they are to survive.

Rabbis Restore Luster to the Maccabees

The events in Charleston presaged future religious divisions elsewhere. Throughout the century, many Jewish congregations fractured as their members disagreed about rules and practices, and clergy struggled to find ways to strengthen Jewish life.[15] Some rabbis compared the contemporary American Jewish dilemma to that faced by Jews in ancient Judea who embraced Hellenic culture yet disagreed about the degree and kind of Hellenic practices one could undertake and still retain Jewish identity.[16] They grasped a moment that seemed to resolve the confusion, the rededication of the Jerusalem Temple by the Maccabees and the fighters whom they led, in 164 B.C.E. With that rededication, Jewish ritual standards replaced the remnants of Greek worship imposed by Antiochus IV. That ancient experience seemed to prefigure the contemporary situation and to provide hope for its resolution. The Jerusalem Temple might be gone, but the image of those Jews who fought for Judaism inspired nineteenth-century rabbis to look at Hanukkah with new eyes.

Antebellum traditionalist Isaac Leeser knew about the battles within Moïse's Charleston congregation and deemed the trend toward religious laxity that washed over the West in the wake of the French Revolution a "calamity." "Instead of illustrating the old methods of worship and making them lovely to the multitude," Leeser said, reformers introduced "changes and modifications unknown . . . and . . . unauthorized . . . [and] unlawful."[17] To the Philadelphian Leeser, the commands and customs of Judaism had been set in place by God. They promoted a sense of personal piety and devotion to God that stirred the heart to more than just sentimentality.[18] Leeser publicized special Hanukkah events and rituals conducted by Jewish congregations around the country to back up his view that most Jews accepted tradition's authority and only needed better resources, such as religious schools, kosher foods, and supportive, committed congregations, to assist them in fulfilling their religious duties. He praised a Cleveland congregation's Hanukkah dedication of its new synagogue and noted that benevolent societies in both Cleveland and Baltimore hosted annual Hanukkah banquets. Leeser scoffed at a reform-minded leader in San Francisco who told his congregation that Hanukkah's meaning was simply to keep "the

light of religion in our hearts" and that Jews need not light the Hanukkah lamps. That synagogue's lamps remained dark. "Is this . . . progress?" Leeser asked his readers. He insisted that many San Franciscans
lit Hanukkah lamps in their homes and contended that the dark synagogue prompted some members to leave and to found another congregation under more traditional principles. Provoking discord like that
was one more way that Leeser felt San Franciscan reformers acted like
modern-day Hellenists who embraced principles opposed to Judaism,
and not like Maccabees.[19]

From Leeser's perspective, reformers "deformed" Judaism to accommodate an uninformed laity, rather than educating the common Jewish person to appreciate Judaism's purpose and meaning.[20] Other traditionalists felt similarly.[21] Tradition-minded New Yorker Samuel Isaacs,
who edited the *Jewish Messenger*, insisted that the Maccabees should be
studied by "[Jewish] children to kindle the spark of [Jewish] patriotism
latent in the hearts of their parents."[22] Traditionalists encouraged Jews
to proudly fulfill their traditional religious duties along with their obligations as citizens of the larger nation.[23]

Like most nineteenth-century American Jews, Leeser came from
central Europe. He served as hazan at Philadelphia's oldest congregation for two decades. Although Leeser had no training as a rabbi, his
religious education far exceeded that of his congregants. He left his
stamp on the Jacksonian era through his monthly periodical on Jewish
affairs, his English translation of the Hebrew Bible, his volumes of sermons, and the various institutions for Jewish education that he helped
to establish, including a short-lived rabbinical school that folded soon
after his death in 1868. In Philadelphia, where Quakers, Presbyterians,
Episcopalians, and Lutherans each maintained schools and supported a
publishing house that produced religious tracts and Bibles, Leeser, rabbis, and lay leaders agreed that Jews needed similar institutional supports to educate them in their historic faith. Only with proper education, they believed, could American Jews understand the importance
of traditional practices such as Sabbath observance and dietary restrictions and so maintain them even though they might be inconvenient.

Tradition-minded rabbi Sabato Morais arrived in Philadelphia in
1851 following Leeser's departure from the congregation he had served

—the city's oldest. Morais remained in Philadelphia for the rest of his life, leading the congregation and leading new organizations to educate American Jews in their traditions. He urged Jews to remember the Maccabees as "illustrious, . . . brave men who ventured their lives to transmit to us unity of religion." He, too, insisted that the Maccabees hoped to preserve Judaism, not transform it.[24] Speaking in 1850, one year before his arrival in Philadelphia from London, England, Morais offered the Maccabees as a symbol of Jewish devotion that might inspire contemporary Jews to rededicate themselves to their ancient faith. A native of the Italian port city of Livorno, Morais felt that he understood Jews in both London and Philadelphia, two port cities where they participated in a cosmopolitan society. He urged them to work for the betterment of both their Jewish and larger communities through religious "self cultivation" which led "away from the self . . . toward political and social activity." The religious self-cultivation he had in mind required education, and Morais developed Philadelphia's Hebrew Literary Society into a lively organization that soon became part of the national Young Men's Hebrew Association.[25] In later years, he established and led a rabbinical school, the Jewish Theological Seminary, to train American rabbis who could educate Jewish congregants and lead them in living observant Jewish lives.

Leeser, Morais, and other traditionalists believed America's freedoms offered Jews an opportunity to embrace their religion even more fully than had been possible under oppressive past conditions. Hanukkah, they felt, because it was the holiday of rededication, ought to provide a vehicle for modern Jews to rededicate themselves to their faith. To Jews scattered around the country and disagreeing over religious practices, these rabbis talked of Maccabees uniting with other Jews to advance and defend their religion and people. Samuel Isaacs, a traditionalist living in New York, fumed that it was "self-abasing" to consider that "here in these shores of freedom, where we have every right guaranteed us by the constitution, where we have every reason to thank God for His goodness to us, and where we have every cause to manifest by our acts that we are Israelites, observing the commandments delegated to us —how humiliating is the idea that [Judaism's] most sacred ordinances [such as dietary laws and Sabbath observance] are totally disregarded."[26]

But other traditionalists held more complex views. Baltimore's Rabbi Benjamin Szold opposed what he saw as radicalism, not change. He compiled a prayer book for his congregation that "closely followed traditional lines" yet included German translations (understood by most American Jews at that time), and it too became popular in America. In Baltimore, it replaced the more radical prayer book, compiled by reform leader Isaac M. Wise, that was used by the congregation before Szold's arrival in 1859. Under Szold's leadership, the membership gained a reputation for strict observance of the Sabbath.[27] Szold's colleague Rabbi Marcus Jastrow of Philadelphia held both rabbinic ordination and a doctorate from the University of Halle, a secular education that might have convinced him to join the ranks of those seeking Judaism's reform. Instead, after coming to Philadelphia in 1866, Jastrow taught Bible and Jewish history at Maimonides College, Leeser's brainchild. Jastrow slowed the pace of his Philadelphia congregation's ultimate embrace of reform.

Traditionalists themselves did not always agree on every matter regarding Judaism. Some traditionalists stepped out of Talmudic norms in their own lives yet wished the synagogue service to remain unchanged.[28] Leeser, a bachelor, rented rooms at the home of a gentile widow, a circumstance that led some members of his congregation to suspect that he could not adhere to Judaism's dietary laws.[29] Leeser and some other traditionalists, such as New York rabbi Morris Raphall, hoped their own congregations would adopt the decorum they noticed in Protestant churches without otherwise changing the Jewish worship service.[30] However, when they compared themselves to their coreligionists who touted reform, they erased their differences and instead conveyed an image of united support for historical Judaism. In their arguments with reformers, they claimed the mantle of the ancient Maccabees who defeated an alien oppressor and restored correct Jewish worship to the Jerusalem Temple.

In the midwestern trading center of Cincinnati, by contrast, other leaders took a different approach. There, rabbis who believed Judaism itself needed to be "modernized" through vernacular worship (at first in German and, later, in English), shorter worship services, and a greater emphasis on ethics to replace complicated distinctive practices such as dietary restrictions established institutions to promote what they called

Reform Judaism. Those rabbis provided weekly lengthy, explanatory, and edifying sermons to instruct Jews in their new approach. Reformers also adorned synagogue worship with instrumental music from the great composers of Europe, such as Bach, Mendelssohn, and Handel, and encouraged family-style seating instead of the separation between men and women that had long marked synagogues. Their emphasis on the synagogue, they believed, also helped Judaism to fit the American environment, where Christians expected religion to focus on church.[31] Many American Jews found those changes appealing, although controversy surrounded them and actual synagogue practices varied widely.

Although reformers, like the traditionalists, aimed to nurture Jewish life in the United States, reformers believed that only their newly reshaped version of Judaism could fit the American environment. Convinced that Talmud-driven Jewish practice could never survive in the modern world, they wrote essays and sermons advancing their cause. Published in various Jewish newspapers and magazines geared to ordinary American Jews, their arguments advised modern Jews navigating their way between American and Jewish customs.

At midcentury, the trend to reform Jewish religion became broadly influential. Led by European-born reform-minded rabbis who had come to the United States, reformers established the first organization to unite American Jewish congregations and a seminary to train rabbis, the only such institutions in the country (Leeser's seminary had folded, and Morais's seminary was not yet born). More than one-third of the country's Jewish congregations identified themselves with the new trend. By 1879, 105 congregations affiliated with Reform's Union of American Hebrew Congregations (UAHC), out of 278 Jewish congregations nationwide.[32] Yet many congregations that did not affiliate with UAHC also experimented with reforms.

Rabbis and Their Worries

Nineteenth-century rabbis studied Jews newly integrating into Western culture in North America and western Europe. Between 1776 and 1840, marriages with Christians reached 28.7 percent of all known Jewish marriages. Adventurous young Jews made their way in a new country that offered them both citizenship and unparalleled economic opportunities. Yet, with immigrants' attention focused on learning a new language, new customs, and new places, Jewish religious obligations sometimes fell by the wayside. Kosher meat was not always available. Most immigrant men began their labors as peddlers who traveled to small towns and across countrysides to serve rural gentile customers, and the large distances could not always be crossed before sundown began each Friday evening's Sabbath.[33] Dozens of new Jewish communities sprang up in trading centers such as Chicago, Buffalo, St. Louis, Atlanta, and Los Angeles. In some cases, peddlers arrived in small outlying towns as bachelors and married local gentile women. Many of those couples raised their children as Christians.[34] Lacking the support of kin and community that Jewish immigrants had left behind and devoid of any authoritative body to teach or enforce religious practices, American Jewish life rested on myriad individual decisions about how —or if—to participate in religion. American rabbis wondered how Judaism would survive.

Most rabbis believed the future of Jewish life in America rested on their own ability to motivate ordinary Jews to greater religious devotion.[35] Talk of ancient Maccabees fighting a great world power in order to restore Jewish practice dotted their rhetoric. Traditionalists more often spoke of the grandeur of the Maccabean past and the duty of modern Jews to honor it. Reforming rabbis used more militaristic Maccabean imagery, drawn from both the Books of the Maccabees and American culture, and dismissed the legend about miracles established in the Talmud. Reformers sometimes claimed that they themselves were the Maccabees of today and often told the ancient story in contemporary language. Both sides also blended America's rhetoric of liberty and revolution into the story of the Maccabean revolt. In doing so, they contributed to a larger trend that dominated American Jewish life as American Jews wove their own story into the fabric of American culture.[36] Those nineteenth-century Hanukkah debates lent new significance to the heretofore minor festival. However, Leeser printed one item in 1845 that signaled the coming trend: a "manifesto" by German rabbis fighting reformers abroad. "At the time of the Maccabees," it said, "Israel . . . valiantly fortified their hearts with courage . . . and saved their holy faith."[37] Rabbis in America soon repeated that image.

Reformers and the Heart of Hanukkah

Most reformers opposed both Jewish nationalism and miracles, two ideas at the core of Hanukkah's celebration. Isaac M. Wise, the most influential reformer in nineteenth-century America, at times sought to eliminate Hanukkah lights. Born in Bohemia in 1819, Wise settled in Cincinnati, where he built institutions to support the Reform movement. He believed that Judaism's "theology" did not depend on a belief in miracles such as the one historically linked to Hanukkah, and he even eliminated mention of miracles from his 1867 prayer book, *Minhag America*. Instead, reformers made a strong appeal to a different element of Hanukkah's story by shifting focus away from the miracle of the oil and toward the Maccabees and their struggle against Hellenism. At the same time, though, they sought legitimacy for their own efforts to revamp Jewish laws in the ancient Maccabean decree allowing Jews to militarily defend themselves on the Sabbath, negating older religious law forbidding it. Wise told American Jews that reformers had "regenerated and rejuvenated" Hanukkah as part of their goal to reshape Judaism itself.[38]

Wise also appreciated the Maccabees' heroism. He ranked their importance to history with that of seventeenth-century British military leader Oliver Cromwell, who had overthrown the monarchy and instituted a short-lived commonwealth with himself in charge. Cromwell had also allowed Jews to live in England, overturning their 1290 expulsion, and so earned the high regard of many Jews. Wise praised the Maccabees for their "indestructible tenacity, strength, power of mind and force of character," attributes he believed they shared with Cromwell. Had "Israel yielded" to Syria, Wise wrote, "the entire history of mankind would have taken another turn. . . . [There would have been] no Jesus of Nazareth and no Mohammet of Mecca. . . . None can say how modern civilization would look now."[39] For that reason, he agreed with the German reforming rabbis who unanimously had decided on "a more suitable and solemn celebration of [Hanukkah]."[40]

Abraham Geiger, a leading voice for Reform in Frankfurt am Main and influential among reformers in nineteenth-century America, depicted Judaism as a tradition that thrives on change. "Wherever a new culture springs up," he wrote, "where the mind develops itself untram-meled, where a fresh nationality or a fresh spiritual development is manifested, there Judaism quickly joins the movement and its profes-sors soon adopt the new culture, digest it, and regard the country which offers them the highest boon, mental and spiritual liberty, as their home." Geiger argued that even Hellenism initially provided that boon, until the "Syrio Grecian" ruler Antiochus IV crushed Judea. The Macca-bean revolt occurred because "the heart of the people could not endure oppression."[41] Geiger and other reformers talked about the Maccabees' strength of heart to suggest to Jewish people that their novel approach to Judaism had an ancient precedent. In both the Talmud and the *Shul-chan Aruch*, Hanukkah's fighters and martyrs alike are simply called Jews willing to die for their faith, people whose devotion convinced God to rescue them.[42] But reformers sought to cultivate an appreciation for religious courage in the language of military heroism and suggested that contemporary Jews could determine their religion's future.[43]

To promote that perspective, in 1860 Wise penned a romantic fiction based on the Maccabean revolt, which he serialized over thirty-nine weeks in his national Jewish magazine, *The Israelite*.[44] In it, he recast the ancient uprising in popular language to appeal to ordinary Ameri-can Jews. His magazine soon reached more Jews in more towns than any other American Jewish publication.[45] Years later, Wise claimed to have written his several works of historical fiction simply to fill the space allotted for them in his magazine, sending them immediately to the press without any editing or revision. By that account, he wrote them quickly and without a second thought.[46] Yet such easily writ-ten pieces suggest his own real views. Wise had worked tirelessly on a scholarly history of the Jewish people that found few readers.[47] His serialized historical romances popularized the approach to the Jewish past that emphasized human agency rather than miracles and divine intervention, the same viewpoint that he had struggled to convey in his scholarly work. In Wise's hands, the Maccabean story looked like other popular fiction in the Victorian era. Victorians expected to find religious virtues, patriotism, and strong gender distinctions in their lit-erary romances, and Wise delivered. On the eve of the Civil War, his novella mixed the language of contemporary political debates about liberty's defense into the Hanukkah story. Like many Jewish writers in

Europe also, Wise created popular fiction with Jewish content that, by bridging modern and Jewish values, helped readers to "navigate . . . a new cultural identity."[48]

Wise was not the first to tell the Maccabean story in the language of liberty and revolution. By 1860, portions of Georg Frederic Handel's oratorio *Judas Maccabaeus* had been performed many times in the United States, probably beginning as early as a 1796 Philadelphia performance of the march alone.[49] Handel, one of the most prolific composers in revolutionary-era Europe, drew on religious themes for his oratorios, which provided nonliturgical, popular religious entertainments. Handel was born in 1685 in Halle and educated in the Lutheran Pietistic tradition noted for its humanistic views and sympathy for Jews, and by the time he relocated to England, where he remained, he seems to have identified "the Jewish cause with the humanitarian strivings of an era dedicated to social progress."[50] Jews in England enjoyed far greater freedoms than he had seen among Jews living on the Continent, and Handel himself knew Jews and often worked with them in his adopted country. When commissioned to write an oratorio to honor the Duke of Cumberland, who had quashed a Jacobite uprising in Scotland, Handel looked to ancient Jewish history and composed *Judas Maccabaeus*, first performed in 1747. Only two years earlier, London's Jewish brokers and merchants had helped England to avert national disaster during an economic panic. Moreover, Jewish merchants had put their ships—fully outfitted—at the government's disposal, and many more Jewish men signed up for the national militia. With *Judas Maccabaeus*, Handel and his librettist, Rev. Thomas Morrell, recalled Jews' service to England and provided the country's stage with a rare image of a heroic Jew, rather than a villain. British Jews flocked to its six performances in its opening year and frequented its thirty performances during Handel's lifetime.[51] Performances of *Judas Maccabaeus* frequently included the aria "See, the Conquering Hero Comes," originally written by Handel for his oratorio *Joshua*.[52] When Judas sings that his father had died urging his sons to "liberty or death!" the oratorio merges the ancient Maccabean military battle to retake the Jerusalem Temple with the eighteenth century's revolutionary values.[53]

Handel's works quickly traveled to North America. By 1818, Bostonians performed his oratorio *Messiah* each year, either at Christmas or Easter, and Handel remained popular throughout the century.[54] By 1873, Bostonians also enjoyed full performances of *Judas Maccabaeus*.[55] A decade later, one person in that city admitted that "now . . . Cincinnati [is] striving for that supremacy which Boston has long been fully entitled to through her Handel and Haydn Society, . . . [and] New York [is] . . . to be credited with the establishment of the American Opera."[56] When nineteenth-century American Jews sought performances of *Judas Maccabaeus* at Hanukkah, they participated in the nation's musical tastes, but in a manner that suited their Jewish sensibilities. Its productions taught them that the Maccabees fought for the same revolutionary values touted in nineteenth-century American culture.

When Wise was writing his historical Jewish fiction, he participated in a movement popular among modernizing Jews on both sides of the Atlantic. In both Europe and the United States, Jewish writers penned fiction and poetry in the vernacular that shaped a modern Jewish culture. In central Europe, some Jewish readers considered Jewish historical fiction important for its capacity to depict "the ethical grandeur of the Jewish past."[57] A Hanukkah poem written in 1848 in German for a Jewish audience praised the Maccabees and their "courageous fight for freedom."[58] Wise drew on Handel's oratorio, American cultural values, and Europe's trend in Jewish historical fiction when writing his fictional Hanukkah narrative. His male Jewish characters exemplified contemporary American masculine values, explaining that they fought for liberty, justice, truth, and manliness itself. One figure explains, "Death is not the greatest evil. . . . [It is] . . . sacrific[ing] truth, justice and liberty." Wise concluded his tale of "First Maccabees" by telling his readers, "kindle your Chanukah lights and forget not your God and country."[59]

Wise also knew that women made up much of the readership for American magazines and fiction, and his romance of the Maccabean revolt provided novel female characters who motivated soldiers and helped to secure victories. Wise encouraged his readers to imagine ancient Jewish women, who, like their men, also embodied the attributes esteemed by Victorian Americans. Wise's female character Miriam, mother to Judah and his brothers, depicted a Victorian maternal ideal. At her husband's deathbed, she describes her faith in his eternal life and hears angels singing as God receives him and grants him "eternal bliss." In the ancient First Book of the Maccabees, Judah's father instructs his sons to continue the revolt. In Wise's story, their mother, Miriam, does so: "I dedicate my five sons to thy service, O God of Israel," she says after her husband's death. For many American Jews, the products of traditional parents and the descendants of even more traditional European communities, a character such as Miriam, an elderly mother who guided her grown sons' religious commitments, would have carried emotional power. Wise also added the character of lovely young Iphegine, named for his daughter born that same year. In his fiction, she provided the love interest for a younger Maccabee brother, Jonathan. Iphegine's spy missions among the invaders, dangerous encounters, and repeated rescues by Jonathan enhance the story's drama. They translate ancient descriptions of female heroism linked to motherhood into a modern idiom in which women support military action. Her women friends discuss their trials under foreign rule, as their husbands, lovers, brothers, and fathers leave to fight or are murdered by their enemies —wartime experiences shared by women throughout history. But Wise points out that despite women's personal sense of Jewish loyalty, they, like men, can be confused about where to draw the line between gentile attitudes and behaviors and Jewish faith. Iphegine expresses the conundrum of many American Jews who adopted much of general American culture, practiced little Judaism, yet considered themselves loyal Jews. She explains that although she acts like a gentile, she believes in Judaism. "I worship no Gods besides the God of Israel," she begins. "I love beauty and chastity, therefore I am a devotee of . . . Venus. . . . But I worship only the God of heaven and earth." The hero, Jonathan, rebukes her for idolizing Venus and urges her to dedicate herself more completely to Jewish traditions.[60]

Although reformers invited women to play a role more equal to that of lay men in the synagogue, they did not allow them to become rabbis and expected that women would continue to require guidance by men. Wise expected some of his readers to see themselves in Iphegine, a young person attracted to the style and form of non-Jewish culture. Jews who read this story got the hint that American values matched Jewish values and that Jewish men and women who remained loyal to Judaism could nevertheless embody them. Thus armed with new hymns, dedicated rabbis, comfortable modifications to Judaism, and an instructive popular press, American Jewish reformers set about saving Judaism for contemporary Jews, thinking of themselves as modern Maccabees.

Both reformers and traditionalists claimed to be Maccabees for the modern era, heroes saving Judaism from extinction in a larger, attractive American culture dominated by foreign beliefs and ideals. In their sermons and their educational organizations, traditionalists aimed to inspire American Jews with a Maccabean model of self-sacrifice and religious devotion. Traditionalists shared an aversion to the sweeping nature of the changes made by reformers. Believing that the Talmudic method by which rabbis adapted biblical law to changing historical circumstances continued to be the best way for Jews to adapt their religious lives to the modern world, they argued that Hanukkah's story justified their trust in God and their loyalty to those traditions.[61] They used Hanukkah's story to refute reformers, pointing out that the Maccabees insisted on maintaining some of the very Jewish "prohibitions" which reformers canceled, such as the dietary laws. Rather than keeping Jews loyal, traditionalists said, reformers provided a route *out* of Judaism and so encouraged its demise. By bringing the Maccabees into the debate over how Judaism might survive in the modern world, all sides revealed the emotions that animated them. Their polemic polarized differences that actually fell along a continuum of approaches to Jewish life.

Young Maccabees Take the Lead

Philadelphia traditionalist Rabbi Sabato Morais and New York's tradition-minded, English-born leader at that city's oldest congregation, Shearith Israel, Henry Pereira Mendes, inspired a small cadre of Young Men's Hebrew Association (YMHA) laymen in their cities. That diverse group included, as they matured, a Semitics scholar, a judge, a physician and poet, a librarian, businessmen, and inventors.[62] In October, 1879, New Yorkers Max Cohen, Philip Cowen, and Mendes met with the Philadelphians Solomon Solis-Cohen, Mayer Sulzberger, Joseph and Samuel Fels, Cyrus Adler, and Cyrus Sulzberger to pledge themselves to "perpetuate and elevate" Judaism. Calling themselves *Keyam Dishmaya*, or loosely, "upholding the dictates of Heaven" in Aramaic, they spearheaded new lay educational and defense organizations that laid the foundation for twentieth-century Jewish intellectual life. Historian Jonathan Sarna explains that the group hoped to launch a revival of Jewish enthusiasm in the United States and aimed, first, "to revitalize and deepen the religious and spiritual lives of American Jews; second, to strengthen Jewish education; and third, to promote the restoration of Jews as a people, including their ultimate restoration to the land of Israel."[63] Their commitment to furthering American Jewish life did not dim as they matured—on the contrary, over the next sixty years these men went on to found or lead significant institutions to reach different audiences across the broad swath of American Jewry. Their achievements included the Jewish Theological Seminary (1886), the Jewish Publication Society (1888) to publish books of Jewish interest, and the American Jewish Historical Society (1892) to study and make known the history of Jews in America and which, through its quarterly publication, also disseminated that knowledge. Using a bequeath from the leading antebellum Philadelphia Jewish Gratz family, they established Gratz College (1893) primarily to train Jewish educators and Dropsie College (1907) to promote advanced Judaic studies, both in Philadelphia. They participated in creating the *Jewish Encyclopedia* (1901–1906) and in "the movement to bring the renowned Jewish scholar Solomon Schechter to America in 1902 to lead the Jewish Theological Seminary after Morais' death."[64] With Schechter at the Seminary, a new, more traditionally focused Jewish denomination emerged that called itself the Conservative movement. In fifty years, it became the largest Jewish denomination. The group similarly strengthened the effort to bring the scholarly journal *Jewish Quarterly Review* from England to the United States in 1910. After establishing the Jewish Publication Society, they further developed its capacity to produce high-quality Hebrew works. That made possible their work in translating the Jewish Bible (1893–1917) and producing the Schiff Library of Jewish Classics (1914–1936).[65] Sarna deems their work nothing less than "a great awakening" for American Jewry.

The group's first step was a new national Jewish magazine, the *American Hebrew*, launched in 1879 to "stir up [their] brethren to pride in [their] time-honored faith."[66] In the young founders' view, previous generations had felt the "crushing impositions and restrictions of a bigoted Europe," and their own parents' generation was burdened by the "all-absorbing cares of bread-and-butter labor." But perhaps thinking of both the Maccabees and the American revolutionists, they described themselves as "combative," like the "youth of every manly nation that has a soul and a history."[67] They saw themselves uniquely suited to "awaken" their coreligionists to greater religious devotion.

The young YMHA men, all American born and raised, spearheaded a new kind of Hanukkah entertainment: the spectacle. The popular civic fetes that celebrated the United States influenced their efforts. Only three years earlier, hundreds of public historical orations delivered in thirty-eight states commemorated the centennial of American independence. Speakers commonly blended religion with nationalism, some comparing the country's destiny to that of ancient Israel and offering their listeners "timeless, universal moral principles" to guide the present. Offering history lessons as "holy heirlooms," orators spoke to crowds from stages elaborately decorated with arches and greenery and flanked by women costumed to depict various virtues. Those events encouraged even more spectacular pageantry that soon appeared in many locations around the country.[68] The YMHA men hoped to rejuvenate commitment to Jewish life among American Jewish men in the same way that the recent American centennial activities aimed to rejuvenate national patriotism. Hanukkah, the holiday of dedication, seemed an ideal occasion to display manly Jewish devotion by performing elaborately costumed scenes from Judaism's ancient drama.

In December 1879, New York YMHA members and their friends staged a massive Hanukkah pageant at New York's Academy of Music, calling it "The Grand Revival of the National Holiday of Chanucka." Their title drew on the popular Christian religious revivals organized in late nineteenth century around the country. But instead of the religious exhortations and hymns that made up Protestant revivals, evidence suggests that the YMHA staged scenes from *Judas Maccabeus*, accompanied by an orchestra and a professional military band. Several hundred costumed men and women composed its six tableaux vivants depicting episodes from Hanukkah's history in a manner designed to inspire the participants and the audience to take up Hanukkah celebrations with new zest. Advertising promised "historically correct" costumes "especially designed to illustrate the Maccabean period."[69] Depicting the Maccabees dressed in battle armor triumphantly reclaiming the Temple

This image of the Hanukkah pageant by the Young Men's Hebrew Association, New York City, December 1879, appeared in *Frank Leslie's Illustrated Newspaper* the following month. (Courtesy Free Library of Philadelphia)

in Jerusalem, cleansing it of Greek gods and sacrificial objects, and rededicating it to the God of the Jews by lighting the sacred candles, it asserted that Jewish religious life was a manly and exciting endeavor. It refuted the Victorian trend toward female-led piety that seemed to contribute to religious apathy among American men and to the popularity of ritual-rich fraternal associations.[70] Evangelical reaction against a seemingly feminized image of a meek and mild Jesus, in addition to a fundamental concern that industrial labor was ruining men's health, supported the popularity of the Young Men's Christian Association to promote a "muscular Christianity."[71] Brought to the United States from England in 1851, the YMCA movement boomed especially after the Civil War. American culture felt the impact of these post–Civil War images of virile masculinity. Although synagogues remained firmly in the hands of men, the Grand Revival of Chanucka reflected the more vigorous and dominant understandings of how men ought to behave. The previous year, New Yorkers had attended a Hanukkah concert featuring *Judas Maccabaeus*.[72] But Cohen and his colleagues hoped that when flesh-and-blood young Jews depicted its themes, it not only would become an anthem for American Jews but would also motivate them to action. The following year, Jews in Baltimore and Philadelphia staged similar events, and New Yorkers repeated their pageant.[73]

Americans around the country reading *Frank Leslie's Illustrated Newspaper* on January 3, 1880, learned about the grand event. Its tableaux offered richly costumed and posed presentations without any actual acting—an art still deemed somewhat disreputable—making it easy for all participants to achieve a fine result. An arranger of children's festivals, the common professional to enlist for pageants such as this one, set up the tableaux.[74] Beginning with an orchestral overture of Chopin's "March funebre, one hundred neatly-clad children from the Hebrew Orphan Asylum marched out upon the large platform" and sang the hymn Adon Olam (God of the World) with orchestral accompaniment, "with excellent effect." After the children left the stage, "the curtain slowly rose and disclosed . . . the first tableau, 'The Country in Mourning,' typifying the Jewish nation . . . under Syrian yoke." To enhance the effect, "brilliant vari-colored lights flashed over the scene." The second tableau, "The Challenge," featured a statue of Jupiter on an altar in an imaginative marketplace at Modein.[75] But for the finale, the arrangers created an even more rousing performance. Two young sisters led off a "grand procession," followed by over a hundred "young ladies with cymbals, incense-bearers, slaves carrying precious vessels and jewels," and Judah Maccabee carrying a banner with Hebrew words meaning "Who Is Like to Thee, Oh, God?" Excerpted from the biblical book of Exodus, the phrase used the first letters of each word to spell "MAKABI." Judah preceded his "brothers, Jewish soldiers, trumpeters, banner bearers, Syrian captives, and young women with harps." According to *Leslie's Newspaper*, "After the parade, forty Jewish maidens with cymbals danced. The dancers [appeared in divisions wearing] blue, red, white and gold, and the fourth silver and white. In the stately [movements], these colors blended or separated like a kaleidoscope. At a stroke from a pair of cymbals behind the scenes, the lights . . . changed from gold to green, or to blue, or to red, while the dancers grouped themselves into motionless statues. Suddenly the curtain at the rear of the stage lifted and a very brilliant light streamed out" to reveal the Temple's interior. "On one side was the *Minorah* [sic], in the center the altar of sacrifice, and on the other side the altar of incense.

High priests and Levites, in Biblical dress, were performing their official duties. Judah and his brothers were in the attitude of worship." The reviewer judged it a "grand work of realistic art." It was nearly midnight when the curtain fell and a grand ball began, inviting the audience to enjoy social dancing.[76]

The sixth tableau earned a particular place in *Leslie's Newspaper*. In its full-page illustration, the women have completed their dances and are bowing, on their knees on the floor below a stage. On the stage, men dressed as priests and as warriors have lit a human-size menorah in a mockup of the Jerusalem Temple. It is a clearly organized scene: male heroes and priests above with the divine light of the Temple shining on them, other warriors standing below, and women kneeling before them all. Such pageantry portrayed the Jewish past with grandeur, along with a Victorian sense of social order and piety. It conveyed to its audience that Judaism deserved admiration and respect and that its ideals could still inspire their own era.

In deeming the Hanukkah tableaux art, Frank Leslie articulated a view shared by most Americans at midcentury. Born in England in 1821 and trained as an engraver and illustrator, he had arrived in the United States as Henry Carter in 1852 to pursue a career in publishing. Three years later, he began publishing his eponymous weekly illustrated magazine, along with several others specially geared to women, boys, and girls. In 1857, he took the name Frank Leslie. For two decades after his magazine's start in 1855, he felt confident that he and his readers shared a "common moral map" based on a gendered and racially divided social order and piety. After his death in January 1880, his wife took the helm at the magazine and even legally renamed herself "Frank Leslie." But the country was changing. By the 1880s, suffragists, immigrant radicals, trade unionists, working women, and freedmen, among others, constituted a new, fractured public with which Leslie's magazine did not communicate. Its style became associated with elite society for whom a hierarchical social order held increasing appeal as threats to its power bubbled up.[77] The Hanukkah revival's tableaux perfectly suited the Leslies' search for moralistic narrative art.

For older Jews viewing the event, the Hanukkah revival countered a common perception that young Jewish people felt alienated from religious life. Many young Jews did indeed prefer YMHA activities to

synagogue worship. Some young people voiced distaste for the dry sermons that had become the centerpiece of many Reform Sabbath services. In more traditional congregations, some young people did not
feel compelled to attend the lengthy services conducted in Hebrew,
a language with which they had little facility. Others accused afflu-
ent congregations of indifference to social ills. Some women resented
their exclusion from formal temple or synagogue membership.[78] Yet
hundreds of Jewish young adults donned costumes for the Hanukkah
revival, a uniquely exciting event. Perhaps even more surprising to their
elders' expectations, by embodying Handel's *Judas Maccabaeus*, young,
nineteenth-century American Jewish activists asked to be seen as modern Maccabees.

Hanukkah's story of military revolt also countered stereotypes of
effeminate male Jews that sometimes appeared in the American and
the German press. Folklore about Jews, brought to America with European immigrants, depicted Jewish men fighting only with their wits,
like women.[79] As the Civil War increased American regard for male
bravery, physical power, and aggression, Hanukkah's militarism became
more meaningful to American Jews.[80] Longfellow's dramatic poem
Judas Maccabaeus, published only eight years before the pageant, provided a similarly heroic image of Jews, despite its focus on Antiochus's
rise and fall.[81] The *Keyam Dishmaya* men also saw the Maccabees as
models for their own courageous devotion to Judaism, proudly identifying their minority status in the face of what many American newspapers called "universal" Christmas celebrations.[82]

The YMHA pageant's parading Maccabean fighters also mirrored a
staple of post–Civil War American culture. Nearly two and a half million men had served in the war, and veterans climbed the country's
social and political ladders. Processions of such leaders opened Philadelphia's Centennial City.[83] Memorial Day, sometimes called Decoration Day, took shape as a national holiday in towns large and small as
veterans paraded, cheered on by women and children. Speeches and
anthems lauding veterans' courage, leadership, and self-sacrifice enhanced each parade's emotional impact.[84] A few months before the Hanukkah revival, New York's Academy of Music hosted that city's Memorial Day exercises. The Hanukkah revival's parade of warriors displayed
Jewish male power and its importance to Judaism in a similar style. Its

parading heroes offered Jews a picture of themselves that refuted the more common images of Jews on America's stages, those of greedy Shylock, the villainous Nathan the Jew, the perfidious Isaac, father of Rebecca in *Ivanhoe*, or the laughable Jew as a junk or old-clothes dealer.[85]

Like many Memorial Day events, the Hanukkah pageant framed soldiers with costumed women who represented cultural ideals. The mourning widow or mother served as the feminine ideal at Memorial Day, and the revival contained no shortage of similar types. But the revival's young organizers also created images of robust youth from Judaism's ancient past. Women became dancing maidens like those who danced before David's army on its successful return to Jerusalem more than eight hundred years before the Maccabean victory. Their dances stamped the Jewish past with beauty and suggested to Jewish men that if they too became courageous Jews, maidens might dance for them. Images of dancing women contrasted with those of parading warriors and the military bands to create distinct gender ideals that mirrored both Jewish and American cultures.

When Baltimore's YMHA mounted a similar event the following year, women found more important roles onstage. A young woman read an "explanatory address" specially written by twenty-year-old Henrietta Szold. She had been educated in Judaism by her father, traditionalist rabbi Benjamin Szold, and went on to become a leading figure in twentieth-century Jewish life. In 1879, she joined the voices urging greater attention to Hanukkah. A second young woman read the poem "Hannah and Her Seven Sons," written by New York philanthropist Minnie Desau Louis and based on the ancient mother who saw her children tortured to death for refusing to eat forbidden food.[86] Women's work in these holiday pageants provided female models of piety within a manly Hanukkah. In contrast to Wise's image of Iphegine, these women revealed no ambiguity about their allegiance to Judaism. Just as the marching Maccabees offered a more appealing image of Jewish men, the pageant's dancing maidens and poets offered more genteel images of Jewish women than commonly were seen on the popular stage, where the frequently performed play *Leah the Forsaken* depicted a wild and uncivilized Jewish woman.[87]

Both Wise and the *Keyam Dishmaya* men elaborated on the image of the Maccabees in their effort to inspire contemporary Jews—though

This drawing of the Genius of Liberty guiding the Maccabees into battle
spiritualized and simplified Eugene Delacroix's famous 1830 painting,
Liberty Leading the People, which also depicted a noble purpose for the
carnage of war. The drawing brings a modest version of France's emblem,
Marianne, associated with both liberty and reason, into Hanukkah's ancient
story. Created by artist G. D. M. Peixotto, it became the frontispiece for a
volume of essays in *The Menorah* in January 1888, less than two years after
France's gift, soon to be known as Lady Liberty, was placed on its pedestal
in New York Harbor. (Courtesy Katz Center for Advanced Judaic Studies,
University of Pennsylvania)

toward very different ends. Wise's extended depiction of the ancient
heroes provided his readers with a different model of Jewish leadership
than the Talmudic rabbinic authority that had guided Jewish life for
more than a millennium. By teaching American Jews about a second
type of Jewish leadership, that of the Maccabees, he helped to legitimate

his own reform movement—which offered a third alternative to both militarism and Talmudic loyalty—in the public mind. Additionally, his fiction's pure entertainment value drew readers to him. Similarly, the young men who staged the Hanukkah pageant aimed to encourage their peers and their audience to greater activism on behalf of contemporary Judaism, in both practicing the religious tradition and contributing to and participating in educational work. The Maccabees offered the most activist and manly model—by contemporary American standards—for motivating American Jews toward the two very different goals.

The *Keyam Dishmaya* men believed a bold Hanukkah event could capture the imagination of ordinary Jews and especially energize Jewish youth. As Max Cohen put it, "Israel must be whatever its children make it."[88] Poet Solomon Solis-Cohen, a *Keyam Dishmaya* member, believed Hanukkah so important that he penned a poem describing a Hanukkah menorah's candles catching the flame from the burning bush on Mt. Sinai that Moses encountered and out of which he heard the voice of God. Solis-Cohen's poem suggested that Hanukkah ought to be considered among Judaism's founding events.[89] Organizers deemed the Hanukkah revival a success. Max Cohen said, "every worker in the cause of a revived Judaism must have felt the inspiration exhaled from the enthusiastic interest evinced by such a mass of Israel's people."[90]

Five separate Hanukkah articles in one December 1888 issue of the *American Hebrew* argued that manly Jews must preserve the Maccabean spirit with self-defense and religious devotion. Many Jewish men felt compelled to labor on the Saturday Jewish Sabbath because American laws banned work on Sunday and they would sacrifice income by opening their shops only five days per week. Yet the young *Keyam Dishmaya* men, few of whom yet supported families, had little sympathy for Jews who "succumb[ed]" to the "so-called force of circumstances." "Pitiful" they called such men.[91] They hoped to move on to reviving Sabbath observance after tackling Hanukkah.

The fervor of *Keyam Dishmaya* becomes even more apparent when we compare their Hanukkah revival to another popular event in the mid-nineteenth century, the Purim ball. Although timed to correspond with the Jewish holiday of Purim, a joyous occasion when it is customary to give sweets to family and neighbors, the balls were simply charitable events. Led by lawyer, judge, and coeditor of the *Jewish Messenger*

Myer S. Isaacs, the Purim Ball Association of New York arranged fancy-dress balls each year to raise funds for Jewish charities, most of them in New York but sometimes also including institutions as distant as the Touro Infirmary and Hebrew Benevolent Society in New Orleans and the Vicksburg Hebrew Relief Society in Mississippi. People of all faiths were invited to the balls. Respectable establishments such as the Metropolitan Opera House, Madison Square Garden, the Academy of Music, and Carnegie Music Hall housed them, and themes chosen for the balls often reflected trends in American society. For the March 1866 ball, attended by an exceptionally large number of Christians, organizers decorated the room in red, white, and blue and staged a procession depicting the history of Jewish persecution, ending in the triumph of "Religious Liberty over Prejudice." Accomplished and wealthy young men founded and led the Purim Ball Association, which achieved its period of greatest activity in the 1870s and 1880s.[92] The ball reflected their interests in philanthropy as well as their desire to create a social event grounded in the Jewish religious calendar. It reflected the popular American elite practice of providing entertainment to raise funds for charities. In contrast, the "Grand Chanucka Revival" mounted by *Keyam Dishmaya* and the YMHA aimed to effect Jews' religious observances by instilling pride in their religious heritage, affirming God's continuing protection, and sparking Jewish national sensibility.

Most latter-nineteenth-century American Jews shared one thing in common with their coreligionists in the United States in every era. Except for a small minority of fervently orthodox people who sought to maintain an insular Jewish society, in each era of American history, American Jews pointed out elements of the broader American culture that seemed to illustrate Judaism's fit with American society and political values. At the same time, Jews used those American principles and cultural forms to reshape their own religious lives in the American style. Their synthesis of Jewish and American culture supported their claim to a rightful place as American citizens and shaped an American Jewish religious culture.[93]

The syntheses they created also expressed Jews' own changing understanding of Judaism's religious principles and forms. An American Judaism took shape in new prayer books, new hymns, and new forms of congregational governance that featured written constitutions.[94] As

American society invented new holidays such as Thanksgiving (1863), Memorial Day (1868), Arbor Day (1885), Labor Day (1886), and Mothers' Day (1914) to inculcate values and behaviors prized in its industrializing, diversifying, and urbanizing society, American Jews took a new look at their own religious holiday calendar.[95]

In that same era, domestic Christmas customs featuring a decorated tree and gifts for children and family members became popular among Christian Americans.[96] Most American Jewish men earned their living through commerce, often providing the gift items, ribbons, wrappers, candles, and tree trimmings used for Christmas celebrations. An unknown number of Jewish families brought those Christian customs into their own homes, eliciting angry condemnations from rabbis.[97] For many Jews, this festive and sentimental trend in post–Civil War American culture seemed to illuminate a new appreciation of Hanukkah's homey celebrations. Those innovations elicited wide-ranging disagreements and discussions about Judaism's religious core versus its husk, about God's commandments versus human invention, and about the demands of modernity. In the midst of the competition over the future of Jewish religious life in the United States, Hanukkah became contested cultural ground as Jews expressed an array of opinions that both redefined the holiday and shaped a new place for it amid their varying attitudes about changes to Jewish life.

The young movement to return Jews to their ancient home in the Judean hills made Hanukkah its chief festival. More than any other event in the Jewish calendar, Hanukkah seemed ideal for promoting Zionist hopes because it celebrated a victory for Jewish political independence. They, too, like the young *Keyam Dishmaya* men, looked to the Maccabees for a Jewish image of virile masculinity that could inspire followers. In 1891, six years before the first Zionist Congress gathered supporters in Basel, Switzerland, to organize leadership for the movement, Bostonians Jacob Askowith and his son Charles created a blue and white Zionist flag with the word "Maccabee" written across the center of its single blue star.[98] A few years later, the father of modern Zionism, Austrian Theodor Herzl, encouraged Jews to take the Maccabees as their model. Vienna's Rabbi Morritz Gudemann pointed him toward that idea when he visited the Herzl home during Hanukkah in 1896 and found the family celebrating Christmas. Christmas trees seemed so much a part of central European life that one Jewish immigrant remembered it as linked to Knight Ruprecht, a German cultural hero, rather than to Jesus.[99] But the rabbi convinced Herzl to remove the tree and to celebrate Hanukkah instead. Banning Christmas from his home, Herzl soon wrote an essay, "The Menorah," arguing that celebrating Hanukkah and avoiding Christmas was central to Jewish self-respect.[100] His story engaged thinkers across a broad spectrum of political views. Herzl placed the celebration of Hanukkah in the center of the modern Jew's capacity to bolster one's own self-respect while living as a minority.

Hanukkah emerged as a newly meaningful holiday for nineteenth-century American Jewish leaders because its story provided images and lessons useful to clergy and lay leaders on all sides of a heated debate about how Judaism should adapt to America. By linking the image of the Maccabees with modernity, they inserted the particularities of their own religious perspectives into the secular universalism espoused by modernist philosophers whose Enlightenment ideals informed the founding documents of the United States.[101] At the same time, they promoted an image of Jewish bravery and faith already admired by some of the country's Christians. Most importantly, rabbis and Hanukkah advocates among ordinary Jews created an image of Jewish military bravery and success comparable to the nation's own patriotic rhetoric, taking another opportunity to assert their own "fit" with American society.[102] They lent Hanukkah's story contemporary importance by drawing parallels between ancient Maccabees and America's own military heroes. Reformers and traditionalists alike drew on the story to support positions for which they argued in their periodicals. Its militaristic history of an unlikely victory over a great power seemed to mirror the American Revolution and so helped American Jewish readers to find American values in Judaism as they sought to synthesize their religion with American culture.[103] In rabbis' hands, Hanukkah became a flash point for the struggle between reformers and traditionalists over how best to promote Judaism among an American Jewish population that seemed disturbingly lax in its religious observance. Traditionalists and

reformers alike claimed the mantle of modern Maccabee, saving Judaism from the acids of an appealing but foreign religious culture corrod-
ing religious practice in American Jews' households and congregations.

Young Jewish laymen finding their way in an American society that
valued both militarism and piety also found that Hanukkah "spoke"
to them. One Jewish soldier's memoir of his Civil War experience
described himself and other Jewish soldiers this way: "descendants of
the . . . Hebrew patriarchs who . . . under the Maccabees, triumphed
over the Syrian despot, . . . quite satisfied to fight with our Christian
comrades for one cause, one country, and the UNION."[104] The *Keyam
Dishmaya* men determined to embody its message of dedication and
to invite their coreligionist to join them by organizing the same sort
of value-laden yet pleasurable entertainment that had become the hallmark of Victorian America's drive to standardize American civilization.[105] These young men aimed to lead American Jewry in a direction
different from the one their elders stood for, and they soon began organizing associations and institutions to accomplish their goals. By claiming the mantle of the Maccabees for themselves, they, like the Reform
rabbis who also aimed to lead American Jewry in a new—but different
—direction, hoped the image of the ancient heroes would help to legitimate their own efforts among their coreligionists.

In 1885, in an open letter to American Jews, Denver, Colorado, Reform Rabbi Emanuel Schreiber summed up his movement's perspective
on a debate about the future of Jewish life in America that had raged
for decades. "Reform Judaism," he said, was "the modern Maccabee"
that "stepped in with a religion of the heart keeping Jews away from
proselytizers" and unbelief and rescuing Judaism from what he believed would have been its certain death in America.[106] Looking back
on Reform's achievements during the past century, Schreiber defended
Reform's changes by comparing its champions to the ancient Maccabees. Mattathias, priest and father of the sons who led the insurrection,
had declared it permissible for Jews to defend themselves on the Sabbath, contravening previous tradition. His insistence that preserving
life should be considered more important than obeying one of the Ten
Commandments became the accepted standard in Jewish law. Reformers also expected their own approach to become the norm. Schreiber
himself hailed from Moravia and studied for his Ph.D. in Berlin. In

his career, he served several American congregations, particularly in smaller cities of the western United States.[107] When he claimed that reformers offered Jews a religion of the heart, he may have had in mind the transformations that accommodated the desire of immigrants like himself and most of his congregants to simplify their religious lives. Religious observances such as dietary laws and lengthy, daily worship services, he felt, "fail to impress the modern Jew with a spirit of priestly holiness."[108] Ten months later, Reform rabbis fully articulated these positions in their statement of principles called the Pittsburgh Platform.[109] Like the Maccabees, it seemed to them, they changed Judaism's rules to improve its chance of survival.

Traditionalists, for their part, pointed to the Maccabees to prove that devotion to Jewish tradition had long been a manly endeavor. At midcentury, traditionalist leaders touted Maccabean devotion to religion as a model of loyalty and devotion to be embraced by contemporary Jews. After the Civil War, however, younger leaders emerged who viewed the Maccabees as young, activist leaders like themselves, who took the action they deemed necessary in order to save Judaism when it faced threats to its health and vigor. In what has been called American Jews' "period of most intense creativity and wrestling over issues of group continuity," they turned to the Maccabees to help them explain and envision their best hopes for American Jewish life.[110]

Yet all the talk about Maccabees remained largely a conversation among leaders who hoped to "revitalize" what had become a "forgotten . . . observance."[111] In New York City, where the nation's largest Jewish community might have supported greater religious observance, Reform Rabbi Dr. Gustav Gottheil noted in 1884 that "the customary candles disappear more and more from Jewish homes."[112] Another New Yorker noted that "not even the Zionists" (the emerging movement that used the Maccabean revolt to bolster support for a Jewish homeland) made much of a "fuss" about the holiday.[113] A recent immigrant to that city complained that it was difficult even to know when the holiday occurred, as he had not noticed other Jews marking the occasion (the Jewish holidays follow a modified lunar calendar), and he had missed it entirely.[114] Although it is impossible to know the rate of Hanukkah's domestic observance in that era, the frequent exhortations to light the Hanukkah menorah, which surfaced annually during the holiday season in the Jewish press, suggest the extent to which the practice had fallen off. The more tradition-minded editor of the *American Hebrew* complained that even those Jews who lit their Hanukkah lamps seemed to "remember their heroes in silence."[115] Jewish leaders would need to move beyond inspirational rhetoric and Maccabean imagery to turn that around.

3

Children Light Up

Reforming rabbis portrayed themselves as Maccabees in order to marshal American Jews to their new approach to Judaism, but, despite that martial imagery, they also sought innovative ways for Jewish children to learn about and participate in Jewish practices that would fit the larger goals of the new movement. For most of the century, reformers focused largely on the synagogue, streamlining and reshaping its worship to attract adults who might have little time to spend there. By making the rabbi's sermon a centerpiece, each Reform worship service also became an occasion for educating Jews in their faith according to the new movement's understanding of Judaism's ideals. The decorous and instructive synagogue environment may have satisfied some adults, but it did little for children. In the century's latter decades, some reformers concluded that if their efforts truly were to invigorate American Jewish life, they would need to do more to attract youngsters.

They focused on Hanukkah, a simple, joyous holiday that could easily be made grand. Traditionalists soon agreed that Hanukkah festivals could encourage American Jewish children to embrace their religion and so also adopted the new custom. Lay leaders, too—especially charitable women and female teachers—also arranged the festivals for the children they served. By the closing years of the century, Jewish children enjoyed these novel Hanukkah events annually in many different congregations as well as in charitable societies around the country. These new festivities added a new way for American Jews to celebrate Hanukkah and another reason for them to do so.

In those latter decades, Isaac M. Wise worked closely with another Cincinnati reformer, Rabbi Max Lilienthal, to create the synagogue-based Hanukkah festival for children. In it, they recounted the exploits of the heroic Maccabees, performed the Hanukkah candle-lighting rite, and provided sweets to the youngsters, hoping to create a happy occasion that would educate the children while instilling Jewish loyalty and strengthening Jewish identity. These new synagogue Hanukkah festivals also set in motion a dynamic relationship between clergy and laity, as women framed the Hanukkah rite—usually conducted by rabbis—with activities they believed children would enjoy, while rabbis strived to oversee the events. Wise and Lilienthal promoted these festivals to Jews around the country, but local congregations implemented them according to their own abilities and desires. The emerging variations shaped the new festivals in ways that reflected local ideals. The rabbis' turn to childhood echoed similar trends in American society, in which domestic and church activities created by women aimed to strengthen religious and familial bonds while also pleasing children.

In fact, post–Civil War American culture increasingly looked to children for emotional rewards. Earlier in the century, Americans began looking to domestic relationships for the emotional honesty that could offset the less trustworthy interaction with strangers that became a growing part of success in urbanizing America.[1] By wartime, "Adults relied on children emotionally to offset personal hardship," explains family historian Anne Carver Rose. Because children were thought to bring feelings "simpler and more innocent" than those of any adult, these feelings "could be returned without reserve."[2] Americans saw that attitude reflected back to them in their cultural products; women's magazines especially promoted it. In the midst of the Civil War, Sara Josepha Hale, editor of *Godey's Ladies' Book*, the most successful women's magazine in the nation, promoted Thanksgiving into a national occasion when familial sentiment might be renewed; Lincoln set the last Thursday in November aside for it in 1863. *Godey's* also joined the even more popular *Harper's Weekly* in promoting domestic Christmas festivities. That same year, *Harper's* illustrator Thomas Nast depicted a Union soldier returning home for "a Christmas furlough," joining his wife and family before a tree laden with gifts. Six years later, the U.S. Congress declared Christmas a federal holiday.[3] In some churches, too, Christian children enjoyed Christmas festivities connected to their religious school. In this era, Christmas became a widely celebrated domestic festival designed to create joyous experiences for children.

While every religious group strived to inculcate its teachings among its children, for Jews, that goal carried particular importance. Since ancient times, the transmission of the religion from parents to their children determined the religion's future. Despite Judaism's popularity in many parts of the ancient Middle East, events ultimately brought Jewish proselytizing to an end. As early as 586 B.C.E., when Babylonia destroyed the First Temple in Jerusalem and exiled many of the country's residents eastward, "marriage with outsiders came to be seen as a threat to Jewish identity and was widely condemned."[4] When the Hasmoneans, who led Judea more than four hundred years later, undertook mass conversions in the areas they conquered, they reversed history's trend. As Judea fell under Roman rule, proselytizing again waned dramatically. When Roman emperor Publius Aelius Hadrian (ruled 117–138) forbade Jews to proselytize, he restored anti-Jewish measures first enacted by Antiochus IV (the villain of Hanukkah's story) three hundred years earlier. Although Hadrian's successor, Antoninus Pius (ruled 138–161), repealed most of those laws and allowed synagogues and schools to reopen, proselytizing remained barred to Jews. Christian rulers carried on that custom.[5]

By the early centuries of the Common Era, therefore, Judaism had already begun its transformation into largely an ethnic tradition passed down through families. Jewish leaders and rabbinic writings urged extensive investigation into a convert's sincerity before any performance of the public conversion ceremony.[6] Although American Jews faced no legal restrictions to proselytizing, the familial tradition that stood for millennia remained ingrained in Jews. Rabbis expected that only marriage could induce a gentile to join them. Christians also assumed that conversion to Judaism was bizarre. In one famous case, when Quaker Warder Cresson converted to Judaism in 1848, his family tried to have him legally declared insane.[7] Without Jews having the option to proselytize, Jewish children were, quite literally, Judaism's only future. And yet few nineteenth-century American Jews living in a country dominated by an enticing evangelical Christianity could take their children's Jewishness—and thus the future of their religion—for granted.

Wise, for his part, believed that American public schools themselves constituted the primary hurdle Jewish children needed to overcome in remaining Jewish. By idealizing national heroes such as George Washington and promoting the simple moral lessons featured in the popular school-book series called *McGuffey's Readers*, he believed American schools neglected the heroes and movements of the more distant past.[8] Wise judged this a "radical error in our American system of education" because children should be taught "to imitate the sublime virtues of classic men." Moreover, the schools' narrow focus on the "spots [of the globe where] the history of the United States was enacted" made it more difficult to teach Jewish children to admire Jewish heroes who lived millennia ago across the planet. He pointed out that every Jewish "feast . . . admonished you . . . [to] Remember the days of old, understand the years of past generations." In a Hanukkah editorial of 1870, Wise exhorted parents to teach Jewish history to their children.[9]

Lilienthal carried the same message about honoring past heroes directly to children in his monthly magazine: "Always mind it, dear young readers, that your own Jewish history is as great and glorious as that of any other nation," he wrote. "You have ample reason to be proud."[10] Lilienthal further blended Hanukkah's story with American history. Linking the libretto for Handel's *Judas Maccabaeus* oratorio to lore about the American revolutionary Patrick Henry, Lilienthal wrote that Mattathias, father of Judah the Maccabee, began the revolt against Antiochus with the battle cry "Give me Liberty or Give me Death!"[11]

But Lilienthal also identified a second challenge, perhaps more consequential than public school, to the development of Jewish identity in children—the growing appeal of Christmas. In the economic boom the North enjoyed after the Civil War, Christmas became the widespread festival with decorated trees, Santa, and gifts we know today. It offered a new tradition in domestic culture. The rising consumer economy and expansion of department stores embraced and promoted the new Christmas customs. Before the nineteenth century, Christmas celebrations, where they occurred at all, tended toward "carnivalesque" revelries sometimes involving alcohol consumption and the firing of muskets in the street, a general rowdiness usually decried by civic and religious elites.[12] But as those celebrations became "genteel," homey occasions, in the century's early decades, attitudes changed. Concerns among some Protestants that the custom was not biblical and therefore should not be practiced by Christians gave way before the desire to unite the country in a shared Christianity and goodwill.[13]

The sentimental and family-oriented trend in celebrations blossomed in nineteenth-century Germany as it did across the industrializing West. When five million German immigrants added to an already substantial German American population over the course of the century, their domestic Christmas customs further reshaped American standards and cemented the prominence of some of the child-centered particulars of the December holiday.[14] The German "tanenbaum" and Kris Kringle figure lent substance and structure to a growing American desire for a Christmas celebration acceptable to the new domestic standards. *Godey's Lady's Book*, whose circulation reached 150,000 at midcentury, featured illustrations of Queen Victoria's family Christmas tree and made the custom fashionable in the United States.[15]

In the heavily German settlement of Cincinnati, Lilienthal noticed that many American Jews, themselves immigrants from Germanic lands, also enjoyed the German Christmas customs. Of the almost 150,000 Jews from central Europe who came to the United States in the half century prior to 1870, nearly 10,000 of them settled in Cincinnati.[16] Most of the city's Jews hailed from Bavaria, Bohemia, and environs, and they stamped the Jewish community with Germanic color.[17] Nonetheless, rabbis and editors of the rapidly growing Jewish press viewed the German Christmas customs as too Christian for Jews.[18] Soon after the Civil War, Lilienthal and Wise decided that they had to address this problem head-on or else risk the slow attrition of Jewish children to the beguiling Kris Kringle. Their solution: a new Hanukkah activity.

Lilienthal was the first American rabbi to preach in Christian pulpits: that experience gave him an idea for Hanukkah.[19] As the December holiday grew more prominent, many Christian Sunday schools developed special Christmas festivals featuring hymns, decorations, and pageants. Observing the celebratory ways Christian churches cultivated interest in religion in their youngsters, Lilienthal noted that festivities, religious socials, and gifts seemed to keep Christian children "in happy expectation" and sparked their interest in their church and in religion. By contrast, he asked Jews, "What are we doing? Nothing!!" Early nineteenth-century reformers, in their rush to modernize Judaism, had eliminated many customs that children enjoyed and reshaped the synagogue service into a more intellectual experience. "The only ceremony which really arouses our youngsters' interest is Confirmation. . . . We must do something, too, to enliven our children. [They] shall have a grand and glorious Chanukah festival nicer than any Christmas festival."[20]

To interest children, Lilienthal came up with a Hanukkah celebration held in the vestry rooms of his own synagogue on Mound Street in the late 1860s. By 1870, Wise instituted a similar event at his Plum Street synagogue for children of the Talmud Yelodim Institute, a Jewish religious school that he led. At both venues, Cincinnati's Jewish children enjoyed a Hanukkah festival where singing and instrumental solos, speeches, and refreshments framed an elaborate version of the holiday's traditional candle-lighting ceremony. More than two hundred children attended. After answering the holiday blessings in a chorus, they enjoyed ice cream and other sweets, all in a room festively decorated by the "ladies of the congregation" who had worked "with a will."[21]

Both Wise and Lilienthal understood that this festival might be the only Hanukkah experience their young charges would encounter. The rabbinic debates touting Maccabean heroism seemed to have little effect on the actions of many ordinary Jews. "Chanukah is entirely neglected in so many of our Jewish families . . . [that] we [should] celebrate it publicly in . . . every congregation. The children shall have it as a day of rejoicing [in] our religion," Lilienthal explained. "Chanukah can be celebrated to delight young and old."[22]

Anthropologists who study ritual in its many forms note that because ritual "is good for conveying a message as if it were unquestionable, it is often used to communicate those things which are most often in doubt."[23] Elaborating on the ritual of this minor, almost forgotten holiday seemed to Lilienthal an ideal way to impress young Jews with its importance and to show youngsters that Judaism held special appeal for them. The new festival also gave the reformers an additional occasion to convey their image of Maccabean heroes for the modern age.

To promote the new festival, Lilienthal and Wise described the first celebrations to readers of the two national Jewish magazines they each edited, beginning with Wise's account in his *American Israelite* in 1870. Lilienthal's magazine for children, the *Hebrew Sabbath School Visitor* (later renamed the *Sabbath Visitor*), followed in 1874. Lilienthal began the festival in his synagogue by offering a prayer and lighting the holiday candles, explaining the candle-lighting rite and its importance and performing it for the assembled group. Then lay leaders took over, as members of the school committee followed with speeches, the choir sang musical selections, and gifts were given to the teachers by the children. Just before the children were sent home, they were treated to oranges and sweets. Their departure signaled the start of an entertainment for adults, planned by the women of the congregation, which "lasted into the night." Wise arranged a similar celebration for children at his synagogue. There, he spoke to a large audience that included 250 students. The cantor (the synagogue's musical director and prayer leader) lit the candles and led the singing, and children recited blessings over food and enjoyed sugary treats. But this congregation's festivities had focused more completely on its youngsters and concluded at ten p.m. These communal Hanukkah celebrations designed to entertain, symbolically instruct, and delight children introduced a new Hanukkah custom to American Jews.[24] From their very start, however, individual congregations stamped them with their own particular desires, strengths, and talents.

Lilienthal and Wise did not invent the new celebration out of whole cloth. Like much of nineteenth-century Jewish innovation, it drew on three sources: customs remembered from Europe, normative Jewish observances, and practices adapted from Christians in America. When the women of Lilienthal's congregation arranged the dance for adults that lasted far into the night, they elaborated on the socializing likely to occur among Ashkenazi Jews in Europe during Hanukkah. In European Jewish communities as distant as Alsace and the Lithuanian *shtetl* of Eishyshok, families and neighbors enjoyed social visits on Hanukkah evenings.[25] The Hanukkah celebration also created another occasion to engage in the convivial charity balls so popular, as we have seen, among American Jews at Purim. Parents who brought their children to the synagogue events in Cincinnati recognized the candle-lighting ceremony and enjoyed a familiar, social atmosphere. Despite the event's novelty, it seemed appropriate.

Lilienthal stands out among nineteenth-century American rabbis for his attention to the needs of children, and he edited his monthly magazine especially for them.[26] In it, he supplemented and expanded on his work at his congregation. The magazine featured his own original didactic fiction, which illustrated the benefits of the innovations he proposed, along with other suggestions for improving Jewish education, and conveyed the same warmth toward children that he showed in his personal character. One such story depicted a synagogue's Hanukkah festival for children, created by teachers in a Jewish Sunday school joined by interested women of the congregation and the rabbi. The story soon shifted from the narrative style in which he painted a picture of the event for his readers to an argument about its benefits. He told readers, "The Chanukah festival, as proposed by the *Visitor*, should be celebrated in every congregation; and the officers of our Sabbath schools throughout the land should take good care that it might be omitted nowhere . . . [because] the children like it."[27] Wise echoed in his *Israelite*, "I would recommend to teachers in our Jewish Sabbath school, that they would try and make the feast of Channukah . . . a feast of joy for our children to which both teachers and children would look forward with longing and delight."[28] A joyous synagogue-based festival also furthered the reformers' goal of enhancing the synagogue's importance in Jewish religious life.[29]

Each year, Lilienthal instructed readers by describing Cincinnati's novel Hanukkah events in ever greater detail. The reports illustrated exactly how they could motivate youngsters to learn and motivate their parents to support the congregational school. No detail was too small to include in these instructive pieces. In 1877, Wise's congregation met at 4:30 p.m. at the synagogue, where the festival began with the choir's rendition of a Hanukkah hymn—perhaps that of Penina Moise. The president of the school board lighted Hanukkah lights, while the children in the two upper classes recited the benediction and its English translation. An organist played the "old Maoz Tsur," and the children recited the evening prayers. Schoolchildren sang more hymns, declaimed speeches in both English and German, and told the story of Hanukkah. Afterward, children feasted on cakes, ice cream, oranges, and other treats prepared by the women of Lilienthal's congregation. Members enjoyed a catered repast and, after discussions enhanced by cigars and wine, addressed more serious issues such as proposals for improving both worship and synagogue operations.[30] The two rabbis regaled their readers with these detailed descriptions in order to promote their new celebration to other congregations. Other reforming rabbis heeded the call, and synagogues in Detroit and St. Paul, Minnesota, among others, soon launched similar events.[31]

Although reformers led the drive to create festive community Hanukkah celebrations for children, tradition-minded Jews quickly joined the effort. Through an article in New York's *Jewish Messenger*, Baltimorean Henrietta Szold urged Jews to reshape Hanukkah in just that way. "Christmas truly fulfills its mission of bringing peace and good will to men. All this and more, Chanuka should be to us," she wrote.[32] Although Szold did not entirely approve of the reformers' approach to Judaism, she, like they, felt that Hanukkah ought to be reshaped along the lines of contemporary Christmas festivities that created good feelings among coreligionists.

The members of the editorial board of the *American Hebrew*, many of whom opposed Reform, included most of the young men who had masterminded the "Grand Chanuka Revival" pageant in 1879, and they enthusiastically touted Hanukkah celebrations of all sorts, private and public. "Glorious Chanukah is here again," it announced cheerfully in 1880. "Let your children celebrate it! . . . Light the lamp and teach them the tune," it urged. To parents skeptical that such a simple domestic rite could have much impact on their child's emotions, the *American Hebrew* insisted, "These little flames will beam, perhaps, through many an hour of fond recollection" when the children have grown up. Moreover, the editors cautioned their readers not "to believe that we shall never need the Maccabee's spirit again. . . . It is a criminal negligence to rock ourselves in the cradle of delusive safety."[33] Was America a welcoming place for Jews or not? Anti-Jewish feeling seemed to be on the rise. Only three years earlier, the Grand Union Hotel in

Saratoga Springs, New York, had refused accommodations to banker Joseph Seligman and his family simply because they were Jews, despite a decade of their previous vacations at that hotel.[34] In the South and Midwest, poor farmers blamed Jews for the economic panic of 1873.[35] The *American Hebrew* editors felt that to face future problems, Jews would need to join together and "nurse every patriotic feeling that can arouse a spark of Judaism in men's hearts." Hanukkah's message might instill the needed courage. "Seize the opportunity of the Chanucka feast to recount its story of valor and devotion . . . [to] provid[e] . . . your children with the wherewithal to answer the demands the future may make upon their national feeling," they proclaimed.[36] For the *American Hebrew* editors, Hanukkah supplied Jews with the courage to live as a sometimes maligned minority.

Rabbis and Jewish leaders across the board, reformers and traditionalists alike, agreed with Lilienthal that a more joyous and child-centered Hanukkah celebration might invigorate religious feeling among American Jews and could dispel the growing attractiveness that Christmas seemed to hold for all American children. The *American Hebrew* argued that Jewish children needed festive Hanukkah experiences to shield them from Christianity's festival and from evangelists who acted like "sneak thieves" stealing Jewish children during the few weeks preceding Christmas.[37] One Reform rabbi, Solomon Sonneschein, suggested that American Jews shift Hanukkah's celebration to December twenty-fifth, to provide real parity with Christmas.[38] Sonneschein's idea found few supporters, and, later, he himself rejected the idea; but it indicated the seriousness with which rabbis and editors alike approached the need to counter Christmas's allure. Like Wise and Lilienthal, the *American Hebrew* editors promoted the new festival by soliciting and printing reports of Hanukkah festivities created by local congregations and charitable institutions around the country. "Practical illustrations such as these, of Israel's feasts and festivals, are worth a thousand sermons," the *American Hebrew* crowed in 1880.

Women who taught in Jewish Sunday schools and who labored for Jewish charitable institutions took up this new responsibility and created Hanukkah festivals for the children in their charge. "In our charitable institutions and in our Sunday Schools . . . the season has been marked by rejoicings and merry makings," the *American Hebrew* reported.[39] At the quarterly meeting of a women's charitable society in New York, the holiday candles gleamed, and "girls sang the Hanukkah hymn" to piano accompaniment; children feasted on cake and ice cream before receiving new clothing from the society. The local Hebrew Free Schools publicly thanked an "unnamed generous donor" who gave twenty-five dollars so that the schools could distribute money and candy to their students. These schools provided vocational training, advice on living in America, and religious education to the children of immigrants, both boys and girls.[40] At their festival, youngsters sang the school hymn, lit holiday candles, and participated in an evening service augmented by a choir of twenty students.[41] In Philadelphia, the traditionalist congregation Beth El Emeth's Sunday-school festival included lighting the Hanukkah lamps and giving a box of candy to each child; that city's Hebrew Sunday School held a similar event.[42]

Over the next decade, reports of Hanukkah festivities such as these appeared in all three national Jewish magazines—Wise's *American Israelite*, Lilienthal's *Sabbath Visitor*, and the *American Hebrew*—tracking their growing popularity. Jews around the country joined in, taking up similar annual celebrations in Boston, Detroit, Rochester, Louisville, Denver, Indianapolis, Cincinnati and Columbus (Ohio), Baltimore, and Buffalo.[43] Local innovations expressed local talents and interests. In Indianapolis, Rabbi Meyer Messing delighted his congregants by leading eight of the smallest children into the synagogue "as they became a menorah carrying tapers and told stories about their candles as they lit them."[44] Most such events featured the candle-lighting ceremony, but most conveners also framed the ceremony with "entertainments" for children. Orphan-asylum festivals, particularly in New York, featured stereopticon exhibitions of biblical scenes, jugglery, and a Punch and Judy marionette show. Detroit's Jews offered children an operetta based on "Red Riding Hood's Rescue." Rochester's celebration featured a magician, while in Denver, Colorado, boys performed a "sword drill" that would have "done genuine soldiers proud." Surveying the range of activities, historian Kenneth White concluded that "some of the entertainment for Chanukah had little to do with the holiday."[45] Yet it may have been the invitation to creativity and the freedom to express local desires that made the festivals popular. By

1900, Jews in Richmond (Virginia), New Orleans, Atlanta, and Dallas also joined in.[46]

The Hanukkah festival began in synagogues, but a growing number of Jewish communal organizations also sponsored them. Immigration raised the number of America's Jews to almost a million by the late nineteenth century, and older organizations such as synagogues, fraternal associations, and women's clubs organized new charitable efforts that provided expanded religious-school activities, industrial schools, penny lunches, orphan asylums, kindergartens, free libraries, and mission schools to new Jewish immigrants and, especially, to their children. In 1890, the *American Hebrew* claimed that ten thousand people participated in these communal Hanukkah events in New York alone, including those sponsored by the Orphan Asylum, Minnie Dessau Louis's Industrial School, and the Ladies' *Bikur Cholim* (Sickness and Aid) Society. The editors concluded, "The happy result was that Chanucka was this year properly celebrated in many a Jewish home where the pleasing rites had for many years lain in abeyance."[47] Even in San Francisco's far smaller community, one observer claimed that Hanukkah had recently "bounded into prominence."[48] Although we cannot prove that characterization is warranted, when we compare its optimism to the gloomy tone in previous decades, it seems something had changed Hanukkah's popularity.

Because no standard liturgy existed for these Hanukkah festivities beyond the basic rite of blessing and lighting the Hanukkah candles, individuals created new songs and liturgies for them. Enthusiasts, even those without advanced training in Judaism, thus found opportunities to shape public religious expressions for these novel events. Philadelphia educator Ella Jacobs hewed closely to standard holiday fare when she compiled a booklet of prayers for children, including special items for Hanukkah. Her booklet paraphrased tradition in praising the "brave Maccabees" who preserved Judaism.[49] But some rabbis blamed lay leaders for bringing "things extraneous and grotesque" into the synagogue and hoped to rein in their exuberance.[50]

Yet, as innovations became increasingly common, rabbis had no choice but to join in. The most effective and simplest way to add religious content, rabbis knew, was in song. However diverse the programming,

whether held in synagogues, in meeting halls owned by the Jewish fraternal society B'nai B'rith, or in schools or homes for the aged, annual
Hanukkah festivals included songs. Group singing also can be counted
on to make participants feel good and to encourage a sense of unity
within the group.[51] Those who organized Hanukkah festivals hoped to
achieve both goals: making children happy and encouraging their sense
of being part of the Jewish community in an instructive manner.

The holiday's most popular tune, as we have seen, was the thirteenth-
century work "Maoz Tsur." In America's growing Jewish communities,
a number of English translations circulated, but one endured. "Rock
of Ages" was the product of a collaboration between rabbis Gustav
Gottheil and Marcus Jastrow, based on a German rewrite of the song
by German reformer Rabbi Leopold Stein. Gottheil and Jastrow shared
much in common. Each had earned his Ph.D. at the University of Halle,
and each served important congregations in the United States. Jastrow's
arrival in Philadelphia to take over the reins of congregation Rodeph
Shalom followed on the heels of his release from European imprison-
ment for participating in a Polish resistance movement. "His thought
was a blend of talmudism, classicism, and modernism," and he hoped
to moderate his congregants' rush toward reform, but not to stop it.[52]
Gottheil came to Temple Emanu-El in New York after serving a Reform
congregation in Manchester, England, and touted far-reaching changes
in Jewish worship. Their work together on "Rock of Ages" reflected
their viewpoints.

The new hymn also fit American culture. It used a popular Christian hymn title to refer to the God of Israel, thereby underscoring the
similarities between American Protestants and Jews. "Rock of Ages"
also cut "Maoz Tsur" from six stanzas to three, increasing the likelihood that busy Americans might take the time to sing the song. The
rabbis also dramatically altered its meaning. Their song did not hope to
again rededicate the Temple in Jerusalem, as did the Hebrew hymn, but
like the older version, it praised God for saving Jews in the past. It also
painted a cheery scene bright with lighted lamps and songs, encouraging American Jews to view the holiday primarily as a joyous occasion.
Finally, using the nineteenth century's idea that each nation formed a
distinct race, it referred to Jews as "children of the martyr race," subtly reminding American Jews that their coreligionists in eastern Europe

still experienced persecution. Like the Hebrew song, it also emphasized God's power over human agency by praising divine rescue "when our own strength failed us." Although it looked forward to a future free of the current dangers Jews faced as a minority, as did "Maoz Tsur," it painted a very different picture. Predicting a future that would see "tyrants disappearing," it reinterpreted Judaism's historical hope for a messiah who would signal Jews' return to their homeland as a messianic age in which all people would be free to practice their religions in peace. Here, too, they linked Judaism's beliefs with an idea that many Americans embraced and gave Judaism's particular historical hope a universal and American meaning. Gottheil published "Rock of Ages" in a widely used hymnal he compiled in 1896, and many other songbooks since then reprinted the hymn, whole or in part, innumerable times throughout the next century.[53]

Yet despite the changes Gottheil and Jastrow made to the lyric, they kept the traditional melody of "Maoz Tsur." By retaining the familiar melody, the authors dulled the new hymn's novelty and afforded Jews an emotional tie to their ancestors and past religious traditions. The *American Hebrew* called the melody "resonantly triumphant" and one which has "a firm hold on the affections of those who from childhood have heard it sung."[54] The melody allowed American Jews to feel that they were singing the "authentic" and "right" song for Hanukkah, even as the lyrics fit their modern sensibilities.[55]

As Wise and Lilienthal promoted the events in their magazines, increasing numbers of American Jews cobbled together programs of songs, entertainments, a brief candle-lighting ritual, recitations that lauded religious heroes, and musical recitals into productions that became annual Hanukkah festivals. Through these events, the rabbis carried the argument for Hanukkah's importance in world history, an argument they had used to support their own legitimacy when they debated other rabbis about Judaism's future, to the children in their congregations. Hanukkah's heroes held significance in the Jewish world and, importantly, in American culture. The Maccabees not only preserved Judaism and made possible the achievements of both Jesus and Mohammad; they fought for such American ideals as liberty and religious freedom. The *American Hebrew* editors therefore asked, "Should Chanuka be a minor festival, or should not Christian and Mohammedan alike join us in its celebration, for the Maccabees were their saviors as well as ours?"[56] This new culture of Hanukkah in America helped Jewish families to feel part of the larger society at the season when they were most likely to feel excluded as non-Christians, and it helped them to appreciate the significance of their own tradition to Western religious history.[57]

Women Prove Pivotal

A dynamic relationship between congregational rabbis and lay women became the engine that developed and promoted these new Hanukkah activities. Whether as financiers or as Sunday-school teachers, in formal ladies' auxiliaries or sisterhoods, or informally as mothers of Sunday-school children, women performed much of the labor needed to mount Hanukkah celebrations. Rabbis turned to women because the celebrations required little specialized religious knowledge, which the rabbis or cantors themselves could provide. But the celebrations demanded a good deal of knowledge about managing and pleasing children. Just as importantly, as New York educator Julia Richman pointed out, "only with the aid of . . . women [could] the Rabbis hope to gain real influence over their flocks."[58] America's market economy pushed men to labor long hours, while the voluntary nature of congregational life pulled women into local leadership. In part, women became necessary especially to rabbis of Reform congregations because they dominated attendance at worship on Saturday mornings.[59] San Francisco's Rabbi Henry A. Henry pleaded with Jewish women, "Draw your husbands to a religious . . . life, and . . . your children will follow in your footsteps."[60] Historically, Judaism's gender hierarchy praised Jewish women for creating a religious atmosphere at home by maintaining dietary laws and blessing Sabbath candles and through their own piety, as well as by encouraging their husbands and children—meaning sons—to study Torah. For example, the "*Brandspigl*, a popular guide for Jewish women in the seventeenth century, portrayed mothers as facilitators in their children's" and their husbands' religiosity by fulfilling their own religious obligations in domestic life.[61] Nineteenth-century reformers, however, who dismissed dietary rules in favor of a more philosophical approach to Judaism and whose male congregants rarely took time for Torah study, enhanced synagogue worship to welcome and inspire women as well as men. Rabbis who hoped to be the maestros of Jewish congregations learned that women would be instrumental to their success. Lilienthal promised women that they would be "loudly praised and cheered for their good will and motherly love" if they worked on Hanukkah synagogue festivals.[62] Speaking to predominantly female gatherings at worship, rabbis could engage and inspire women to undertake synagogue-based Hanukkah responsibilities.

Elements of Jewish tradition also suggested women's particular interest in Hanukkah. The *Shulchan Aruch* claimed that women especially benefited from the Maccabean victory because it ended a Greek practice of "forced sexual immorality" that targeted women.[63] Therefore, rabbis historically had encouraged Jewish women not to perform any housework while the Hanukkah candles burned, and this was understood to be a particularly strict observance of the holiday.[64] Elsewhere, the *Shulchan Aruch* declares that the high priest Yochanan's daughter, Judith, captured and beheaded the Assyrian general Holofernes to aid the larger Maccabean effort. This account relocated both Judith and Holofernes from the era of Babylonian conquest of Judea, as it appears in the Apocryphal Book of Judith, to the era of the Maccabees. Other traditions placed Judith within the Hasmonean family, as a sister to Judah the Maccabee.[65] Judah and Judith are forms of the Hebrew word meaning "Jewish person." Both figures take great risks to defeat foreign oppressors, and both achieve victory. Judith's tale therefore provided women a place in Hanukkah lore.[66]

Congregations often treated children to ice cream at the new Hanukkah festivities, and that reflected more than the popularity of the creamy sweet treat among American children. Judith fed cheese to Holofernes to intensify his thirst, which she slaked with wine to make him sleepy. She then chopped off his head, thereby preventing the siege of her village, set for the next day.[67] Her story made it customary to eat dairy foods at Hanukkah.

In many locales, girls took leading roles in the events. Many Jews looked to Sunday schools to create Hanukkah festivals, and Jewish girls constituted the majority of Sunday-school students. These schools were first adapted to Jewish purposes by a group of Philadelphia women in 1838—and thereafter were taught primarily by women—and parents seem to have been more willing to send their daughters to these novel

institutions than to send their sons.[68] Girls did not become bar mitzvah, as boys might, and so did not need to learn to read Hebrew to prepare them for that rite. Sunday schools did not attempt to instruct their
charges in reading Torah in its original Hebrew, a skill far beyond most
of the teachers. Instead, their curriculum focused largely on holidays,
basic Jewish principles, and Bible stories. The Hanukkah festivals soon
became popular vehicles for attracting both parental support and new
students for the schools. In Evansville and Quincy, Illinois, therefore,
girls performed most of the Hanukkah songs and instrumental pieces
at their festival.[69] Women in Lancaster, Pennsylvania, organized a Hanukkah festival in order to convince local Jews to establish a Sunday
school for their children.[70] The programming at various Hanukkah festivals sometimes strayed far beyond the strictures of the customary curriculum and brought in elements of children's culture popular among
their charges. Performances by girls dominated the 1887 Sabbath School
Hanukkah program in Detroit, for example, which included a juvenile
operetta based on the story of Little Red Riding Hood.

When these schools implemented Hanukkah festivals, the manly
Maccabean vigor touted by many rabbis and male leaders inevitably
became muted. Women teachers often selected the programming that
supplemented the traditional candle lighting and blessings and the
account of the Maccabees' heroic acts, elements which together would
not take long to conduct. "Rock of Ages" or "Maoz Tsur" would not
add more than ten minutes. Instrumental music, played by the students
—mostly girls—soon became common, but so did children's performances of highly gender-coded stories for girls, such as Little Red Riding Hood. In these programs, femininity framed the commemoration
of a divinely powered military victory and dulled its masculine code.
Some rabbis decried the trend to incorporate so much of American
children's culture that had no link to Judaism, but the festivals could
hardly be produced without the labor of women and the performances
of the largely female cast of schoolchildren. Moreover, because these
festivals aimed to delight both the children and their parents while
conducting a Jewish rite and conveying Jewish values, the promoters
could not ignore either the stories popular among American schoolchildren or the children's musical abilities, which made their parents

proud. In these festivals, then, the Maccabean drama and its historical significance, so important to rabbis, when framed by very different contemporary elements selected and performed by females, lost some of its masculine punch. The overall program underscored the importance of a gender boundary, an idea shared by both nineteenth-century America and Judaism, as much as it conveyed a message about the importance of Hanukkah.

Popular fiction in the English-language Jewish press suggested that Hanukkah festivals for young people could rekindle Judaism among a new wave of Jewish immigrants who began entering the country in large numbers after 1881. The newcomers came from eastern Europe, spoke little English, and entered an industrial America that quickly utilized their skills. Most were impoverished families, and the Jewish press emphasized the long working hours that seemed to quash the immigrants' time for religious practices.[71] An 1891 investigation found that New York's many garment workers, overwhelmingly Jewish, labored sixty-six to seventy-two hours each week during the slack season and sixteen to nineteen hours each day, seven days each week, during the busy season.[72] In many households, entire families worked on piecework completed at home. New York's newspapers soon informed their readers of the immigrants' struggles, and among Jews, new charitable efforts swiftly mobilized to assist the newcomers.

American Jews organized day nurseries, afternoon schools, night schools, and trade schools, along with settlement houses and visiting nurse services, for immigrants and poorer Jews.[73] Women in New York's wealthy congregations uptown also organized elaborate Hanukkah entertainments for children of the Lower East Side, where most of the new Jewish immigrants lived; these entertainments were sometimes held in large, uptown synagogues or in industrial schools run by uptown's Jewish charities.[74] Featuring stereopticon displays of exotic landscapes and scenes of the Holy Land, as well as puppet shows, songs, and sweets, these events seldom pretended to do more than provide children with holiday cheer. Memory of the Maccabees drifted further from the central meaning of the event, as the organizers focused on the increasingly important matter of making Jewish children happy in December. Christmas was becoming an almost universally celebrated and child-centered holiday for most Christian Americans, and organizers wanted to be sure that immigrants' children enjoyed an appropriately Jewish—but equally fun—occasion.

These popular communal Hanukkah celebrations replaced the holiday's eight-day, domestic candle-lighting ritual that had fallen into neglect among many American Jews with a one-day, communal, child-centered festival more easily scheduled for a convenient time during the week of Hanukkah.[75] Usually, these occurred on a Sunday morning in conjunction with Sunday-school activities. Reformers and traditionalists alike offered the event to American Jews who seemed to have little time for the fullness of Jewish traditional observances; reformers felt tradition itself had become "overgrown with ceremonies."[76] Yet few religious leaders felt the new festival could be truly sufficient to replace the nightly, home-based, family celebration.

"Judaism is not safe if relegated only to synagogue celebrations and elaborate public festivals," argued the *American Hebrew* editors, because "the true . . . best place for religion is the home."[77] For that reason, tradition-minded Rabbi Sabato Morais felt sure that Judaism's future in America would be determined by Jewish mothers.[78] Some Reform leaders also agreed that their movement had erred by neglecting Judaism's many domestic rituals. Early reformers who reshaped Judaism to be more philosophical missed a countertrend changing religious life in the Western world. Over the course of the nineteenth century, urbanization and industrialization drew economic production away from households and segregated the genders by their labor; women in middle-class families usually did not labor for wages outside the home. In response to those changes, sentimental, domestic occasions, sanctified by religious custom, enhanced the religious purpose of family life and expanded women's responsibilities within it. American society, "criss-crossed with religious, linguistic, regional and ethnic differences," embraced these regular holiday occasions that gave its diverse people a shared experience and that sweetened their acquiescence to the rule of the clock.[79] Thanksgiving, Christmas, and Sunday dinners, along with children's birthday parties each year, became significant events enhancing emotional bonds in family life. These increasingly valuable events depended on the labor of a family's women, especially mothers.

As the nineteenth century came to a close, the influential reformer

Rabbi Kaufman Kohler longed for the Jewish home rites that the Reform movement had eliminated but that he felt could "touch the soul and heart."[80] One girl recalled that at the time of her 1889 confirmation in a Reform synagogue, her family practiced no Jewish domestic rituals at all, except lighting of the Hanukkah candles.[81] Kohler urged such families not only to "kindle the Chanukah lights anew" but to "make the festival more than ever before radiant with the brightness and beauty of love and charity."[82]

Religious leaders such as Kohler agreed that synagogue activities alone could not instill Judaism in young people who did not experience Jewish rites within their families. Some doubted that communal Hanukkah festivals actually imparted any religious education at all, because the "little ones . . . think more of the cakes and cream than of the heroic deeds of the Maccabees."[83] But American rabbis had little control over Jews' domestic religious observances, and actual practices varied widely. Sara Liebenstein recalled that despite her father's lack of interest in Judaism, each year her mother lighted the Hanukkah candles with her seven children every evening, sang the traditional blessings, and sent the youngsters to visit the Jewish neighbors on their Chicago street to collect gifts of fruit.[84] Even those who vigorously advocated communal Hanukkah festivals agreed that they must "be rendered null and void by the irreligious attitudes of the parents" that leave the children without "Jewish devotion and religious training at home."[85]

The same traditionalist and reformer leaders who advocated communal Hanukkah festivals also urged Jewish women to create domestic Hanukkah celebrations. Using a gentler touch to encourage these domestic rites, Lilienthal again used semifictional accounts in his magazine to sketch appealing religious domestic scenes for his readers. He described a Hanukkah celebration in a home whose elegant parlor featured silver candlesticks with eight wax candles on the mantelpiece and lithographs with Jewish content hanging on the walls. "Grandpa" visits and joins the family in singing blessings and songs, lighting candles, and playing dreidel games; the children are impressed and have fun, too.[86] The story showed readers that Hanukkah could provide occasions for memorable and warm family togetherness, but the obvious wealth of the family in this story also conveyed the message that Hanukkah could be fashionable. Other writers simply rebuked Jews who neglected domestic celebrations. An unnamed *American Hebrew* writer acidly satirized wealthy Reform Jews content to doze through the rabbi's Hanukkah sermon and to buy Hanukkah tapers from "a poor old Jew" but never put them to use. "What would the servants think?" asked the fictional family in this story, "not to mention the grown up boys and girls who would be poking fun . . . at mama getting religious —all of a sudden."[87] The writer made plain his contempt for Jews who lacked the courage to practice their religion in their own homes.

Adapting Hanukkah to the Christmas Season

As Lilienthal suspected, the choice of which December holiday Jews would celebrate may have had as much to do with fashion as with fortitude. In America, Christmas was the fashionable holiday, not Hanukkah. When President Franklin Pierce set up a Christmas tree for his family in the White House in 1856, he lent the custom legitimacy and status.[88] Increasingly, Christmas imagery appeared in the leading national magazines. The influential *Harper's Weekly*, billing itself as a "Journal of Civilization," filled an 1860 December cover with scenes from a prosperous family's Christmas celebration.[89] Over the following decades, other important magazines depicted posh Christmas parties enjoyed by adults dressed in tuxedos and gowns, parlor Christmas trees filled with beautifully wrapped packages, and clean, pajama-clad children opening gifts or peering up chimneys looking for Santa Claus.[90]

As the nineteenth century wore on, it seemed more and more difficult to escape Christmas's lure. "Sponsorship of [national] holidays by retailers and trades, already incipient in the antebellum period, became a foregone conclusion in the half century after the Civil War," explains one historian.[91] Each December, merchants repackaged their ordinary goods for sale as holiday items and elaborated on the normal utilitarian decor to transform their stores into seasonal Christmas "bazaars." John Wanamaker used religious statuary and a pipe organ sounding out religious music to turn his large New York and Philadelphia department stores into sacred arenas for commerce. Many shop owners hired specialists to produce displays that could attract shoppers. In New York, though countless stores added decorations in December, none produced the spectacular results of R. H. Macy, whose holiday store windows themselves became a destination. Unlike Wanamaker's religious themes that might appeal to adult Christian shoppers, Macy's windows aimed to delight children and their parents and often featured puppets and machines with moving parts that depicted characters and events in children stories such as Jack in the Beanstalk. Visits to Macy's windows became annual December events for many families.[92] Christmas also turned many municipal public spaces into holiday marketplaces. In 1881, trees cut for sale at Christmastime filled New York City's Washington Square. Twenty years later, "one American in five was estimated to have a Christmas tree."[93]

So many of the Christmas images that Jews encountered on their streets each December, and in their mailboxes via magazines and circulars, dealt with shopping, decorating, and making children smile—it was surprisingly easy to overlook the Christian content. By late century, Santa Claus had been transformed from the Christian St. Nicholas to a pudgy shopkeeper with magical powers for gift giving.[94] Further blurring the holiday boundaries, Jewish merchants—from the wealthy Strauss family that owned R. H. Macy's to the many small shopkeepers such as Sam M. Lederer, who owned a modest dry-goods store— used Santa Claus images in their advertising each December.[95] These customs turned Christmas into what one Reform rabbi in Philadelphia called a "universal Volkfest" with a secular spirit. He thought that Jews should participate in those customs in order to "knit . . . [themselves] with the rest of rejoicing humanity into a bond of social brotherhood." A reformer in St. Louis, Missouri, agreed. He suggested that Christmas was only an adaptation of Hanukkah, because both are joyous, light-filled, winter rededications to religion; his own children enjoyed Christmas.[96] From the many comments in the Jewish press each year, it seems that many Jews celebrated the secular elements of Christmas celebrations—trees, shopping, and Santa Claus—even those who also celebrated Hanukkah.

But most rabbis and other Jewish leaders argued strenuously against Jews participating in even the most secular Christmas customs and felt offended that so many Jews did so. They argued their case from several different directions, amounting to a barrage of tactics and points, hoping to influence as many Jews as possible. Lilienthal told his young readers that "Grandpa does not like a Christmas tree and Christmas presents in Jewish families."[97] For most of his young readers, grandparents resided in Europe, and their actual likes and dislikes remained a mysterious matter. Although Lilienthal aimed the *Sabbath Visitor* primarily at children, he expected that parents read it. A "Grandpa" character proved a useful narrative device for instilling a little guilt in families that might have lapsed from ancestral standards.

Religious leaders writing for adult audiences often pointed out the Christian meaning of the seemingly secular Christmas customs. While Jews might see a decorated and lighted tree simply as a lovely sight to cheer wintry gloom, "the Christmas tree reminds the Christian world of Jesus of Nazareth," explained Lilienthal.[98] Its evergreen nature represents the eternal life that Christians believe Jesus's death brought to the world. Therefore, all Christmas trees are an "implied concession to . . . [the] . . . creed of our Christian neighbors," another editor explained.[99] Why would Jews bring an emblem of Christianity into their homes? he implied incredulously. Moreover, these leaders argued, because Christianity teaches that all other religions are false, Jews who celebrate Christmas are actually insulting themselves.[100] Another rabbi took an entirely different route and pointed out that the Christmas tree began as part of a "heathen" festival. Jews should be contemptuous of it, not admire it. Another noted that Christmas itself is founded on shoddy history, because no one knew Jesus's actual birth date.[101] Whether Christmas trees were emblems of Christian faith or remnants of heathen nature worship, Jews should keep them out of their homes. Religious leaders among Jews in Germany took a similar stand. One story in a journal promoting a modern traditionalist Jewish viewpoint used the main character's envy for a friend's Christmas tree and contempt for her own family's old Hanukkah menorah to illustrate how badly she had been educated in Judaism.[102]

American rabbis and others also asked their readers to consider the impression that having a Christmas tree might make on Jewish youngsters. By celebrating the birth of the founder of Christianity, Jews not only taught their children to "ape" Christian customs but "set a premium" on their child's ultimate conversion to Christianity.[103] If Jews shared the holiday with their gentile neighbors in hopes of cultivating friendships, these editors insisted they would fail. "You will gain more respect from your neighbors" by observing the tenets of your own faith and being virtuous than by copying theirs, the *American Hebrew* advised.[104]

Finally, the Jewish press explained that in the not too distant past —and in parts of contemporary eastern Europe—Jews expected to be attacked by Christian mobs on the holiday. It did not bring "peace on earth, good will to men," as American Christians touted each year. The chilling poem called "In the Name of Jesus of Nazareth," by American Jewish poet Emma Lazarus, reminded readers that in Russia, Christmas had become "a blood red . . . day of hate."[105] Those who used this argument implied that violence and antisemitism lay beneath the outward Christmas cheer, and American Jews should not expect their own participation in the holiday to promote goodwill. Each December, rabbis and editors dew on this arsenal of arguments in the hope of influencing their readers to celebrate only Hanukkah in their homes.

In 1881, a correspondent to the *American Israelite* from Buffalo, New York, suggested a solution to the problem. Noting that "Christmas . . . here . . . was observed as usual among the Israelites by plentiful presents to the children"—a practice he condemned—he thought to shift the occasion for parental benevolence to "one of our own holidays. Chanuca or Purim might well serve the purpose." Jews customarily exchanged gifts (usually baked goods) on Purim, but its timing did not coincide with the December hoopla surrounding the national gift giving at Christmas; Hanukkah did.[106] Some Jewish women's charitable organizations already gave Hanukkah gifts of clothing to children in foster and orphan homes, in sewing and industrial schools, and to those youngsters whose families received general benevolence. Donors began using Hanukkah to exhibit their charity's largess toward the children.[107] The idea caught on quickly, as the suggestion from Buffalo was repeated in more and more local papers in the following years. We have no idea when the first families began to exchange gifts as the menorah candles burned, but it seemed to grow more common in the 1880s.

The Jewish press agreed that books made the best gifts for Jews of all ages. Reform Rabbi Jacob Voorsanger, who became editor of the *Sabbath Visitor* after Lilienthal's death, recommended "Grace Aguilar's works, first, last and all the time." A British novelist, poet, liturgist, and theologian, Aguilar articulated a religious perspective that defended Judaism, Jewish women's spirituality, and Judaism's fit with modern

Western culture. Her works remained popular and available long after her death in 1847. All but three of her fifteen books dealt with either Judaism or women's religious influence in the home. She found many readers in the United States; her *Women of Israel* was reissued twenty-two times by a New York press into the twentieth century. It provided an image of family devotion linked to religious piety that resonated with Jewish memory, yet it echoed the sentimental rhetoric popular in Victorian Christian literature for women.[108] American Jewish religious leaders, male and female, admired her work.

The *American Hebrew* expanded on Voorsanger's suggestion a few years later. In 1890, its editors urged parents to purchase books for their children and also for "relatives, and friends" at Hanukkah. Having recently helped to launch the Jewish Publication Society in order to make high-quality English-language books with Jewish content available to American Jews, the editors seized on the season's commercial benefits to promote the new press. The purchase of "new books . . . issuing from the press" would be "excellent . . . to add to the Chanukah festivities," they wrote. Eager to sell books, they did not discuss the edification or knowledge that might come from actually reading a high-quality book. Instead, they pointed out that books signified a cultured and fashionable home. They asked readers to consider "what ornaments could possibly equal books in . . . decorating the home in the truest sense [?]" Nothing could match them. Only books offered emotionally and intellectually satisfying experiences to their owners. "Neither bric-a-brac nor pictures, nor rugs nor tapestries, can make any such appeal to us for close companionship as the printed volumes on our shelves," the *American Hebrew* insisted.[109] The Jewish Publication Society made it easy for rabbis and editors to promote Hanukkah as a gift-giving occasion for Jews. It made it possible for Jews to join the national shopping spree while performing acts that reminded them of their Jewish identity, brought a marker of that identity into their homes, and perhaps expanded their Jewish knowledge. By exchanging books at Hanukkah, Jewish families could share a common experience of generosity that also united them in a religious bond.

Those who urged parents to make Hanukkah an occasion for exchanging gifts soon turned their attention to women. Rabbi Sabato Morais explained that mothers are the "first and principal teachers of their offspring" and "consequently . . . [have] the power to fashion [children's] hearts in . . . piety."[110] Just as communal Hanukkah festivals depended on women's ability to manage small children, so, too, did a gift-centered domestic Hanukkah require women's labor. Women shopped to fulfill their families' needs and desires, along with their own. By the 1890s, some American women spent the two to three weeks before Christmas shopping almost daily.[111] Advocates called on American Jewish women to shop for Hanukkah, by first impressing women with the power they wielded at home. Over the nineteenth century's last two decades, articles increasingly appeared in the Jewish press that drew women's attention to their own importance to Jewish life in their homes. Voorsanger refuted the claim of a gentile lecturer who said Judaism placed women's status below that of men, asserting that "but for [mothers] Jewish men would not occupy the high moral position that they do." A Jewish woman is "queen and mother both!" he said, explaining that at home "she rules." He argued that Jewish women's situation was no different from that of American women who also lacked political rights yet nonetheless were esteemed in their families.[112] Voorsanger published this heated essay in the *Sabbath Visitor*, where mothers of Sunday-school children in Reform congregations could read it. The *Sabbath Visitor* also prominently displayed poetry for Hanukkah by Emma Lazarus. Most often it featured her stirring "Feast of Lights." While the bulk of the poem recounted the Maccabean revolt, its opening line made the main point: "kindle the taper like a steadfast star." The poem offered readers a model of an acculturated, accomplished American Jewish woman unafraid to express her deep loyalties to Judaism and the Jewish people. But most importantly, it told readers what to do—light the candles each Hanukkah evening.[113]

By creating new ways of celebrating Hanukkah in order to delight Jewish children during the Christmas season, Jews added conviviality to synagogue life and brought more children and their families within its walls. Reformers found a new way to express a religious sentiment at Hanukkah that linked that holiday to the Victorian religious mood. In the booming midwestern city of Cincinnati, reformers reshaped the holiday to align with the child-centered and domestic sentimental values of the post–Civil War era in America. Amid the growing postwar popularity of Christmas festivities, new communal Hanukkah festivals offered Jewish children celebrations comparable to those enjoyed by their Christian friends. Yet Jewish culture had, for many centuries, strived to bring children into religious life, and the new Hanukkah festivals found ready participants in many Jewish communities. Both reforming and traditionalist rabbis encouraged Jews to expand Hanukkah's importance for Jewish children, in big cities such as New York and Philadelphia, in midsized Cincinnati, and even in small communities with few resources such as Lancaster, Pennsylvania.

The holiday commemorating military success and divine rescue surprisingly also held new opportunities for women. In the nineteenth century, when few congregations counted women as members, their efforts in Hanukkah events emerged from their increased presence in their synagogues and from the common concern for the future of Jewish children shared by many rabbis and lay members alike. Yet, because women's new activity at Hanukkah festivals concerned itself with children and focused on a novel activity not historically part of Jewish worship, it did not directly threaten traditionalist sensibilities or mandates. Their work seemed appropriate by many standards—reforming, traditionalist, and Victorian.

Those changes framed the historical Hanukkah, an occasion commemorating God's rescue of faithful Jews from dangers inflicted by gentile powers, with activities Jews could share with gentile Americans at the same season. As Christmas developed as a national celebration, those who did not participate in its festivities came to be seen as outsiders. Changes in Hanukkah redefined the holiday so that Jews could participate in activities that paralleled Christmas. Synagogue children's festivals and elaborate domestic Hanukkah celebrations that featured gift giving adapted the national activities to Jewish religious circumstances. Lilienthal suggested that Jewish parents might choose red, white, and blue candles for their home celebrations, reassuring themselves, their visitors, and the merchant from whom they purchased the candles that their holiday was not alien to American society.[114] An American variety of Hanukkah began to take shape.

Philadelphia's oldest congregation, which had always opposed reforms in its worship, hosted a 1907 celebration for its schoolchildren that framed the candle-lighting ceremony with a three-act play about a workshop that produced Hanukkah toys for Jewish children. It adapted the vivid images of Santa's workshop. (Courtesy American Jewish Historical Society)

These changes also suggest how a national Jewish culture emerged. The Jewish press linked Jews around the county and encouraged activities and attitudes promoted by the editors. By printing reports of local Hanukkah celebrations in diverse communities, those magazines created a conversation about Hanukkah's importance and about the variations in ways American Jews might appropriately commemorate the ancient event. The press urged Jews who hailed from various towns in Europe and from various regions of the United States toward common activities. Local variations in the national trend show that American Jews across the country found it intriguing and attractive and applicable to their own particular customs. They were ultimately part of the overall movement of Hanukkah toward greater significance in the lives of American Jews.

Reformers especially engaged in the effort to enhance Hanukkah, to reshape it from a minor festival to one which children would eagerly anticipate, which mothers would labor to produce in their homes and in synagogues, and which fathers would be drawn to share with their families. Few American Jewish children received formal religious instruction —in 1880, "no more than fifteen thousand out of nearly fifty thousand Jewish children"—so that edifying, child-centered Hanukkah celebrations became one valuable tool to instill Jewish knowledge as well as an emotional bond to tradition and the synagogue.[115] This underscored Reform's sense of providing an alternative to assimilation.[116] Yet the more religiously traditional group of editors at the *American Hebrew* also urged Jewish parents to "surround the observance with such innocent yet gladsome festivities as their own skill will suggest and devise."[117] In augmenting Hanukkah's simple rite, Reform rabbis and tradition-minded American Jews alike elaborated on an element within Judaism that corresponded to an element of Christianity in order to *resist* Christianity. Lilienthal provided Jewish children with a fun Hanukkah to help them embrace Judaism at a time when their Christian friends seemed to be having all the fun. Hanukkah gifts, especially gifts of books on Jewish themes, gave Jews a shopping experience that supported each other's Jewish identity while joining the national shopping season. Those new Hanukkah customs also provided Jews with a way to explain and defend their Jewish religious life to inquiring gentile neighbors, by referring to ideas or activities they held in common.

Those American Hanukkah elaborations helped Jews to feel part of a national celebration as Jews and as Americans. These new Hanukkah customs voiced little of the fear of non-Jews suggested by the holiday's traditional rite and its historical songs. Synagogue festivals, home parties with decorations, specialized foods, and nightly gifts lent Jews' engagement with the American Christmas season a lighthearted tone. Through those Hanukkah recastings, Jews provided themselves with a way to talk easily with their gentile neighbors about their own religious lives at any December party.

These developments became the foundation on which later Jews built their own Hanukkah celebrations with special meaning for themselves. Synagogues became locations for Hanukkah festivities for children and

In 1914, children attending the religious school at the congregation popularly called simply The Temple in Atlanta, Georgia, a Reform Jewish congregation, posed for this photo that documented their Hanukkah celebration, which included funny hats. (Courtesy Cuba Archives, The William Breman Jewish Heritage and Holocaust Museum)

social events for their parents. These events, and others like them that sometimes occurred at Purim in midwinter, promoted the turn-of-the-century transformation of some American synagogues from their historical purpose as locations for prayer and Torah study into multiuse centers for Jewish communities. Although this trend began among Reform congregations, more traditional groups soon joined in.[118] At children's festivals, rabbis and leaders repeated the holiday's revised narrative that touted a Maccabean fight for freedom. For those who grew up hearing this story at festivals, it became the standard account of the ancient events. That narrative and the festivals together reframed and reshaped Hanukkah into an authentic Jewish version of the American holidays that proliferated after the Civil War. In this form, it became ever more ingrained as an American Jewish tradition throughout the next century.

In the closing years of the nineteenth century, the English-language Jewish press began losing its role as the key forum for debate about the condition of American Jewish life. New Jewish immigrants had begun to arrive in massive numbers, speaking different languages and publishing their own newspapers in those tongues. After the turn of the twentieth century, their distinctive perspectives and their customs further embellished Hanukkah in America—but in new directions.

4

Remade in America

In the forty-three short years between 1881 and 1924, the American Jewish world underwent a transformation. Nineteenth-century rabbis who touted Maccabean heroism and who, along with religious-school teachers, organized Hanukkah festivals for their youngsters, and the young men in *Keyam Dishmaya* who aimed for a broader revival of Jewish religion and commitment watched a vastly larger new group of Jews change the shape and the culture of Jewish life in the United States. In 1880, American Jewry counted roughly 250,000 souls, most of whom traced their heritage to the Germanic areas of central Europe. By the time the U.S. government restricted immigration in 1924, more than two million Jews lived in America, the vast majority from eastern Europe and imbued with an identity distinctly Jewish. They were *Yidden* (Jews) in their language of Yiddish, or Jewish. The diverse Hanukkah celebrations they created in America reflected their own particular memories and hopes.

Yet their Hanukkah celebrations, too, like those enjoyed by earlier American Jews, reshaped and reinterpreted the holiday to express their own understanding of the needs and possibilities of American Jewish life. Over the course of the holiday's eight days, they crafted customs that sometimes recalled traditions from Europe but at other times drew on American models of December festivities. Some of their new public gatherings aggrandized Europe's more humble versions of Hanukkah celebrations, while others offered utterly American creations tailored to their own Jewish sensibilities. Seldom guided by rabbis in these efforts, the new Jewish immigrants elaborated as they wished to on the European customs they recalled. Encountering American abundance, they augmented their holiday celebrations with gifts, foods, songs, and concerts, along with poetry, inspirational writings, and admonishments penned by a cadre of lay intellectuals and newspaper editors. Free to remake Hanukkah according to their own desires, they reached into the Jewish past to create a religiously sanctioned cluster of ways that adapted their distinct culture to turn-of-the-twentieth-century America.

Those immigrants began arriving when a combination of political tumult in Europe and relative economic prosperity in the United States propelled them to emigrate. Their massive relocation ended, with shocking suddenness, when an isolationist U.S. Congress sharply curtailed immigration. But in these intervening years, as we will see, arrived Jews who brought with them a much richer Hanukkah experience than most American Jews had ever known. Once settled in America, they developed an array of Hanukkah practices far different from the Sunday-school festivals and occasional Hanukkah spectacles so popular in older, wealthier American Jewish congregations in more comfortable parts of town. Yet, as the new immigrants established their communities in the United States, their own Hanukkah customs underwent change. Some aspects of their celebrations provided nostalgic recollections of the town life and families left behind, while other, newer customs emerged that integrated American culture into the holiday. An ethnic economy arose to provide the goods, venues, and foods needed for the celebrations. As the immigrants established a foothold in the New World, their Hanukkah customs helped to identify and enrich their distinctive neighborhoods.

Perhaps because few immigrant laborers could obtain time off from work to properly observe the Saturday Sabbath in synagogue and home, this more easily scheduled, formerly minor holiday took on added significance for expressing Jewish identity and faith. As an annual event celebrated in evenings, and without requiring abstaining from work like the more important Jewish holy days, Hanukkah could more easily fit the time demands of immigrant life. For adults perhaps more than for children, the holiday's concerts, games, social gatherings, and feasts brightened winter evenings. Immigrants told Hanukkah stories about the ancient past but also turned Hanukkah objects into metaphors with which to consider their own experience. The simple doing of Hanukkah's special activities, performing its rites as well as singing songs, playing games, and savoring foods, and even shopping for holiday items, became bridges between the Old World and the New. Needing the familiar as ballast and the new as reassurance that they were in fact adjusting to America, these Jews shaped Hanukkah into a cluster of rituals and events that fit their new lives. The Hanukkah stories they told reflected their particular hopes and anxieties.

The New Immigrants

The world's largest Jewish settlement had evolved over several centuries in eastern Europe. But, as the feudal world there collapsed in the nineteenth century, its Jews endured widespread impoverishment, violence, and expulsions.[1] Nearly seventy-five percent of the world's estimated 7.7 million Jews lived in eastern Europe in 1880, but emigration and violence in Europe reduced that figure to less than forty-six percent by 1920.[2] For Jewish refugees, any element of Hanukkah could become a metaphor for a facet of their lives. One such man counted himself not a Maccabee, as did the men who hoped to lead nineteenth-century American Jews, but something far more humble. "I am a Khanike dreidel," he wrote. "It may appear that I am but a plaything, . . . but I witness . . . to the . . . sons of Abraham, Isaac and Jacob remain[ing on] . . . the path which their ancestors blazed."[3] That simple toy that determines good fortune or bad by the circumstances of its fall seemed to perfectly illustrate this immigrant's lot. Turned this way and that by hostile forces, he nonetheless felt he carried within himself a noble heritage.

Romanian-born David Moses Hermalin, another new immigrant to America, found inspiration for his own life especially in the figure of Judah in Hanukkah's story. "Ah, how I love this hero and admire his courage! . . . that one, who . . . mocks danger . . . and . . . senses no . . . fearfulness! . . . This is Yude Maccabee!"[4] Such bravery amazed Hermalin, who recounted the Maccabean revolt in the *Idisher Zhurnal*, a religiously oriented Yiddish-language paper published in New York. Hermalin arrived in New York in 1885 at age twenty and built a career in Jewish letters through essays, plays, translations, and editorial work just as Yiddish literary culture blossomed there. Other Yiddish writers found religious devotion or nationalist fervor in the Maccabees' story, or a thirst for freedom, or a commitment to universal brotherhood. Yet, whatever larger goals they saw in the Maccabean account, some Jewish writers perceived a bravery that they themselves aspired to attain. They, like other American Jews, molded Hanukkah into a multifaceted occasion with diverse meanings that reflected their own lives.

For the adults among those immigrants, Hanukkah held an importance far beyond its possible worth as a Jewish child's antidote to Christmas. It provided a rich trove of memories, new political meanings, familiar rituals, and simple joys. Torn from old pleasures, the immigrants sought new ones.[5] Those who remade the holiday with activities that fitted their new situation imagined themselves as modern Jews with a Hanukkah suitable to their new home. At the same time, by carrying out the rite, they also acted on their desire to continue Jewish religious life. Their culturally rich Hanukkah helped these immigrants to understand their tumultuous lives within Judaism's chain of tradition.

These were not the first Yiddish-speaking Jews to settle in America. Such Jews had lived in North America since colonial days. To name just one example, the Silesia-born brothers Michael and Barnard Gratz, who settled in Philadelphia in the 1760s when fewer than three hundred Jews lived there, relied on a Yiddish business correspondence to protect the confidence of their plans for shipping on the Delaware River and land speculating in the Midwest.[6] Yet the late nineteenth-century Yiddish-speaking immigrants seemed different. Many clustered near urban factories, where they found employment and created distinct Yiddish-speaking neighborhoods. Another tiny percentage of new Jewish immigrants, perhaps sixty thousand, hailed from areas of southern Europe,

North Africa, and the eastern Mediterranean, including Greece and the Ottoman Empire. Their worship customs shared much in common with practices familiar to many colonial American Jews, and some, eventually, joined those venerable congregations. In contrast to the Yiddish-speaking Ashkenazim, these immigrants spoke Jewish languages such as Ladino (which combined Hebrew with Spanish) and Judeo-Turkish that few other American Jews understood.[7] Among the Sephardi immigrants, the tiny percentage of people who emigrated from Arabic lands spoke Judeo-Arabic. The linguistic distinctiveness among these immigrants forced them to create their own small enclaves.

These diverse Jewish newcomers arrived amid eighteen million non-Jewish immigrants from eastern and southern Europe, mostly Roman Catholic or Orthodox Christian, many of whom also clustered in urban neighborhoods near employment. Their number, languages, religions, and residential patterns distinguished all these immigrants from the English-speaking Protestants who dominated American culture. Social analysts dubbed them "new immigrants" and worried about their effect on the country.

Jews pooled their resources in varying ways to escape Europe's problems. Boys in Odessa's Ascanazy family emigrated to elude conscription, a fate that haunted Russia's Jews long after the end of Czar Nicholas I's policy of forced military service, which could last more than a decade and usually included forced conversion to Christianity.[8] Jacob left while still an adolescent, traveling first to a married sister living in Cleveland but settling finally in Buffalo, New York, and ultimately opening a tailor shop there. For many years, he sent money to bring his younger brothers, Mike, Reuben, and Harry, to join him. He never again saw his parents.[9] Some Jewish communities pooled resources to aid emigrants. In Socheczew, now in Poland, the community hired Pinchas Keller, a resident who spoke six languages, to accompany its members on their journeys from their town to New York. Keller's wife and five children joined him there after he had made several crossings.[10] In other cases, extended kin groups supported each other. From the outskirts of Kiev, carpenter Max Kaminker and his wife, Deenah Beilis Kaminker, a milliner, brought their many children to Englewood, New Jersey, after the bloody Kishinev massacre in 1903. The Beilises organized a family circle to assist their large clan in moving to the New World.[11] In those ways and others like them, the percentage of world Jewry that lived in the United States jumped from three percent to twenty-three percent by 1920.[12] Once in the United States, they stayed. The rate of return for Russian Jewish immigrants was the lowest of all immigrant groups.[13] Moreover, Jewish immigrants to the United States were among the poorest of newcomers. Because they often depended on kinfolk already in the New World to help them settle, find work, and adjust, they could risk the journey with less cash. Dense social relations subsidized their survival.[14] Holidays such as Hanukkah, particularly with its new brand of public activities, further cemented the crucial role of kin and communal networks.

Ports in Boston, Philadelphia, Baltimore, and Galveston accepted and processed immigrants, but approximately seventy percent of all immigrants arrived through New York.[15] Many Jews settled in portions of the three wards that made up Manhattan's Lower East Side, not far from disembarkation. But neighborhoods composed of these immigrants also appeared in many cities and towns around the country. They so expanded the Jewish presence in locations nationwide that thirty-seven percent of U.S. cities with Jewish populations of one thousand or more in 1927 had no Jewish residents at all just a few decades prior.[16] Yet, for size, density, and depth of misery, none could match the Lower Ease Side. In its twenty-square-block area, the number of Jews at one point in 1910 climbed to 542,000.[17] In its overcrowded tenement apartments, parents sometimes shared their beds with their small children, while older siblings slept on cots or kitchen chairs.[18]

Few tolerated the congestion for long, and Jews left it when they could. By 1905, two-thirds of the Lower East Side's Jews had relocated to neighborhoods such as Harlem, the Bronx, Washington Heights, Williamsburg, or Brownsville.[19] New Jewish immigrants soon took their places. So many immigrant families had passed through the Lower East Side, living for a time and moving on, that historian Hasia Diner judges that it became the American Jewish version of the "old country" for later generations, engendering Jewish nostalgia in a way that Europe, with its anti-Jewish outbursts, seldom did.[20] The neighborhood's restaurants, theaters, and shops continued to draw people to it. By 1914, New York's various Jewish neighborhoods counted more than 1.4 million residents, making it the largest Jewish center in the world.[21]

Many Lower East Side Jewish immigrants found their first employment in the garment industry, whose Jewish industrialists were more likely than other employers to understand Yiddish. Conditions often were so bad that reporters coined the term "sweatshop" to describe them. Jews laboring in Philadelphia's clothing sweatshops and cigar-rolling factories and in similar industries in Chicago and Boston shared similar difficulties and, like the New Yorkers, often participated in trade unions to improve working conditions and pay. The small manufacturers who employed those workers lacked the power enjoyed by big industrialists, and trade unions made greater headway against them.[22] One significant result was that these new immigrants, though quite poor relative to previous generations of Jews, had a bit of disposable income and leisure time, enabling them to create lively Hanukkah celebrations with material goods, distinctive foods, and special cultural events.

Hanukkah Shopping and Eating

American observers sometimes assumed that these Jews, unless stripped of time for religious observances by work demands, lived in lockstep with traditions mandated in the Talmud. But the immigrants actually held a wide range of religious attitudes. Some activities considered shameful in European communities because they flouted Jewish law or custom became commonplace in New York. Historian Moses Rischin pointed out that "by 1913, almost sixty percent of the stores on the Lower East Side did a brisk business on Saturdays," despite religious proscriptions against such activities.[23] Many immigrant congregations urged their coreligionists to maintain proper Sabbath observance, yet, by one estimate, only forty percent of these immigrant Jews still did so.[24] From a certain perspective, though, religion seemed to be booming. By 1910, approximately six hundred new congregations had formed, each following traditions, melodies, and Hebrew dialects familiar in the home-towns of their congregants. At least at first, these followed traditionally observant standards. Many among them soon made compromises. Some, for example, offered early Sabbath-morning worship to members who wanted to say their prayers before heading off to work. Despite congregations that tried to keep religious observances alive, the trend to laxity continued.[25]

Just a few decades earlier, as we have seen, traditional and Reform rabbis alike expressed great concern about the Jewish flock deserting its roots, and rabbis among the new immigrants felt similarly. Because rabbis found no governmental and little communal financial support in America, their influence seemed to wither. The laity wielded more power than the clergy.[26] In short, by the start of the twentieth century, rabbis across the ideological gamut held far less power than rabbis had exercised in earlier eras of Jewish history and in other parts of the world.

Poverty and violence hounded Jewish immigrants out of Europe; abundance, security, and access to new places marked their Americanization. "Presents" was among the first English words to appear in Yiddish newspapers. Many scholars have pointed out that "the prospect of material abundance . . . made America different" for many immigrants.[27] These Jews had arrived "with an intense desire to fit quickly into American society" and, as cultural historian Andrew Heinze points out, they expected to enjoy the "fruits of the economic system in with they labored."[28] By 1906, the *Forverts* (Jewish Daily Forward) advertised Hanukkah gift objects, or "presents," for sale at K. Rez's Tea and Coffee Stores.[29] The religiously conservative *Yiddishe Tageblatt*, like Jewish presses across the religious and secular spectrum, urged Jewish parents to give gifts to their youngsters at Hanukkah to increase children's enthusiasm for the Jewish holiday.[30] A gift signified a new American Jewish trend. Instead of the European custom of bestowing *gelt* on children at Hanukkah, which many parents in turn expected children to give to their teachers, objects specially selected to please children or fulfill their needs became popular. The shopping experience became integral to Hanukkah. "If it does not touch the heart, it does not touch the pocket," noted one editor, and advertisers wasted no time in linking the new immigrants' holiday emotions to goods for sale.[31] The *Tageblatt*'s most faithful advertiser, Ridley's Department Store, explained that Christmas gifts and Hanukkah gifts go hand in hand, in a joyous, "ecumenical spirit of buying and giving."[32] One Lower Manhattan store promised affordable phonographs "for Hanukkah," and another claimed a piano the ideal Hanukkah gift.[33] A third offered a free Hanukkah "present" for each customer.[34] Holiday gifts became another way in which to enjoy American abundance and to measure one's own success.

Many Jews living in New York City's Lower East Side would have purchased candles and gifts for Hanukkah from pushcart vendors like the one shown here, from whom goods could be obtained more cheaply than in stores. (Courtesy American Jewish Historical Society)

Only a decade or two earlier, the editors of the English-language press had urged parents to buy books on Jewish themes for Hanukkah gifts. But the Yiddish press now voiced no such restrictions. The *Tageblatt*, for example, needed Christmas advertising and, like most Jewish periodicals, wove Hanukkah into the broad December marketplace through extensive advertising, but without steering readers toward specific holiday purchases.

Yet some editors in the Jewish press did voice concerns. Ever perceptive and wary of capitalism's snares, *Forverts* editor Abraham Cahan warned Jewish immigrants away from too much gift giving by cautioning readers against buying on the installment plan. American materialism could be as deadly to Jewish life as persecution, he said. Perhaps contradicting the paper's own advertising, the *Tageblatt* put it more succinctly when it warned readers, "we do not want death from pleasure!"[35] America's abundance played havoc with Jewish culture's ability to mark sacred occasions with goods of superior quality, argues Andrew Heinze. Tradition urged Jews to beautify the Commandments, and European Jews reserved their choicest meats, best clothes, and loveliest tableware for Sabbath and festivals. American goods made the everyday look as good as holidays did back home.[36] America's abundant material culture flattened the Jewish one, but Hanukkah presents offered a way to once again distinguish a Jewish holiday from the mundane world through more luxurious material objects.

The *Tageblatt* editors' worries may also have been provoked by the many Christmas trees they noted in Jewish homes in Lower Manhattan. These secular items bore no Christian markings yet identified the Christmas season. They seemed ubiquitous. The problems that American rabbis had struggled with as early as the 1880s were now even harder to avoid. How could a Jewish immigrant distinguish between an item of American culture and a Christian symbol? Observers remarked that most kindergartens in New York, including those in Jewish neighborhoods, featured Christmas trees, and even mothers of Jewish schoolchildren helped in their decoration. The paper tried to turn Jews away from the practice, suggesting it symbolized everything the Maccabees fought against. The ancient struggle of the Jews "against the turbulent forces of Antiochus" found no better parallel than "the struggle between the poor, quiet, little Khanike lights and the brightly illuminated, dressed-up and decorated Christmas tree."[37]

Jews had, of course, encountered Christmas celebrations in Europe. The holiday was most often referred to as *nittel nacht* (natal night), but the dangers Jews sometimes faced on the day led to other slang terms for it. One scholar counted twenty different terms for Christmas in varying Yiddish dialects.[38] In Poland, Jesus's divine birth became a wicked birth (*beyz geboyrenish*), and in central and southern Europe, Christmas Eve was known as *goyeimnacht*—gentile's night. New immigrants harbored European-bred fears about Christmas but soon faced a far different experience in the United States. In Chicago, the Christmas party at Hull-House filled Jewish immigrant Hilda Satt Polacheck with terror. Yet she overcame her fear to attend. Finding herself welcomed by the settlement's founder, Jane Addams, and "cheery strangers," her attitude changed. "I became an American at that party," she recalled.[39] Cahan noted that for Jewish immigrants in New York, "the first thing that shows you're not a greenhorn is buying Christmas presents."[40] For an untold number of Jewish immigrants, participating in Christmas pleasures indicated that they had learned American ways.

Judaica shops like the one owned by D. Leibowitz, shown here, sold the items used in religious observances, such as Hanukkah menorahs. Many such shops could be found in New York's Lower East Side. Leibowitz communicated with potential customers in Hebrew, Yiddish, and English. When Jews relocated to suburbs, these shops lost most of their local Jewish clientele and soon closed. Suburban Jews could purchase necessary religious items from miniature Judaica shops located within synagogue buildings. (Courtesy American Jewish Historical Society)

Yet one historian concludes that despite Jewish immigrants' Christmas trees, they had "no intention of adopting Christmas" in its religious meaning.[41] Most of them firmly resisted suggestions to do so. Public school curricula aimed to Americanize the children of immigrants by instilling an ideal image of the American past that would elicit affection for the nation. "They left out all the terrible things that happened," recalled one student. "Minorities and their pasts had no place." Schools also strived to instill patriotism in their charges through the recently established national holidays of Columbus Day (established in fifteen states by 1910), Lincoln's Birthday, and the older commemoration of Washington's Birthday. Thanksgiving, established as a national day of homecoming and dedication in 1863, also became an occasion to instruct immigrants and, through public schools, their children in the values and history lessons of American heritage. Most Jewish parents understood that these lessons on national holidays would assist their children. Few objected.[42]

Yet, while many immigrants seem to have accepted holidays commemorating the American past, some of them used political muscle to shield their children from Christian influence in the public schools. Between 1903 and 1906, New York's Jewish press covered the increasing savagery and frequency of Europe's pogroms against its Jews, and some immigrants found it difficult to entrust their children to the gentile teachers and staffs of the city's schools.[43] Moreover, while Jews embraced civic holidays as part of their new American world, they drew the line at efforts to inculcate Christianity. They expected the U.S. Constitution to protect their children from forced conversions, just as it protected themselves.

In the Brownsville section of Brooklyn, New York, Jewish families protested the Christian activities conducted in the public school each year just before the Christmas vacation. The problem began in 1905 when the school principal told children at a school assembly that they should be more like Christ. Jews perceived his remarks as coercing their children to become Christians. One hundred outraged Jewish parents signed a petition asking for his dismissal. When the local school board did not help them, they took their case to the New York Board of Education, which passed a resolution disapproving his action. Hoping to ensure that it did not happen again, Jewish parents asked the board to direct the school to eliminate all Christmas ceremonies in which Jewish children would be expected to sing Christian hymns and hear Christian religious instruction. The next year, after teachers told students to wear their best clothes for the special Christmas assembly on the last day before vacation, Jewish parents called for a strike. The *Yiddishe Tageblatt* and the orthodox *Morgen Zhurnal* (Morning Journal) publicized the strike in their Sunday editions and urged parents to keep their children home that day. Both newspapers accused the Board of Education of trying to convert their children to Christianity. The newspapers assured worried parents that the school planned no academic work for that day, which would be devoted entirely to Christmas special events. As a result, one-third of the school population, between twenty and twenty-five thousand children, stayed home.

The event received wide coverage in Jewish newspapers around the country.[44] In Los Angeles, the editor of a Jewish newspaper recommended that Jews in other parts of the country also keep their children home from school on days when parents know that Christian teachings will be heard. But he admitted that it is "only in New York as Jews are one fifth of the population . . . [and are] strengthened by other liberal elements and in some instances by Catholics, that they at least get a respectful hearing."[45] The New Yorkers not only were heard; they prevailed. The next year, the Brownsville school specifically excluded Christian hymns and the reading of religious tracts and confined the celebration to less doctrinaire items such as Santa Claus and Christmas trees. News of New Yorkers' success emboldened Jewish teachers in California to begin a dialogue with their gentile co-workers about the impact of school Christmas celebrations on their Jewish students.[46]

Jews' resistance to Christmas in public schools indicates their willingness to pick and choose among elements of American culture and thus to navigate their own routes toward Americanization. Nowhere was this more evident than in their food choices. Jewish law regulates foods, banning some items entirely (such as pigs and shellfish) and some only in combination (such as meat and milk). As a result, food became a marker of Jewish identity as well as religious loyalty, and holiday foods especially so.[47] Eastern European Jews commonly ate latkes (pancakes) at Hanukkah—a popular and inexpensive dish whose simplicity made it available even to the poor. The oil in which they are fried symbolizes the small amount of oil that miraculously lasted for eight days when the Maccabees rededicated the ancient Jerusalem Temple. Other American Jews did not seem to share this custom. A late nineteenth-century cookbook produced by an earlier generation of English-speaking American Jews provided recipes for special foods for many holidays, including Purim cookies, but none for Hanukkah.[48] However, eastern European immigrants across the board consumed the simple pancakes at Hanukkah. Lithuanian-born Cahan described "buckwheat pancakes . . . dripping with fat," while Jews in Poland and Russia usually ate the potato pancakes popular in that region.[49] That food staple of eastern Europe was a reminder of immigrants' former homes. But that was soon to change. Whether the pancakes were made of buckwheat or potato, cooks often produced the cooking oil by rendering chicken fat, a time-consuming and messy process. New York's food purveyors soon adapted their marketing to reach Jewish customers. Yiddish advertising urged cooks to use Crisco, but ads for Mazola Oil seemed to understand their labors when it told them, "End Your Slavery to a Cup of *Shmalts*" (chicken fat).[50] Ads for Aunt Jemima Pancake Flour encouraged cooks to prepare the holiday specialty, claiming, "The taste of latkes gives everyone an appetite."[51] By using Yiddish words, these companies sought the huge eastern European customer market and ignored the far smaller number of Sephardim, Jewish immigrants from the Levant who did not speak Yiddish and did not eat latkes. Immigrants benefited from the fact that since the last decades of the nineteenth century, the cost of food in America continued to decline, allowing a more varied diet.[52] By 1903, advertisers in Yiddish newspapers touted gastronomic gifts such as fruit to augment traditional Hanukkah latkes, along with tea and coffee to complete the meal.[53] In eastern European Jews' latke recipes, desserts, and even their tea, they could enact a range of identities either by selecting these new American products, by cooking with new American ingredients, or by making holiday dinners the old-fashioned way to taste more like those they remembered eating in Europe.[54]

Many Jews combined food products available in America with recipes they deemed appropriate for Hanukkah meals.[55] Even with a simple meal at home, immigrants could imagine a different Hanukkah past than the one in eastern Europe. They could envision a personal bond with Judah Maccabee by selecting Carmel wine, which claimed to be "what the Maccabees drank."[56] Local food shops such as Goldman's Tea and Coffee Store held special sales in honor of Sabbath Hanukkah. Jewish restauranteurs sometimes targeted immigrants' desires for American foods at special occasions. Perhaps no food is so identified with America as the turkey, an animal native to North America and the featured dish of the Thanksgiving dinners that take place across the country only a few weeks before Hanukkah. When Gorfein's, a kosher restaurant, advertised a deluxe Hanukkah turkey dinner in the *Forverts*, it apologized in print the next day to "hundreds [who had to be] turned away" because the restaurant "had no space or food left for them." Gorfein's offered the same dinner a second night.[57] Dining in restaurants

—or "eating out" as it was soon called, *oysessen* in Yiddish—became a hallmark of Jewish American lives.[58] Few had experienced such pleasures in Europe.

For the many immigrants who dropped religious dietary restrictions as they Americanized, traditional holiday foods could provide a gastronomic bridge to their more pious past, or to their kinfolk still in Europe, and could deepen any festival's emotional impact. Hanukkah's food customs, whether old recipes prepared with new products or enjoyed in restaurants, cooked up an American-style Jewish holiday. For immigrants just a few years removed from the hunger of the Old World, such food luxuries could be a deeply gratifying element of their new American Jewishness.

Singing the New World

Hanukkah celebrations among the new immigrants seldom discussed the holiday's broad historical significance. Moreover, except for "Maoz Tsur's" recitation of past divine rescues and Psalm 30's pronouncement of dedication to the faith, their Hanukkah melodies evoked neither religious prayer nor sacred devotions but wove themselves around the activities that constituted the holiday's celebration itself. Thus, Hanukkah music reflected the immigrants' own celebrations while it enlivened them. Myriad musical programs often reflected the different roots of immigrant cultures, revealing Jewish, European, and American influences in the immigrants' lives.[59] Well-known melodies held "sad and sweet memories, thoughts of much that is dearest to the Jewish heart and home."[60] As immigrants took advantage of a burgeoning music industry, Jewish music became a key element in expanding Hanukkah celebrations both in their dense Jewish network of clubs and institutions and in Jewish homes.

Despite the growing repertoire of Jewish tunes, on both sides of the Atlantic, Jews often heard and sang the same handful of Hanukkah songs. Most popular was the sprightly "Khanike, Oy Khanike," which praised the festival's good food, games, and song while also thanking both God and Judah Maccabee. Its quick, regular beat lent itself to the circle dances often enjoyed by Hasidic (fervently Orthodox and mystical) men at their gatherings and, later, to the Zionist circle dances shared by women and men together. In another popular ditty, "Kha-nike," father sings the blessing and lights the candles, before the fun and games begin. One children's song came from the point of view of the dreidel—"I'm a spinning top. . . . I invite you all to play"—while another encouraged children to light the candles. Displaying more fear than cheer, immigrant poet Morris Rosenfeld composed a more plain-tive song that described lights of the Hanukkah candles stirring him to recall ancient times. It ended, "With a heavy heart I ask, what will happen now?"[61] These simple songs most often could be heard in the myriad clubs formed by the new immigrants, where they shared their common hometown backgrounds, political aspirations, or trade-union solidarity, as well as at home, where they amused their families.[62] The songs remained popular in Yiddish schools and clubs for many decades to come.[63]

The new immigrants brought with them a rich musical tradition that soon expanded and enlivened their Hanukkah events. The Social-ist, Communist, Anarchist, and Zionist political movements popu-lar among Russia's disenfranchised Jews inculcated zest and devotion among their members through workers' choruses, Zionist singing soci-eties, mandolin orchestras, and other such musical efforts. Immigrants also brought with them a rich folk-music repertoire that included lul-labies, love songs, holiday songs, and work songs, arriving just as the American piano market burgeoned. Between 1900 and 1910, piano sales in the United States increased 6.2 times the rate of population growth.[64] Rosenfeld, the poet who became beloved as the "voice of the sweatshop," portrayed an immigrant father's wish to provide a piano for his daughter and a guitar for his son, purchasing the items on credit although the children have little time to practice. They play for him in the evenings after they, like their father, toil "daytime in the factory." Though they play poorly, their "sweet tones hover and fill the heart."[65] His poem captured immigrants' delight in music's pleasures.

Within the vast world of Jewish music, these changes—and thus the ways that Jews celebrated their holidays—were matched in the late nineteenth century by the growing significance of the cantor, the professional religious singer. Some historians think the cantor's role as the congregation's sweet-voiced messenger to God was firmly estab-lished by the Middle Ages. Others disagree. We know that at least three different musical styles emerged by the mid-nineteenth century. In the Iberian peninsula and the Levant, congregations expected the cantor to lead the congregation in prayer and to avoid solo performances except when liturgically required, such as on Yom Kippur. In modernizing central European areas, cantors employed standardized notations and "harmonies familiar to western art music norms," sometimes including instrumental accompaniment. The young Reform movement, which grew up in central Europe, embraced those changes. In eastern Europe, however, where a "penchant for oral tradition" remained, boy singers learned an extensive repertoire through apprenticeships to multiple cantors.[66] Perhaps because a cantor's music could elicit strong emotional responses from a congregation, rabbis insisted that a cantor must be of good character, be married, sport a beard (cantors were always male), and have real musical ability.[67]

In America, however, eastern-European-style cantors sang to Jewish audiences in many venues in addition to synagogues, including concert halls, vaudeville shows, fund-raising events for communal organizations, and on recordings. Outside the synagogue, cantors often drew on German, Mediterranean, Russian, or Polish tunes to build their own distinctive repertoire of melodies. They also worked with musical groups emerging within social movements and on the secular stage. These opportunities sometimes "enlarged the cantor's profile from communal messenger to star."[68] Yet cantors needed those opportunities to retain their stature and income in the face of the new sheet-music industry, which democratized cantorial music and made even specialized liturgical music available to anyone.[69]

The Jewish musical repertoire experienced dramatic growth in New York, where immigrants heard songs from many towns and shtetls. Sheet music for Jewish songs proliferated. In the earliest years, Jews bought mostly liturgical songs, and "Kol Nidre," the prayer intoned by the cantor with great solemnity on Yom Kippur, became the best seller.[70] Sheet music made the correct musical performance of "Kol Nidre" possible in homes, clubs, and, more importantly, the many auditoriums around the city that offered inexpensive Yom Kippur worship services to anyone who purchased their tickets. At Hanukkah, eastern Europe's synagogues attracted crowds for special holiday concerts —the only time of the year when instrumental music was permitted within them. Those synagogue concerts, often recalled by immigrants, made similar events—even outside the synagogue—seem especially appropriate for Hanukkah. In immigrant neighborhoods, the rise in sheet music for Hanukkah resulted in holiday songfests in homes, halls, clubs, and schools.

Among Jewish immigrants, sheet music "was in almost constant use, leafed through at the piano (a surprisingly common fixture in poor immigrant homes), passed around for family sing-alongs, opened and closed and opened again."[71] New York became the commercial center for religious recordings and for Jewish-themed sheet music, adding to its growing luster as the national center for Jewish life. Cantors, too, recognized the growing power of sheet music, and some self-published small "songsters" for public sale to supplement their often meager incomes from a synagogue. Cantor S. Zeemachson's thirty-five-page songster called "Chanukah Habajis" (Hanukkah at Home) offered arrangements for four Hebrew songs commonly sung on the holiday, including the candle blessings, Psalm 30, and a blessing for the home.[72] Other songsters provided a larger assortment of songs associated with Yom Kippur, Passover, Hanukkah, and Shabbat to be performed in homes, schools, and clubs, further enhancing the popularity of holiday music among American Jews. Although Hanukkah is religiously less important than the other three occasions, its customary songfests and concerts boosted it into more august company in various holiday songbooks. By the turn of the century, as the English language made its way into Yiddish life, Jewish-owned Globe Music and the Hebrew Publishing Company romanized lyrics to many Yiddish melodies.[73]

By 1919, New York's Jewish religious schools serving immigrants' children often arranged holiday celebrations featuring choral singing by the young students to elicit donations. With those festivals in mind, Rabbi Israel Goldfarb and his brother, Samuel E. Goldfarb, head of the Music Department at New York's Bureau of Jewish Education, compiled a songbook published by religious schools in Brooklyn. Hanukkah melodies constituted seven of its fifty-three songs, more than for any other single holiday or topic in the collection. One among them, "Hear the Voice of Israel's Elders," asked who will complete what the fathers started when they are gone. It voiced the immigrant generation's sense of a cultural gap emerging between themselves and their own children.[74] Its plaintive melody could be heard in immigrant communities until after World War II, when American Jewish culture took a new direction.

A cantor's persona confirmed the audiences' expectation of an authentic Jewish performance.[75] Yet, through cantors' commercial success in America, they also modeled a successful synthesis between customs that reflected values of the Old World and the New. Some of the most famous cantors performed at New York's Hanukkah concerts. For example, Yosele (Joseph) Rosenblatt drew on the art music created by operatic singers such as Enrico Caruso in some performances, but he regularly also sang liturgical and folk melodies at a New York synagogue.[76] Leading cantors also performed at Hanukkah concerts on the Lower East Side. There, they embodied the Jewish song tradition, and their dress and deportment marked them as its authoritative carriers. American immigrant audiences understood such men as avatars of Jewish tradition and their own version of opera stars, but many rabbis denounced these cantors for turning a devotional experience into one of sensual pleasure.[77] Nonetheless, cantors dominated the Jewish musical world at the turn of the twentieth century and enjoyed widespread popularity.[78]

Annual Hanukkah concerts became the norm in new immigrant communities in early twentieth-century New York. "It is Hanukkah when the entire Jewish quarter has en masse attended a musical concert," wrote Lithuanian-born Getsl Zelikovitsch in 1900. A linguist and Egyptologist, Zelikovitsch mocked the ads for Hanukkah concerts which boasted "Kings of Cantors" and "Princes of Tuning Forks," but he expounded at length on music's central place in Jewish worship. He could imagine that "in no other religion has music been represented so officially as in Judaism," pointing to the ancient Jerusalem Temple where the Levites, he said, constituted "the largest choir in the world" and where both string and wind instruments regularly played in its orchestra. Music had been "since ancient times the most beautiful part of Judaism," he went on, "for music . . . [reflects] the harmony of the six days of . . . creation and . . . the language of our cells."[79] Zelikovitsch despaired of the Lower East Side's annual Hanukkah concerts for the same reasons that ordinary Jews loved them. Comprising mostly familiar, uncomplicated melodies, they typified an ideal of Jewish tradition that appealed to the emotions. Zelikovitsch longed for serious orchestral concerts that also engaged the mind. But in the era of singing stars, cheap sheet music, and relative poverty among the mass of Jewish immigrants, expensive, serious orchestral performances could never become as popular as cantorial concerts. American Hanukkah concerts ensured that standard holiday songs would survive the era's upheavals by providing annual occasions for their performance along with opportunities for new songs to be sung.[80]

Zelikovitsch also wanted Hanukkah music to inspire Jews. Unlike the music produced by the ancient Levites, Hanukkah's music "has nothing to do with adoration," Zelikovitsch explained, and so is entirely different from that heard on other Jewish holidays. This holiday about dedication focused more on recounting the strength Jews find when they remain loyal to the faith than on praising God or asking for spiritual bounties. Hanukkah's music is "a historical drama in notes which the Cantor tells us," he continued. The music depicts the "heroic Hasmoneans . . . march[ing] from the battle-field to the [Temple] singing, 'Who Is Like to Thee Among The Mighty, O Lord?'" But cantorial performances with these now-familiar tunes are not what today's Jews need, he insisted. Claiming that the French regiments attributed their heroism on the battlefield in Crimea to their stirring Marseillaise, he asked, "Where is the cantor . . . who can return us that forgotten Marseillaise" that the Hasmoneans sang? "Ancient, sweet lost musical string, where are you?"[81] He sought a cantor who could stir Jews to heroic action, not simply please them with well-sung familiar melodies.

Zelikovitsch's dissatisfaction with the general run of Hanukkah concerts did not dissuade Jewish New Yorkers from organizing them each year. Traditional religious schools, synagogues, and cantors depended on the income they generated.[82] In 1912, a Talmud Torah community religious school in Williamsburg, Brooklyn, timed the laying of the cornerstone for its large new building to its public Hanukkah celebration, thus hoping to garner funds to complete its construction. The Brooklyn Jewish School for Girls, too, counted on donations made at its Hanukkah concert at a popular music hall to defray its expenses. There, an orchestra of thirty-five boys accompanied its female students, who sang, recited orations, and performed two playlets.[83] School performances such as these were different from the earlier Hanuk-

kah festivals in Reform congregations that generally framed the holiday's candle-lighting ceremony with a host of activities to please their
children, rather than to raise funds from adults. The early twentieth-
century religious schools created by the new immigrants commonly
showcased their students' accomplishments at public Hanukkah events
when soliciting funds and promised that donors could "earn the biggest
mitsve [spiritual reward]" by both purchasing tickets and donating to
the school.[84] Immigrant assistance agencies, including the city's almost
two thousand associations of townspeople, called *landsmanschaftn*,
arranged similar festivities featuring cantors or Jewish singers with
piano accompaniment, speakers, and candle-lighting ceremonies.[85]
Perhaps the grandest of those Hanukkah concerts was one arranged
by the Ladies Auxiliary of Rabbi Jacob Joseph School in 1918 to fund
its effort to clothe and feed the school's students. Combining Hanukkah's celebration with a commemoration of the end of World War I,
the Ladies Auxiliary arranged a program boasting seventy-five cantors
from the Cantor's Union of America along with an orchestra.[86] Few of
the city's many poor congregations could support a cantor's services on
a regular basis, but some tried to do so for special holiday services and
holiday concerts.[87] Special Hanukkah events such as these helped very
traditional religious institutions to thrive in the United States, where
they lacked the broad financial support of a centrally organized Jewish community—their mainstay in Europe. These sorts of Hanukkah
fund-raising concerts could never offer the stirring and serious concert
music that Zelikovitsch thought Jews needed most.

Famous cantors sometimes arranged their own Hanukkah concerts
in theaters to supplement their personal income. When they acted
independently, cantors enjoyed more freedom to arrange performances
that showcased their own abilities. Yosele Rosenblatt expected his fame
would draw an audience to a 1920 double concert in Brownsville. The
commercial setting of these Hanukkah concerts permitted transgres-
sions that might not have been allowed to occur in eastern Europe's Jewish communities, where religious authorities wielded more influence.
In New York, more unusual performers also hoped to find an audience
amid the thousands of concertgoers. The same year that Rosenblatt
sang in Brownsville, a female cantor from Odessa penned an open letter
to the women of New York asking them to attend her free Hanukkah

concert at Cooper Union Hall on the Lower East Side and to bring their husbands along. "If your husbands love and respect you, they will consent to this," she told her readers. Singing with a choir of twenty-seven men and women, "Cantoress" Madame Sofia Kurtser promised "an evening of great spiritual fulfillment."[88] Her advertising assured Jews that she was not flouting traditional mores, despite the religious ban on women cantors. Because Kurtser performed in a secular auditorium, not in a synagogue, she did not violate any rules. Yet the unusual nature of her performance undoubtedly aroused suspicion among many Jews. She expected that men would stay away, but she hoped Jewish women would come to hear her sing.

Most Hanukkah concerts promised religious rewards along with pure enjoyment because their repertoire generally included both religious and secular songs and because they usually asked for donations to a charitable institution, thereby helping Jews to fulfill the religious obligation for charity. By 1927, the program had become so standardized that an unnamed essayist could satirize the typical Hanukkah concert performed at old-age homes, orphanages, synagogues, seminaries, and schools for children. The first half of a typical program featured Hanukkah blessings, candle lightings, and familiar Hanukkah songs heard at synagogue or at home, sung by the cantor with an accompanying choir and some sort of instrumental accompaniment always referred to as an "orchestra." But these "few ditties aren't enough to comprise an entire concert program, and as the holiday isn't a religious one, and a concert isn't a religious service, the rest of the program is based on the cantor's taste, meaning, whatever is his whim." For this writer, as for Zelikovitsch, Hanukkah's focus on an ancient episode of national liberation moved it outside the realm of other Jewish holidays that focus much more directly on God. Hymns and excerpts of prayers from other holidays, including Rosh Hashanah, Yom Kippur, and Passover, along with Yiddish folk tunes, were likely to constitute the next portion of the event, more to fill out the program than to promote an experience of the divine. Finally, popular songs taken from vaudeville commonly rounded out the evening.[89] This mishmash of music sung at Hanukkah, drawn from more devotional Jewish practices and borrowed from American popular culture, could be heard at many concerts.

Hanukkah concert advertising touted musical pleasures, but most events also included speeches by rabbis, editors, or leaders of various Jewish organizations expounding on the meanings to be derived from Hanukkah's story. Political groups such as the *Paoli Tsion* (Labor Zionist) offered serious speeches to deepen members' dedication to their cause. By linking a holiday message to their own goals, these organizations hoped to attract new members. By putting the children of members onstage in these concerts, they could count on their parents' attendance and perhaps win a chance to revitalize their commitment to the organization.[90]

These trends—the availability of sheet music and cantorial soloists, some amount of leisure time and income, nostalgia for a Jewish life left behind, the desire for reassurance that one's venture to America need not mean an entire loss of Jewish identity, and the expanding knowledge of a Jewish song repertoire—enhanced simple holiday hymn traditions and made Hanukkah concerts into a staple of Jewish immigrant life. Music historian Mark Slobin concludes that the many concerts, classes, musical associations, newspapers, and theatrical productions supported by impoverished immigrants indicated a need for entertainment as great as their desire to succeed.[91] Hearing and singing the "old melodies" allowed immigrants to recall their lost world among fellow "bewildered" newcomers to America. In an immigrant novella, one woman is nearly moved to return to Europe by the sound of a local rabbi chanting the Hanukkah blessings.[92] These events also provided occasions for different immigrants to come together. In 1914, the Hanukkah concert organized by the Sephardic Zionist Union drew over a thousand attendees, including more than a hundred eastern European Jewish immigrants.[93] These Hanukkah concerts became so much a part of Jewish life that the next year, New York's Jews arranged them for Jewish prisoners in Sing Sing.[94]

Immigrant Intellectuals Promote New Hanukkah Meanings

The Yiddish language created an immediate bond among Jewish immigrants despite the fact that they hailed from myriad towns and regions across eastern Europe. Over 150 Yiddish periodicals, including 20 dailies, defined their readers' common identity as Jews. They eased the transition to America for many newcomers by offering advice on accommodating to American ways.[95] Simply reading Yiddish newspapers was itself an American activity. While nineteenth-century European Jews "produced and consumed a vast amount of popularly oriented literature that was specifically Jewish in its content, audience, and objectives," in eastern Europe, this usually meant Hebrew, not Yiddish.[96] As the everyday language of the common folk, Yiddish earned little regard from the region's educated writing class. In the United States, by contrast, Yiddish-speaking immigrants easily published materials in their lingua franca. The *Forverts* became the largest ethnic newspaper in the United States with a circulation reaching half a million; half that number lived in New York alone.[97] Its readership among Jews in towns and cities around the United States further promoted New York City's rising status as the nation's leading Jewish city. The paper's editor, Abraham Cahan, considered himself a Socialist yet limited the paper's political tone in favor of concrete news about daily events. His paper's advice column made it especially helpful to new immigrants, whom he urged to enjoy life.[98] Jewish men should let their sons play baseball and get good at it, he wrote, and let their daughters and wives enroll in night school.[99] The Yiddish press made itself essential and so became immensely popular.[100]

Many newspapers offered readers Hanukkah essays, short fiction, and poetry conveying the views of diverse rabbis, along with those of intellectuals, political thinkers, socialists, scholars, and poets. These essayists expounded on Hanukkah's imagery to enhance its contemporary meaning for the immigrants' own lives. One explained that the original Hanukkah lights were "one of the most magnificent illuminations in world history." They dwindled to small flickering candles only when Jews "were forced to take up their walking sticks and set off on their wanderings throughout the world." Yet, even in their contemporary form, they served as beacons. Like the light that guided ancient Hebrews from Egypt to the Promised Land, he said, they "served [the Jew] as did the pillar of light in the desert, to guide his way."[101]

Several religious scholars published pamphlets to instruct ordinary Jews about Hanukkah's importance. Polish-born Judah David Eisenstein advertised his newly published Hebrew-language anthology of Hanukkah sermons in the Yiddish press. Asserting that "God is completely light," he explained that in the diaspora, the Hanukkah candles brighten the dark night of exile with the promise of redemption.[102] Eisenstein's essay urged Jews to see divinity itself within the Hanukkah lights in their homes. With those elaborations on Hanukkah and its ritual objects, Jewish immigrants could find holiday inspiration in their daily newspaper. They need not attend synagogue to encounter a Hanukkah sermon.

Yiddish newspapers offered an array of different perspectives on the immigrants' lot and often voiced an anxiety about how life in America might impact Jewish customs. Some authors questioned Hanukkah's relevance in the New World. A more conservative paper, the *Tageblatt*, called the Hanukkah candles only "poor, quiet, little . . . lights."[103] The menorah's row of candles reminded Socialist poet Morris Rosenfeld that Jews once lived orderly lives, instead of the tumultuous confusion they now faced. "How strange it seems!" he wrote.[104] The holiday seemed to fit best in the Old World, where even the design of its ritual object reflected its culture. Many menorahs brought to the United States by immigrants reflected a premodern taste for ornamentation and religious iconography, but nearly all arranged their small receptacles for either oil or candles in a neat, single row. Social commentator Ephraim Kaplan complained that American technology spoiled Jewish children's appreciation of Hanukkah's small candles. The candle lights looked dim to today's children because their "eyes . . . are . . . pampered [by the] . . . luxury, . . . comfort, . . . [and] splendor [of] large magical electric lights [which] have weakened their sense of sight," he wrote.[105] By 1920, electrical lighting, which delivered more than one hundred times more brightness than candle power, could be found in forty-seven percent of urban homes.[106] Kaplan believed that the Old World's hardships made Jews appreciate even the simple candle light of a Hanukkah menorah. Unless Judaism could incorporate modernity's marvels, he seemed to warn, it will be left behind by modern American Jews. In a few years, electric menorahs appeared and by midcentury became a popular holiday fixture.[107] But in the century's early years, Kaplan could not envision a home for Hanukkah in America.

Newspaper editor Abraham Cahan also believed that despite the charm of Old World Hanukkah practices, they were too simple and quotidian to survive in the twentieth-century West. In December 1906, Cahan eulogized Hanukkah's pleasures because he saw little future in

America for them. "The old Jew will light candles, make a *brocha* [blessing] and end with singing every evening," he began.[108] Cahan consigned the traditional practices to the past by linking them to the "old Jew." His rhetorical flourish discounted the many Jewish immigrants who remained faithful to tradition. Between 1900 and 1925, the members of the Union of Orthodox Jewish Congregations (committed to tradition) doubled from about one hundred to two hundred, but many other observant congregations remained outside that umbrella.[109] For those traditional Jews, Hanukkah customs likely remained fully alive. Cahan, however, was a Socialist, and his political ideology expected religion's demise, an idea which seemed to be supported by the obstacles to orderly religious life created by both the upheavals of immigration and the abundance, openness, and time demands of American culture.

Despite Cahan's inability to see a future for traditional Judaism in America, he admitted that Hanukkah's customs could lend enchantment to many Jewish homes. "Hearing the father's tunes as he sanctifies" the candles is a "delight," he wrote. From the kitchen, women of the family produce the "fat *latkes*" fried in oil that remind the household of the miraculous oil that burned for eight days—and that taste "exquisite." The "jingle of money at the card game" played by adults while children play dreidel and the "urchins" who "thank the uncle for the Hanukkah *gelt* [coins], all that is music," Cahan wrote. Hanukkah also lent a distinctive sensual pleasure to synagogues, where "the Cantor's concert . . . by the menorah awakens the blood."[110] Cahan's paean to Hanukkah's pleasures acknowledged that most Jews enjoyed it.

But Cahan thought that few among the Jewish immigrants actually understood the holiday's meaning. He claimed that because Hanukkah's rite lacks the formal questioning and lengthy answer that mark Passover, "what the holiday is about is known by only one Jew out of ten."[111] Hanukkah's brevity itself seemed to invite Jews to augment and aggrandize the holiday in various ways, but without clear instruction about its significance, it also became easy to misunderstand. As we have seen, nineteenth-century American Jews found it easy both to ignore Hanukkah and to add elements of American culture to its celebration. The new immigrants brought Hanukkah celebrations which primarily had offered them cheer in wintry and hostile Europe with little instruction as to its deeper meaning. Editors with more traditional religious viewpoints also felt Hanukkah deserved greater attention. The religious *Idisher Zhurnal* complained that compared to the other Jewish holidays, Hanukkah is "like a step-child" and likely to be neglected.[112] It seems that the editors of both sorts of Jewish newspapers—Socialist and religious—agreed that for Hanukkah to survive as a holiday with religious meaning, rather than only as a folk custom whose popularity could easily rise and fall, its rite needed to be augmented with instruction about its larger meaning. Nineteenth-century American rabbis across the board had voiced similar concerns and arrived at the same conclusion. But Cahan, who held a different vision of Judaism's importance to the world than rabbis did, took Hanukkah in a different direction.

Taking Hanukkah in a Political Route

To save the holiday from demise, Cahan suggested several new ideas to revivify it. While "old Jews" simply delighted in Hanukkah's rituals, he explained, younger, politically minded Jews found a new meaning in the holiday. "For the young nationalistic element it's the most important holiday, . . . similar to the Fourth of July."[113] The young movement to return Jews to their ancient home in the Judean hills made Hanukkah its chief festival. Hanukkah seemed ideal for promoting Zionist hopes because it celebrated a victory for Jewish political independence. Zionists claimed the Maccabean mantle of Jewish power, thereby reimagining themselves as a powerful movement, just as nineteenth-century American reforming rabbis and lay leaders had done for their own efforts to revitalize Jews' future in the modern world.

But Cahan personally held a different view. He explained to his readers that the Socialist vision of a worldwide future of peace and economic justice could find a model for its success in the ancient Jewish past. "For us Socialists, Hanukkah unfolds in a new, timely, much wider . . . manner." He portrayed the Maccabees as forerunners to larger revolutionary efforts then emerging in Russia. "Maccabees . . . purified a religious house of worship," but Socialists in Russia, Lithuania, and Poland "will purify the entire human spirit of greed, bloodlust, and power," he wrote enthusiastically. Voicing the hopes for a utopian future that marked the Socialist movement at the turn of the twentieth century, Cahan called the Maccabees predecessors to the revolution that he believed would improve living conditions for everyone. The Maccabees "were just Jewish heroes," he said. But the "current Jewish heroes" fighting for revolution in Russia "are humanity's Maccabees!"[114]

Socialist and poet Abraham Liesen took things a step further. He turned his own Hanukkah essay into a lesson in a Marxist understanding of Jewish history that emphasized the economic class differences between ancient Jews, differences that motivated the poor to overthrow the Jewish upper class allied with Antiochus and his minions. It was the aristocracy among the ancient Jews that collaborated with the "oppressors at the cost of their oppressed people," he argued.[115] Born in Minsk, Liesen had been expelled from a Talmudic academy for his heretical ideas. Saddened and angered by the poverty and injustice Jews endured in eastern Europe, he painted a sad picture of Hanukkah there. While Cahan penned a homey image of holiday charm, Liesen, on the other hand, tore away Cahan's veil of nostalgia to reveal the poverty and fear permeating eastern European Jewish life, even at Hanukkah. The holiday's candles "flicker . . . in mouldy ghettos like a mournful embodiment of the entire existence of the Jewish people." Their menorah's flames are "abandoned, desolate."[116] Jews endured Russia's dangers and trials because they had forgotten Hanukkah's message, he told his readers. He hoped that revolutionary changes would free Jews from the political and economic disadvantages they faced and end widespread anti-Jewish attitudes there. Moreover, Liesen blamed Jews' ignorance about the Maccabees' successful revolution on rabbis who reduced the heroic revolt to a miraculous vial of oil and consigned that oil story to "some corner of a Talmud page." Doing so, they "expelled Khanike from Jewish hearts." It is the "modern, worldly, self-proclaimed nationalist Jew," Liesen said, who "gave the holiday . . . a place among the most beautiful of Jewish holidays." These modern Jews embraced the idea of "Jewish fighters . . . for a holy thing—their freedom and their beliefs."[117] Liesen's perspective wrested religious idealism from rabbinic discourse and claimed it for revolutionaries like himself, who redefined it for the Jewish nationalist movement and, even more so, Jewish revolutionaries in Russia.

Hanukkah found champions among the new immigrants across a spectrum of thinkers, from religious writers such as Eisenstein to radical Marxists such as Liesen. But Cahan admitted that some Jews simply did not care about the holiday that elicited such eloquence and passion from intellectuals. For them, "Khanike has no significance and is not even a holiday." These Jews have "freed themselves from . . . feelings." They neither light candles nor "hold nationalistic speeches." He marveled at their lack of emotion. Is Hanukkah "the same as all other days of the year" for them? How could it not "make any impression at all" on them? he asked his readers. To reach those Jews, and to subtly mock them, too, Cahan published a short story, "What Is Hanukkah?" by beloved humorist Sholem Aleichem (Solomon Rabinowitz) that spoofed the Hanukkah celebrations typical to such Jews. For them, card parties entirely replaced candles, blessings, and even dreidels.[118]

It is not difficult to understand why some Jews ignored Hanukkah. A significant number of Jewish immigrants came to America hoping to loosen the hold of the Jewish authorities that they felt had bound them too tightly in Europe. Galician-born Fanny Edelman recalled that she emigrated primarily to escape the arranged-marriage customs that overruled her own desires.[119] Russia's poorer Jewish families grew to resent their community's leaders who sometimes offered up their sons, rather than the sons of the wealthier classes, to fill the czar's quota of boys for the military.[120] Long after Jacob Ascanazy had settled in Buffalo, New York, he remained apart from the local Jewish leadership and chose to live in an Italian neighborhood, where his tailor shop remained open on the Sabbath. On the Lower East Side, other immigrants shared a similar resentment toward authoritative Jewish bodies.[121] Individuals such as those young women who escaped parental authority and the businessmen who ordered their lives according to America's economic demands placed their own personal freedom uppermost. They provoked anxiety among Jewish thinkers. Intellectuals and rabbis alike agreed that Jews ought to be guided by principles derived from some inspirational vision, whether of a new era of freedom and justice or by God and divine commandments. Jewish political radicals often understood their views as extensions of Judaism's religious values.[122] One man who grew up in this immigrant milieu thought of Socialism as simply a "moral idea" and its promised utopian future akin to a "supernatural event which one might await with perfect faith" and toward which many around him ordered their lives.[123] But disaffected

Jews seeking more personal freedom in America could easily ignore the whole Hanukkah event.

Desperate to reach those immigrants who cast off everything from the "old country" in order to fit into America, Cahan offered another explanation for Hanukkah, this time in American terms he knew they would appreciate. The Maccabean revolt "was purely an uprising for freedom," he said.[124] Others among the Yiddish-speaking immigrants claimed likewise. Philologist, poet, and editor Alexander Harkavy's lengthy 1892 pamphlet *The Jewish Revolution* had compared Judah Maccabee to George Washington.[125] Like nineteenth-century American rabbis, Harkavy linked the Maccabees with American liberty. Written for fellow Yiddish-speaking immigrants and published in New York, Harkavy's essay claimed that the two military leaders fought for similar goals and suggested that immigrants could develop American values by participating in Hanukkah rites.

Although Harkavy echoed the approach to Hanukkah promoted by Reform rabbis such as Lilienthal and Wise a few decades earlier, he opposed Reform. In his popular account of the Maccabean revolt, Harkavy compared ancient Jews who collaborated with Judea's Greek oppressors to modern Reform Jews because they compromised Jewish practice to fit American culture, just as some ancient Jews adopted some Greek customs to make Judaism fit more seamlessly into the Hellenic world.[126] Like many other Jews in America, Harkavy cast his own view of Judaism's foes and allies into the holiday's array of characters —heroes, loyalists, traitors, and collaborators. Yet his Hanukkah message echoed Lilienthal's. The story of the American Revolution and the freedoms offered by the country's founding documents captivated these new Jewish immigrants as they had earlier Jewish generations in America. Just like earlier Jews, though perhaps more gradually and with greater diversity in their perspectives, these immigrants came to view Hanukkah through the lenses of American values and heroes.

For turn-of-the-century immigrants, Hanukkah became an occasion to enact their adjustment to American life while, at the same time, performing activities generated by Judaism's rites and customs. Each

Among the duties of the National Jewish Welfare Board was providing items used by chaplains who ministered to Jewish men who served in the American military throughout the twentieth century and into the twenty-first. Here, Jewish soldiers serving in World War 1 celebrate Hanukkah in 1917 using items provided by the NJWB. (Courtesy American Jewish Historical Society)

Hanukkah called forth their literary skills, their political dreams, and their enjoyment of American standards of material abundance. It occasioned eating American foods in a Jewish atmosphere. With eight nights of celebration, both "eating out" and eating home meals made according to recipes both old and new could be part of an American Hanukkah. In retelling Hanukkah's story, Jews also allied the ancient holiday with intellectual currents swirling around them, reflecting new nationalist, revolutionary, and utopian movements inflected both by Jewish faith and American ideals. In the many Hanukkah concert venues that appeared each year at schools, old-age homes, synagogues, meeting rooms, theaters, and halls, they quenched their thirst for entertainment while uniting in songs that defined both their various political and regional subcultures and their shared Jewish identity. Hanukkah provided them with lively occasions for celebrating their Jewishness and an identity that they could imagine to be as constant as the carved letters on a dreidel, despite the new turns their lives had taken.

For the vast majority of the newcomers, the Yiddish-speaking Ashkenazim, "Maoz Tsur" was only one of many Hanukkah melodies. Local choruses, schoolchildren, and visiting professional soloists regaled audiences with religious songs, folk melodies, new political anthems, and operatic compositions. Concertgoers might attend such events after dining at a Jewish restaurant or at home. They may have indulged a feeling of satisfaction that they were able to give their offspring "presents" for the holiday, perhaps purchasing items advertised in a Yiddish newspaper. Taken together, these activities constituted Hanukkah celebrations that helped Jewish immigrants to feel at home in their new country while nurturing their distinctive Yiddish-in-America culture. The bustling life of America's Yiddishland created exuberant Hanukkah celebrations far different from the children's festivals that had become the focus of Hanukkah celebrations among wealthier, American-born, Jews.

This broad range of American Hanukkah customs embedded the holiday in New York's commercial culture and, in that process, democratized it. Rabbis retained authoritative control over religious activities only if Jews chose to attend to them. For at least one immigrant rabbi new to New York, this situation created an upside-down world where "people walk on their heads."[127] The new authority of the market economy offered a different leadership. Newspaper editors could provide Hanukkah sermons that conveyed any number of secular or religious messages—but just as with rabbis, people could choose to ignore them, too. New public spaces for Hanukkah gatherings, such as restaurants that placed special holiday foods on their menus and concert halls that arranged special cantorial performances, likewise depended on customers who might or might not pay the tab. Songbook publishers, too, hoped to please a buying public. In their efforts, these editors, restauranteurs, publishers, and producers shaped their offerings in ways that would please the largest number of customers. Most restaurants offered potato latkes, using the simplest recipe that would be enjoyed by the most Jews, rather than the buckwheat pancakes special to Abraham Cahan's childhood memories. Companies selling cooking shortening promoted its usefulness in preparing the latkes of eastern Europeans, not the *burmuelos* (fritters) or *burekas* (turnovers) eaten by the smaller numbers of Sephardim. Songsters grew larger but repeated the same few of the most popular ditties each time, before adding new creations. Likewise, the cantorial repertoire at Hanukkah concerts featured favorites expected to please the largest audience. In this way, the reins of the new Hanukkah activities rested to an unprecedented degree in the hands of ordinary Jews.

Religious traditions had no choice but to work with market forces. Now, not only rabbis but editors, restauranteurs, producers, and shopkeepers determined the range of purchasing options from which Jews could choose and the holiday meanings they could learn. The Hanukkah culture that blossomed in the early twentieth century thus changed the experience of being Jewish in America, simultaneously undermining traditional religious authority, empowering ordinary Jews, and tying religion inextricably to the market. Jews raised with this Yiddishland's culturally rich Hanukkah experiences later created different holiday cultural products in a new language to voice their own concerns about Jewish life in America after World War I, when new attitudes toward immigrants in general and Jews in particular challenged the very nature of what it meant to be an American.

5

Homegrown Heroism

In the decades between 1924, when the U.S. Congress restricted immigration, and 1945, when the Allies defeated Nazism in World War II, American Jews began to tell Hanukkah's story of Jewish victory and divine rescue in a different way than they had in the past. In original plays, in the correspondence of women's organizations, in sermons, in advice manuals, and in songs, American Jews approached Hanukkah with new urgency and experimented with new ways to think about its meaning in this more dangerous time. Their worries about their children and their own futures in America replaced the concerns of earlier eras.

Old arguments over who should carry the reins of religious leadership in America, debates that had been so acrimonious in the nineteenth century, reached a stalemate in the early twentieth, when each side in those debates developed Jewish denominations to support their own particular religious style. By the 1920s, Reform (most liberal), Conservative (the middle of the road), and Orthodox (the most traditionally observant) branches of Judaism each produced rabbis trained in their distinct approaches, who served affiliated congregations composed of dues-paying members. Now, rabbis seldom battled each other. They usually reserved their rhetoric about Maccabean heroism for inspiring their own congregants to greater religious devotion, rather than to confront rabbis linked to other denominations over Jewish leadership.

Nor did American Jews in the twenties and thirties talk much about the importance of synagogue and charitable-society Hanukkah festivals for Jewish children—those had become commonplace. Among Jewish adults, the great exuberance with which new immigrants had aggrandized Hanukkah with public concerts, poetry, songbooks, food, and presents, by the twenties, also had subsided into familiar, but smaller, annual activities. New media technologies such as records and movies drew audiences away from large Hanukkah concerts that had been so popular only a decade before. As immigrants and their grown children relocated to new neighborhoods far from the very dense Jewish enclaves immigrants had created, distances further diminished the likelihood of gathering a large audience for a Hanukkah concert.

Yet, in the confusing and challenging years between the end of World War I and the end of World War II, American Jews once again found that Hanukkah provided a vehicle for thinking about their own contemporary Jewish issues. The holiday about dedication became a palimpsest for expressing their own concerns. For example, original amateur Hanukkah dramas for adults and children, performed in myriad clubs and schools, expressed fears of another kind of "death from pleasure" than the *Yiddishe Tageblatt* had warned against in 1907. Then, that newspapers' editors had told immigrants that indulging too much in America's abundance might erase the special luxury that holidays typically brought to Jewish homes and thus emotionally flatten the religious high points in the Jewish calendar. Now, in the twenties, through creative dramas and plays, Jews voiced fears that some of their peers, and many of their children, might abandon both their religion and their religious community in its time of need as they stepped into the welcoming arms of America's larger gentile culture to enjoy the pleasure of total acceptance.

But how welcoming was America? Original Hanukkah dramas from this era reveal Jews' anxieties about rising antisemitism and the country's growing distrust of immigrants and their children, at the same time that they warned Jews against too much assimilation. When the U.S. Congress sharply limited immigration from eastern and southern Europe and the Levant (along with most parts of the world outside western Europe) in an effort to restore the ethnic makeup that prevailed in the United States in 1890, it signaled that the limit to its welcome had been reached. Antisemitic ideas could be read in American newspapers and, by the 1930s, heard on radios. Select universities instituted quotas that kept many Jewish students out. As Jews watched Nazism rise in Europe and sometimes violent antisemitism rear its head in America, original dramas performed by amateurs in Jewish social organizations and clubs, as well as in religious schools, provided vehicles for expressing fears while also containing them. Some Jews, especially mothers, also strived to cultivate more religiously rich domestic experiences that provided emotional support and inculcated Jewish identity amid familial bonds. Hanukkah's domestic rites, easily embellished, became pivotal in the effort to strengthen children's Jewish identity. In communal settings and in homes, Jews in this era shaped Hanukkah into a festival uniquely suited to address the uncertainties they faced.

Often, Hanukkah festivities occurred in an array of associations that provided camaraderie and emotional support while reaffirming common values. Individuals from long-established American Jewish families as well as immigrants and their children found voluntary associations to join. In women's clubs, charitable societies, Jewish community centers, fraternities, *landsmanschaftn*, religious associations, and synagogues, in clubs for youth and for political ends, Jews gathered together. For small communities, annual Hanukkah events reinforced important social ties. Among Sephardi Jews in both Seattle and Los Angeles, Hanukkah activities in local religious schools became major festive occasions to gather together.[1]

Those myriad associations provided venues for expressing Jewish identity, sharing common concerns, and relaxing among companions. Social warmth and acceptance became precious commodities for Jews in this era. After World War I, Americans became more fearful of threats from Europe. "The so-called Red Scare generated an irrational fear of Bolshevism," explains historian Charles Lippy, and "resulted in immigration quotas."[2] Those quotas ultimately made it impossible for all but a comparative handful of Europe's Jews to escape Nazism.

Groups also often organized entertaining holiday events to keep their members involved despite the popular attractions of theater and the newfound intrigue of movies. The leisure time of Jews, like all Americans, was ever more contested as the century wore on. Rates of membership in all kinds of organizations dipped across the country during the Great Depression, as incomes dropped, but picked up again, at least for women, during World War II. At Hanukkah, otherwise lighthearted social events could turn serious, as the story about loyalists and Hellenists became a metaphor for the growing anxieties about the Jewish future.

Just as alarming as antisemitism was that the American Jewish population had stopped growing. First, severe immigration restrictions cut off new arrivals. Second, many Jews in the United States successfully used the techniques made available by the new birth-control movement that emerged in this era. When Deenah and Max Kaminker came to America from the Ukraine shortly after the turn of the century, they brought their five young children. Yet their three daughters collectively produced only four children.[3] Now, more than ever, it seemed, the loyalty of every American Jew mattered. New original short dramas performed by amateurs addressed those concerns amid otherwise convivial occasions.

Lively Hanukkah events helped many Jewish organizations retain members despite changing conditions. *Landsmanschaftn*, for example, began as new immigrants helped each other adjust to America but continued to provide a warm social life long after their members ceased to look to them for aid. For the Boyerke *landsmanschaft* in New York, for example, the annual Hanukkah party became the largest social event of their year and drew people from new homes far from immigrant neighborhoods.[4]

In the 1920s and 1930s, many Jews joined the Boyerkes in scattering beyond immigrant enclaves. In New York, new apartment buildings and neighborhoods grew up along new subway and bus lines and new highway routes. As Jews wended their way around neighborhoods and apartment buildings restricted to white Christians, they identified welcoming locations. They moved into Pelham Parkway in the Bronx, Yorkville in Queens, or Eastern Parkway in Brooklyn.[5] Similar changes occurred in other cities. In Philadelphia, the children of Jewish eastern European immigrants who had clustered in the city's southern section for the past four decades began to move north. In Chicago, Jews from the Maxwell Street area, mostly eastern European immigrants and their children, moved west, especially to Lawndale. Nearly forty-five Chicago synagogues relocated there by the 1940s.[6] Yet many Jews remained in poorer neighborhoods. As late as World War II, New York's Seward Park High School drew seventy-four percent of its students from Jewish families that lived in the "tenements and alleys of the lower East Side."[7]

American Jewish culture changed. With few Yiddish-speaking newcomers, the Yiddish press dwindled, and by the end of World War II, few remained but the *Forverts*.[8] American society placed greater pressure on immigrants to assimilate, to blend into its culture as quickly as possible. The national rush to assimilate immigrants extended to public schools, where new curricula designed around cultural holidays such as Arbor Day and Thanksgiving were designed to "build . . . community spirit, patriotism, and Americanism."[9] Thus, Jewish adults and children alike felt the press of American culture.

Scripts for Survival

As always, Jewish culture manifested itself in myriad ways. But one particularly revealing creation that blossomed after World War I was the original drama specifically created for Hanukkah that centered on issues of religious dedication and community defense. Worries about instilling a strong Jewish identity and religious commitment in children emerged with particular force in these years and inspired original Hanukkah dramas and songs performed by both club members and schoolchildren. The taste for dramatic entertainments satisfied through the Yiddish- and English-language theater earlier in the century was, in the twenties and thirties, enhanced by movies, radio, and widely popular amateur dramatics.

Original plays depicted the drama in Jews' own lives as they explored the borders that might exist between Jewish and gentile ways of life. For some, this exploration entailed profoundly disturbing and emotional issues. Would the way parents drew that border be meaningful for their children? And if children moved into gentile milieus, how would they navigate those boundaries? Under those uncertainties, could Judaism survive? Dramatic formulas heightened the urgency conveyed in these plays. Hanukkah's cast of ancient characters—loyalists, Hellenizers, traitors, and foes—became metaphors for contemporary characters in America. They provided a way for twentieth-century Jews to consider the perplexing demands of Jewish dedication in the United States. With those larger questions waiting in the shadows, children's skits strived to inculcate a strong personal identification with the ancient Maccabees. Adults hoped that these pleasures would build children's emotional tie to Jewish life. One observer noted that "almost every Hebrew school has a Hanukkah play in which young pupils participate" and that "youth clubs generally present Hanukkah plays."[10] Staged in club meetings and classrooms, Hanukkah plays conveyed serious meanings beneath the lighthearted atmosphere.

American Jews drew on a long Jewish tradition of original drama, but that tradition did not center on Hanukkah. As early as the fifth century, Jews near Antioch celebrated Purim with songs, jokes, and reenactments of the final scene of the Book of Esther, whose events Purim commemorates.[11] By the seventeenth century, these became more like actual dramas, and two hundred years later, the repertoire outgrew imaginative versions of Bible stories.[12]

But beginning in the 1920s, many new plays written for Hanukkah became available to American Jews. The holiday about dedication became an ideal vehicle for raising issues about American Jews' religious loyalties, as well as evaluating threats to Jewish life and survival. Jews selected from an easily obtained stock of plays produced by small publishing houses such as Bloch and the Hebrew Publishing Company, which printed and promoted these skits along with their line of songbooks, prayer books, literature, and other religious and educational materials. Advertisements for these items often filled each back cover. Nearly all were in English, another signpost of the demise of Yiddish. The Reform movement's publishing house also produced plays, juvenile literature, and textbooks which, in the interwar years, reflected respect for various styles of Jewish observance and the importance of Jewish peoplehood, making them useful to many different groups.[13] To ease the search for new and useful plays, annotated listings of these original productions appeared in 1937; by 1945, another compilation listed

250 "Selected Plays of Jewish Interest." Only three years later, an additional listing offered 100 plays specially for Hanukkah. The Jewish Welfare Board, which coordinated activities in the country's Jewish community centers and which first printed that compilation, advised that
such dramatizations "are particularly effective for interpretation and
identification with the Jewish experience." Hanukkah's "story, ceremonial, heroism, . . . [and] idealism [can] stimulate creative dramatics and
improvisations," the JWB explained. A play or pageant "recounting the
historic event interpreting the struggle for freedom of worship and for
internal unity, depicting the ancient heroes or their modern counter-
parts can add much meaning to the Hanuka festival." The plays could
be used by groups, in many different settings. They might "even stimulate discussion, creative writing, and improvisation" and so significantly
enliven religious-school classrooms or club meetings.[14] In one or two
acts, these dramas conveyed lessons about Jewish survival, either by
drawing on Hanukkah's story, its customs and rites, or on the social
uneasiness derived from being Jewish in the interwar era, when antisemitism increased.

Despite those common themes, each play reflected its author's ability
and imagination. Settings ranged from grand homes to impoverished
apartments, from big cities to small towns, from Europe to America.
Characters included Maccabees and Antiochus, important men in Jewish history, children, adults, grandparents, and even phantoms. Most
depicted adults—usually parents, neighbors, or teachers—instructing
children in Hanukkah's meaning and importance. Some playwrights
intended their work to be used in classrooms or youth groups where
Jewish youngsters gathered under adult supervision. Their casts of characters sometimes reveal their authors' assumptions about the gendered
nature of boys versus girls. Some writers adapted literary devices popular in juvenile fiction and in trends in American culture to enrich their
Hanukkah dramas. Many used the play-within-a-play technique common to Western drama since the ancient Greeks and through William
Shakespeare or used dream sequences popularized by Charles Dickens
in *A Christmas Carol* and by Frank Baum in his *Wonderful Wizard of
Oz* (book, 1900; movie, 1939). Many incorporated instrumental music
and singing. All didactic, they nonetheless wrapped their messages
in entertainment.

While occasionally applying the devices used in high or popular culture, the Hanukkah plays written for adults often tackled serious issues.
A grim Hanukkah melodrama published in 1924, just as political rhetoric denouncing immigrants culminated in severe restrictions, insisted
that America could be a dangerous place for Jews, especially in small
towns where Jews are vastly outnumbered. Entanglements with gentiles
could lead to tragedy. Written by Rabbi Goodman Lipkind, its forty
pages made it an unusually long Hanukkah play. No music softens its
impact, and little artistry complicates its message.

Lipkind experienced firsthand the contrast between life in the dense
Jewish neighborhoods of New York, where he usually resided, and
small-town life in the Midwest. In New York, he participated in ambi-
tious Jewish projects. He contributed to the multivolume *Jewish Encyclopedia* published in 1906 and served on the Executive Committee of
the American Federation of the Jewish Territorial Organization, one of
the early groups that sought a homeland for Jews. But between 1912 and
1914, Lipkind served as rabbi for the United Hebrew Congregation of
Chesterfield, Missouri, a venerable group formed in 1836. His play is
heavy with the Christian imagery so prevalent in the culture of many
small southern and midwestern towns. For the rabbi, pervasively Christian environments such as this one are menacing locales for Jews.

Lipkind called his one-act play *What Happened on Chanukah: A
Play for Adults* and set it in the home of the Gersons, a fictional Jewish family (whose name means "stranger" in Hebrew) living in a small
town.[15] Despite the play's length, the action moves quickly. Its tragedy
begins when the oldest son, Gerald, home from university for Christmas break, reveals that he has rejected Judaism. As the family lights
the Hanukkah candles, an argument begins. "God doesn't help [Jews],"
he says. Why should he suffer along with them? At college, he attends
church and pretends to be Protestant. Moreover, Gerald wants to marry
the daughter of the head of the local Ku Klux Klan. He points out that
his own mother converted from Christianity to Judaism and argues
that "he feels his gentile blood" within. His mother angrily insists that
she is a loyal Jew and that "just because Jews are despised doesn't mean
they're wrong." Ironically she draws on Christian theology to refute her
son's condemnation of Jews. "Jesus," she says, "was the most despised
and downtrodden of men, . . . and his name is a magnet that attracts

all hearts. The fate of the Jew is the same!" Insisting that Judaism is "faith not blood," Gerald's parents point out that his younger sister was adopted and raised as Jewish, further refuting the possibility of "Christian blood." Lipkind uses the mother's character to contrast ideas about racial antisemitism with Christian ideals and values. Her speech reveals her love for both her Jewish family and for Jesus, despite her conversion.

This family argument is interrupted when a friend runs in to announce that local Klan members accused Gerald's eight-year-old brother of vandalizing a statue of Jesus that stands in the town center and had beat him badly. The ringleader was the father of the girl Gerald loves. Hearing this news, Gerald collapses.

On recovering, Gerald tells the assembled cast that he now sees antisemitism must be opposed and that it takes courage to do so. "Perhaps this is God's way of bringing you back to us," his mother says. "Someone had to suffer so that the truth shall be revealed." In the play's final speech, Gerald explains that he now sees that Israel's suffering served to "bring divine Revelation to the whole world. . . . That is our purpose." Asking his father's forgiveness, he promises that the household "shall never be divided." His perspective, like the one voiced by his mother, views Jews and Jesus as sharing a common role in the religious history of the world.

This brutal play reveals more than Lipkind's distrust of small-town America. It suggests that Christians who are antisemitic are also misunderstanding Jesus. With so much of this play espousing a particular vision of Christianity, it seems likely that Lipkind intended it to be performed before audiences of both Christians and Jews. For a Jewish audience, however, it conveys an image of confusion and danger that can result from close association with Christians, even those who are loving. It also reflects Lipkind's thoughts about the dilemmas faced by Jewish university students. In the decade after World War I, overall enrollment in the country's colleges jumped from six hundred thousand to more than one million.[16] Numbers further increased in the next decade despite the economic challenges posed by the Great Depression. By then, Jews provided roughly ten percent of the nation's college students despite constituting only three and a half percent of its population.[17]

But many colleges did not welcome Jews. At Harvard, the new president, A. Lawrence Lowell, believed that "no democracy could be successful unless it was tolerably homogenous" and firmly believed that a quota sharply limiting the number of Jewish students would help them to integrate into the larger Christian class. Admit too many Jews, he believed, and they would neither socialize with gentiles nor adopt the gentile American cultural style.[18] Other colleges joined the trend. Decrying the "invasion" of Jews via a new subway from Lower Manhattan, Columbia University cut Jewish students from forty to twenty percent of its student body.[19] While the majority of young Jews who sought advanced training attended business schools, many others opted for universities. Jewish newspapers cast the Harvard conflict in the "language of the American ideal of democracy and merit," asserting that a core American value was at stake.[20] Jews faced similar, if not worse, restrictions against their employment at large businesses, firms, and hospitals that similarly barred Jewish employees, attorneys, and physicians. When the country's best schools limited Jewish students, they made it unlikely that Jews could surmount those employment barriers through a better education.

The Jewish press often argued that antisemitism at universities threatened Jews' ability to participate in American life, but Lipkind's play suggested that it posed a more profound threat to *Jewish* life. It asked audiences to consider that gentile college campuses posed the same threats to Jewish students as do small, largely Christian towns because the students are expected to erase their Jewish distinctiveness. Lipkind's play forced its audience to consider the special stresses faced by younger Jews. This problem could not be solved simply by providing children with Hanukkah presents so that they will not envy their gentile friends at Christmas. Young adults need to be able to withstand outright hostility, he implied. If they cannot face it, they will leave Judaism.

Lipkind's play also offered a position on the thorny issue of conversion and intermarriage, as Gerald's mother affirms her commitment to Judaism in a way that also discloses her continued regard for Jesus. Several years earlier, the Reform rabbinate supported congregations whose bylaws insisted that "no person married to a non-Jew may be a member" because "forbidden marriages have disastrous results, especially in regard to the offspring."[21] Lipkind's play suggested that a marriage between a convert to Judaism and a person raised Jewish is in some respects an intermarriage, yet it also can produce a cohort of people able to articulate a theologically sophisticated condemnation of anti-semitism. Even so, those marriages can confuse children about Jewish identity.

Another play for adults featured a famous Jewish family to tackle the same question. Elma Ehrlich Levinger's drama *The Unlighted Menorah* forced her audience to reflect on the threat to Judaism's future in America by pointing out how similar circumstances ended in the past, when post-Enlightenment Germany had extended political rights to some of its Jews. The play's action takes place in the home of Abraham Mendelssohn, son of the famous eighteenth-century Jewish Enlightenment philosopher Moses Mendelssohn and father of music composer Felix Mendelssohn. Moses Mendelssohn translated the Hebrew Bible into German, a work that helped many Jews learn that language, and explained Judaism in such a way that it could survive in a modernizing Germany. Yet his children did not remain Jews. Levinger's play imagines Mendelssohn's son, Abraham, filled with regret when faced with his own son Felix's great distance from Judaism.

Like Lipkind, Elma Ehrlich experienced Jewish American life in both small towns and big cities. Born in Chicago in 1887, Ehrlich taught in rural schools in Iowa and Illinois and studied English and drama at the University of Chicago and at Radcliffe College. After marrying Reform Rabbi Lee Levinger, she went on to author over thirty books, most for children but several for adults, all conveying the importance of maintaining Jewish identity. Her brief, one-act Hanukkah play is erudite and graceful, effectively using props and music and drawing on the dramatic device so successfully used by Charles Dickens in *A Christmas Carol*—a voice of the dead that advises the living during a dream.

The play opens with Abraham Mendelssohn, aged fifty-nine, sitting in his library in his home in Berlin. Nearby, a table is covered with sheet music and books, and the room is lit by many "handsome and fantastic candle holders."[22] An array of candelabra, some far more ornate and larger than the Hanukkah menorah, presents a visual metaphor of the religious choices available to Jews in modern Germany. Grand cathedrals and gothic stone churches offered more architectural beauty than most synagogues provided. Abraham's wife, Leah, tells Abraham that they were right to "turn Christian" because "Felix has never known the hardship of being a Jew with wealth and education," who can find no welcome anywhere. She finds their old Hanukkah menorah behind some books, and Abraham remembers the "old Hebrew song, Maoz Tsur." Leah hums it and leaves.

Felix enters, and Abraham asks him if he can play the melody he heard his mother hum, but he replies, "I don't know anything about Jewish music, father." Moreover, Felix explains that he is working on a new piece about St. Paul for the church and exits, leaving Abraham alone once again. As Abraham falls into a reverie, the ghost of Moses Mendelssohn appears. The phantom asks, "Do you still light the Chanukah candles my son?" Abraham admits that he does not, explaining that "it is not always easy to be a Jew," and stops, ashamed. Moses's reply constitutes the purpose of the play—conveying Levinger's message to convince her audience that by diminishing Judaism's role in their lives they were losing a source of joy. Despite poverty, hatred, and injustice, Mendelssohn says, "it is a great joy to be a Jew. . . . I was happy through all my miseries for I loved my people." Taking an image from classical sports, he says, "Every Jew is a torch-bearer. . . . Which he thrusts into the hand of the man who follows him." The phantom moves to light the menorah, but there is no candle. He says, "I gave you the light but you have not been able to renew it." Seeing Abraham's sadness, Mendelssohn assures him, "If you remain a good Jew, . . . the light of Torah will always give you comfort." The phantom disappears, just as Felix enters to see his father attempting to light the menorah. Listening to his mother playing "Maoz Tsur" on a piano offstage (which the audience hears), he exclaims happily that he will use the melody for his new cantata, hoping it will be played in all the churches of Europe. The play ends as Abraham replies, "and the menorah will never be lighted." Levinger's play challenged Jewish parents to see the larger impact that their own child-rearing decisions will have on the long-term Jewish future and the impact for happiness or sadness those decisions may have in their own lives.

The Hebrew Publishing Company brought out Levinger's play in conjunction with the Reform movement's Department of Synagogue and School Extension. The majority of Reform Jews claimed central European ancestry, and, for them, Mendelssohn and his family remained well-known figures. During the 1920s, Jews who traced their ancestry to eastern Europe began joining Reform congregations, and they, too, contemplated the Mendelssohn family's decline when they saw this play. Reformers used it in their continuing campaign, begun in the nineteenth century, to urge their members to light Hanukkah candles in their homes. Annette Kohn, a regular contributor to the Reform newspaper the *American Israelite* echoed Levinger's point. She lamented the "spectacle " in "modern Jewish homes" of parents neglecting to light Hanukkah lamps for themselves and their children but, instead, "letting their children light the candles on the Christian Christmas trees in their own Jewish homes." Kohn argued that such behavior brings the Hanukkah story "naturally" and "sadly to an end."[23] It seems that Christmas trees appeared in an unknown number of Jewish homes, but especially among those with German heritage.[24] Yet writer Moise Soulam also urged members of his own Sephardi community, whose worship style did not undergo the changes initiated by Reform, to "abandon these Christian customs" of buying Christmas trees, decorating their houses, and giving presents and instead raise children with "Jewish spirit."[25] He, too, would have endorsed the message of Levinger's drama.

A very different sort of Hanukkah play for adults tried to convince skeptical adults that they were missing out on a lot of fun by neglecting the holiday's celebrations. Marketed by Behrman's Jewish Book House and set in the distant future of 1950, it is the only Hanukkah play that features a cast of science professors—a group typifying rational thought, seriousness, and skepticism. As it opens, the group debates the wisdom of using the time machine that one of them has built. A member's child says, "Tomorrow in Sunday School we are celebrating Chanukah," and the adults, who had forgotten about the holiday, decide to use the machine. But instead of going to ancient Judea, they go to the future, to the end of time. They appear costumed as characters in the Hanukkah story standing in a court before the Judge of History—a secularized version of the God of History. The judge is to decide the ultimate importance of the battle between the Maccabees and Antiochus, who symbolizes antisemitism in general. Embodying the past, each person speaks for a different viewpoint. The judge rules, not surprisingly, that the Maccabees shall rule in the hearts and minds of the Jews "unto eternity." The professors are quickly restored to their meeting and to modern dress, and they agree that the Maccabean story can revive religious fervor among secular Jews because it makes Judaism exciting and is historically significant. One concludes, "There is color, beauty, romance, thrill, everything you wish—in Jewish history."[26] Interestingly, they find a place for the Jewish past in their lives not by dislodging their commitment to scientific truth but by valuing Judaism for its aesthetic and emotional satisfaction.

This play suggests that even sober Jewish scientists occasionally need the excitement Hanukkah can provide. Modern science and its rigors serve as foils for the much more exciting realm of Jewish religious history. The play's author, Samuel M. Segal, who obtained rabbinical ordination in America from the Jewish Institute of Religion, sympathetic to both Reform and Zionism, offered psychological and emotional reasons to appreciate the holiday. Few people expected scientists to believe the story of the miraculous oil, and Jewishness itself seemed unappealing among some college students, even at heavily Jewish New York University.[27] Rather than attempting to instill guilt for not observing the holiday, Segal enticed skeptics to just enjoy it because Hanukkah can be just as entertaining as movies. Some of the most popular films shown in the movie palaces that appeared in the twenties featured larger-than-life heroes who triumphed in thrilling escapades.[28] Segal's play encouraged adults to experience Hanukkah as they would a film, approaching it as a fun escape from daily tedium.

Children's Plays

Most of the plays written in this time period were designed for children and reflected the era's concern to instill Jewish identity. The Conservative movement's Deborah Marcus Melamed challenged "any mother with a little initiative" to take charge of her family's holiday events and to coordinate activities. "In many homes each child has his [sic] own menorah. . . . In others children take turns lighting the family menorah." Gather a few children for a Hanukkah play, she said, and use Hanukkah "to make children glory in their own traditions and be happy they are Jews."[29] A close look at a sample of typical plays reveals that most were written for use by religious schools and clubs or in larger domestic gatherings.

Four plays from the 1920s demonstrate both the range and the limitations of these simple creations for children. *Too Much Noise*, by

Conservative Rabbi Abraham Burnstein, is set in the living room of a Jewish family's apartment, where Jewish neighbors live above. Eight boys gather there on a Hanukkah evening. No adults are present at first, for the parents have gone to a nearby train station to meet a visitor from Palestine. While the boys wait, they decide to act out the Hanukkah story. Pushing the furniture aside, they assume the roles of shepherds in Jerusalem's hills, Antiochus's soldiers, and Maccabees. As that play-within-a-play concludes, the upstairs neighbors, Mr. and Mrs. Gold-hammer (played by two older children), knock on the door. They have been awakened by the noise from below, so decide to come sing "Maoz Tsur" with the children, which concludes the play. Stage directions advise that the Hebrew song can be replaced with the English "Rock of Ages." Like most plays for children, this one entertainingly frames a simple enactment of the Maccabean revolt and victory.

The play presents a dense, urban Jewish environment familiar to many American Jews in that decade. Here, Jewish neighbors monitor nearby children when parents are absent and easily reinforce Jewish activities. This presents a sharp contrast to Lipkind's play about the dangers small towns posed to Jewish children. Teachers or parents could explain the hidden reference to Judah the Maccabee—the Hammer—in the neighbors' names. The cast reflected the typical religious-school population. Families more often provided formal religious education for their sons, who might achieve bar mitzvah, than for their daughters. Many urban Jewish families felt their children did not need a religious school, because they easily met Jewish friends living nearby.[30] Plays such as this one could both educate and entertain children at home.

Another play by Samuel Segal is set in a Reform religious-school classroom and includes parts for fourteen children and a female Sunday-school teacher. As the play opens, the cast sings an original Hanukkah ditty by Segal which admonishes students to attend these classes. The play's central lesson is the meaning of the word *Maccabee*, and this play, too, employs the familiar play-within-a-play device. While the teacher is instructing students about Hanukkah, the audience learns that the Hebrew letters *Mem, Kof, Bet*, and *Yod*, which read "Maccabee," stand for "Who is like thee, O Lord, Among the mighty?" The teacher asks the children to think of a second meaning for the word.[31]

The lesson is interrupted at various times by David, a student who has fallen asleep and dreams about the Maccabean revolt. The lights dim, and students change into costumes to act out the dream that David relates while talking in his sleep. In his dream, Judah Maccabee is searching for a special hammer. Judah himself had dreamt that the hammer, now hidden in a cave, would be used for rebuilding the Temple in Jerusalem. Lights come back up, students remove their costumes, the teacher wakens David, and he relates that Judah was called the Hammer because he was a "great fighter." The teacher adds that the hammer he searched for that would rebuild the Jerusalem Temple is also David's treasure. Laughingly, she tells him that she hopes his dreams come true, and she wishes everyone a happy Hanukkah as the students leave for home.

This play reflects Segal's desire to reach a broad audience, and it offers a striking mixture of Jewish perspectives. The play's setting, a mixed Sunday-school class with a female teacher, suggests a Reform congregation's educational system. But, while Reform had long renounced hope for restoration of the Jerusalem Temple, the idea remained a cornerstone of Orthodox prayers for the Messianic Age. Moreover, Hanukkah celebrates rededication and purifying the Temple, not rebuilding it. Segal's play spans denominations with its setting of a mixed-gender Sunday-school class led by a woman but with an espousal of a goal long rejected by Reform. Orthodox groups could easily adapt the play by selecting a single-gender cast. Most importantly, it provided an entertaining, instructive vehicle adaptable for many Jewish classrooms.

Dreams and make-believe shaped most Hanukkah dramas for children, reflecting the continuing popularity of these devices in children's literature despite the "terrible honesty" that became the rule for modernist adult literature.[32] Sunday-school teacher Henry Woolf adapted the way L. Frank Baum used one girl's dream of a fantastic world in *The Wonderful Wizard of OZ* to create a Hanukkah play with central roles for girls. By adapting an icon of American children's culture to help Jewish children embrace Hanukkah, Woolf's play subtly reshaped and subverted American juvenile culture and created an American Jewish cultural product. Baum's story about leaving the farm for city life and returning home to the rural American heartland became, in Woolf's hands, a story about American Jews' ties to their ancient past. Reform's UAHC Department of Synagogue and School Extension distributed the play. Offering parts for thirteen children, plus a chorus and music for eight songs, it is an extravaganza.

Action begins when a girl, Miriam, falls asleep in a chair after reading about Hanukkah. As she dreams, Jewish characters step out of a large book, talk, and sing. The action is led by the Queen of Jewish History, reminiscent of the good witch Glenda, who tells Dorothy how to get home in Baum's tale. The characters of the Maccabean revolt help the Queen tell their story. Even Antiochus praises the Maccabees. He says, "I was mad! . . . I slaughtered and butchered them," provoking "an honest nation [to] rise in revolt against [me]."[33]

This play, like the others, also aimed to make contemporary Jewish children see themselves in the ancient story by providing vehicles in which they themselves embody Hanukkah's heroes and villains. Woolf made a special effort to bring this experience to girls. When the character of Judah Maccabee steps out of the book, he points to Miriam (who is now awake) and says, "I knew an ancestor of yours whom you resemble exactly!" Woolf also echoed the now oft-repeated link between the Maccabean revolt and American values. In a six-stanza song, Judah explains that "a freeman born would never die a slave!" More soldiers and individuals step out of the book, explaining their motivations and experiences. But Woolf's play aimed to instruct its audience—likely composed of the child-actors' parents—as well as its performers. As the play closes, Woolf reminds adults that they will be judged on their ability to hand on Jewish tradition to their children. "Posterity never forgets, but judges" our deeds, says Judah. Reminding adults in the audience that history will judge them, the play suggests that Hanukkah's real miracle is that Jews remember it.

These plays for children set dreamy, idealized reenactments of the Maccabean story within idealized versions of an American Jewish child's world. But in 1929, Fanny Evelyn Freehof published an eleven-page play that owed more to O'Henry's poignant short story "Gift of the Magi" than to children's literature. In three scenes, she depicts a family of impoverished, orphaned Jewish children whose love for Hanukkah surpasses their desire for their own physical comfort. They dream only to be able to one day celebrate the holiday with greater material pleasure than is currently possible for them.[34] Freehof's own family emigrated from the Ukraine to London's immigrant neighborhood, where she was born, and then ultimately settled in Baltimore, enduring hardship along the way. Her father maintained close ties to the Lubavitcher Hasidim, who strived to punctiliously observe all religious commandments in joy, regardless of the cost to one's earning power, and to bring other Jews into their fold. Yet her brother, Solomon, studied for the rabbinate in Cincinnati and believed Reform held the future for Judaism in the modern West.[35] Those divergent perspectives emerge in Freehof's drama. Her play depicts the devotion to Jewish ritual regardless of cost that was so idealized by the Lubavitch, but its cast of children made it suitable for any religious school. Published on the eve of the Great Depression, this play may have carried greater resonance than even Freehof expected. Her play suggests that children are specially devoted to Hanukkah and subtly urged adults in the audience to sacrifice, if necessary, in order to make the holiday joyful for their children.

These didactic, brief, Hanukkah plays lacked much artistic merit, but their authors really aimed instead for emotional impact. The playwrights depicted familiar settings and used well-known cultural references to send simple messages. They hoped to influence their audience's behaviors, emotions, and ideas toward Judaism and did not expect literary or dramatic critics to ever encounter their work. Segal's *Scientific Chanukah*, for example, gave the grown-ups in his audience permission not only to enjoy the fun that Hanukkah could bring but to allow themselves to be emotionally moved by its story. He is not giving them permission to reduce Hanukkah to a card party of the sort Sholem Aleichem famously ridiculed in his short story of twenty years earlier. Segal wanted adults to open themselves up to the emotional power of the Hanukkah myth and to the pleasure to be obtained by imagining it. His play itself invited them into the fun of a Hanukkah play that gives them permission to simply enjoy the holiday.

The plays offering children the opportunity to act out a synopsis of the Maccabean story helped them to feel that they themselves were Jewish heroes and to feel themselves cheered for it. The plays might also have reinforced the children's emotional bond with Judaism, as the playwrights hoped, or simply strengthened the children's camaraderie. Anthropologist Victor Tuner, whose studies of ritual dramas and performances led him to conclude that such events often entail intense emotional experiences and a loosening of social boundaries, would have expected the actors themselves to have undergone a memorable experience. His ideas further suggest that, in the case of these Hanukkah plays, there is slippage from the make-believe setting of the play into the Hanukkah story that comes during—and is reinforced by—the holiday's ritual.[36] In the twenties, when many Jews relied on their social ties to support them emotionally amid antisemitism, these children's plays provided supportive group experiences while inculcating the community's values, customs, and beliefs. Convinced of the worth of these skits, by 1937, the Reform movement's women's organization, the National Federation of Temple Sisterhoods, marketed eleven original dramas, supplying congregations, schools, and associations across the spectrum of religious styles.[37]

Organized Women Advocate for Hanukkah

Few women displayed Elma Levinger's literary gifts, but many acted on her play's sentiments. Beginning in the 1920s, Jewish women in their own organizations aggrandized Hanukkah in order to educate their children, to build devotion to Judaism in their families, to enhance synagogue life, to fund their various projects, and to promote their own authority in their homes and in their congregations. The National Federation of Temple Sisterhoods (NFTS), a vibrant and formidable organization, energetically promoted domestic Sabbath and holiday observances, especially Hanukkah, each year. Its national leadership shared ideas, information, and resources with local chapters to generate activities for children. By 1925, the NFTS counted fifty thousand members, and the organization's network of chapters soon provided a profitable base for selling new Hanukkah products.[38] Although membership dropped during the Great Depression, as it did among most American organizations, it surged upward again in the 1940s. Through the NFTS, women claimed more influence in their own synagogues and the Reform movement as a whole than they were able to achieve only a few decades earlier, when only Sunday-school teachers, interested mothers, or local synagogue sisterhoods could offer suggestions affecting their own congregations. Now, with a national organization, Reform women had also achieved the right to vote in their synagogues, mirroring women's recent gain of the franchise in American national politics.

Hanukkah programming became an opportunity to promote good relations between NFTS women and the teachers in synagogue religious schools. An "entertainment given by the religious school children to the sisterhood . . . forms a splendid contact between your organization and the school," the chair of the Committee on Religion explained. She reminded members that appropriate plays could be purchased from the Board of Jewish Education in New York City and listed Levinger's play among the ideal candidates to select.[39]

The NFTS guided women in assisting their local synagogues, religious schools, and rabbis and in promoting religious activities among their congregants. Its records reveal the national body's effort to make Hanukkah more widely celebrated among Reform's families. Chair of the Committee on Religion Mrs. Leon Goodman (as she appeared in the records), of Louisville, Kentucky, instructed local chapters on implementing the national organization's agenda. In December 1921, she counseled that they would soon celebrate "one of the most joyful of all Jewish holidays." She urged members to explain Hanukkah to their children and to "observe the beautiful ceremony with kindling the . . . candles." At the meetings of each NFTS chapter, she said, women should "announce the holiday and make a plea for its observance," suggesting that a significant number of members did not generally do so. Goodman further urged the women to ask their rabbis to "make an announcement from the pulpit" echoing the NFTS goal.[40] Praising the many pleasures to be derived from the holiday's celebration, she reminded members that despite the energy they devoted to fundraising and the social rewards of membership, the NFTS "is primarily a religious organization."[41]

Mrs. Henry Nathan chaired the Committee on Religious Schools from her home in Buffalo, New York, and her lengthy and impassioned plea for Hanukkah observance offered each local chapter several programming suggestions to implement. Hanukkah gives the Committee on Religious Schools "more scope for work" than any other Jewish holiday, she wrote, suggesting that Reform's religious schools involved the NFTS more at Hanukkah than at any other season. Nathan expected them to get busy. "Cooperate with your rabbi and teachers," she said. Both leaders instructed members to provide every child with "little tin candle holders," each available for twenty cents from Reform's

Department of Synagogue and School Extension office in Cincinnati, along with a box of candles. These menorahs, usually painted a
bronzelike color and embellished with a Jewish symbol, such as a Star
of David, a lion of Judah, or a menorah centered on a back plate behind
a row of candle holders, simulated grander Hanukkah menorahs. In
Buffalo, Nathan said, women are "presenting these . . . attractive" items
to the kindergarten children so they will have them "throughout their
school career."[42]

The NFTS women aimed to make home, religious school, and synagogue work together to enhance Jewish religious life. In this era, religious instruction for children offered by Reform congregations seldom
totaled more than four hours per week and continued only during
the public school year. Many congregations supported only Sabbath
schools, which offered perhaps half that time. Nathan therefore urged
the women to increase their domestic religious observances to reinforce
and enliven their children's religious training. Echoing Reform's overall
effort to promote Jewish domestic rituals among the laity, she explained
that women must themselves "bring this beautiful religious spirit of
the Feast of Lights into" their homes. "It is there that the impressions
are made upon our young people. . . . Make it a happy week for your
children and burn Chanucka lights with them throughout the eight
days." She urged parents, "Form the habit of giving Chanucka gifts to
your children."[43]

The NFTS approached Hanukkah with two linked goals: increasing the numbers of Jewish families that celebrated the holiday in their
homes and decreasing the number of those that celebrated Christmas.
After General Electric began to produce electric lights useable outdoors
in 1925, public Christmas-tree displays became even more attractive and
dazzling than they had in the past.[44] They also turned Christmas into a
holiday associated with lights, just as Hanukkah was, and blurred the
iconic differences of the two distinct occasions. NFTS women felt that
the situation called for ever greater effort to promote broad knowledge
of Hanukkah's Jewish meaning. At the NFTS's fifth Biennial Assembly, leaders urged "the revival of religious ceremonies in the home" in
order to stimulate a "greater desire for Temple attendance" and a greater
appreciation in general for Jewish religious practices. A special resolution, passed that year and reaffirmed at each assembly throughout the

decade, explained Hanukkah's special significance in achieving those goals. Beginning by insisting that Christmas is a Christian holiday, the Executive Board "went on record" opposing its celebration by Jews and urging sisterhoods to use "every effort" to "discourage such practices." The board recommended that Hanukkah "be more generally celebrated" and that the "spirit of good will" could be encouraged by gift giving then, at Purim, and through celebrating the "Festival of Trees" (Tu B'Shvat, another minor winter holiday) in religious schools.[45] By observing more of Judaism's holiday calendar than was common among most Reform Jews, the NFTS Executive Board hoped to enliven Reform synagogues, to make religious schools more festive and interesting, and to make Judaism more enjoyable for children and families. Its move also mirrors the public schools' use of American national holidays to impart civic values and lessons on national history. By bringing American pedagogical styles to the Jewish schools' curriculum, the board hoped to make the schools more attractive to Jewish students and to imbue congregations and families with greater regard for Judaism and its values.

The NFTS's attention to children, families, and schools reflects the fact that most members were also mothers. By creating home-based Hanukkah activities, mothers also participated in the effort to provide safe, edifying play for their children, as urged by the new experts in child psychology who popularized work by Stanley Hall, John Dewey, and Sigmund Freud.[46] Attitudes about children promulgated by experts increasingly warned parents—particularly mothers—about a child's vulnerabilities. Social changes contributed to this new attitude. Urban environments seemed especially dangerous for children, according to those experts, and smaller families made each child the object of greater parental attention. *Parents Magazine* emerged in the twenties to provide ongoing advice from researchers and pediatricians. Experts advised parents to reinforce good behavior rather than punish misdeeds and to create environments that made wrongdoing unlikely. Promote the good, do not instill guilt, and use bribes if necessary to bring children into conformity with parental goals, they advised.[47] Following that advice, Reform Jewish women placed great importance on moralistic domestic rites that children would enjoy, such as Hanukkah celebrations.

Most rabbis agreed with the NFTS's efforts. Cincinnati's Rabbi David

Philipson, a leading voice in the Reform movement, agreed that "children are especially impressed with all this [Christmas] excitement. It makes an emotional appeal that is stronger than all arguments" and that can only be countered by Hanukkah celebrations.[48] Other leaders in Reform disagreed. The editor of the *American Israelite* (possibly Louis Wise) did not seem to consider children's emotional experiences to be significant factors in the larger issue of Jewish life in America. In 1925, while the NFTS women passed resolutions insisting that their members must banish Christmas from their homes and celebrate only Hanukkah, he told his readers that the custom of giving Christmas gifts "prevails among Jews only to a limited extent." Most often, Jews who did so gave the gifts only to servants, employees, and children, he wrote. For him, Christmas gifts seemed to be simple gestures of generosity made by those with power (fathers and employers) to those without power (servants, employees, and children). Because Christmas gifts simply placated the powerless and possibly increased affection toward those who truly did wield authority, he believed Christmas gifts posed little threat to established Judaism itself.[49]

But the *American Israelite* could not tolerate the idea of Jews setting up and decorating Christmas trees in their homes. In years when Hanukkah comes early in the American calendar, both holidays could be easily celebrated. To counter the claim that some people made, that they simply joined many other Jews in a popular American custom —one encouraged by President Coolidge's lighting of the first national Christmas tree in 1923—the newspaper insisted that it only occurred in a "very few [Jewish] families." Again revealing the view that children are less important than adults, the paper added that it was only in those families with children. Yet it called the practice "absurd" and ignorant. "These people have not the remotest idea of the significance of the Christmas tree and are merely aping Christian customs," it said.[50] Since the latter decades of the nineteenth century, this paper frequently pointed out the Christian symbolism of the tree, even to the extent of educating their Jewish readers in Christian theology.

As in the nineteenth century, many Jewish men earned their livelihoods in businesses that sold the very items used for Christmas celebrations, especially gifts items and trimmings for trees. Sometimes, after laboring to make their shops attractive to Christmas buyers, they brought these items into their own homes. Moreover, Jews could easily put up a tree and exchange gifts without using any more obvious symbols of Christian faith. While their Christian neighbors might place a nativity scene near the tree or hang crosses, crucifixes, or images of angels from its branches, there is no evidence that Jews ever did any of that. But the *American Israelite* editors hoped to convince Jews that *any* item associated with a Christian celebration should remain off-limits to them.

Other rabbis sometimes further confused the issue. When explaining Judaism to the general public, they sometimes confounded listeners who sought simple guidance. A *New York Times* reporter sent to cover a public lecture about Hanukkah by Dr. Nathan Krass at the flagship Reform synagogue Temple Emanu-El concluded that the "Jewish feast [is] like Christmas. . . . Their differences . . . were largely philosophical." Krass advised Jews to participate in any demonstration of "kindness, freedom and good cheer," such as might be encountered in the workplace or in a public park, but told them to ignore all "theological interpretations."[51] Some Reform rabbis had repeated this perspective since the late nineteenth century. Over the intervening years, it had become a staple in the speeches that some rabbis made to answer questions about the differences between Judaism and Christianity that commonly arose during the Christmas season, when Jews seemed to be among the only Americans not joining in the holiday. Krass may have outlined exactly what those "theological interpretations" were in the speech itself, but his more subtle points escaped the *Times* reporter. The newspaper article offered little substance to help readers figure out precisely what to do.

But the NFTS did not equivocate. By focusing on domestic objects, it easily determined appropriate identifiers for Jewish households: Hanukkah menorahs were in; Christmas trees were out. Its leaders insisted that women carried special religious responsibilities because "today many things . . . send our children away from their ancestral faith." Public schools, sports clubs, musical groups, and other activities competed with religious school and home life for children's attention and time. Therefore, "it becomes the fundamental obligation of the mother to revitalize our faith," and domestic Jewish rituals became key to that effort. Pointing out that symbols provide a "powerful means to educating both adults and children," the NFTS board resolved that "Jewish ideals be made more concrete, . . . more effective, through an intelligent use of ceremonial objects." These things "feed and strengthen sentiment, touch the heart, and carry . . . all the devotion and reverence which . . . belong to our religion and our heritage," it said. The NFTS board distributed this emphatic resolution to each chapter, insisting that mothers should take the lead in carrying out Hanukkah ceremonies in their homes. It aimed to motivate Reform families across the country toward greater religious commitment through increased holiday observance. For the next several years, Goodman included copies of that resolution in her regular letters outlining the Hanukkah activities she expected members to accomplish.[52] "As the tree is bent, so the twig is inclined," she reminded her members. Children who experience religious ceremonials in their childhood homes will "instinctively be religious."[53] Mothers should consider Hanukkah ceremonies among their parental duties. "The remembrance" of holiday observances in the childhood home "must be a lasting influence for good," Goodman explained. She assured members that if they made the effort to light the candles and tell their children the Hanukkah stories, they would find their youngsters "proud to celebrate their own holidays."[54]

In 1926, the NFTS created and sold a new Hanukkah product designed to politely remind congregants and friends to celebrate Hanukkah. It arranged for a printer to manufacture Hanukkah greeting cards for NFTS members to purchase for their own use and to sell in their congregations. Fifty years earlier, Louis Prang began manufacturing Christmas cards for purchase in America. Now, the NFTS adapted that custom for Hanukkah, creating the first Hanukkah cards. Two designs offered buyers a choice. One featured a single lit candle in a dish adorned with flowers and seemed to modify a simple Christmas card. The second placed the opening stanza of Emma Lazarus's Hanukkah poem "The Feast of Lights" on its cover. "Kindle the taper like a steadfast star; Ablaze on evening's forehead o'er the earth," it began. The poetic instructions on when and where to light a Hanukkah menorah continued, "Send through the night its luster till afar, An eightfold splendor shine above thy hearth."[55] Lazarus, who died in 1887, had become a familiar, illustrious American Jewish name by the 1920s. Her poem subtly encouraged Jews to follow its instructions by suggesting that this admired woman did so.

Goodman urged members to sell the cards at two for five cents and to report their totals to the Executive Office, and she enclosed order blanks with her letter. The cards proved so popular that the following year the NFTS offered four style selections at fifteen to forty-five cents per dozen. Goodman urged members to encourage the "children of the religious school" to buy and send the cards and asked Reform rabbis to permit sisterhoods to arrange Hanukkah-card sales as part of their holiday programming. These sales soon became annual events and initiated a new Hanukkah activity. Greeting cards formalized a way for Jews to acknowledge each other and to underscore their shared identity in the midst of the Christmas season. By sending Hanukkah cards, individuals gently reminded others to celebrate the holiday and signaled that the sender did so. This new Hanukkah embellishment eliminated one element from the list of Christmas customs that contributed to the general feeling that Christmas was so much bigger and more fun than Hanukkah. Goodman concluded her letter with one more suggestion to adapt Christmas's style. "The use of the menorah hung with presents as a substitute for the Christmas tree is becoming popular in many cities," she wrote. While it is difficult to see how small menorahs used in homes could be made to serve this purpose, the larger Hanukkah menorahs in synagogues could satisfy a religious school class.[56]

NFTS women, by making themselves essential to their congregational religious schools, providing financial support for their congregations, and assisting their rabbis, wielded unusual influence in their congregations and were sometimes counted in prayer quorums.[57] Emboldened by the passage of the Nineteenth Amendment and the rhetoric of women's rights surrounding it, they pressed for women's ordination. Although Reform rabbis considered the question in 1922, they did not endorse it.[58]

The NFTS's significance in its own Reform movement influenced other Jewish women. Deborah Marcus Melamed, president of the Conservative movement's Women's League for Conservative Judaism (WLCJ), founded in 1918, urged her members to follow the pattern set by the NFTS. By putting greater effort into assisting their synagogues, she suggested, they could obtain a greater voice in congregational affairs.[59] Hanukkah festivals and the marketing of Hanukkah goods to congregants became one route toward that political goal. Moreover, while Conservative synagogues usually offered more hours of religious education to their members' children than Reform provided, this too, was deemed insufficient by most religious leaders. Conservative women, then, also came to value home instruction through holiday celebrations as a vital part of their children's religious education. For them, as for Reform women, Hanukkah provided the means to enhance women's influence in the synagogue and at home.

Conservative women also produced holiday materials, but theirs' reflected different religious expectations than those produced by Reform women. The WLCJ made educational programming for women their centerpiece, rather than focusing on assisting in congregational religious schools. Like most women's religious groups, the WLCJ usually sought rabbinic approval for its publications on religious topics. It soon published a ritual guide to Jewish holidays titled *The Three Pillars: Thought, Worship, Practice*, which underwent nine printings and became a cornerstone for its work. The guide was written by Melamed, who hoped to "instill in other women the love she felt for Jewish tradition."[60] Her lengthy book aimed to motivate and instruct women about observing each religious rite.

Melamed told readers that just as on "Independence Day we take pride in United States traditions" that "ennoble" us, we should take similar pride in edifying Jewish holidays such as Hanukkah. Like Greenberg, Melamed presented the emotional and psychological benefits to be obtained by carrying out Judaism's religious celebrations.[61] Just as Independence Day venerates the state while reaffirming a shared commitment among Americans, Hanukkah can generate commitment to Jewish communal feeling, she explained. Moreover, Jews ought to revere Hanukkah, she argued, because its importance to Western civilization cannot be overestimated. With formal training in both Latin and Hebrew, Melamed served as supervisor of foreign languages in the Elizabeth, New Jersey, school district, where she lived with her husband, Rabbi Raphael Melamed.[62] Her knowledge about the classics of Western civilization influenced her assessment of Hanukkah's significance. If Judea had been defeated by the forces of Hellenism, "civilization today would have been totally different," she wrote. Drawing on the analyses of Hebraic versus Hellenic values that were much discussed in classical studies of her day and that could be traced to an idea that first appeared in the Second Book of Maccabees, she explained that the sense of "duty, sacrifice, . . . [and] spiritual discipline [central to Hebraism] were altogether foreign to the Greek view." She asked her readers to consider, "To what end [would have] a degenerated Hellenism led us?" The Hebraic values, transmitted through Judaism to Christianity and Islam, govern our lives today, she said.[63]

While acknowledging that "Mankind" draws ideals from the moral standards of many people, Melamed insisted that the "chief contribution to the [world's] moral vision was made by the prophets of Israel. . . . Were it not for the Maccabees, it would have been destroyed." In her view, Hanukkah celebrated not only the political rescue of ancient Judea but the rescue of the world's moral standards, especially the virtue of liberty. Therefore, Hanukkah lights are really "little flames of faith . . . that liberty in all its aspects, religious, cultural, and moral, will one day become the unchallenged right of every human being."[64] Melamed's readers may have understood her hope for universal liberty not only as a paean to American values but also as a not-so-veiled reference to Jews in eastern Europe, where the new Communist regime banned religion and diminished Jews' political rights. Additionally, after World War I, pogroms had occurred in areas of Ukraine and Poland. Those conditions in eastern Europe fueled the Zionist movement. Jews' oppression in Europe became part of the backdrop for Melamed's argument and cast the difference between oppression and liberty into sharp relief.

Melamed's logic turned Hanukkah into a holiday whose universal importance surpassed that of Christmas. Her discussion also aimed to change Jews' self perceptions. Day-to-day experience as a minority might lead them to conclude, incorrectly, that their heritage is relatively inconsequential. Hanukkah convinces us otherwise, Melamed insisted, because the course of world history depended on the events it commemorates.

Orthodox women, on the other hand, looked to the nineteenth century's Victorian ideal of "true womanhood" that had shaped women's gender ideal in that earlier era. Like the pious-toned nineteenth-century American and British women's literature and advice manuals, Orthodox guide books urged women to liken their effort in creating Jewish homes to "service at the altar" that "consecrated" their homes to religion. Yet, as some Orthodox synagogues, like Reform and Conservative ones, expanded into community centers, their sisterhoods undertook obligations similar to those common among Conservative and Reform women. Attending Sabbath worship, adorning the synagogue with attractive ritual items, assisting with activities for children, and raising funds became their route to participation in the life of their congregations. In 1923, the Union of Orthodox Jewish Congregations in America organized a Women's Branch to link its congregational sisterhoods. Like the NFTS and the WLCJ, the Women's Branch soon published a holiday manual that aimed to create a "highly motivated observant American Jewish woman." Books such as *Symbols and Ceremonies of the Jewish Home* and *The Jewish Home Beautiful*, the latter produced originally by Conservative women but used also by Orthodox women, promoted religious observances along with stylish good taste.[65] *The Jewish Home Beautiful* urged readers to create a Hanukkah atmosphere "bright with candles and gay with parties and the exchange of gifts."[66] Rabbi and religious educator Hyman E. Goldin underscored women's special interest in Hanukkah. Basing his advice on the *Kitzur Shulchan Aruch*—the 1864 compilation of Jewish laws and customs compiled by Hungarian Rabbi Solomon Ganzfried—he pointed out that songs and praises are to be sung, that charity is to be dispensed, and that women are not to work while the candles are burning, not only in their homes but also in the menorah in the synagogue.[67]

Thus, in the interwar years, Reform, Conservative, and Orthodox women's organizations alike encouraged their members to set a domestic stage for Hanukkah through attractive menorahs, foods, and gifts. Each group deemed these events important to educating their children and, just as importantly, instilling a love for Judaism in their families. The NFTS circulated an argument for Hanukkah's importance that appeared in a volume by professor of Jewish music A. Z. Idelsohn. "This festival buoys up the Jew's spirit that he may withstand the waves of assimilation," Idelsohn wrote, "that being a small minority, . . . he may not be made timid" or "underestimate his own spiritual culture."[68] Both the NFTS and the National Federation of Temple Brotherhoods circulated Idelsohn's work among their members. In 1928, one study found that only thirty percent of the eight hundred thousand school-age Jewish children in America received a formal religious education.[69] For these youngsters, and more so for those who received no instruction, elaborate home Hanukkah events came to be seen as important to their development as Jews.

Women's organized work at Hanukkah also applied the holiday's story to their own lives. Just as the Maccabees had cleansed the Temple to dedicate it to God with ritually correct oil, so these American Jewish women urged each other to dedicate their homes to God by clearing them of Christmas trees (emblems of another religion) and by using and displaying menorahs. In 1930, the WLCJ urged members to purchase items produced by the Jewish settlements in Palestine for Hanukkah and to display them in their homes, creating additional domestic emblems for their Jewish identity.[70] The holiday's story, full of allusions to ritual purity and pollution, lent itself to women's effort to make their own homes ritually pure. Their Hanukkah decisions adapted in a much simpler way the rigorous holiday preparations involving domestic purification expected at Passover. Moreover, they provided a different way, on an annual calendar, for women to implement other spiritual routes to religious domestic purity. Historians have found little evidence that many American Jewish women in that era maintained the traditional rites of family purity that required married women to undergo ritual immersion in a special public bath (*mikveh*) each month. But women's Hanukkah messages to each other encouraged them to create a purely Jewish domestic space where the holiday rite, with its accompanying foods, games, and songs, could be performed to create happy, religiously correct experiences that they could enjoy with their families.

Finding the Present in Hanukkah's Past

While women focused their efforts on creating joyous Hanukkah celebrations for their families and congregations, rabbis dreamed up new ways to convince Jewish men and women of Hanukkah's significance. As Conservative Jews articulated their positions on Jewish practice, they voiced new ways to understand Hanukkah. Unlike both Reform and Orthodoxy, Conservative Judaism rarely codified a distinctive theological doctrine. The movement strived instead for religious understandings and practices that could maintain the practices of the Jewish mainstream.

Conservative Rabbi S. Greenberg's 1927 Hanukkah sermon provides a perfect example; it used scientific language to support a religious idea. He explained to his recently formed suburban Philadelphia congregation that the Maccabean victory provided "evidence of the reality of the Spirit." How else can it be explained? he asked his congregants. Using details in the First Book of Maccabees, he seemed to defend the Talmudic interpretation that credited the victory to divine intervention. It was the only logical conclusion. "Mattathias was well over seventy years old," he began, and "force must be met with force if it is to be overthrown, but . . . the Maccabees were far outnumbered. What was the additional force?" he asked rhetorically. His full answer elided the difference between religious and secular perspectives. "We say they had morale. . . . Our fathers said that they had God. . . . Both are true." By consigning religious language to his parents' generation, he suggested its heyday had passed, not that its meaning was wrong. Thus, the holiday's larger meaning remained relevant. Greenberg's congregation published his sermon in its newsletter so that members who had not attended religious services could read it.[71]

To explain how "morale" could be the same as "God," Greenberg employed the psychological perspective that became popular in the twenties. Freud's ideas reached the United States near the turn of the twentieth century, and the language of "moral fiber" that had been so much a part of Protestant American discourse about personality slowly was replaced by psychological concepts. Joseph Jastrow, a rabbi's son who held a Ph.D. in psychology from Johns Hopkins University, played a key role in popularizing psychological thinking. From his home in Wisconsin, where he taught at the university, Jastrow established a national reputation through his books advising readers about ways that psychology could improve their lives. Clergy such as Rabbi Greenberg used Jastrow's concepts to argue that religion promoted psychological health.[72]

Greenberg explained that the words *morale* and *God* attempted to "express altogether too inadequately the feeling that it was the ideals that animated the Maccabees which proved more than a match for . . . [the] forces pitched against them." It made little difference, he said, whether Jews believed that the Maccabees won because they had superior morale or because the ideals that motivated them carried more power than those believed by Antiochus's army or because the God of

Israel "delivered the strong into the hands of the weak," as the liturgy says. Greenberg gathered up morale, ideals, and the divine into a single conceptual bundle which he labeled "Spirit." His thinking also reflected that of nineteenth-century Jewish philosopher Nachman Krochmal, who himself learned from philosophers of German idealism such as Georg Friedrich Hegel.[73] Greenberg's ideas could appeal to college-educated or intellectual Jews as well as to those simply skeptical about religious claims.

By redefining religious terms, Greenberg hoped that Jews with different religious perspectives could unite in a common Hanukkah ritual. Many Conservative synagogues, like Reform synagogues, provided Hanukkah entertainments for members and their children. At Greenberg's congregation, the 1927 festival included poems, songs, dances, recitations, a play about early Jewish settlers in Palestine, and lighting of the Hanukkah candles. Under his tutelage, congregants differing in age and attitude could enjoy the festivities together.

A growing chorus of rabbis and women's groups argued that Hanukkah's story held even greater contemporary meaning than it had in the past—even if they had to redefine key terms in order to prove it. But at least one rabbi remained doubtful. On the Thursday before Sabbath Hanukkah, 1928, Mordecai M. Kaplan struggled to come up with a topic for a sermon to deliver to the Society for the Advancement of Judaism, a congregation that had gathered around him based on his innovative ideas for American Judaism. He knew that the group expected the "regulation type of . . . sermon" that told them to "emulate the . . . Maccabees." But Kaplan found very little analogy between the Jewish "situation then and the Jewish situation today." Yet, after sleeping on the problem, Kaplan came up with a Hanukkah sermon about moral courage, but probably not the sort his congregants expected. Instead of lauding the Maccabees, he spoke about "the lack of moral courage in the wealthy and influential Jews that brought on . . . the tyrannical decrees of [Antiochus IV] to suppress the Jewish religion. . . . [His decrees were] the culmination of a campaign against Judaism carried on by the Hellenizing Jews, . . . [and] they were more to blame . . . than Antiochus." Kaplan felt sure that at least one of the leaders of his congregation had garnered all his knowledge about the Maccabean revolt from "Sunday School Hanukkah plays." As we have seen, those simple

dramas encouraged Jewish children to identify with the ancient Maccabees. But Kaplan hoped this sermon would challenge his congregants to
see themselves as Hellenizers and so to rededicate themselves to greater
effort in the service of Judaism. The group's Hanukkah celebration itself
did not dim his contempt for his congregants that year. Although the
140 people who had gathered to celebrate Hanukkah with hymns, dinner, entertainment, and dancing had declared the evening a success,
Kaplan was convinced their satisfaction had only to do with the ample
amount of red meat and not the religious edification he provided.[74]

Six years later, Kaplan understood things differently. He had come
to believe that the evolving Jewish civilization that he envisioned
needed lighthearted yet value-laden occasions such as Hanukkah that
heightened a sense of participation in the generations of Jewish life.
Hanukkah, he wrote, "should be observed with more elan than at present." Echoing many earlier rabbis, he said, "Since [it] falls so near the
Christmas season, it must be made as interesting and joyful for the
Jewish child as Christmas is for the Christian child. . . . It should be
the season for paying social calls, playing home games, and holding
communal entertainments."[75] As American Jews watched legal and
physical attacks on Jews in Germany unfold after 1933, he believed they
needed occasions to enjoy their religious lives, to recount the ancient
divine rescue from Antiochus, and to renew their commitment to the
faith and to each other. Whether they believed Hanukkah commemorated divine rescue or an unlikely victory, the hope for rescue that the
holiday offered remained valuable in assuaging the generally "gloomy
attitude."[76] Kaplan, along with so many others in those times, appreciated that.

Standing Their Ground

As the national economy collapsed, Jewish charities measured financial woes in their growing caseloads. Dependency on the largest Jewish
family services jumped from twenty-five thousand families in 1930 to
thirty-one thousand only two years later. New York's Hebrew Orphan
Asylum sheltered more children in the 1930s than at any time since the
1860s, and nearly every congregation in that city found itself unable to
pay its bills.[77] One Hanukkah play urged Jews to extend aid to children,

depicting a wealthy Jewish family bringing a poor child into their home to be raised by them—with the permission of the child's impoverished mother living in a poor part of town.[78] While few, if any, audience members would undertake such a responsibility, many could donate to a charity. Yet, on the whole, most Jews weathered the Depression with less destitution than was suffered by unskilled workers and farm laborers. Small-business owners often turned to Jewish free-loan societies to meet their expenses and remain solvent.[79]

Yet old stereotypes of wealthy Jews secretly controlling the world's banks resounded again. Father Charles E. Coughlin cobbled together an ideology of conspiracy theories, isolationism, and antisemitism in a campaign against "the Money Power" and broadcast his ideas on radio; by 1932, his fan mail, "much of it stuffed with cash, . . . required . . . one hundred six clerks and four personal secretaries" to handle it. Tens of millions listened to him each Sunday afternoon.[80] Four years later, B'nai B'rith's Anti-Defamation League counted seventy different antisemitic groups operating in the United States.[81]

Parents, rabbis, and psychologists worried about the impact that blatant antisemitism might have on Jewish children. Jewish boys often faced physical attacks from gentile boys as they walked home from school, stores, or other places that took them out of their Jewish neighborhoods. "We felt hunted," one recalled.[82] In that climate of fear, many Jewish adults and religious leaders once again turned their attention to the problem of securing the well-being of Jewish children. In 1935, Reform Rabbi Samuel H. Markowitz, who had earned a Ph.D. at the University of Chicago and served a congregation in Santa Fe, New Mexico, published a series of lectures called *Adjusting the Jewish Child to His World*, from which the NFTS drew advice, rhetoric, and programming direction. For Jewish children to be happy Jews, Markowitz said, parents needed to bring "color and joy into Jewish home life." He described games, decorations, food, and novelties, along with prayers and ceremonies that children would enjoy.[83] Rabbis sometimes bought Markowitz's pamphlet series for teachers to use in their religious schools.

Psychology soon began to support the wisdom of making Hanukkah —as well as other religious events—happy occasions for Jewish children. Five years after Markowitz's series appeared, Kurt Lewin, a Jewish social psychologist who came to the United States from Germany

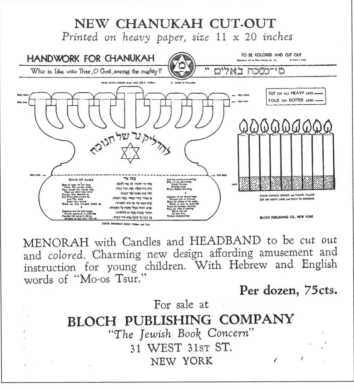

A simple headband in the shape of a menorah with candles provided Jewish children with an inexpensive Hanukkah cut-and-color play experience during the Great Depression. *Women's League Outlook*, December 1931. (Courtesy National Women's League of the United Synagogue of America)

in 1932, urged parents to strive to instill positive feelings, "group pride, and loyalty" in their children. This would help to "minimize the ambiguity" inherent in being a minority and to promote their children's future happiness.[84]

An array of Jewish leaders insisted that especially in the current climate, Jews needed to celebrate Hanukkah. That act now, more than ever, symbolized their own religious loyalty and lent it dignity. Alexander Dushkin, superintendent of Jewish education in New York City, linked Hanukkah to both the Maccabean struggle against Hellenism and the desire for light in the depth of winter. But he went further. "Just as the life-giving light conquers the deadly, cold darkness of winter, so the light of Torah has conquered the devastating forces of antisemitism and assimilation," he wrote.[85] Reform Rabbi Samuel S. Cohon tapped the pugilistic mood when he told Jewish parents to "discipline themselves" to "stand their own ground" and resist their children's pleadings for Christmas gifts.[86] New York's Governor Herbert H. Lehman echoed their sentiments in 1937, when he told guests at a Hanukkah dinner that adherence to "tradition" and to Jewish ideals was the best way to combat antisemitism.[87]

Denominational boundaries and political ideologies blurred when Jewish associations promoted Hanukkah celebrations as a brake on assimilation. Hanukkah is important to the future of Judaism, most agreed, not only because it gives Jewish children a joyous occasion at the same season when Christian children seemed to be having so much fun but also because it provides the best occasion for training Jewish children to resist the allure of Christianity. While Jewish leaders had argued this point as early as the late nineteenth century, now, because of increased pressure on Jews to assimilate and increased threats to their security, those arguments seemed even more important. Common explanations aimed to counteract the influence of the broader American culture that radio now brought into each home. Historian David M. Kennedy points out that in the 1930s "radio assaulted the insularity of local communities . . . to bypass and shrink the influence of leaders and institutions" that represented religious and ethnic loyalties.[88] Hanukkah and other Jewish domestic rites became an important tool in deflecting radio's power.

Other Jewish religious organizations' Hanukkah messages asserted Judaism's importance to Jews and to world history. For example, Hadassah, the women's Zionist organization, repeated Melamed's point that Hanukkah reflected the superiority of Hebraic to Hellenic values. The ancient conflict between those two forces is "analogous to the present struggle to . . . maintain the continuity of the Jewish people," Hadassah told its members. Therefore "light . . . the candles" and "sing . . . Maoz Tsur and other melodies" to keep the Jewish people alive.[89] In 1938, the Reform movement brought out a book called *The Jewish Festivals*, by Lithuanian-born Hayyim Schauss, an educator who taught for more than a quarter century at the Conservative movement's seminary. Schauss explained that Hanukkah stood for two ideals. First, it commemorated the "achievement of religious liberty," an idea Reform had touted for half a century. But "in the minds of large masses of Jewry," Schauss went on, Hanukkah also "stood for a revival of sentiment for the national development of the Jewish people."[90] Thus, in varying ways, interwar Jewish thinkers tied Hanukkah ever more tightly to the matter of Jewish survival.

Advancing Hanukkah in Jewish Schools

Educators applied ideas about children's emotional needs for a festive Hanukkah to nearly every variety of Jewish school and once again turned to songs to instill values, to convey knowledge, and to promote camaraderie. In 1930, nationwide, 604 congregations supported weekday schools, with almost sixty-five thousand pupils.[91] Instructors in Talmud Torahs, the community-supported religious schools for teens and grade-school children that met weekday afternoons and on weekends, also turned to songs to enliven classrooms and promote educational goals.[92] The *Jewish Teacher*, a new periodical that appeared in the thirties, printed full texts of plays and original songs by teachers.[93] Ben M. Edidin, president of the National Council for Jewish Education and director of New York's Jewish Education Commission, compiled a volume chock full of ideas for holiday-based projects that could be used by each school.[94]

Soon, musicians published songbooks to be used by Jewish schools and by the new youth groups such as Reform's National Federation of Temple Youth (NIFTY, begun 1939) and Young Judea, a Zionist group (begun 1918). Clubs for Jewish teens aimed to instill Jewish identity, a sense of civic duty, and a fondness for Jewish life while creating friendly ties among a new generation of Jews. They also relied on songs.[95] The *Judean Songbook* of 1934 told its readers that "Jewish song voices the spirit and history of a people who for three thousand years has been fighting bitterly, but hopefully, for its preservation. . . . Its music always [was] a genuine echo of [its] . . . inner life."[96] That compilation included Yiddish folk tunes, religious tunes, and rhythmic melodies for the circle dances like those popular in the Jewish settlements in Palestine.

One new song immediately became among the most reprinted. In 1939, it appeared in two very different songbooks. One offered more

At a Jewish community center's Hanukkah festival in 1955, children pull
strings that move homemade marionettes in order to retell the story of
Hanukkah (Courtesy American Jewish Historical Society)

than two hundred melodies that included Yiddish folk tunes for adult
audiences. The second collection provided simple melodies for very
young children; its compilers were closely linked to the fledgling movement growing around Mordecai M. Kaplan. The new song featured in
both collections shared Kaplan's emphasis on human responsibility and
the importance of Jews' collective effort to maintain their own religious
civilization. Sung in Hebrew as "Mi Yimalel," as well as in an English
version by Edidin, it was called "Who Can Retell?" Its sprightly tune
modified a traditional hymn and never mentions God. Instead, it claims
that human effort has aided Jews in every age. Although heroes and

sages saved Jews in the past, now "all Israel" must "arise" and "redeem itself through deed and sacrifice," suggesting that only a mass movement will be effective in the modern world. Like Hanukkah itself, the song promises success in the face of daunting dangers. It appeared the same year that Germany conquered Poland, Britain blocked the Jewish settlements in Palestine from admitting Jewish refugees, and the United States admitted far fewer Jewish immigrants than its own small quota from eastern Europe should have allowed. Yet this song, sung in a round, created an impression of the richness and power of the human voice and a sense of unity and power among singers. Its liveliness and its lyric seemed to promise victory.[97] "Mi Yimalel / Who Can Retell?" soon became a standard Hanukkah melody, reprinted in songbooks and sung on new recordings of religious music. Mordecai Kaplan included it under a new title, "The Maccabean Spirit Today," in the prayer book he compiled in 1945 that reflected his own revision of Judaism.[98]

Embracing Hanukkah during World War II

World War II sharpened many Jews' appreciation for Hanukkah's story of a military victory. "At no time . . . has its celebration been of larger and clearer significance than . . . this year," proclaimed Kaplan's movement's magazine, the *Reconstructionist*, in 1940.[99] If the antisemitism of the interwar years called forth Hanukkah's capacity to raise Jewish morale, wartime seemed to prove morale's power to determine the fate of nations. While Hitler's armies threatened Poland and France, Roosevelt and the U.S. Congress debated whether to become involved in Europe's affairs. The low state of French morale proved a stark contrast to British determination to resist invaders at any cost. The United Kingdom's attitude influenced Roosevelt's decision to answer Churchill's pleas for arms. "Both [Roosevelt and Churchill] knew that morale and perception were scarcely less important than metal and firepower," concludes historian David M. Kennedy.[100] In 1942, when victory seemed distant, the *Reconstructionist* told readers that the "lack of a morale-giving religion is what the democratic nations have most to fear." The "Maccabean war [shows us] what a religion can do to save even a small and weak people from being overwhelmed by a powerful enemy." France's "collapse" proved that without a "cause or religion to inspire it," a nation is lost. The editors felt it "extremely urgent" that Protestantism, Catholicism, and Judaism "be made relevant to the issues at stake in the war."[101] Kaplan explained that Judaism's religious observances could only be said to "serve [their] purpose" when they contributed both to the preservation of the Jewish people and to the "satisfaction of the personal spiritual needs of Jews."[102]

With hostility toward Jews increasing, Jewish leaders remade Hanukkah to accomplish the goals that Kaplan identified. The voice of the Jewish "Y" in New Orleans told local Jews, [Hanukkah . . . rallies] us . . . to a rededication to our faith in faith. It has brought home to the world that as Jews we will insist in living despite the horrible catastrophes which have befallen us."[103] As American Jews watched calamity descend on the Jews of Europe, Hanukkah offered hope for some sort of Jewish survival. Rabbi Isaac Klein told his Buffalo, New York, radio audience that Hanukkah urges Jews "not to lose hope . . . [or] fall into despair."[104]

The mobilization for war lifted the U.S. economy out of its doldrums, and new materials to invigorate Jewish education and home celebrations quickly became available. Hanukkah products provided a winter boost to the ethnic economy and became ever more elaborate. The prestigious Jewish Publication Society had recently issued three volumes for holiday enrichment, including one cornucopia of Hanukkah essays, poems, songs, stories, blessings, and recipes. Edited by Emily Solis-Cohen, it stands out for offering a significant selection of items drawn from her own Sephardi tradition, along with many items already familiar to many American Jews.[105] Yet one reviewer remarked that it "provided little guidance for parents and teachers," as it lacked rabbinic instruction in the holiday's rules.[106] By omitting that, though, the publisher made the volume attractive to a broader number of potential Jewish buyers.

Three years later, Ben Edidin produced a richly illustrated, thick volume called *Jewish Holidays and Festivals* and intended for teachers and parents to use in instructing children. Discussing customs among Jews in many parts of the world, including the young Jewish communities in Palestine, he insisted, "Not in twenty centuries has Hanukkah been so important a festival as it has become in our own day." He explained, "We understand a little better, perhaps, what it means to enjoy liberty and have heroes and heroines." Contemporary American Jews now comprehend the whole historical context of the Maccabean revolt much better than had Jews in other eras, he said. They "realize what it means to have Hellenists." He continued, "Today we call them assimilationists—Jews who do not care whether the holidays and customs are observed."[107] His volume could help families, clubs, congregations, and schools to create a broad selection of Hanukkah celebrations and customs and to attain a deeper understanding of the holiday's contemporary relevance. Colorful, instructional songbooks to use with very young children also became more available to help parents and preschool teachers instruct children in the holiday customs.[108]

Women of the NFTS also marshaled resources and energy to create and promote new Hanukkah music. Each year, Samuel Markowitz's wisdom appeared in the organization's memos, letters, and minutes urging women to turn this "half remembered date on the Jewish calendar" into one of the "outstanding occasions in the life of a Jewish family." It also told members to purchase a new recording for Hanukkah, produced by the sisterhood at Temple Israel in New Rochelle, New York. Featuring "traditional holiday music," the candle blessings sung by the rabbi, and holiday songs performed by the sisterhood, the recording "inspires a home ceremony by providing a beautiful blessing" and "invites your family to join in singing the hymn."[109] The record sold for only one dollar plus shipping expenses, and the NFTS Committee on Religion accepted orders on behalf of the group in New Rochelle. These recordings and others like them brought the Hanukkah music customs so popular among eastern European immigrants into the homes of many American Reform Jewish families with different ancestry. Now, parents unfamiliar with Hanukkah songs could provide their families with the growing repertoire of holiday music.

Other Jewish organizations quickly understood the programming possibilities that recorded holiday music offered. In 1941, the Hillel Foundation's anthology of recordings of Jewish interest listed productions of Handel's *Judas Maccabaeus* along with Hanukkah ditties for small children as well as a rendition of the blessings and "Rock of Ages" sung by a cantor and choir.[110] These enterprises raised funds for local initiatives and congregations and expanded the Hanukkah marketplace as abundance slowly returned to American life. Just as importantly, they brought lighthearted pleasures to Hanukkah celebrations in an era marked by fear.

Wartime infused the fight against Christmas trees in Jewish homes with a new vigor as big-budget films such as the frothy musical *Meet Me in St. Louis* and the black-and-white tearjerker *Since You Went Away*, among others, portrayed the domestic Christmas tree as an emblem of familial love.[111] Just as national war rhetoric asked all Americans to be emotionally tough to be able to make personal sacrifices for the nation's survival, so Jewish spokespeople challenged American Jews to be firm in their religious commitments at Hanukkah. Rabbi Theodore H. Gordon, working at the Hillel at the University of California, insisted that the lure of Christmas was a problem for Jewish parents, not Jewish children. The "same mother who insists upon her child's eating spinach and washing behind the ears is somehow helpless to oppose his whims in the matter of a Christmas tree," he fumed to readers of the *Reconstructionist*.[112] Parents should deem fidelity to Jewish customs as important as matters of physical health. An unnamed contributor to the Conservative *Women's League Outlook* asked whether "Jewish mothers who blithely celebrate the birth of a Jew whose martyrdom caused the martyrdom of millions of other Jews throughout the ages know what they are doing" by celebrating Christmas in their homes. "Forgive them, O Lord, they know not what they do," she commented with angry sarcasm. Their behavior shows a lack of "self respect." Especially "at these times," she continued, "our Hanukkah candles must burn ever brighter in our homes and the bravery of the Maccabees be emphasized more than ever."[113]

During World War II, the Jewish media embedded contemporary world events in Hanukkah's story. The *Reconstructionist* said that the United States entered the war to defend freedom, rather than for revenge or to protect the nation's physical defense, just as the Maccabees had militarily defended Judaism.[114] Similarly, a spring editorial drew on Passover's imagery to argue that a " 'tabernacle of peace' must be reared upon the moral foundation of freedom."[115] Accounts of Jewish heroes seemed necessary, especially for children. Letty Cottin Pogrebin, who grew up in the 1940s, explained why during Hanukkah she painted the Maccabean revolt on her family's dining-room mirror: "so that, despite

news of Hitler's atrocities reaching us daily, I might imbibe Jewish heroism along with my gefilte fish."[116]

Despite all the talk of contemporary Maccabees, the Jewish press
usually referred to the half million Jewish soldiers serving in the U.S.
Armed Services in more familiar terms. They were the community's
children. Stateside Jewish organizations strived to cheer them and to
boost their morale with Hanukkah parties, gifts, extra food, uniongrams (cash or messages sent via Western Union), and greeting cards.
In Honolulu, just a few days after the attack on Pearl Harbor, the local
synagogue's Hanukkah celebration included the Kaddish (the prayer for
the dead), which the entire congregation stood to recite. Many Jews in
uniform attended the service, which preceded a social dance. Each soldier returned to base carrying gifts of cigarettes, cookies, and candy.[117]
In Abilene, Texas, near Camp Barkeley, the Ladies Auxiliary of the small
synagogue "served High Holiday meals to approximately 250 soldiers
and sponsored suppers every other Sunday for 200 to 400. . . . They
also organized parties for Chanukah and Purim and, . . . most spectacu-
larly, prepared Passover Seder meals for hundreds of participants."[118]
The NFTS urged its members to send Hanukkah uniongrams "when so
many Jewish men and some Jewish girls [who] serve in every branch of
the armed forces" needed to hear a cheery message from home.[119] With
more than a third of the world's Jews facing imminent death in Europe,
and most young Jewish American men risking their lives in military
service, it seemed even more crucial than ever to keep each American
Jew loyal to the faith. Hanukkah gifts and celebrations for young men in
military service seemed a crucial part of the larger Hanukkah effort to
strengthen Jews' ties to their religion and their community.

During wartime, the image of traitors and Hellenists appeared in
many Jewish periodicals. Editors of the *Reconstructionist* agreed that
the "historic similarity" between the Maccabean revolt and the "present conflict is deeper than would appear at first sight." Today as in the
past, some Jews are so "impressed by the brilliance of Greek civilization" that they consider those who "persist in their ancestral ways as
narrow-minded." The editors heaped special derision on a congregation
in Houston, Texas, that adhered so closely to the Reform movement's
late-nineteenth-century version of principles that it refused membership to anyone who supported Zionism or maintained Judaism's dietary

During World War II, this cover of the program for Chicago's Annual
Chanukah Festival depicted a landscape nearly empty of people.
The couple who survey it suggest Adam and Eve alone in Paradise.
Yet, with tilled farmland and distant mountains, it could also recall
the western United States. The image supported the Zionist goal
of providing a haven for Jewish refugees by addressing the qualms
of American donors. (Courtesy Chicago Jewish Archives, Spertus
Institute for Jewish Studies)

laws.[120] By contrast, the Reform movement itself published a set of holiday sermons for use by military chaplains and other rabbis that urged
Jews, "Beware of Hellenism in the Ranks." Comparing the Maccabean
"struggle for freedom" with the current "fight against the Axis powers
for the freedom of the world," the author claimed that modern Jew-

ish Hellenists are materialists, opposing spirituality. Materialists set up Christmas trees in their homes, thinking of them as toys to "amuse the children." This is "an insult to Christians and Christianity," the author claimed.[121] He argued that Jews who fail to grasp spiritual values should be considered supporters of Nazi ideas.

In the closing days of 1944, images of Hanukkah celebrations in Palestine offered American Jews "hope for the future." Scarcely five months before Germany surrendered, American Jews began to grasp the devastation that had befallen Europe's Jewry. Chicago's *Sentinel* featured two Hanukkah images that captured the moment. One depicted children who had been rescued from Europe celebrating Hanukkah in Palestine. The children's photo evoked the dependency of the Jewish settlements in Palestine on American Jews' largess. Before Nazism, Jewry in the United States often relied on Europe's Jewish resources, its religious publishing firms, its leading rabbinic academies, and its energetic and diverse Jewish population. Now, just as the United States emerged from World War II shouldering heavier responsibilities for the well-being of Europe, American Jews sensed that the future of world Jewry depended on them. Alongside that image of children in Palestine, the *Sentinel* placed one from the annual meeting of the American Joint Distribution Committee, which collected funds for charitable distribution to Jewish refugees overseas. Two men light the last candle in a menorah several feet tall. The unusual size of the menorah, with its lighted long tapers, before two men standing upright to light it suggested the power of American Jews to fulfill their new responsibilities and their dedication to that task.[122]

In the interwar period and through World War II, many trends lent Hanukkah added significance. Everywhere Jews looked, it seemed, life was easier if they jettisoned markers of Jewish identity. The heady possibilities of American culture and the social pressure to assimilate appeared to replicate the circumstances surrounding the ancient Maccabean revolt. American Jews, as they had in the nineteenth century but now with even greater fervor, mined Hanukkah's story for imagery with which to oppose Jews whose religious practices seemed too negligible to keep their children within the fold. The ancient story, with its fundamental clash between a dominant culture, a religious minority, and traitors within that minority, proved as durable as ever.

Jews' responses to threats against them that emerged in the interwar years elicited new, more nuanced cultural creations and activities. While parents' desire to synthesize Jewish and American culture remained, they came to believe that the most important place for that synthesis to occur was in their children's psyches. The synthesis needed to be a healthy one. The nineteenth century's assertion that the Maccabees fought for religious freedom continued to be repeated. But, at the same time, Jews believed that Judaism's distinction needed to be maintained so that Jewish children could develop a healthy self-respect. Thus, spokespeople pointed out Judaism's significance as the foundation for both Christianity and Western civilization.

Most Jews seem to have accepted the idea that the Christmas season challenged them to create memorable Jewish experiences for their children, now ever more precious in smaller families. Presents became de rigueur. Women's organizations urged mothers to create a holiday atmosphere in their homes by arranging festive tableware, foods, and decorations as well as by creating fun parties for their children. The result was a Hanukkah filled with objects—from sheet music to recordings, from a panoply of published dramas to bound collections of poetry and readings, from branded cooking products to Hanukkah cards and tin menorahs, Hanukkah and the American marketplace had become interwoven to an unprecedented degree. An American Jew from the 1850s would scarcely have recognized this holiday, less than a hundred years later.

Simple, one-act, original dramas entertained children while instructing them in Hanukkah lore and promoting the grandeur of the Maccabees. Children's plays were largely upbeat and cheerful. Yet dramas written for adults reveal complex considerations and conflicting emotions. They provided imaginative vehicles by which adults could consider the costs, the benefits, and the limits of their own emancipation within American society. Each one strived to convince performers and audiences alike that Hanukkah ought to play a significant role in their Jewish lives.

Reform, Conservative, and Orthodox rabbis and women's organizations insisted that, in December, the thresholds of Jewish homes should mark the boundary between Jewish and gentile culture. Some enlisted new experts in psychology to support their arguments. Hanukkah goods identified Jewish space just as Christmas goods identified Christian space, they argued, and the two were incompatible. The most tradition-minded Jews asserted that Christmas would hold little temptation for Jewish children who experienced the full year of Judaism's Sabbaths, holy days, and festivals. Orthodox leaders, therefore, evinced little interest in magnifying Hanukkah but, rather, promoted full observance of all Jewish ritual events. To this end, in 1927, religious educator Hyman E. Goldin translated the *Kitzur Shulchan Aruch* into English.[123] Nonetheless, Orthodox Jews joined others in asking women to undertake special duties. In 1941, Goldin explained in a volume just for women that in the hands of the Jewish woman, as "mistress of the house, . . . perhaps more than any other, lies the future of Jewish life."[124] The Jewish home, the Women's Branch argued, should magnify a Jewish child's emotional tie to Jewishness. Christmas culture seemed to require all Jews to create comparably enthralling but distinctively Jewish experiences whether at Hanukkah or at other Jewish occasions. The violence that erupted against Jews after World War I and that Jews saw magnified in horrendous form in Nazi-occupied Europe seemed to demand that they themselves not abandon Jewish life. Synthesis had its limits. The conviction that emerged in this era that American Jews especially needed an emotionally rich domestic Judaism was reinforced by the circumstances they encountered in the postwar world.

6

Forging a Common Tradition

In the two decades after World War II, Jews, like other Americans, joined religious congregations in increasing numbers. As new congregations sprouted in postwar suburbs, rabbis' messages reached more people and women's organizations linked to congregations saw their numbers mushroom. In the 1950s, synagogues—often in suburbs—became the communal centers of Jewish life. They benefited from the national rush to join organizations that continued from the postwar years through the 1960s. Indeed, membership in groups of all kinds, from religious associations to bowling leagues, marked that era of American history.[1] When television's three major national broadcast networks rose to dominate the national airwaves, they lent an aura of mass culture that augmented the drive toward conformity that supported the era's clubbiness. In those postwar years, as in previous decades, Jews in America came to see Judaism through the lenses of their American experience. Once again, they tinkered with Hanukkah to make it serve their own needs and reflect their own values, ideals, and concerns.

Postwar congregational rabbis, women's groups, and denominational presses joined in a more sophisticated effort to promote the religious home life that could be created through holiday rites. Now, instead of debating whether American assimilation resembled the traitorous Hellenism of ancient times, as some interwar and wartime voices had argued, the expanding religious institutions and agencies found more ways to promote the performance of Hanukkah's rite itself. They repeatedly pointed out that domestic rites—especially Hanukkah—played a significant role in raising moral children and creating happy families. To create Hanukkah celebrations powerful enough to broadly impact Jewish children, families, and adults and to improve the quality of their lives as Jews and as individuals, Jewish leaders marshaled arguments, customs, and material goods from earlier eras, adapted items most associated with other Jewish holidays, and defended Hanukkah in public arenas. Earlier assertions that Hanukkah marked an event with worldwide significance were heard again, now to support the broader effort in advocating that serious attention be paid to creating psychologically powerful domestic religious rites.

In 1946, Sarah Kopelman, president of the Women's League for Conservative Judaism, challenged her members to maintain their wartime diligence. "Do we not need the same unquestioning faith . . . [and] courage . . . that helped us to perform herculean duties" during the war years? she asked them. Jewish women, she said, now faced a problem as daunting as their wartime experiences. Wartime had challenged them to manage restricted household economies and, often, to raise funds for war bonds and agencies such as the USO and Red Cross Canteens, activities shared broadly by Americans. Jewish women also collected donations for refugee aid and other charitable work. Some women carried increased responsibilities for small, family-owned businesses when their menfolk served in the military. A few Jewish women joined the Women's Airforce Service Pilots (WASP), Women's Army Auxiliary Corps (WAAC), and the Women Accepted for Volunteer Emergency Service (WAVES).[2] Kopelman had doubled her own organization's membership during the war years. Marshaling the organizational and speaking skills she had learned as an attorney and former schoolteacher, she developed new leadership programs to train WLCJ members to speak on Jewish topics to the general public. She also strengthened the league's educational programs.[3] Yet those accomplishments did not earn women a postwar rest.

Emotional stress added to Jewish women's burdens. They grieved, as did other American women, for loved ones in the armed services who were lost in the war—eight thousand American Jewish men died as war casualties.[4] Jews constituted "roughly nine percent of the U.S. uniformed personnel," almost triple their percentage of the U.S. population.[5] Until the war ended, fear remained that Germany could win the war and then annihilate America's Jews. Jubilation came at the defeat of the Axis powers. But the immensity of Europe's Jewish losses "exceeded even the most pessimistic previous reports" of their deaths made during the war. Howard Fasts's 1948 fictionalized account of the Maccabean revolt, *My Glorious Brothers*, with its anguished descriptions of Jewish carnage, captured a general mood.[6]

Women's religious groups had, for decades, as we have seen, urged their members to celebrate Judaism's domestic rites. They echoed rabbis—Reform, Conservative, and some Orthodox—whose reminders had become fixtures of rabbinic messages to their congregations since the mid-nineteenth century. Home rites could help women accomplish the "Herculean" duty Kopelman had in mind: raising Jewish children. Unprecedented complications and emotional burdens seemed to be involved. The shrinking numbers of American Jews and threats to world Jewry that elicited such worry about child-rearing in the interwar years set the stage for concerted and serious attention to children after the war. In the interwar years, every American Jewish child had become even more precious because Jewish immigration had been reduced to a trickle and because American Jews tended toward smaller families. Now, after World War II, Jews felt increasing urgency that each Jewish child must now grow into a healthy adult with a strong Jewish identity because one-third of the world's Jews had been murdered. Yet, although postwar parents found more expert advice, as we will see, they could rely on less hands-on familial support. In response, many women's groups and rabbis further reshaped home festivals such as Hanukkah from religious celebrations into tools for parenting.

Former Jewish generations, Kopelman claimed, passed on to their children "precepts of good character . . . and responsibilities," through "painful and crude" methods that modern parents could no longer use.

Arthur Szyk painted this 1948 depiction of a Polish Hasidic family's Hanukkah celebration to eulogize a lost world. Part of a series illustrating Jewish holidays, this one features a menorah ready to be lighted at right and a chess/checkerboard at the bottom. Szyk focuses on the family gathering, rather than the ritual items he pushed to the edges. (Reproduced with the cooperation of the Arthur Szyk Society, www.szyk.org; courtesy Yeshiva University Museum)

We, she said, "must make use of modern child psychology and pedagogy if children are to grow up normal, healthy and happy." Yet, she said wistfully, those former methods instilled an unwavering dedication to Judaism. "Neither degradation nor enmity, nor pogrom could swerve [a Jew] from his faith."[7] Her idealized description of Jewish devotion certainly did not describe the diverse attitudes toward Judaism among the immigrants from eastern Europe who came to the United States before 1924, most likely including Kopelman's own parents or grandparents. More likely, she used this image both to eulogize Europe's Jews and to idealize their abilities. It also offered hope: if loyal Jews could emerge in Europe's hostile environment, then it should be possible to instill loyalty and enthusiasm in American Jewish children. Hanukkah once again assumed significance as a tool in achieving a goal that seemed more important than ever.[8]

Kopelman also may have thought it more difficult to raise postwar children because new mothers received less help from extended kin. Few suburban homes provided sufficient space for three generations. Increasingly, as older people lived longer and housing patterns changed, nuclear families lived apart from more experienced parents. Moreover, as child-rearing styles changed, by the 1940s, "a majority of American parents, when polled, claimed it was vital to raise their children differently from the way their own parents had raised them."[9] Few may have wanted grandparents around. Yet that left new parents to solve problems on their own. Not surprisingly, the 1946 book *Baby and Child Care*, which opened with the comforting words "You know more than you think you do," made its author, Dr. Benjamin Spock, a household name.

In the 1950s, it seemed that Jews did not participate in the postwar baby boom to the same degree as Protestant or Catholic families and so may not have grown comfortably at ease about child-rearing simply by experience. One 1950 study noted an "increase in the number of [Jewish] infants" but considered it a "purely temporary phenomenon." Jewish marriages in 1949 declined by nineteen percent compared with the previous year, the author noted. Moreover, Jews remained mostly urbanites, and such people tend toward smaller families.[10] By the late fifties, it was clear that, on average, Jewish women of childbearing age did not produce enough children to replace the current Jewish population. Despite Jews' move to the suburbs, they behaved like urbanites. Eighty-four percent of them still lived in metropolitan areas with populations of a million or more.[11] Some moved as far as the sunnier cities of Los Angeles or San Diego, California, or Miami, Florida. Few chose small towns, and almost none selected a rural scene.[12] Yet, by the mid 1960s, when the boom had ended, new surveys discovered that Jewish women had taken longer to complete their families, but they had, nonetheless, attained a fertility replacement rate of 2.8 children.[13]

The conviction that religion could achieve social goals became an article of faith in midcentury America. When the Cold War emerged, American social analysts and politicians expressed concern that Western societies remain stable, and they believed religion could help.[14]

Congress added "under God" to the Pledge of Allegiance recited by schoolchildren each morning. The next year, they put "In God We Trust" on the nation's currency.[15] Believing that strong societies rested on stable families, sociologists such as Julius Draschler and Ruby Jo Reeves Kennedy studied the factors contributing to strong marriages. Draschler suggested that the rush to assimilate immigrants that had marked the early decades of the century actually had made America *less* stable. Strong unions most often occurred when couples shared a common cultural and religious background. America should take a gradual approach to assimilation, he said—the more gradual, the better. Kennedy's 1944 study of marriages in New Haven, Connecticut, supported Draschler, who had attributed Jewish "cohesiveness" to Jews' tendency to marry within their group.[16] Rabbis and women's groups in the 1940s and 1950s drew on those studies to advise Jews not only to avoid marriage to gentiles but also to create domestic religious festivals that strengthened a family's emotional bonds. Sociologists and rabbis, along with other American clergy, now shared the same message; they repeated it in magazines such as *Time* and *Ladies' Home Journal* and in Jewish venues.[17] Now, it seemed, Jews could strengthen America by forming strong Jewish families.

Concerns about revitalizing Jewish family life grew amid national interest in the factors that influenced personal motivations. In 1950, the Midcentury White House Conference on Children and Youth drew "almost six thousand delegates from all parts of the country and many foreign nations" to assess "factors . . . shaping the health and welfare movements as related to children." Conferees took as a "fact " that they acted "under the shadow of one of the most critical world crises of our time." The nature of the crisis seemed so obvious that the authors wasted no ink in identifying it. Minority groups sent delegates, and the Women's League for Conservative Judaism participated. The conference "focused a clear spotlight on the key importance of personality development" and "the influence of . . . educational, social, health, recreational, and religious institutions and practices on [it]."[18] Kopelman's concern for Jewish children seemed only a Jewish version of a national worry.

In that climate, the self became a focus of expert attention. In the influential book *Childhood and Society*, Erik Erikson stressed the importance of a healthy ego and argued that a child's environment exerted a critical influence on the youngster's ability to develop a sound identity. By extending Freud's five stages of development of the self in childhood to eight, Erikson identified further growth in an adult's capacity to care for others and to achieve wisdom.[19] His advice found ready audiences among Americans. The recent rise and expansion of the corporate and the service sectors of the national economy meant that social skills, in addition to technical abilities, became crucial factors in finding and keeping employment. That same year, David Riesman explained that this increasing "other-directedness" required healthy self-esteem to navigate the subtleties of those situations.[20] The quest for an authentic identity, a "solid core of personality that would allow the individual to withstand pressures toward mindless conformity—that was the defining question of the postwar era," explains historian Andrew Heinze.[21]

Postwar Religious Realignments

Sarah Kopelman's worry about raising Jewish children reflected a concern for the future voiced by most Jewish religious groups. The catastrophe in Europe, combined with the end of significant growth through immigration, contributed to realignments among American Jewish denominations. Now, in a new social landscape, religious organizations mobilized to educate Jews and non-Jews about Judaism. Conservative Judaism attracted significant numbers of nominally Orthodox Jews and undertook formal and informal adult educational programs. At the same time, over twenty-five hundred adults enrolled in Reform's courses on Jewish religion and issues. Meanwhile, in the Yiddish presses, discussion about the Jewish future led a number of intellectuals to strongly support traditional religious practices and ideologies, as Yiddish secularists also reexamined their positions and assumptions.[22] By 1949, the socialist Workmen's Circle schools instructed students about Jewish holidays and celebrated them in their classrooms.[23] Yet that did not mean they embraced religion. Some taught Hanukkah as the commemoration of a revolt by Jews who would not allow themselves to be made slaves to an exploitive king.[24]

Among the Orthodox, divisions hardened. Those willing to accommodate some of Judaism's precepts to modern exigencies—often epitomized in coeducational schools—felt ever more alienated from those with a fervent devotion to creating Jewish communities that lived strictly according to Talmudic norms. From the interwar years through the aftermath of World War II, a thin but "steady stream of European Orthodox congregations and rabbis made their way to America." Some Orthodox American families that respected Talmudic traditions even though they did not entirely live according to them sent their children to religious day schools set up in part to provide employment to fervently Orthodox rabbis among the recent refugees from Europe. Five hundred such schools thrived by the end of World War II.[25] Many of the children trained in these schools later grew up to be much more traditionally observant than their own parents. Defining themselves against the accommodationist style shared by most of American Jewry, ultra-Orthodox Jewish immigrants also set up *yeshivot* to train older boys and men in Talmud.[26] Their schools became the centers of their local communities in Brooklyn, Lakewood, New Jersey, Cleveland, Chicago, and other areas. By 1946, 17,500 men studied at eighty-four *yeshivot.* At the same time, mystical, ultra-Orthodox Jewish individuals also came to the United States, where they, too, set up their own *yeshivot* that, along with their *rebbes* who led their communities, generated distinctive, often Yiddish-speaking worlds.[27] One observer concludes that they "set out to reconstruct the religious civilization they had seen burned before their very eyes. . . . Their holy quest was to recapture the past."[28] Those changes among Orthodox Jews influenced American Jewish life in the coming decades, despite the fact that their numbers seldom reached as much as ten percent of American Jewry.

Those realignments did not change the arguments for Hanukkah's contemporary relevance that had become standard fare across more liberal denominations. Thoughtful religious leaders of different stripes drew on Hanukkah's story to advise Jews in coping with the postwar challenges. Robert Gordis, editor of the journal *Judaism,* published by the Jewish rights advocacy group the American Jewish Congress, argued that for "virtually all" modern Jews, two problems loomed: the preservation of the gains of emancipation on one hand and "retention of their Jewish identity and some form of Jewish distinctiveness on the other." Yet, he argued, this problem that seems to mark modernity is not really new. "Assimilation was powerfully at work" even long ago, when the "assimilation which characterized the Hellenizers in the period of

Antiochus IV and the Maccabees" threatened Judaism.[29] Gordis did not say anything novel—this had become a standard American Hanukkah theme. Telling the story in this way gave this holiday particular relevance in the American Jewish calendar. It suggested that if Jews in the ancient world could overcome the conundrum of resisting assimilation, modern Jews could also overcome it, and so this lesson provided reassurance and encouragement to contemporary Jews.

Prolific author and Reform rabbi Abba Hillel Silver also counseled hope for overcoming the lure of assimilation. Pointing to the Maccabean revolt, which he called the "only successful revolt in defense of religion known to the ancient world," he defended Judaism against disparagements by Christian intellectuals who claimed that Judaism withered after the period of the prophets. Following that victory, Silver said, "Judaism gained in power and in confidence with the resurgence of national pride." Indeed, he claimed that the "victory of the Maccabees did for the spirit of the Jewish people . . . what the victory at Marathon had done for the Greeks."[30] Hanukkah records Jews' spiritual rescue and Purim their physical rescue, agreed both Conservative Rabbi Morris Kertzer and religion scholar Theodor H. Gaster.[31] Each man taught consolation for contemporary problems in his own understanding of the Maccabean revolt.

Even thinkers who doubted that much useful guidance could be elicited from Hanukkah's story repeated the view that Jews who considered Hanukkah to be only a children's holiday misunderstood its significance to Western civilization. Joachim Prinz, who had trained for the rabbinate in Breslau and became a great defender of civil liberties in the United States, disagreed with the optimists. He pointed out that "freedom is an untested Jewish experience." Jews had never really faced circumstances quite like their situation in the United States. Judaism could survive in America only if Jews "liberate" themselves from "kindergarten approaches" and "celebrate their Hanukkah, not in the shadow of the Christmas tree" but for its own value, knowing that "without the Maccabees there would have been neither Jesus nor Paul nor Christianity."[32] Prinz's assertion about Hanukkah's importance to world history echoed those made by earlier rabbis. In 1857, as we have seen, Isaac M. Wise told it to readers of his newspaper, the *Israelite*. It also echoed Deborah Melamed's more general argument that the Maccabees preserved for Western civilization the moral traditions propounded by the Hebrew prophets. It seems unlikely that Prinz meant to suggest that Judaism is great because it made Christianity possible. Rather, he —like Wise and Melamed—hoped to instill a sense of pride and dignity in Jews by showcasing their venerable history. Now, as this argument emerged again in the postwar era, it became a standard understanding of Hanukkah's significance that supported other reasons to make the holiday a more important Jewish occasion.

Guiding Home Celebrations

Rabbis and Jewish leaders wanted every Jew's "core of personality" to be self-identified as Jewish. Religious celebrations held at home, such as Hanukkah, where identity is shaped in fundamental ways, became especially valuable. After the war ended, the Conservative movement promoted domestic religion even more energetically than in the past. Some Conservative congregations arranged congregational Passover seders and other normally domestic holiday rituals in their synagogues because they feared that some members did not celebrate them at home.[33] They hoped those experiences would give attendees the confidence to replicate those rites domestically.

In 1947, Minneapolis's Rabbi Albert Gordon, trained in sociology, published a sixteen-page manual for families to use in creating emotionally and spiritually meaningful domestic occasions. His confidence-boosting prose applied the new experts' advice to mold behavior by encouragement and praise.[34] He urged American Jews to find historical and divine significance in their own commitment to a Jewish future. Hanukkah proved that "no matter how numerous are the obstacles against the champions of the right," one should never despair but must persevere until victory is achieved. That lesson seemed underscored by the Allies' long struggle to defeat Nazism. The Hanukkah lights should "inspire us to learn and to study, to work and to live, so that the Judaism which the Maccabees preserved may be preserved by us in these difficult hours."[35] Gordon hoped his Hanukkah guide would convince people to commit to that goal.

Gordon's manual marked postwar rabbis' efforts to infuse more educational and inspirational material into domestic celebrations. They built on similar earlier work by women, published in organizational newsletters and in works such as *The Three Pillars* and *The Jewish Home Beautiful*—volumes that continued to be reprinted throughout the 1950s. Since the early days of the first synagogue festivals for children in 1870, rabbis and women had been working together to promote Hanukkah and to enrich its educational impact. Their dynamic relationship continued to be the engine that drove Hanukkah to greater significance in the post–World War II years. Although they shared a common goal, women also continued their independent work toward the same end.

The WLCJ initiated a special project to promote "Judaism in the home" among its members; the project built on the organization's interwar work in educating Jewish women in religion.[36] One nationwide study in 1950 concluded that "perhaps one-fifth to one-third of American Jews receive no instruction in things Jewish." A rabbi trained at the Conservative movement's seminary deemed the widespread "lack of knowledge of the spiritual elements of Jewish life . . . appalling." Religious leaders agreed on a "glaring need of the American Jewish community for religious direction and informal leadership." Rabbis and women's groups, following the trend set by Deborah Melamed's publications, soon published heftier manuals, and more of them, on special topics for adult education than had previously appeared as features in synagogue or organizational newsletters. Synagogue men's clubs and sisterhoods marketed them.[37]

American rabbis and teachers could no longer look to Europe's Jewish schools for guidance and leadership; those had been destroyed under Nazi rule.[38] The Conservative movement's leaders therefore hoped to "transform" the Jewish "settlement" in America, which before the Holocaust had been on the periphery of the Jewish world, into a coherent "Jewish society" united by "self-identification with Jewish culture."[39] Now, in light of America's radically increased responsibility, Lithuania-trained American Orthodox rabbi Hyman E. Goldin took another look at his twenty-year-old translation of the abridged *Shulchan Aruch,* condensed it even more, and emphasized its ethical meaning in order to reach wavering Orthodox American Jews. "Hanukkah has become . . . more important," he told readers, describing its message as one of "idealism, courage, and hope."[40] At Hanukkah, "Every Jew should retell amid feasting the miracles that were wrought for our fathers," he wrote.[41] "Every man and woman must observe the commandment of lighting the Hanukkah lamp, . . . even children."[42] Yet we have no idea how many people read or used either Gordon's or Goldin's manual. Both works succeeded enough to be reprinted—Goldin's as late as 1985. Gordon's appeared—with an additional thirty pages—in 2007, as access to Hanukkah items expanded through Internet marketing.[43]

Gordon opened his 1947 manual with a hopeful quote from former U.S. Supreme Court justice Louis D. Brandeis, whose stature lent authority to his words and whose recent death during the war lent them poignancy. The Maccabean victory, Brandeis had insisted, "proved that the Jews—then already an old people, possessed the secret of eternal youth: the ability to rejuvenate itself through courage, hope, enthusiasm, devotion, and self-sacrifice of the plain people. This will bring again a Jewish Renaissance." His assurance encouraged optimism. Gordon asked readers to believe that Jewish life would be renewed if they celebrated festivals such as Hanukkah. Although the Holocaust triggered a crisis of faith among many Jews who wondered how God could have allowed the tragedy, Gordon told readers, "[That] our fathers and we too have been able to maintain our identity and our faith, despite the numerous attempts to annihilate us, is nothing short of a miracle." Gordon hoped to shift readers' attention from the catastrophe in Europe to the religious import of their own lives.[44] Another new Hanukkah manual, specifically to be used as a guide to expanding the standard Jewish grace after meals, repeated that message. Compiled by playwright and film director Dore Schary, it foregrounded Hanukkah's ceremony, with lavish praise for Jews who conducted its rite. "Our own devotion to Torah parallels that of the Maccabees," Schary claimed.[45] Echoing a Hanukkah theme used in America since the early nineteenth century, Schary encouraged contemporary Jews to see themselves as being like the Maccabees. His grace thanked God but also rewarded Jews with praise for the divine significance of their own actions.

Gordon expanded the Hanukkah rite into a formal lesson in Jewish values and religious figures. Each night's light added a religious ideal linked to a person and event in the Torah. The first night's stood for God's words "Let there be light," which began the process of creation, as well as the Jewish people's "radiant knowledge of God." Other candles stood for Torah, justice, mercy, holiness, love, patience, and courage.

A muscular and learned group of Maccabees forms the core of the menorah in this stained-glass window about Hanukkah in the Temple of the Valley Jewish Community Center, North Hollywood, California, 1949. Designed by Mischa Kallis. (Courtesy Congregation Adat Ari El; reproduction from the Collections of the Library of Congress)

To impress youngsters with the importance of this straightforward lesson in religious values, Gordon advised parents to "see to it that their children receive . . . nicely wrapped [gifts] indicating . . . that the parent has taken pains to make the occasion memorable." Parents also should "make a ceremony of the distribution of the gifts" each night to enhance the experience. Finally, he reminded readers to give Hanukkah charity and suggested a donation be made to the Jewish National Fund, which aided the Jewish settlements in British Palestine. His manual encompassed many Hanukkah themes and customs that had emerged among

Jews over the past several decades. But in the postwar climate, those behaviors and ideas served more than religious goals. Gordon hoped his manual could help Jews to create psychologically supportive, religiously inspiring, and emotionally satisfying celebrations. Those should assist every family member in attaining a healthy Jewish self, he argued, while strengthening their ties to each other.[46]

Gordon's enriched domestic Hanukkah festival also offered instructions for creating Hanukkah parties. Recipes for foods, songs lyrics, decorating advice about blue and white lights and crepe paper, details of guessing games, lists of Hanukkah children's books, songbooks, and recordings of Hanukkah music now available from Victor, Columbia, and Decca record companies filled many pages. As the postwar consumer market expanded, more Jewishly coded commodities became available for enacting Jewish religious and cultural life. Like the cards, records, and candies marketed by the NFTS in the interwar years, these items provided markers for Jewish identity. Through the purchasing, displaying, and giving of these objects, they provided material ways for Jews to recognize each other and to validate their shared understandings of Jewish culture. Gordon showed Jews how to use them to create idyllic Jewish worlds in their homes.

Hallmark sold its first Hanukkah card in the 1940s, but most Jews turned to the ethnic economy for Hanukkah goods. Jewish women sold most holiday items in synagogue gift shops and through their religious organizations.[47] These commercial additions to most newly built suburban synagogues provided the specialty objects to adorn religious observances, objects that had recently become available to the broad Jewish consumer market. Almost universally, synagogue sisterhoods ran the gift shops. The NFTS advised its members on marketing the many new objects for sale. It suggested silver *mezuzahs* for housewarming gifts, Palestinian olive-wood matzah holders for the Passover seder hostess, Hanukkah menorahs and Sabbath candleholders for newlyweds, and Hanukkah gifts for children.[48]

In autumn, those shops filled with goods for Hanukkah. Menorahs and candles, greeting cards, decorations, games, books and records, napkins with special holiday designs, and items made in Israel found their places on display shelves. In 1960, the shops featured miniature Israeli character dolls that embodied figures in religious stories. The

Ziontalis company offered forty-seven styles of Hanukkah menorahs and promised that those made from chromium retained their gleam without the polishing required by silver. The publisher KTAV supplied holiday gift wrapping. The NFTS sold special holiday name tags for use at large parties. After 1951, Barton's Candy produced chocolate latkes, before hitting on the more iconic chocolate coins wrapped in gold-colored foil that turned Hanukkah *gelt* from something to save to something to savor.[49]

By 1960, the NFTS regularly coached its members on the details of running an enticing and profitable gift shop. Allow sufficient time for special holiday displays to be set up and for goods to arrive, it advised, and remind customers to shop early if they are planning to mail a gift. NFTS conferences often featured model Judaica shops that showed members exactly how to do it. The shop "ought to be an educational and religious device attuned to the programs of the congregation," the NFTS told its members.[50] Some observers began thinking that "all the problems of the commercialization of Christmas . . . began to manifest themselves . . . [at Hanukkah] as well."[51] Yet income from these sales contributed to synagogues as well as women's group programming, charity, and special projects. Those organizations welcomed the proliferating variety of Hanukkah goods. Moreover, the items themselves, the location of their sale, and the exchange between Jews in their purchase all amplified Jewish identity.

Denominational trends shifted after the war. Many nominally Orthodox Jews—those who preferred the Orthodox worship service but did not maintain many daily religious observances—found a place in Conservative synagogues. These congregations welcomed nominally Orthodox Jews without making them feel guilty for driving to synagogue on the Sabbath instead of walking there.[52] Offering a middle way between Orthodoxy and Reform, the Conservative movement experienced its greatest growth in the postwar era, as young families moved into new areas, usually suburbs. Single-family-housing starts numbered only 114,000 during wartime in 1944 but jumped to 1,692,000 in 1950.[53] Synagogues sprang up in new Jewish suburban settlements. Between 1940 and 1965, the number of Conservative congregations jumped from 350 to 800. The American-born children of eastern European immigrants composed the vast majority of their members.[54] Similar growth occurred in Reform. During roughly the same years, Reform congregations expanded and new ones emerged, growing to 700 by 1975.[55]

These suburban synagogues offered central locations for Jewish socializing and religious education along with worship. Members looked forward to the coffee and cookies in the social halls that encouraged shmoozing after Friday-evening worship. Women's organizations and men's clubs could be found in every congregation. Congregants also formed social-action clubs, bowling leagues, and choirs and served on various committees to keep the synagogues humming. Membership lists rose as synagogues became communities. This trend toward reshaping synagogues into centers of Jewish life began near the turn of the twentieth century but became the norm only when most Jews relocated far from their familiar, Jewishly dense urban neighborhoods.

Despite the impressive growth in synagogues, their sanctuaries remained vastly underused most of the year. One 1961 study found that only thirteen percent of Jews attended synagogue once a week or more; fifty-one percent attended only for the High Holidays of Rosh Hashanah and Yom Kippur each fall. Fifteen percent never attended synagogue at all. Two years later, a study of New York City's Jews found the American-born far less likely to attend synagogue than foreign-born Jews.[56] Few new congregations formed after the mid 1960s.[57] The trend looked bad for synagogues, despite the building and membership boom. Rabbis and religious groups looked for other ways to instill interest in religion, including the holiday guides that promoted and expanded Judaism's domestic rites.

The Conservative movement published Gordon's and Schary's manuals, and its men's and women's clubs made them available, but it is unclear who purchased or used them. For, that same year, the movement's women's association included its own Hanukkah advice in the *Women's League Handbook and Guide*. Because it usually fell to women to create these festive events at home, this guide may have been the most widely used. Compiled by WLCJ founder and leader Sarah Kussy, it featured women's voices. Instead of Brandeis's words, she opened its ten-page section on Hanukkah with an excerpt from Emma Lazarus's poem for the holiday: "Clash, Israel, the cymbals, touch the lyre, blow the brass trumpet and the harsh-tongued horn; chant psalms of victory till the heart take fire, The Maccabean spirit leaps new born." The poem set the tone for the guide, meant to create Hanukkah events that "stir the imagination." Kussy told readers that their first step was to shop. Rarely did the general American marketplace feature Hanukkah items, so Kussy advised women to buy prayer books with the traditional Hanukkah service at synagogue gift shops. They could find suggestions for setting a festive table and home decorations in *The Three Pillars* and *The Jewish Home Beautiful*. Each publication had been produced by the Conservative movement, and Kussy promoted them along with holiday objects. Women could find "games, skits, and other Hanukkah material" at the National Jewish Welfare Board, whose address she provided.[58]

Kussy especially urged her readers to engage their children in the Hanukkah rite. Mothers should provide "enough menorahs to enable each child to light his [*sic*] own candles every night." She echoed Gordon's manual but replaced the eastern European custom whereby men lit the candles for their households—familiar to most American Jews—with this advice from the *Shulchan Aruch*.[59] To children, lighting their own candles in their own menorahs would signal the holiday's exceptional importance and deepen the experience, for youngsters usually were told not to touch matches because of fire's danger. Gordon's manual had advised only that "all members of the family be present" at the lighting of the menorah and that children should be involved through games. Kussy and Goldin put the candles into children's hands. That change also made it possible for candles to be lighted despite a father's absence—December marketplaces kept many businessmen at work through evening hours. Long commutes brought many others home later than a small child's bedtime. Yet, even without dad, Hanukkah could be impressive.

According to Kussy, time ordinarily spent listening to the radio or watching television should be used to extend the family's Hanukkah experience. "Play games in the evening," she said.[60] By shutting access to December's mass culture, with its Christmas programming, women could block both secular and Christian ideas. Few Americans owned a television set in the late 1940s, when radio had sixteen hundred stations but television only twenty-eight. Television stations served New York City, where over two million Jews lived, long before small towns. But television spread quickly. By 1955, roughly three-fourths of American households owned a television.[61] While Jewish families

The children in this 1955 photo are seated before holiday decorations that won "honorable mention" in the Hanukkah Home Decorating Contest sponsored by a synagogue in Tampa, Florida. They were then the only Jewish children in their small town of Zephyrhills, thirty miles away. (Courtesy Helen Chenkin Hill)

might join the mass viewing audience on other evenings, at Hanukkah, women should turn the set off in order to create a Jewish environment for their families.

Nor should a family spend Hanukkah evenings working on separate tasks—whether school work, business duties, or housework. Those labors divided families. To strengthen their emotional bonds, family members must put shared Hanukkah activities uppermost. Playing Hanukkah games, singing songs, and eating traditional foods gave the holiday power to strengthen family life. Kussy's guide urged WLCJ members to accept these familial religious goals as their special responsibilities as Jewish wives and mothers.

Yet, ironically, women seemed least able to shoulder a new religious responsibility. Few American women had obtained a formal education in Judaism. A 1935 study estimated that only twenty-five percent of the eight hundred thousand Jewish school-age children in the United States studied in Jewish religious schools. A similar study ten years later noted that students seldom stayed in school more than two years.[62] Most students were boys. Some immigrant families embraced secular ideologies and working-class loyalties, and their daughters learned to celebrate Hanukkah only as an occasion to rejoice in political emancipation.[63] Migration also took its toll on memories. Women in Miami, Florida, it seemed, "had lost the skills to celebrate home rituals." One Reform rabbi there inaugurated a program to train women in domestic rites, first with Hanukkah; instructions for Passover and the Sabbath came later.[64] Kussy told her readers, "Familiarize yourselves with the story of Hanukkah." Then, instruct your children and "follow it with a quiz," reinforcing new knowledge in both mother and child.[65]

Women also could learn about Hanukkah by attending WLCJ meetings. Posters with Hanukkah sayings, such as Zechariah's "Not by might, nor by power, but by My Spirit, sayeth the Lord of Hosts," Kussy said, should adorn the walls. Appropriate readings from the prayer book should be recited, and songs from a popular Hanukkah songster should be sung. Women should discuss "Civilization's Debt to the Maccabees" and consider the revolt as part of the "world-wide struggle for democracy." Although the Maccabean revolt ultimately installed the Hasmoneans as Judea's kings, Kussy linked it to the American values long touted by the country's rabbis. Women who participated in these activities could be impressed with Hanukkah's significance for their families, for Judaism, and for Western civilization.[66]

These three guides to Hanukkah, published by the burgeoning Conservative movement and written by Gordon, Schary, and Kussy, aimed to turn each Jewish household into a small Jewish world. These works stand out among the myriad postwar pamphlets and newsletter essays on religious topics issued by many Jewish organizations for their imaginative and extensive compilation of Hanukkah activities for families.[67] Yet, despite their novelty, they used identifiably Jewish forms. From Passover, they adapted the idea of the guide used to tell the holiday's meaning and the order of the evening's events. Special Hanukkah guides expanded the holiday's evenings into something more like Passover and Sabbath evenings. Their familiar Jewish style made them easy to understand and to use. The authors hoped that this kind of Hanukkah experience could help Jews accomplish their "Herculean" task—raising psychologically healthy children with strong Jewish identities.

Such manuals continued to proliferate and expand until, in 1959, one ran to more than one hundred pages.[68]

Hanukkah advocates wanted Jewish homes to be locations for comfort, solace, and support that countered the estrangement of the Christmas season. Mothers, once again, shouldered much of the Hanukkah work. One woman urged Jewish mothers to be ambassadors to their gentile neighbors and to explain the Jewish customs to parents of their children's gentile playmates. Invite all the children to a Hanukkah party where they can both learn and play games, she said, and where they can also see a home with Jewish markers of religious identity. This may "take a bit of educating" on the part of the Jewish mother, but it will certainly help her child feel "part of the gang" without submerging his or her own heritage.[69] Child-rearing experts told all American mothers to create "safe play" experiences, such as home parties, for their children.[70] Hanukkah parties helped Jewish mothers to display their own informed parenting skills to their neighbors along with their Jewishly identified households. One mother resented it; resistance to Christmas changed Hanukkah from a festival of freedom into a festival of "refuge," she complained. Jews in her town "violently amplify" Hanukkah celebrations only because of an "accident of timing."[71]

Understanding the Child's Hanukkah

Jews' postwar relocations set the stage for religious changes. Two years after Albert Gordon wrote his Hanukkah manual, he published his analysis of Jewish life "in transition" in Minneapolis.[72] Among the changes he noted was a deliberate effort to create Hanukkah celebrations within synagogues, religious schools, and homes. By 1951, instructors found "an abundance of material available" for use in classroom celebrations.[73] One woman recalled that during her own childhood in the 1930s, she "missed what the Christian children had," perhaps because her father and brothers were engaged in a "Christmas business" that kept her aware of all the goods that made that holiday so glamorous. Hanukkah seemed "drab" in comparison. After she married, her Hanukkah experiences improved. Her own family now attended a synagogue that, unlike the congregation her parents had belonged to, made Hanukkah "fun for the kids." In the local public schools, holiday assemblies added

Children at the Strawberry Mansion Day Nursery's Hanukkah party in Philadelphia are clearly enjoying themselves, circa 1955. (Courtesy Philadelphia Jewish Archives Center)

Hanukkah songs to the usual roster of Christmas carols. In addition, two nearby Conservative synagogues began to urge a "greater degree of special home decoration for Chanukah and . . . conducted home lighting and . . . decoration contests" that bestowed awards and prizes. As a result, this woman felt that "there is a greater awareness of the beauty and meaning of Chanukah today" than when she was a girl. Amazed by the changes, she admitted with surprise that "you can revive a holiday." But you have to "work away at it."[74]

"Of course, there are still a great number of Jews who do not observe Chanukah," Gordon admitted, and there are some who "light the Chanukah candles and yet decorate their homes with Christmas trees," doing so, they say, "for the children."[75] In New York City, young Lois Greene confessed to her diary her enthusiasm for her own family's celebration of Christmas in 1946, for which she received seventeen gifts on Christmas Eve and five more the next morning, concluding. "Ain't life grand?" By contrast, she admitted her confusion about how to spell Hanukkah when she noted lighting its first candle the previous week —with a palpable lack of enthusiasm.[76] Both Conservative and Reform rabbis aimed to change the experience of children like Lois. In San Diego, Reform Rabbi Morton Cohn, a former navy chaplain, told his congregants that "Hanukkah isn't for cowards" and prepared a mimeographed booklet on the holiday for them to use. "We undermine the survival of American Jewry and Judaism—and we confuse our children —if we do not develop in them respect for their own festivals . . . by practicing the customs and ceremonies . . . at home," he insisted.[77]

Hanukkah Music to Create a Jewish Esprit de Corps

Postwar Jews argued that religious instruction belonged in homes and in synagogues, and they enrolled their children in religious schools in record numbers. Schools in all Jewish denominations experienced rising enrollment. In 1959, the combined increase reached more than 131 percent over previous years. By the early 1960s, "approximately 590,000 children nationwide studied in synagogue schools."[78]

Religious educators understood that Jews expected much from them. They improved their teaching style despite the fact that only a quarter of instructors held teaching licenses. Thanks to a teacher exchange with Israel, teachers from that country constituted a quarter of the instructors in weekday Jewish schools in the 1950s, supplementing the short supply of American instructors.[79] These schools aimed not only to educate but to create in their charges a "will" to be Jewish.[80]

The schools turned to music to reinforce lessons, to help students practice Hebrew pronunciation, to enliven the classroom experience, and, especially, to promote Jewish spirit. "Schools of all types taught customs and ceremonies," and Hanukkah's musical repertoire expanded.[81] Harry Coopersmith, a Chicago musician and director of music for the local Board of Jewish Education, compiled songbooks used by Conservative synagogues and religious schools; the compilations mark the details of that expansion over time. From four Hanukkah songs in his small 1939 collection to fifteen in his 1950 two-volume work to eighteen in 1971, the holiday's proportion grew in relation to other songs. By 1950, the number of Hanukkah songs equaled those for Passover—one more than for Purim and many more than other holiday songs. Only Sabbath liturgical selections outnumbered those, as did folk songs. By 1971, however, Coopersmith included more songs for Hanukkah than for Passover.[82] In 1955, Reform published a new songbook for synagogues as well as a short pamphlet of brief worship services and songs for religious schools. Reformers hoped the children's service would "make [Jewish] children learn and love to speak to God."[83] As with past generations, Reform students spent less time in religious school than did Conservative students, and the Reform songbook is smaller.

But the books offered many of the same tunes, and that overlap determined that Jewish students from many different backgrounds would, to some degree, share a common holiday experience and perspective. Reform's twelve songs for Hanukkah, including the candle blessings, brought together items from a complex heritage of Jewish music, as did Coopersmith's eighteen. Items such as "Rock of Ages" blended nineteenth-century American values with a traditional European melody, while another called "My Candles (in the Window)" set English words to a Hasidic *nigun* (melody). Reform congregations purchased more than three thousand copies of the pamphlet.[84]

Both collections included the 1930s tune "Who Can Retell?" which first had become popular in the interwar years. It said that today's challenges required "all Israel" (meaning Jewry as a whole) to solve them, and this tune grew increasingly popular in the postwar era, a time when appeals for funds to assist Israel reached into nearly every congregation. Most collections identified it as a folk song associated with the Zionist movement and sung by Jewish settlers in Palestine. Its Hebrew version, "Mi Yimalel," proved as popular as the English. The song's "buoyant," quick, rhythmic melody, sung in a round, made it fun to sing. Its major key, different from the minor keys of many Jewish tunes from eastern Europe, lent it optimism and force. One observer argued that songs in Hebrew, sung by Jews in different parts of the globe, provided a "spiritual bridge which binds Jews in many lands to one another."[85] This one signaled Jews' urgent new historical challenge and told them to face it together.[86]

Coopersmith expanded his songbooks to match Jews' growing use for school music. Their sense that singing should be part of Jewish education reflected the wide range of musical events in Jewish communities. As with past generations, music enlivened celebrations in multiple settings, from homes to schools, community centers, and synagogues. "Feverish" musical activities among Jewish organizations surrounding the establishment of the state of Israel in 1948 aimed to bring Jewish music to the public. Israeli pronunciation of Hebrew became fashionable. Called "the most cheerful and meaningful Chanukah since the triumph of Judah Maccabee," that year's holiday meant for one observer the emptying of Displaced Persons camps by welcoming Europe's Jewish refugees in Israel.[87] Recalling the eastern European and immigrant neighborhood traditions of Hanukkah concerts, by 1950, more than a thousand Jewish community centers, synagogues, and religious schools supported symphonic, choral, and chamber concerts, lectures and exhibits to educate about Jewish music, and contests and radio programs to entertain. New musical institutes formed to improve the quality of Jewish music and to promote its importance. Cantors associated with Conservative congregations formed their own association to advance their work, and the Reform rabbinical seminary established a School of Jewish Sacred Music to train cantors who served its congregations. The National Jewish Music Council published theoretical material and guides to appreciating Jewish music, along with program aids.[88]

These efforts contributed to the sophistication of the Ninth Annual Hanukkah Festival commemorating the three hundredth Hanukkah celebrated in America, in 1954, the tercentenary of Jewish life in North America. Held at Chicago's Civic Opera House and opening with the "Star-Spangled Banner" followed by "Hatikvah" (the Israeli anthem), it offered orchestral and operatic selections along with sophisticated arrangements of *klezmer freilachs* (lively eastern European Jewish tunes) and selections from Hanukkah's liturgy sung by Metropolitan Opera tenor and cantor Richard Tucker.[89]

"Jews have always been a singing people," said folklorist Ruth Rubin, and new Hanukkah songs stretched the holiday's meaning in many directions.[90] If "Who Can Retell? / Mi Yimalel" roused Jews to think of self-defense, other tunes encouraged them to laugh. In a collection of parodies by Ben Aronin, a Chicago music teacher associated with the College of Jewish Studies, well-known Hanukkah songs refocused on the simple latke. The collection brought together melodies from European, Zionist, and American music traditions. In Aronin's hands, songs about military bravery became songs about Jewish food. "Mrs. Maccabee" made the latkes that "gave brave Judah a soul." To the melody of "Mi Yimalel," he said, "latke is the food of bravery." Even in Israel, Aronin wrote, Jews fighting in Israel's war of independence relied on latkes to "make the *Palmach* [an elite Israeli military unit] hustle."[91] His silly tunes affirmed the one Hanukkah experience familiar to most American Jewish children—moms cooking latkes. Although it might have been a stretch for postwar, suburban Jewish children to imagine the bravery required for a military revolt, they all ate. They could sing with gusto about food. The books implemented Samuel Markowitz's message, reprinted once again by the NFTS in 1961, that "Jewish life can flourish in America only if Jews find pleasure in Jewish living."[92]

Aronin's songs worked within the now-established folk tradition shared by most American Jews. They voiced a Hanukkah that showed its eastern European roots in both food and music, as well as its contemporary context in postwar American suburbs. Despite appearing in the wake of the Holocaust and alongside Israel's independence after two millennia, Aronin's songs paid little attention to those momentous events. For all their use of the word "Maccabee," they nonetheless focused on Jews' suburban experience of households, where domestic religious rites devolved on the ceremonial foods of eastern Europe. Other collections of Hanukkah tunes that emerged in this era brought together Hanukkah melodies and traditions from Mediterranean and Arabic cultures, reflecting the new awareness of the broader world of Jewish customs.[93] But Aronin aimed simply to increase the delight of the many American Jews who shared his own heritage.

Aronin's simple tunes served small groups well. They provided occasions for the unisonance achieved in group singing that evoked feelings of strength and community. Hanukkah records, however, provided a different musical experience. An increasing array of recorded music adapted the holiday's tradition of cantorial concerts to suburban home life. One of the most famous among those who created special Hanukkah records was Moyshe Oysher, who identified himself as sixth in a cantorial lineage founded by a rabbi seven generations past. Oysher's unique musical persona became a valuable commodity. As high-quality recordings became available and inexpensive, the "expert model" created a "climate in which the majority of the population have been relegated to 'procurers' rather than 'producers' of music."[94] Oysher's albums promised performances authorized by his personal identity as much as by his ability and assured purchasers that they would hear an authentic cantorial concert.[95]

Kinor Records, on the other hand, "encourag[ed] the active participation of young children through singing and dramatization." It's *Chanukah Music Box* asked them to spin like a dreidel and march like a Maccabee while they sang along with the music. Seven sprightly tunes followed the brief blessings. Marketers hoped the "unbreakable" album's red cover with drawings of dancing children would make it an attractive Hanukkah gift.[96] The famed composer of liturgical and popular Jewish music Sholom Secunda also offered his own recordings of holiday songs for children, which, like Kinor's, provided lots of activities. Four years after a small Chicago Jewish organization brought out his 1960 recording, Twentieth Century Fox Records produced his special Hanukkah album, indicating that Jews purchased these records in significant numbers, and so attracted the interest of a major label.[97] Jewish organizations publicized the new music. In musician Judith Kaplan Eisenstein's regular column in *Hadassah Magazine*, she recommended a much broader selection of Hanukkah music, including Handel's oratorio *Judas Maccabaeus*, Israeli music, recordings for children, and "Music of the French Synagogue."[98] Songbooks and albums used in homes, schools, and clubs not only promoted a buoyant Hanukkah spirit, but, more importantly perhaps, they also promoted an esprit de corps among Jews by providing a singing experience that gave voice to shared communal experiences and religious perspectives.

Drawing and Erasing a Christmas Boundary

Just as had been the case since before the turn of the twentieth century, two items continued to identify the December holidays: the decorated Christmas tree and the Hanukkah menorah. Americans' religious identities might be invisible to each other most other times of the year, but in December, these items literally marked religious territories. The overwhelming preponderance of Christmas trees seemed to identify the nation itself as Christian. Even in Brooklyn, Cary Hillebrand recalled, they made him feel like a stranger in his own country.[99] Postwar American Jews believed that the destruction of Europe's Jews meant they must be vigilant about defending their rights in America. Feeling emboldened by their own U.S. military service, Jews engaged December's challenges in varying ways. Increasingly, they displayed their own religious identity and insisted on boundaries between America's Jewish, Christian, and secular arenas.[100]

Clashes between tree worlds and menorah worlds popped up. In Brooklyn, home to almost nine hundred thousand Jews in 1955, the Jewish Community Council urged Jews to display Hanukkah menorahs in front of synagogues. It praised residents of apartment houses in Flatbush and on Eastern Parkway (where Jews predominated) who erected large menorahs in front of their buildings. Such displays fulfilled the religious requirement to publicize the Hanukkah miracle, and the council also hoped the displays would encourage more Jews to celebrate Hanukkah at home. But, at Christmas, the placement of menorahs and trees also carried a more political implication because they identified the religious group that dominated local spaces. In apartment houses where both Jews and non-Jews resided, lobbies sometimes became contested territories. The absence of either item suggested a rapprochement had been reached. Building superintendents customarily set up Christmas trees in these common spaces to signal tenants about yearly Christmas cash gifts to them. A Flatbush group suggested that Jewish tenants offer their gifts before Christmas, to let the superintendent know that "it is unnecessary for him to erect a Christmas tree to collect" them.[101] A lobby empty of religious markers could signal mutual respect.

Reform Rabbi Morton Cohn also aimed to help Jewish youngsters develop their own ability and willingness to police the boundary between Jewishness and Christianity in their everyday encounters, while still participating fully in American life. His Temple Youth League held a Christmas-Hanukkah meeting that brought together teens of their synagogue and those of the local Unitarian church.[102] That very liberal Christian group could be trusted not to evangelize the Jewish youngsters. The encounter therefore underscored Rabbi Cohn's position that the boundary between Judaism and Christianity could be maintained by both parties. A positive experience in publicly maintaining Jewish identity could embolden young Jews to deal with more uncomfortable situations that might arise during the Christmas season. Cohn's Reform movement also organized interfaith institutes to instruct ministers of all faiths about Judaism, emphasizing common ideals shared with Christianity. Such knowledge might ease Jewish children's December encounters with Christian children.

Postwar Reform and Conservative rabbis and women's organizations repeated their decades-old instructions to keep Christmas trees out of Jewish homes and to prominently display Hanukkah menorahs. "No right-minded faithful Jew can permit a Christmas tree in the home if he stops to think of the untold misery this celebration has betoken [sic] for the Jews," wrote the *Women's League Outlook*. "The Women's League pleads" that every member use her influence to dissuade Jewish mothers from "bringing Christmas trees into their homes." Instead, Jewish women should "let the . . . lights from the menorah strengthen our Jewish pride."[103] As Reform rabbis had done since the late nineteenth century, one in Philadelphia described the Christian symbolism of the tree to help his congregants see it as filled with Christian meaning and not as simply a pretty item of American culture.[104] In Rochester, New York, Rabbi Abraham Karp wrote a pamphlet with simple ways parents could keep trees and Santa Claus out of their homes, along with an etiquette guide that allowed Jewish children to participate in their gentile friends' Christmas parties. The pamphlet's simplicity pasted over deeper confusions. Its title, *Our December Dilemma*, became the phrase most used by Jews to describe their situation for the next fifty years.[105]

The situation seemed complicated, and children who attended public schools sometimes felt the confusion most pointedly. Edward Cohen described the holiday season of his youth in Jackson, Mississippi, this way: "Christmas seemed not only alien, but dangerous, and staying away from it in some way integral to my very identity." His own house, the only one on his street lacking Christmas lights, stood alone and dark, "conspicuously." He wanted a tree. His parents finally relented, allowing a "small artificial tree" in his room, where he plugged in its blinking lights. After saving up his eight Hanukkah gifts to open at once, Cohen found it all "profoundly dispiriting."[106] Without his family's participation, his Christmas tree became an emblem of his own isolation in December.

An untold number of postwar Jewish families incorporated decorated trees into their December celebrations, as Lois Greene did in New
York. In Minneapolis, some Jews insisted that "the fir tree . . . does not
belong to Christmas exclusively," and if it helps to "make the holiday
beautiful, that's all that matters."[107] Aesthetic appeal trumped religious
boundaries. In suburban Buffalo, New York, the Klein family placed a
small, pink, aluminum tree on a round table in front of their suburban home's picture window, ringing it with colored electric lights. They
dubbed it their "Hanukkah bush." That neologism proclaimed the family's authority to construct and identify its own ritual objects. Peter
Lemish's Northern California home boasted a tall evergreen hung with
ornaments that "transformed the house" by its aroma and colors. Each
Hanukkah night, the family pulled their wrapped gifts from beneath it.
"Quite a few Jews who grew up as part of the post–World War II baby
boom, as second- or third-generation Jewish Americans, . . . tell stories about their Hanukkah bushes," Lemish recalled.[108] The ready-made
Christmas decorations along with smaller and less expensive decorative
lights that appeared in the early 1950s made it easier and more tempt-
ing to set up a well-appointed tree.[109] Some Jews redrew the boundary
between Christmas and their own Jewish homes by simply renaming
their tree. Placing it inside their own home, they felt it was now under
their own control and ripe for redefinition.

Places marked as Jewish with menorahs, or welcoming to Jews
through their conspicuous lack of Christmas trees, could provide positive emotional experiences that countered the sense of exclusion provoked by Christmas-tree-marked territories. The larger the place, the
more intense the experience. In 1954, Grace Goldin, a writer who lived
in the Midwest before moving to Manhattan, described the "heady
experience" of belonging to a majority, something she felt only upon
moving to New York City. There, for the first time, she saw what she
described as "Judaism as an unself-conscious civilization," with the "Jew
inside the man [finding] expression as full as he can bear." Growing
up in Tulsa, Oklahoma, that was something she "would not have supposed . . . possible."[110] Buffalo's Irving Ascanazy, who changed his sur-
name to Ashton in 1952 to find employment after his military service,
marveled that in New York City, Jewish businessmen could put their
own long Jewish names on storefronts and still turn a profit. In New

York, stores made commercial Hanukkah greeting cards available long before they appeared in other parts of the country.[111] New York housed so many Jews that their identity displays welcomed others to it. There and around the country, most Jews preferred to live in Jewish neighborhoods and usually counted other Jews among their closest friends.[112] The more comfortable Jews felt living among Christians, the more likely they were to set up Christmas trees in their own homes.[113]

If many Jews felt that the boundary between Jewish and Christian worlds was their own front door, in New Orleans, some Jewish garden-club members felt that those doors should be used to display Jewish identity and to instruct their gentile neighbors in Judaism. Calling them "Hanukkah doors," these members decorated them for the holiday season. After covering the entire door with brown paper or gift-wrapping paper, they applied inexpensive, everyday materials: paint, bottle tops, egg cartons, plastic spoons, drinking straws, rice, beans, Mardi Gras beads, acorns, pine cones, popcorn, cardboard, typewriter spools, nuts, or flash cubes. Out of those humble objects, they created Hanukkah menorahs, scenes of Moses receiving the Ten Commandments on Mt. Sinai, the Western Wall in Jerusalem, or the Eternal Light. To help neighbors understand an image, each homeowner placed an explanation beside the door.[114] Through Hanukkah's material presence, it carried educational and political implications in suburban homes, urban apartment buildings, and in cities such as New Orleans where Jews lived amid a much larger gentile population.

But Jews disagreed about what to do at public school holiday celebrations. They could not achieve their "overriding [goal] of social inclusion" by angering Christian neighbors and the schoolteachers who often loved the Christmas assemblies.[115] Moreover, the brunt of the conflict would be felt by their own children. Annual school Christmas pageants became a point of contention for many adults, leaving Jewish children themselves to navigate the boundary issues.

In Mississippi, Edward Cohen solved the problem one year by declining a role in the school Christmas play, but he participated by operating the stage curtains. Only when he saw his parents in the audience, smiling and clapping along with other parents, did he feel that he and his family were "just like everybody else."[116] But that solution could not work for every child.

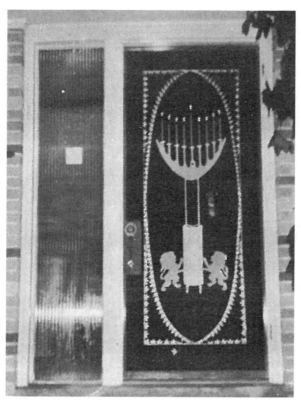

A Torah made of egg shells stands beneath a menorah of
hominy grits on the front door of this New Orleans home
for Hanukkah. Glittered pine cones form the candle flames.
Women's League Outlook (December 1963). (Courtesy National
Women's League of the United Synagogue of America)

Conflicts over this issue abounded. The American Jewish Congress,
founded in 1918 to defend Jewish rights, opposed holiday celebrations in public schools, but the Anti-Defamation League distinguished
between religious assemblies and those that aimed to promote interfaith understanding. Rabbis pointed out that public school teachers
are "ill equipped" to teach about religion.[117] Jewish parents lined up
on both sides of the issue. Many Jews objected to school activities that
asked their children to sing Christmas carols, seeing it as an infringe-
ment of their child's religious freedom. Other parents, however, felt it
more important that their youngsters participate in school activities

The "Living Menorah" formed by these children onstage at Chicago's Covenant Club became a popular element of congregational Hanukkah festival performances in the mid-twentieth century. (Courtesy Chicago Jewish Archives, Spertus Institute for Jewish Studies)

along with the other children. Joint celebrations where children sang both Christmas and Hanukkah songs became a more acceptable solution. When Cleveland's Jewish Community Relations Council opposed school plans to conduct a joint Christmas-Hanukkah assembly, local parents voiced their own support for the plan.[118] The "overwhelming conviction" of American parents, educators, and lawyers favored the December holiday school events. Many Jewish parents, concerned for their children's self-respect, simply wanted Hanukkah included.[119] As public school Christmas assemblies slowly became holiday assemblies, Hanukkah became a vehicle for interfaith understanding that also reached into Christian religious schools.

The postwar movement to promote interfaith tolerance, begun in the 1930s with the formation of the National Council of Christians and Jews, turned to chaplains' experiences in World War II. Military chaplains had ministered to soldiers who practiced many different religions, and organizations such as the Jewish Welfare Board provided materials to guide them in serving those new constituencies. After the war, the Chicago branch of the Anti-Defamation League's Department of Interreligious Cooperation adapted the concise style of chaplaincy materials for its postwar series called *Your Neighbor Celebrates: The Jewish Holidays*, to be used by gentile leaders in creating accurate interfaith programming, as well as by Jewish chaplains. It was compiled by Rabbi Irving J. Rosenbaum, the first executive director of the Chicago Board of Rabbis, an organization that comforted Jews in hospitals, nursing homes, old-age homes, and prisons. Rosenbaum often served as the religious spokesperson for Chicago Jews. When *Your Neighbor Celebrates* first appeared in 1945, it explained only the High Holidays and the major festivals, reflecting Judaism's ranking of important occasions. But Christian educators who needed to answer their students' questions about Jews' obvious difference at Christmas asked Rosenbaum to expand it.

The Hanukkah celebration of a Jewish family in Flint, Michigan, became the focus of *Look* magazine's feature "The Vanishing American Jew" in 1964. Here, Mom supervises as four of her five children create home decorations. This large family paralleled those of many Americans in this era. By the 1960s, Hanukkah had become a holiday that identified Jews to most Americans. (Photograph Collection, Library of Congress)

His larger version appeared in 1947. There, Hanukkah receives lengthy treatment. Its Jewish meaning is described in ways that also indicated the holiday's value for Christians.

Rosenbaum's explanation conveyed the historical and theological links between Judaism and Christianity for American Christian children. First, it described the Maccabees as a "small but brave army of Jewish patriots," shaping the Maccabees as underdogs with good character—a popular image in American movies and in narratives of the country's founding. Rosenbaum's Antiochus is not only "wicked" like the witches of children's stories, but he is a pagan, a word that signified an outsider who lacked morals because of false religious beliefs. In many Catholic schools of that era, children donated funds to support missionaries who would save "pagan babies."[120] Rosenbaum then described the Maccabees restoring worship of "God" to the Temple, using the neutral word for the divine shared by both Christians and Jews. Without specifying any content, "God" seemed to work perfectly in interfaith efforts as part of both Christian and Jewish theologies. Rosenbaum pointed out that the New Testament mentioned Hanukkah as the Feast of Dedication in John 10:22, thereby granting it authority by Christian standards. Finally, he explained Hanukkah's rite of lighting candles.[121] This expanded volume aimed to inform as well as to promote harmony between religious groups. Ten years later, an even larger version of the pamphlet described twelve Jewish holidays as well as bar mitzvah, confirmation, and the role of the synagogue. It even included a glossary of Hebrew words.[122] Published with the support of the Anti-Defamation League of B'nai B'rith, it featured a foreword by Episcopal Reverend James A. Pike.

Soon, a book published to a wider market by the Macmillan publishing company joined the interfaith effort. In *Told under the Christmas Tree*, the Literature Committee of the Association for Childhood Education, which authorized and edited the volume, offered fourteen short selections about Hanukkah in its hefty compilation of Christmas tales and verse. This "brings together other peoples and races in good fellowship," the editors told readers. It "should bring to you all a richer, more significant feeling about this winter holy-day." To the "love, laughter, and rejoicing" that Christmas usually entails, they said the Jewish people "added one more thing in their festival . . . *Freedom*, something

Dressed for a special event, these Flint, Michigan, siblings concentrate on lighting the Hanukkah candles in their home. The sister, eldest, does the lighting. (Photograph Collection, Library of Congress)

the Christian world often forgets." After explaining to readers that the sources from Judaism will improve their Christmas, the editors went even further. Long before both Judaism and Christianity, people celebrated the dark season with light, they said, and that element of the festival seems to unite most people. With this book by a major publisher, the effort to promote interfaith harmony at Christmas became another way to market books for children in December.[123]

In 1968, New York City's mayor, John Lindsey lighted a large, ornate Hanukkah menorah in City Hall near a Christmas tree. His side-by-side solution was an explicit attempt to please his large Jewish constituency, whose support for him had waned, as he faced reelection the following autumn. Placing these two markers of separate holiday traditions in the same room suggested that they belonged together. Because the tree had been draped with the Christmas lights that had become increasingly popular in the years since General Electric began producing them in the twenties, the two religious icons of December seemed to be recast as similar nature festivals meant to create light in winter's shortest days.[124] This politically deft solution mirrored many public schools' change

DANCE A MONTH'S

Chanuka *Dance*

Sunday,   December 14, 1952

KEYSTONE   ROOM   HOTEL   TEXAS

**DANCE TO THE MUSIC OF
DICK JOHNSON**

EXTRA!   FLOOR   SHOW   FEATURING
TOM   KENNY, COMEDIAN

FOR RESERVATIONS PHONE JERRY LEFF AT WI-1569
BEFORE 12 P. M. SUNDAY

Texas couples who enjoyed ballroom dancing hired a come-dian to make their Hanukkah Dance a special event in 1952. (Courtesy Max Kaye Collection, Congregation Ahavath Sholom, Fort Worth, Texas)

from Christmas assemblies with carols and hymns to winter assemblies with songs about Santa, dreidels, and snow.

Hanukkah Stories Americanize Its History

New collections of Hanukkah stories for young people helped them to imagine and to identify with Jews in other eras of American and world history. Some, like the plays of the interwar era still performed in some religious schools, encouraged them to see people like themselves par-ticipating in the Maccabean revolt. Other stories wove tales set in later eras of Jewish history. "Legend and history are inseparable," said compiler Kinneret Chiel. "Ever since the world began . . . storytellers . . . have been delighting their listeners with good tales and . . . morals." The stories she chose for her lengthy Hanukkah collection helped American Jewish children to see beyond their own neighborhoods and schools and to identify with other Jewish children in other eras who solved conflicts at Hanukkah.[125] Like Deborah Marcus Melamed in an earlier era, Chiel, also married to a rabbi, produced items that she hoped would enrich Jews' religious domesticity. Such women often married rabbis with hopes of assuming a leadership role.[126]

Chiel's publisher, a Jewish press based in New York, hoped her hundred-page paperback might pull some market share from the well-known *Hanukkah: The Feast of Lights*, the four-hundred-page tome published by Philadelphia's venerable Jewish Publication Society, a book

The Women's Division of the American Jewish Congress, a Jewish defense and rights organization, seated its special guests, former first lady Eleanor Roosevelt and Judge Justine Wise Polier, next to each other at its annual Hanukkah luncheon in 1955. By the mid-twentieth century, many Jewish organizations in America organized special events at Hanukkah. (Courtesy American Jewish Historical Society)

that in 1955 saw its fourth printing. Both volumes included Hanukkah tales featuring Jewish children living during the American Revolution, underscoring Jews' place in the country's founding. In Chiel's selection, Rebecca Gratz, described as a mere "slip of a girl," solved her synagogue's inability to celebrate Hanukkah by urging her elders to invite the leader of New York's congregation to join them—and to bring along his synagogue's Hanukkah menorah. In fact, the New York leader and many of his congregation did go to Philadelphia while British troops held their city to the north. However, Gratz, born in 1781, could never have made any such suggestion. No matter—the story gave Jewish girls an American Jewish heroine for Hanukkah.[127] Emily Solis-Cohen's original bit of fiction features a Philadelphia boy named Judah taking his own Hanukkah lamp to his father, camped with George Washington's men at Valley Forge. "We are all Maccabees here," Washington says encouragingly to Judah when he arrives.[128] Surgeon's-mate Phillip Moses Russell did serve at Valley Forge that winter, but this story turns on a boy's devotion.[129]

The two tales conveyed to Jewish youngsters the same message of Jews' American patriotism that filled speeches and essays by Jewish leaders at the tercentenary of Jewish life in North America in 1954. For a century, American Jews had explained Hanukkah's link to American history by saying it commemorated the first battle for religious freedom. These new little stories helped Jewish children merge those two traditions in "real" American Jewish children. They constructed "memories" of a Jewish American past that furthered what one observer calls the "coalescence" of their Jewish and American identities.[130] Two years later, when New York City's Jewish Education Committee published a massive collection of 658 stories on Jewish themes, Solis-Cohen's story appeared along with an imaginative sequel in which Washington brings a medal inscribed with a Hanukkah menorah to a Jewish soldier who had served at Valley Forge. Another tale depicts Asser Levy of New Amsterdam—a real person—saving the city from Indian attack on a Hanukkah night (a fictional event). These imaginative short stories wove Hanukkah into the American Jewish past and became part of American Jewish heritage.[131] The volume included tales set in the ancient world, in the Warsaw ghetto, in Russia, and in modern Israel.[132] But those set in major episodes of American history supplemented the lessons in national history that Jewish students learned in public school and encouraged them to see their own place in the nation's pivotal events.

Hanukkah Brings Teens into Real Events

Few Jewish children remained in religious schools beyond elementary school, and Jews tried a variety of ways to keep teenagers involved in Jewish life. Clubs for teens such as the B'nai B'rith Youth Organization (BBYO), Young Judea, and teen groups linked to Reform and Conservative movements increased their membership. Synagogues arranged special worship services themed to appeal to teens.[133] *World Over*, a magazine for Jewish youth often distributed in religious schools, offered older students features on real places and events. In 1964, its photos and descriptions of archeological digs in Israel lent the retelling of Hanukkah's story a reality that might appeal to skeptical adolescents.[134] The next year, the WLCJ told its members that older children should learn that the Maccabean revolt was more than a struggle against Antiochus. It also pitted Jews "steeped in and enamored of Jewish cultural values" against Jews "won over" to the dominant Greek culture. The women's group advised instructors to help teens to see Hanukkah's parallel to contemporary American Jewish life, in which "intermarriage and outside acculturation" are both "stronger than ever." At the same time, it said, hopeful signs should be pointed out to teens. These included the much-improved Jewish educational opportunities for all ages, the growing number of universities offering courses and programs in "Hebrew culture," increasing numbers of books on Jewish subjects, Jewish camping programs, and more kosher foods in markets. All indicate "hopefulness" for Jewish survival in America that contrasted sharply with the fears about rising antisemitism that marked the interwar years. Teens should be urged to see the impact that their own personal decisions have on Jewish survival, and that they alone would determine how the Jewish "story" would end.[135]

Congregations also involved teens in the growing coalition to improve the lot of Jews in the Soviet Union. The Soviet Jewry Movement, as it became known, aimed to convince the USSR to allow its Jews to practice Judaism or, ideally, to allow them to leave. A midsixties Hanukkah play by the director of dramatics at Washington Hebrew Congregation's religious school offered older students a "current and meaningful celebration of Hanukkah" based on that larger political drama. Opening with a television newscaster covering Israeli and American protests against Soviet antisemitism, the scene quickly shifts to a Jewish home in the USSR. The play's action brings together Jews from all classes of Soviet life who learn that they must escape across the border through a little-known tunnel to avoid arrest by the KGB. The characters find courage in recounting the Hanukkah story, eating latkes, and singing "O Hanukkah." The play's contemporary, international perspective underscored the common Hanukkah lesson that Jews must work together to survive threats to themselves and their religion.[136]

The play expressed attitudes widely shared by the Soviet Jewry Movement leaders and by its youthful members, who often organized their own events. Yaakov Birnbaum, who escaped Nazi Germany at fourteen, organized the Student Struggle for Soviet Jewry (SSSJ). He sometimes turned protests into religious pageants. When protesting the recent Soviet restriction on importation of Jewish food, in spring 1965, near Passover, he brought two thousand people to march near the Soviet mission to the United Nations, carrying signs asking, "Why are Matzos subversive?" Seven men carried Torah scrolls; others blew shofars (the ram's horn ceremoniously blown on the fall holidays Rosh Hashanah and Yom Kippur). Only a few months earlier, the Menorah March he had organized drew a thousand students who marched across Central Park on a bitter cold December evening. Four young men holding a two-hundred-pound lead-pipe Hanukkah menorah led the procession. Carrying flashlights covered in red cellophane, marchers sang the Hebrew words of Isaiah's prophecy: "Nation shall not lift up sword against nation and shall study war no more." The next year, in December 1966, three thousand high school and college students marched from the United Nations to rally at Cooper Union Hall, protesting the USSR's treatment of its Jews. They, too, carried a large Hanukkah menorah aloft before them.[137] More than a symbol of the holiday, those menorahs carried political and religious import. Paralleling the 1965 civil rights movement's Selma-to-Montgomery march, also made up of "neat columns of young people singing religious hymns and asking for liberation," observers described the young SSSJ movement as energized by the American climate, the desperate need of the Soviet Jews, and their own determination to be more vocal in securing their core-ligionists' safety than they believed their parents had been during the Nazi era.[138]

Many American Jews who had experienced the challenges of the inter-war era and World War II emerged from those struggles with a commitment to securing their own and their children's place in America —as committed Jews. Hanukkah became an important tool for raising happy, devoted Jewish children and enriching family life. As Jews joined many other Americans who moved out of cities and into sub urbs, their nuclear families—like those of other Americans—drew the attention of both religious leaders and women's religious groups. At the same time that the country as a whole embraced religion as a vehicle to strengthen civic life, American Jews amplified Hanukkah celebrations in many different ways. They repeated interpretations of the Maccabean revolt that had emerged in earlier eras of American Jewish history to promote the holiday's significance to the United States and even to Western civilization.

Synagogues and religious schools continued to create Hanukkah festivals to delight children. Composers created a range of new songs to enliven holiday lessons and celebrations in religious classrooms, as well as to create camaraderie in Jewish clubs and among family members. Recorded music provided individuals and families with a way to create traditional cantorial Hanukkah concerts in their own homes, along with Jewish-themed musical fun for their children. Synagogues reaped the funds raised in gift shops that sold a growing diversity of Hanukkah items for families and individuals to display, to use, and to give to others. Increasingly, the Hanukkah menorah became an emblem of Jewish identity that emerged most importantly in December, when the ubiquitous Christmas decorations identified the vast majority of Americans as Christians and, by extension, identified local spaces as Christian. Confrontations between the two emblems sometimes involved eliding their distinctions by identifying both objects—the lighted menorah and the Christmas tree decorated with small lights—as signifiers of similar winter, family-based festivals about light.

All those efforts to evoke pride, to raise morale, and to spread delight in being Jewish indicate that the state of American Jewish life worried its religious leaders. In 1964, despite almost twenty years of synagogue expansion, advancing numbers of children who obtained a religious education, and efforts to revitalize religious life in families, Mordecai Kaplan continued to be utterly pessimistic about Judaism's future in the United States. "The Jewish people today . . . is in danger . . . of a slow . . . process of erosion . . . of any Jewish consciousness," he warned. He agreed with Joachim Prinz that freedom was a new experience for Jews and pointed out its challenges. By and large, Jews are neither guided in their daily lives by fixed laws of religion nor restricted by persecutions from leaving the fold. Those with a "yearning" to rejuvenate a lively sense of Jewish meaning and purpose needed a "planned effort to resuscitate whatever life still inheres in the Jewish people, and to re-motivate whatever urge to go on living still remains."[139] Without clear boundaries between Jewish and non-Jewish worlds, Jewish distinctiveness became muddled and confused. And each December, it seemed, despite a century of collective experience, Jews had a hard time clarifying the issue.

Did the effort to instill a will to be Jewish and a "core" Jewish personality take effect in post–World War II children? Had a magnified Hanukkah deflected Christmas's temptations? One study found that, more than any other goal, parents hoped a religious education would instill in their children a strong Jewish identity and pride in Jewry.[140] As postwar Jewish children grew into their teens, they became subjects for study.

In 1961, researcher Irving Cantor thought he spotted a new trend. Instead of assimilating, Jewish teenagers he studied evidenced "selective acculturation," picking and choosing among December's various customs. Most did not consider completely jettisoning Jewish life. Studying 868 teenage members of BBYO (B'nai B'rith Youth Organization), he found that the teens easily articulated their own standards. Although eleven percent reported some kind of Christmas decoration at home, most often a Christmas tree, none displayed a "distinctly religious" Christian symbol such as a nativity scene or a cross. Most teens "rejected Christmas symbols for intra-Jewish purposes." Almost half of them "found it objectionable" to receive Hanukkah cards from Jewish friends because it mimicked a Christmas custom, while more than a third liked it. Less than ten percent attended Christmas parties sponsored by other Jews or sent Christmas gifts or cards to relatives or friends. Forty percent sang Christmas songs, either religious or non-religious—probably at public school. The same percentage discussed Christmas within their BBYO group, although only half that number discussed it with their parents. Most importantly, over ninety percent of the teens reported observing Hanukkah at home, in their BBYO group, or in their synagogue. Cantor concluded that the teens' own sense of a proper boundary between Jewish standards and Christmas practices would ultimately "defeat" not only the "outright acceptance of Christmas" but also the popularity of such sillier Hanukkah creations as "Hanukkah Harry," an imaginary fellow whom some Jewish parents said brought their children's Hanukkah gifts. In both England and the United States, this fiction could be heard. One woman who remembered her postwar childhood in England recalled being told that Harry was Santa Claus's cousin. She happily continued that tradition for her own children, just for the sheer fun of it.[141] But Cantor expected the next generation of parents to let that myth die.

Cantor's study of the members of a Jewish club could hardly reflect the broad general teen population, and other experts soon stepped in to prognosticate. Sociologist Milton Matz used an idea forwarded by social theorist Marcus L. Hansen, who argued that the grandchildren of immigrants are more open to elements of the immigrant culture than are immigrants' own children because they do not feel caught between two worlds. Only a few years earlier, the important Jewish periodical *Commentary* published Hansen's idea, and now Matz applied it to contemporary Jewish teens. They feel fully American, Matz said, and they want a religious identity—something American culture promoted. But teens also considered the decorated tree an attractive American symbol. Although teens did not see it as the marker of Christianity as many of their parents' generation did, Matz expected them to give up Christmas trees as they matured and learned how divisive the trees were among Jews.[142]

Predictions about the future seldom prove accurate. As Prinz pointed out, freedom was a new experience for Jews. How effectively would Jewish educational, religious, and communal groups—forged in the first half of the century—serve Jews into the 1970s and beyond? The American Jewish Committee (AJC), begun in 1906 to defend Jewish rights, funded studies about American Jewish life by esteemed sociologist Marshall Sklare. Choosing to study a suburban Jewish community near Chicago, rather than the dense Jewish worlds in metropolitan New York City, he found that ninety-nine percent believed that to be a good Jew one must promote "civic improvement." Clearly, the AJC of the future would serve Jews who felt responsibilities to both American society and Jewish communities.[143] Sklare also pondered why some Jewish rituals and holidays thrived in the suburbs, while others died. He identified five characteristics shared by the lucky events chosen to be maintained by many suburban Jews. Each one evidenced a capacity to be redefined in modern terms, and none demanded social isolation or the adoption of a unique lifestyle. Indeed, they accorded well with the culture of the larger American community and provided a "Jewish alternative" to American practices when one was felt to be needed. Just as importantly, each was centered on the child and was performed annually or infrequently.[144] Hanukkah shares each attribute. Yet, as we have seen, Hanukkah's special prominence among American Jewry also rested on other distinct characteristics. In each era of Jews' history in the United States, from the early decades of the nineteenth century through the post–World War II era, advocates argued for Hanukkah's special relevance to American Jews, its singular importance to their children, and its special capacity to generate enjoyment in Jewish life. The turbulent sixties were to leave their mark on American Jewry, just as they did on the rest of the nation, but Hanukkah continued to find advocates for its special importance. Nonetheless, after the sixties, Hanukkah was taken in different directions.

7

Hippies, Hasidim, and Havurot

The sixties' political and social upheavals set the stage for different religious values and practices to emerge toward the century's end. Critiques of American society that developed with the civil rights and anti–Vietnam War movements posed significant challenges to the country's sense of a social, political, and legal status quo. New immigration laws enacted during the decade meant that by the year 2000, fifty-six million Americans were either foreign-born or had one foreign-born parent, constituting twenty percent of the U.S. population. Most came from either East Asia or Latin America, bringing new cultures and religions to the country.[1] Among Jews, too, diverse experiences of American life generated more diverse understandings of Hanukkah's significance than in previous years. That diversity included new assessments of Judaism and the nature of its faith in the divine. By the end of the century, in a surprise to most American Jews, one small Jewish mystical group became widely recognized for public Hanukkah celebrations aiming to completely change the quality of American Jews' December experience.

Observers of the postsixties era have called it a "restless" time, when many individuals turned away from communal institutions and felt more "alone," far different from the national mood in the post–World War II era leading to that momentous decade. People who had previously joined myriad Jewish organizations that forged a broad consensus in strong Jewish institutions watched American Jewish life develop in new—and opposing—directions. By the last decade of the century, the Conservative movement lost its premier place as the largest denomination. Its membership dropped from forty-six percent of congregational Jewry to thirty-six percent, as some Jews left for either Orthodoxy on the right or, more often, Reform on the left.[2] In the late century's widely divergent Jewish world, Hanukkah's story about conflict between ancient Jews who differed in the ways that they faced a compelling and powerful gentile society seemed to mirror current realities more than ever before. By the 1990s, American Jewry, like the nation as a whole, looked like a more religiously diverse people, who practiced many "varieties of Jewishness," over which denominational organizations exercised little control.[3] Surprising to many American Jews, interest in highly traditional and even mystical forms of Judaism flourished alongside liberal incarnations that exhibited little traditional religiosity but a strong commitment to Jewish versions of contemporary American values. Jews at opposing ends of the religious spectrum energetically touted Hanukkah, but the similarities and differences in the ways they did so reveal that the holiday remained a uniquely pliable and timely occasion able to promote distinctive visions of American Jewish life.

Dramatic economic shifts in the 1970s and 1980s that shuttered industries in northern cities drew America's population southward and westward. Just prior to World War II, forty percent of America's Jews lived in New York City, with another ten percent in Chicago, and, along with populations in New Jersey, Philadelphia, and Boston, these locations "accounted for the preponderance" of the nation's Jewish population.[4] By the 1990s, by contrast, sixty percent of American Jewry resided outside the Northeast.[5] But the small percentage of Jews who had lived in small towns of the South also found themselves relocating. Big-box discount chain stores drove small, family-owned retail shops out of business and pushed many Jewish families away from the small, southern and midwestern towns that had welcomed them many decades earlier. In Blythedale, Arkansas, for example, Temple Israel disbanded its annual children's festival and congregational Hanukkah party in 1990 because young families had moved away.[6] Together, those trends in the American economy meant that many older Jewish communities felt the ground shift beneath them as national forces swept their members to new locales.

Emerging from the 1960s, a new generation carried Judaism in new directions, bringing new ways to deal with Hanukkah and modifying previous explanations of its significance. In earlier eras, American Jews had expressed their own anxieties for the Jewish future through Hanukkah. Now, more confident than ever before about their place in American society, Jews found in it an array of meanings that reflected a broad swath of Jewish perspectives about the divine, about miracles, about modernity, and about themselves as individuals. Just as in earlier eras, in the latter decades of the twentieth century too, Hanukkah became what people made of it. Now, however, Hanukkah celebrations revealed not only changes in the ways Jews practiced Judaism but also the widening differences between them. One observer who assessed the state of American Jewry at the close of the century judged it to be "a people divided."[7] Not surprisingly, just as American Jews differed on what their relationship to American society ought to be, they also explained Hanukkah's message, meaning, and purpose in different ways and enacted new ways to celebrate the holiday.

Family life shared in an overall disarray affecting many American homes. The country's divorce rate rose sharply, and, as people complained of being overscheduled, family dinners seemed a relic of 1950s nostalgia. Some American religious groups decried the ebbing of "family values." Proponents of more traditional ways of Jewish living found stronger voices as many Americans promoted religion as the answer to their country's ills. For Jews, Hanukkah's ability to bring family members together became increasingly valuable. Synagogues continued to arrange Hanukkah events aimed at children—but now also especially encouraged whole families to participate.

Once again, Hanukkah's timing, its story, its domesticity, and its joyfulness became signal factors in its embrace by American Jews. Ohio's Reform Rabbi Mark Oppenheimer insisted that they could not "overdo the celebration of Chanukah." It not only turns people's "feelings from

winter doldrums to sunny rejoicing"; it also reflects "the acceptance of
. . . Chanukah's theme—freedom to celebrate fully the religion of our
choice." Embellishing Hanukkah is not "the mimicry of our neighbors," as some earlier rabbis had insisted. Instead, he said, by adding to
Hanukkah's activities, Jews show how much its message of freedom of
religion means to them. Since the mid-nineteenth century, American
rabbis had repeated the idea that the Maccabees fought for freedom of
religion, a national ideal enshrined in the First Amendment to the U.S.
Constitution, and so suggested that Judaism itself promoted the country's values and goals. Yet Oppenheimer shifted the language to a more
contemporary attitude. Earlier rabbis touted Jews' freedom to practice
the religion of their fathers or their ancestors; but he hailed freedom
of religious choice. Personal choice and a heightened appreciation for
individual experience emerged from the sixties as key American values,
and Oppenheimer found them also at Hanukkah's core. If we choose
to remain Jewish "in the midst of a world of reasons not to be Jews," he
said, then we can "duplicate" the Hanukkah miracle.[8] Now, although he
echoed the interwar Hanukkah advocates who suggested that the holiday's real miracle was Judaism's survival, he meant a miracle created by
individual Jews who maintain their religious commitments, not by a
divine power. Yet the emphasis on individual choice lent cultural support to those who were seeking new ways to enact their religious lives.

A Jewish Counterculture's Hanukkah

As far back as the nineteenth century, when American rabbis argued
over how Judaism could be maintained in America's open society,
and through the twentieth century, when generations of parents worried about how to keep their children interested in Judaism, Jews
assumed that they might see their religion disappear. Surely, many of
them thought, children imbued with American cultural values and free
to choose any religion, or none, would be unlikely to select Judaism
because it demanded so much that did not fit with the larger culture's
trends. Its Sabbath, for example, asked Jews to "pull the plug" on gentile society and shut off electricity, cars, and jobs for twenty-four hours
every week. Its dietary laws banned such American staples as cheese-
burgers and ham and eggs. Those demands and others like them drove

generations of Jews away from observant living. Most Jews expected their children to respond similarly. Those worries motivated many parents to come up with less demanding styles of Judaism that would hold their children's interest and loyalty.

But when the American counterculture emerged in the sixties, a generation gap marked both the country and Jewry. In 1968, young, counterculture Jews deemed the big synagogues and federations of Jewish agencies that absorbed their parents' energies to be more bourgeois than Jewish. Some of these young Jews, raised with so much care and concern for their Jewishness in the postwar era, rejected the large suburban synagogues they had known as children. Instead, they wove antiestablishment values into Hanukkah celebrations in their own religious fellowships, called *havurot* (Hebrew; singular, *havurah*). By organizing their own groups for religious observances from among their like-minded friends, they refuted the need for both synagogues and ordained rabbis. College-educated people, they trusted their own abilities to study and understand Judaism. Many of them had been raised and educated in Conservative congregations, yet they resisted denominational organizations and preferred to see themselves simply as Jews. Through their informal, communal prayer groups, they strived to create an intimate, supportive, and richly Jewish alternative to the large and impersonal suburban synagogues that each one of them recalled from their childhoods. Although these counterculture *havurah* people constituted only a small percentage of college-age Jews, they were part of the broad generational change in values among young Americans.

Havurah people also believed that the most inspirational Hanukkah celebration would be free of the mass-produced consumer goods through which mainstream Jews enacted their Jewish identity and that were also sold to raise funds for Jewish causes. Instead, they rejected both American commercialism and the large Jewish institutions that required endless fund-raising. They advised other young people to act on very different values. "Forage in the woods to find your own menorah," urged *The Jewish Catalog* in 1973. It is a "nice reason to go into the woods."[9] The *Catalog*'s compilers—Michael Strassfeld, recently graduated from Brandeis University with a major in Judaic studies; Sharon Strassfeld, with whom Strassfeld also compiled two later editions of the *Catalog*; and friend Richard Siegel—counted themselves members of the Jewish counterculture and were *havurah* members. The catalog they produced served the new *havurot* especially well, but it also found a broad readership. "Plug in wherever you want," it told readers, and it offered something for varied interests: halakhic, psychological, mythical, spiritual, and artistic facets of Judaism.[10] The compilers promised a far richer religious experience than could be obtained through buying a menorah from a synagogue gift shop. Judging the ethnic market to be only an arm—and a tool—of the vast, mass-production consumer industry, they urged their readers to bypass it entirely. Jews could obtain a far richer experience by turning to the natural world that God created. At the same time, by crafting objects for their own use, they participated in the broad "do-it-yourself" American subculture that emerged during their childhoods, when suburbanites maintained their homes. Public school "shop" classes for boys trained them in using the simple woodworking tools described in the *Catalog*. Called "one of the key documents to emerge from the Jewish counterculture," *The Jewish Catalog* signaled a different religious perspective as well as a new Jewish aesthetic.[11]

Like most young counterculture people, the compilers prized both personal creativity and the natural world.[12] Those values shaped the publication they produced. For young Jews like them, it seemed that mass-produced items barred an avenue for connection to the divine.[13] They hoped to "get back to nature," as the saying went, to restore their sense of awe. By instructing readers in creating their own ritual objects, *The Jewish Catalog* promised an enriched and personalized religious life. With instructions for making candles and wine (in the section on Shabbat) and dreidels, along with recipes for latkes and cheese dishes, its section on Hanukkah guided a full holiday experience. The compilers' recommend reading list drew on their university educations and suggested new perspectives. Citing leading scholars on religion, they advised readers that the menorah "may be understood as a stylized tree which bears light" and so can function as a "powerful stimulus to . . . religious imagination."[14] *The Jewish Catalog* was modeled on *The Whole Earth Catalog*, the counterculture volume that offered instructions for creatively avoiding mass-produced items, and its compilers promised to enrich Jewish experience by avoiding the consumer society that they felt deadened the soul.

Three experiences motivated these Jewish young people to turn their energies to creative Jewish living. First, they felt comfortable being Jewish in America. This was the case despite continuing antisemitism in the United States. Although the decades immediately after World War II saw a marked decline in antisemitism, it was never eradicated and continued throughout the century. Nearly a thousand "antisemitic incidents nationally, including cemetery desecrations, threats, and arson" occurred during the late 1980s and early 1990s, and openly antisemitic speeches by "militant Black separatists and marginal neo-Nazi hate groups" could be regularly heard.[15] Yet those were fringe sentiments, and mainstream American society did not echo those hostilities. One Jewish activist of that era explained that he felt he "belonged" equally to his Jewish community and American society.[16] Jews had overwhelmingly supported the civil rights movement, and the language of pride in ethnic identity that it generated "spoke" to them. The whole country "experienced a new enthusiasm for ethnic particularism" and expected Jews to "cultivate some distinctiveness."[17] That mood made it easy for college-age Jews to be openly Jewish, something Jews in the first half of the twentieth century only dreamed about. Even after World War II, despite talk of interfaith cooperation, social customs and hiring practices at large firms through the 1950s could be described as following a "gentlemen's agreement" that barred Jews as wells as blacks. Anti-discrimination laws implemented in the sixties, along with a new mood accepting diversity, created a more welcoming atmosphere.

Second, young Jews became aware that they viewed the world somewhat differently from their gentile peers. Although many of them joined the New Left in opposing the war in Vietnam, the New Left's response to the Six-Day War in 1967 revealed a rift between Jewish youth and the larger antiwar movement. As Israel defended itself against attacks by six Arab nations, American Jews feared another Holocaust. The New Left, by contrast, held little sympathy for an Israel that they judged to be only another in a long line of Western imperialist adventures. Jews concluded that they needed to act on their own behalf. Since that war, "thousands of American Jews have gone to Israel for a summer, a semester, or a year of study."[18] Among these young people, a new understanding of Israel's isolation deepened Jewish identity.

Finally, by 1970, more than eighty percent of Jews attended college, and sometimes that experience shaped their attitudes about being Jews.[19] Their university educations sometimes included formal or informal Jewish studies that revealed an intellectually sophisticated and spiritually broad Judaism that their previous, child-oriented religious instruction had lacked. One observer judged that students who enrolled in Jewish studies courses indicated a "willingness . . . to go public with their Jewishness," different from earlier generations of college students.[20] Some of these young people insisted that the boundary between Judaism and Christianity must be more stringently maintained, especially at the Christmas season. The *University Jewish Voice* castigated a mainstream Jewish newspaper in Dallas, Texas, for running Christmas advertising, an act the *Voice* considered "disrespectful of Jewish tradition."[21] Counterculture Jews frequently "accused their elders of failing to adopt a more learned, reflective, and spiritual approach to being Jewish."[22] Hanukkah activities that centered on gift giving and latkes did not earn their respect. These young people purchased *The Jewish Catalog*—130,000 copies sold soon after its release. Together, its three editions sold over a million copies.[23]

In addition, some Jewish faculty modeled an easygoing openness for their Jewish students. In 1945, just after World War II, University of Chicago Hillel director Rabbi Danny Leifer found himself in a debate with two faculty friends to determine whether the latke or the stuffed pastry called *hamantash* eaten on Purim was the more delicious. They enjoyed their conversation so much that they decided to open it to others—Jewish and gentile—at the university. The annual event became a popular occasion when scholars spoofed their own academic methodologies in constructing their arguments. Absurdist topics have ranged from "The Hamantash in Shakespeare" to "The Latke's Role in the Renaissance." Students' votes determined the winner of each annual debate. By the 1970s, other schools joined the fun. The Great Latke-Hamantash Debate became an annual event at many schools and often drew large interfaith crowds of students and faculty.[24]

The first counterculture *havurah* began in 1968, but adventurous denominations and synagogues organized small prayer groups as early as 1960. By 1963, ten *havurot* counted themselves in the Reconstructionist camp. California's Reform Rabbi Harold Schulweiss believed *havurot* could rejuvenate interest among congregants who belonged to

very large synagogues but spent little time in them. Through his influence, by 1975, some five hundred *havurot* existed in that state alone.
As many as "twenty percent of American synagogues had at least one
havurah"; the figure doubled for California. Synagogue-based *havurot*
usually did not hold their own Saturday-morning worship so as not to
compete with the synagogue.

Young Jews in the counterculture created independent *havurot* in
order to harmonize Judaism with their own values. Beginning in Boston and New York City, and soon in Philadelphia and Washington, D.C.,
many of these early *havurah*-niks had attended the Conservative movement's Ramah summer camps. Some were children of rabbis. Members
expected the *havurah* experience to combine holiday celebrations and
religious learning with the warm, friendly, community support reminiscent of summer camps. They preferred these leaderless small groups
where they could tailor religious worship and holiday celebrations to fit
their own values and interests. Often, they used lively melodies drawn
from Hasidic traditions which they had learned at camp or in university rather than from the songbooks produced and marketed to synagogue religious schools by Reform or Conservative presses. The mystical Jewish movement called Hasidism (pietism) arose in eastern Europe
in the eighteenth century and rapidly drew adherents to its joyous style
of worship. Hasidic music offered an authentically Jewish alternative to
the melodies that *havurah* young people had learned in synagogue religious schools and that sometimes bored them.

Since the sixties, musical tastes identified various American subcultures, and young *havurah* Jews explored Jewish music just as new
avenues to Hasidic music became available. As in the past, Hanukkah
became an occasion for Jews to enjoy Jewish music, and in the late sixties, a new interest in Hasidic music became increasingly evident. Rabbi
Schlomo Carlebach, an Orthodox rabbi who had adopted the Hasidic
world before undertaking a public career in Jewish music, visited campuses, synagogues, and Jewish communities in North America and
Israel to teach traditional Hasidic melodies along with his own original
songs.[25] In 1971, ethnomusicologist Velvel Pasternak judged the time
ripe for publication of his two-volume anthology of Hasidic music. He
also founded Tara Books, which specialized in Jewish musical traditions. Hasidic music, Pasternak said, "is a living testament" that bears

eloquent witness to the "conviction that the sacred encompasses all of life."[26] Along with Carlebach's more than twenty-five record albums, Pasternak provided resources that enabled counterculture Jews to incorporate Hasidic music into their own groups, enlivening their own worship gatherings without joining the Hasidic world. When the Milken Archive of Jewish Music began producing CD compilations in 1990, it included one called *Echoes of Ecstasy* devoted to melodies inspired by Hasidic traditions. Six years later, Six Degrees Records, which produced world, folk, and contemporary classical music, produced a compilation for Hanukkah filled with updated uses of Hasidic melodies; another similar compilation appeared three years later.[27] Interest in Hasidic style, in other words, moved well beyond its own communities.

A number of students learned about Hasidic religious attitudes in their college classrooms. Philosopher Martin Buber's classic study of Judaism's imagining of the human encounter with the divine, *I and Thou*, found a broad readership in Jewish studies programs and in general classes in philosophy of religion. Buber drew heavily on Hasidic perspectives. His *Tales of the Hasidim* also found a place in university libraries and curricula. When these ideas moved out of the Hasidic world that framed them with the authority of biblical and Talmudic teachings and communal customs, the critical, analytical approaches of university scholarship encouraged students to assess them according to different intellectual standards. Those scholarly challenges made them exciting, especially for students accustomed to simplistic, elementary school versions of Jewish thought. People who had obtained those educational experiences tended to be more open to the theological explanations for divine power at work in the Maccabean effort, rather than the political and social understandings that had reigned among American Jews since the mid-nineteenth century.

Other intellectual currents also opened a door to Hasidic ideas. More philosophical critiques of Jewish theology in light of the Holocaust, such as Richard Rubenstein's controversial *After Auschwitz*, questioned a theistic conception of God and urged a close analysis of the human condition. "Our experience of tragedy, guilt, conflict, and the inherent limitations of human decency have been far too profound to warrant rejecting existentialism's insights as irrelevant," he argued. He agreed with Kierkegaard that "religious life hovers over a sea of doubt."[28] Now,

Judaism shared in the "death of God" trend that some Protestant thinkers asserted, but Rubenstein carefully maintained that for Judaism, it meant the end of any meaningful and convincing way to talk about a theistic God who acts morally, not the actual death of the divine itself. Published by Bobbs-Merrill's college division, Rubenstein's book nonetheless reached lay readers and stirred so much controversy that he became "virtually unemployable" as a rabbi, despite ordination from the Jewish Theological Seminary and training at Harvard University. Instead, Rubenstein found an academic home at Florida State University.[29] A decade later, Holocaust theologian Irving Greenberg called the Holocaust the "most radical countertestimony to religious faith, both Jewish and Christian."[30] Buber's description of the experience of a personal encounter with the divine remained compelling, because it discussed an experience-based encounter with the holy that bypassed the Holocaust's challenge to the theistic view of God as the judge of history.

The Jewish Student Press Service that flourished on more than sixty campuses shared news from a broad network of young people who combined Jewish values with social action. It spread news about *havurot* to its readers. In the early, 1967–1972, period of counterculture *havurot* creativity, the movement probably never drew more than twenty-five hundred, but through the *Catalog* and the Jewish Student Press Service and the eventual career choices of some of its leaders, it influenced broader trends in late-twentieth-century American Jewish life.[31] In Philadelphia, one Conservative congregation shared its space with a *havurah* that grew so large by 1981 that it divided into three different groups that met together only for special occasions such as life-cycle celebrations and some holidays. These lay-led groups implemented a broad range of approaches to Jewish practice. Four years later, the National Havurah Committee brought together both independent and synagogue-based *havurot* under one umbrella.[32] Independent or semi-independent prayer groups continued to flourish into the twenty-first century.

Many *havurot* members also espoused the egalitarian views promulgated by the era's women's movement, despite a sometimes bumpy ride in implementing them. Future rabbi Art Waskow lent his name to a piece in *The Jewish Catalog* called "How to Bring Moshiach" (Messiah), which was entirely written by women and advocated enhanced rights

and roles for them. In the wake of Betty Friedan's powerful 1963 description of what she termed "the feminine mystique," which kept American
women from the jobs and financial resources available to men, Jewish
women articulated some of the women's movement's core perspectives
and goals. They challenged Jewish organizations, and enhanced roles
for women soon became standard. The Reconstructionist Rabbinical College welcomed women since its inception in 1968, and Reform's
Hebrew Union College ordained America's first woman rabbi in 1972.
After years of lengthy debate, the Conservative Jewish Theological Seminary also ordained women. By 1990, all Jewish groups benefited from
the markedly higher degree of Jewish education among women under
age forty. It is fair to say that no previous generation of women had
benefited so broadly from a formal education in Judaism. In the willingness of each of these Jewish subgroups to see women's equality as
a religious value, they embraced and promoted a new value reshaping
American society.[33]

By the 1980s, some younger, college-educated Jews, women and men,
joined small religious groups that brought Hasidic singing, dancing,
and mystical teachings into their worship. Loosely led by Polish-born
Zalman Schachter-Shalomi, they used *havurah*-style communities to
develop what they called Jewish Renewal, a movement to "re-energize
Jewish piety by making it more emotionally satisfying, inclusive, exper-
imental, experiential, and compelling."[34] Carlebach's work also provided inspiration. A decade later, this movement supported a journal
called *Menorah: Sparks of Jewish Renewal*, utilizing the image of sparks
of divine light that Jewish mystical traditions describe as scattered
through the world and in its people, especially in Jews.[35]

An umbrella organization called ALEPH: Alliance for Jewish Renewal formed in 1993 to coordinate and provide resources for its member groups. Its 1994 Hanukkah messages offered "kabbalistic musings"
about darkness and light drawn from Judaism's mystical teachings,
along with advice on protecting the earth through focused candle lighting, urging people to concentrate on the act of candle lighting as they
conducted the rite. This organization, too, viewed the natural world
as a vehicle for spiritual growth. Yet, like the NFTS of earlier decades,
the organization's journal also urged readers to order Hanukkah gifts

from it. Hanukkah's decades-old capacity to generate funds for Jewish purposes could not be ignored by this young and small organization. It promised readers that a purchase from ALEPH would incur a "triple mitzvah"—an act that provided spiritual benefits three ways. Using the authority of the biblical and Talmudic language of religious commandment (mitzvah), it explained the triple mitzvah this way: "heartening the lives of yourself and your friends; supporting the writers and artists [of the journal] and supporting Aleph."[36]

The New Hasidim Enjoin Hanukkah Debates

Both Carlebach and Schachter-Shalomi shared a sense of mission that characterized the Chabad Lubavitch, the Hasidic group among whom both men had lived and worshiped for a time. In eighteenth-century Europe, distinct Hasidic dynasties developed around different rebbes, but only Chabad undertook a mission to "seek out other Jews in order to . . . bring them into the [fully observant] fold."[37] At least half a dozen different Hasidic traditions thrived in the United States, most of whose followers arrived during or immediately after World War II. By the 1980s, they constituted roughly five percent of the eight to ten percent of the American Jews considered Orthodox.[38] Believing that each Jew retains "a spark of Judaism and is worthy of reformation," Chabad seeks out Jews for chance encounters that might kindle interest in the faith. It sees its work as part of "loving one's fellow Jew as oneself."[39] The mission to increase all Jews' level of religious observance defined Chabad's self-identity. Its use of singing and dancing to heighten devotion in worship had attracted many followers in eastern Europe—some historians think it especially appealed to young people.[40]

In the United States, Chabad conducted outreach in Jewish areas and on college campuses. Interest in Chabad among some former student radicals astounded members of San Diego's Reform Congregation Beth Israel. In November 1973, they invited the University of California–Los Angeles Hillel director and a graduate student from the University of California–San Diego to speak to the congregation about it. "A few years ago young Jews carrying placards against war in Vietnam, now are inhabitants of Chabad house or Jewish communes," they pointed out to congregants in advance of the talk. Hoping to attract both synagogue members and college students from the nearby campus, they offered refreshments to attendees.[41]

Some Americans reacted against what seemed in the sixties and seventies to be a breakdown of social mores by advocating a larger role for religion in the public arena. The growing respect for religion and religious language in American public discourse emboldened Chabad to stage public Hanukkah rites. It did not aim for a simple display of a Hanukkah menorah, as did some postwar Jews, but to conduct a full ritual candle-lighting ceremony and to create a festive Hanukkah celebration open to the general public. One ethnologist who studied Chabad summed up its attitude this way: "If anybody else can display whatever they want to, why do we have to be shy?"[42] Despite being one of the country's smallest religious groups, Chabad nonetheless undertook a mission to increase all Jews' level of religious observance. Toward that goal, it brought public menorah lighting to new heights that elicited new rulings from the U.S. Supreme Court.

In 1974, Chabad set up the first of its annual gigantic Hanukkah menorahs for a public lighting at a community celebration of Hanukkah in Philadelphia's Independence Mall, near the Liberty Bell. The following year, it lighted one at the opposite end of the country, in San Francisco, and many new lightings emerged after that. In 1978, Lubavitch Rebbe Menahem M. Schneerson urged his emissaries to erect gigantic Hanukkah lamps around the world as a way not only to publicize the miracle but also to further the Lubavitch goal of "spreading the wellsprings" of Hasidism. In 1979, Chabad erected a thirty-foot menorah in Lafayette Park near the White House. President Jimmy Carter, then consumed with the Iran hostage crisis, attended the lighting and delivered a speech about the "forces of light and darkness." Chabad's menorah design replicates one created by the eleventh-century rabbinic leader and philosopher Moses Ben Maimon (Maimonides), rather than the more common, rounded shape which also is seen in the large, seven-branched menorah that stands outside Israel's parliament (Knesset) building. Chabadniks are not Zionists.[43] Within their own communities, Lubavitchers strive to perform deeds of kindness as well as every Jewish ritual, each one of which, they believe, will help bring the

Messiah. For example, one Brooklyn Hasidic teenage girl brought a large box of jelly doughnuts to a local hospital so that patients might have a Hanukkah treat. Were many of the patients too ill to eat doughnuts? No matter. She felt sure her act would hasten the Messiah's arrival. "Moshiach [Messiah] will be here soon, and all the sick will be healed, and all the dead will be brought to life," she assured the interviewer who asked her about it.[44] Local Chabad leaders came to see the new custom of lighting gigantic menorahs in public squares as an ideal way to further their goal of enticing Jews to take a greater interest in their religion and, ultimately, to invigorate American Jewish life.

Chabad publications supported its Hanukkah outreach efforts. Schneerson explained that Hanukkah's story provided members with a vivid way to understand their own lives. "Let's picture ourselves members of the little band of Hasmoneans," he began. Since the mid-nineteenth century, most American rabbis had asked Jews to identify with the Hasmoneans, and in this Schneerson echoed what had become the American Hanukkah heritage. But he soon diverged sharply from his forebears outside the Lubavitch camp. Whereas other rabbis encouraged Jews to understand the Maccabees as fighters for religious freedom, a value that legitimated Jews' place in America, Schneerson asked readers to see things very differently. He asked them to admit their discomfort. "We are under the domination of a powerful Syrian King," he said. He not only erased differences between the U.S. government and Antiochus IV; his imaginative construction equated them: both are powerful, and neither is guided by Judaism's teachings. The very fact that so few American Jews maintained an Orthodox Jewish life seemed to support his contention that America exerted a pernicious power over them. Like the ancient Hellenists, he said, "many of our brethren have left us and accepted idolatry as a way of life." But he did not ostracize those Jews as did other, more inward-looking Hasidim and Orthodox practitioners. Instead, Hanukkah's story provided him with metaphors for explaining their situation. Their inner "sanctuary"—their "attachment to and identification with God"—had been "invaded and contaminated." Hanukkah, he said, reminds us that "the greatest danger to the Jewish way of life" lies in "defil[ing] it" with what he called "unholy oil."[45] Schneerson's followers understood him to mean rational universalistic ideals accepted by many unaffiliated Jews as well as by those in liberal branches of Judaism, such as Reform, Reconstructionist, and Conservative. Those people were the central focus of Chabad's mission.

Chabad's sense of mission distinguished it from most Jewish groups, but some others agreed that observant Jews carried a responsibility to help their lax coreligionists take up more of Judaism's practices. Orthodox Rabbi Bernard A. Poupko, for example, encouraged observant Jews to help the nonobservant "banish some of the darkness of religious illiteracy and . . . complacency from [their] home[s]." In a 1974 collection of sermons by Orthodox rabbis, he pointed out that the rabbinic sage called the Chofetz Chaim (Hebrew: Seeker of Life; Yisrael Meir Kagan, 1838–1933) taught that if a Jew has "just enough oil for the eight days of Chanukah . . . and his neighbor has none at all, let him share his oil with his neighbor even though, as a result of it, he will be able to kindle only one light" each night. Such generosity was especially important in light of a recent decision by Orthodox rabbis that electric menorahs did not fulfill the requirement of lighting a fire each evening. The Chofetz Chaim's ruling, Poupko explained, shows the importance of "involv[ing] another Jew in the performance of a mitzvah even when it will reduce one's own status" as a highly observant Jew.[46] Some among the Orthodox aimed to shape their American Jewish lives to reflect those they recalled or read about existing in pre–World War II Europe. They looked inward, strengthening their own communities, educating their children in their own private schools, and avoiding contact with less observant Jews. They weighted each holiday's importance according to its Talmudic designation. Hanukkah engaged far less of their energy than did more religiously significant events, such as the Sabbath, the High Holidays, or, among the festivals, Passover and Sukkot.

Poupko's remarks addressed the dramatic changes in American Orthodoxy since World War II. Enrollment in Orthodox Jewish schools jumped from fourteen thousand in 1946 to approximately sixty-seven thousand children in 330 schools by the beginning of the 1970s, and they existed "within nearly every Jewish community larger than 7500."[47] Women and men benefited. By 1990, Orthodox women under age forty were ten times more likely to have obtained a day-school education than were Orthodox women over sixty.[48] Yet many of these graduates left the larger Orthodox synagogues behind to form their own, smaller congregations, where they worshiped among others who maintained equally punctilious levels of devotion. Poupko deplored that situation. Although individuals may achieve a "higher level of . . . spiritual ecstasy" praying only among like-minded, highly observant people, they are ignoring an ethical duty, he said. By depriving others of the good example and influence they might provide, they are robbing them of their "ancestral possession." Hanukkah especially "demands" that Jews "deny" themselves the "prestige and joy" of being "super observant" in order that they "share [their] oil with those that have none." That is the real meaning of the command to publicize the miracle, Poupko told readers. In the closing decades of the century, Orthodox Jews found themselves choosing between congregations with higher standards of observance or leaving for those aligned with the more liberal Conservative movement. Orthodoxy had moved right, but Poupko deplored its inwardness, feeling it revealed little regard for the religious well-being of other Jews.[49]

As American Jewry divided into highly observant and minimally observant camps, the Chabad Lubavitch Hasidim stood out. They acted on their felt obligation toward less observant Jews. Schneerson told his followers—people already committed to Chabad's mission —that Hanukkah's story advised them on how to reach the less faithful. "We must always be like that faithful band of Hasmoneans," he said. Lubavitchers must "remember that there is always a drop of . . . pure olive oil" hidden deep in the heart of every Jew, which, if kindled, "bursts into a big flame." Those flames "must and will pierce the darkness of our present night, until every one of us will behold the fulfillment of our prophets' promise for our ultimate redemption."[50] Hanukkah provided Lubavitch Hasidim with a way to lend their mission the authority of divine rescue drawn from Jews' ancient past. Hanukkah also gave Lubavitchers an image with which to understand their own identity, made especially vivid then. A Hasid "is like a street lamp lighter," Schneerson said. Because the soul is like a candle of God, a Hasid lights up "the souls of Jews with the light of torah and *mitzvot*."[51]

Chabad made special use of Jewish holidays in its task of enticing Jews to greater observance. The group in Skokie, Illinois, for example, invited people to regular Sabbath meals and observances, including Saturday-evening coffee houses. The Friday-evening events included dinner along with religious services, as well as a lecture on a topic that explained Chabad's views. By 1985, the Skokie group renovated and enlarged its Chabad House for these activities (referring to it as a house made it less intimidating) and named it after a local benefactor. But public, holiday-linked events that drew curious onlookers improved Chabad's chances of kindling Jewish "sparks." These occasions supplemented the Chabad vans, sometimes dubbed "mitzvah tanks," which could be driven to various areas where Jews might be found, such as Miami Beach's famed Lincoln Road, a broad pedestrian boulevard with restaurants and shopping. Chabad men invite male Jewish passersby into the van to recite daily prayers and to receive a ritual object—small Hanukkah menorahs for them and pairs of Sabbath candle holders for their wives.

Hanukkah's rule to "publicize the miracle" by placing lighted menorahs in doorways or where they could be seen by the public served Chabad's goals well. The huge menorahs Chabad erected in public squares made news, and local newspapers and television stations reported on them.[52] "These Menorahs have been singularly successful in reminding Jews of the festival of Chanukah and encouraging a feeling of pride in being part of the Jewish people," Schneerson said. They also provided excellent publicity for Chabad. The public menorahs also accomplished another, more political goal. They conveyed to "all citizens," he said, "the Chanukah message of the triumph of freedom over the forces of oppression."[53] The first evening's menorah lighting in Chicago's Daley Plaza that year anchored a choreographed event that framed the ritual in a total ceremony that seemed to provide American support for Hanukkah. While the Chabad rabbi who oversaw its Illinois activities lighted the huge menorah, a local alderman served as master of ceremonies in an event that included speeches from "civic dignitaries." To create the cheery mood of a Hanukkah celebration, a local klezmer band played Jewish musical selections, and Chabad members served hot latkes to the assembled crowd. Chabad added an additional light each night. Finally, Chabad distributed five thousand Hanukkah menorahs for "personal use to Jews in hospitals, nursing homes, religious schools, prisons, and on the street."[54]

Chabad's Hanukkah events performed a Jewish aesthetic based on the group's own self-identity as authentic emissaries of eastern European

Jewish religious tradition. Since the Middle Ages, when clothing styles identified one's class, gender, and labor, many areas of Europe demanded that Jews wear identifying markers. Over time, clothing became one more aspect of Jewish identity. Biblical and Talmudic strictures further constrained Jewish choices. Among Chabad, men and women dress modestly in subdued tones and keep their heads covered. Men do not shave. The long fringes of their *tallit kattan* (ritual undershirt whose fringes remind Jewish males of religious commandments) are visible. Yet, because Chabad aims to interact with modern Jews, Lubavitchers' attire also reflects contemporary styles. Chabad men wear black suits with white shirts and wide-brimmed, black fedora hats, a relatively modern fashion. Those choices seem au currant when compared to the knee socks, short pants, and large, fur-trimmed hats called *streimels* preferred for special occasions by Satmar Hasidim, who avoid contact with both unobservant Jews and gentiles. The clothing of the Satmar Hasidim marks them as people with no interest in accommodating the tastes of the broader society. Unlike Satmar, Chabad invites conversation.

Standing in a municipal plaza and flanked by civil dignitaries, the Chabad spectacle presents an image of American society endorsing the fully observant Jewish practices that are being modeled. Handing out hot latkes to everyone in the crowd, Lubavitchers invite Jewish and gentile spectators to eat together, a nearly universal practice to mark shared openness and mutual regard. Moreover, their generosity seems to echo the motto of "goodwill to men" so often touted at Christmas. America's cultural calendar sets this season for lighthearted, friendly celebrations, and Chabad's public events convey Judaism's own version of those practices. The public celebrations offer Hanukkah's rite itself as the ideal way for Jews to enjoy the country's happy December mood. They imply, by contrast, that the enthusiastic Hanukkah gift giving which for many decades American Jews had promoted as the way to bring the Jewish holiday in line with the larger national activity was an irrelevant diversion.

In Pittsburgh, in December 1989, Chabad placed its eighteen-foot-tall menorah along with a sign proclaiming a "Salute to Religious Liberty" next to a forty-five-foot tall decorated Christmas tree on the steps of the city courthouse. A nativity scene had been set up inside the courthouse. When the American Civil Liberties Union objected to all three displays because they exhibited religious symbols on government property, the Supreme Court agreed to hear the case. Justice Brennan explained the Court's decision to allow both menorah and tree. While the crèche clearly endorsed particular religious beliefs by displaying images of divinities, which the court banned from the courthouse, the religious meaning of the two other items seemed less obvious. While each item, tree and menorah, might be seen as particular religious symbols under some circumstances, when they are displayed together, that is not necessarily the case. "The menorah here stands next to a Christmas tree and a sign saluting liberty," he wrote. That turns the display into "simply a recognition of cultural diversity." The objects remained.[55] Like the much smaller menorah and decorated tree that had adorned Mayor Lindsey's New York City Hall in the sixties, these two gigantic versions in Pittsburgh created a single visual message that said more about seasonal diversity than religious faith. Alone, each one is an emblem of a religion, but paired they become a unit that conveys a message about good interreligious relations.

While other lawsuits against the display of menorahs and other religious items on public land sometimes drew different rulings, this High Court judgment pointed a way forward for Chabad. It allowed gigantic Hanukkah menorahs to be erected and lighted in cities around the country, although legal challenges continued. Some Jews felt that Chabad opened "a dangerous can of worms" that could undermine religious freedoms. Others viewed Chabad's actions as "aggressive exhibitionism" not authorized by Jewish tradition.[56] The president of Reform's Central Conference of American Rabbis implored Rebbe Schneerson to end the practice because it jeopardized constitutional limitations on governmental interference in religion.[57] Only about a third of Jews approved of erecting menorahs in public places. By contrast, American non-Jews felt positively about it by a much higher percentage—four-fifths of white Americans and three-fifths of black Americans favored it.[58] We have no figures about the displays' impact on Jews' personal decisions about worship or about the degree to which those who did take up a more observant lifestyle—a trend noticed with some shock —had been influenced by Lubavitch's Hanukkah activities.[59] Nonetheless, by the end of the century, these events became fixtures in the season's calendar.

The increasing national acceptance of lighted Hanukkah menorahs can also be marked by a parallel acceptance of them in the White House. In 1979, as we have seen, Jimmy Carter walked to Lafayette Park to join the lighting of the new "National Menorah" erected there by Chabad members. A decade later, when George H. W. Bush received a menorah from the Synagogue Council of America, he chose to display it within the White House. Taking things further, Bill Clinton invited school-children into the Oval Office for a small candle-lighting ceremony and photo opportunity.[60] Later presidents have continued and embellished this custom.

Once the Supreme Court determined that when the decorated Christmas tree and the Hanukkah menorah are placed together, they convey a different message than when either one is displayed alone, public schools could create a festive atmosphere with less fear of legal problems. As early as 1972, the San Diego school district established a policy of "simple non-sectarian and nondenominational" programs and plays, which typified this solution. The three rabbis at Reform Congregation Beth Israel asked their congregants to contact them about any problems their children encountered.[61] That year, the American Jewish Committee issued its guidelines for parents to bring to their schools to be sure that Jewish children did not feel "pressure[d] . . . into action inconsistent with their beliefs." Public school teachers should not be offering religious instruction, the AJC said, presumably because they are not trained in religions. Listing three kinds of activities that should be avoided, it included nativity scenes, clergy offering religious teaching in classrooms, and religious songs.[62] The AJC worried most about direct indoctrination, rather than the simple presence of a Christmas tree or menorah.

Variations in local standards created different school experiences for Jewish students. In a Buffalo, New York, suburb, a very Catholic area, for example, no Bible readings occurred in public schools of the 1950s. Catholics read a different Bible translation and canon than Protestants and discourage Bible study without the guidance of Catholic clergy. On that basis, they had won a legal ban on Bible readings in public schools many decades earlier. Yet daily Bible readings remained standard fare in New York City into the 1960s. In Miami a decade later, Easter assemblies still reenacted Christ's death on the cross, complete with blanket condemnations of Jews. Moreover, in parts of both Georgia and Pennsylvania, students in the early twenty-first century still sing religious Christmas carols each year.[63]

Despite pronouncements by Jewish defense organizations, when it came to music, it is unclear just how pressured or uncomfortable Jewish children actually felt. The future chancellor of the Jewish Theological Seminary recalled no special anxieties. He simply did not sing any specifically Christian lyrics, such as the final three words to "O Come All Ye Faithful" ("Christ the Lord").[64] At least one Jewish public high school music instructor determined that if the students were to sing Christian music at a December concert, then it would be the best Christian music. Rather than carols, each year, the "Hallelujah Chorus" from Handel's oratorio *The Messiah* more than satisfied the audience's desire for real Christmas music despite a repertoire of tunes otherwise heavy on snow and reindeer.[65]

Hanukkah Devotion amid New Challenges

While the Supreme Court determined the religious content allowed in public spaces, rabbis felt confident in their own authority to guide Jews' domestic religious lives. Like a century of American rabbis before them, they denounced Christmas trees in Jewish homes. But now armed with social-scientific analyses of American Jews' religious practices, they grew more alarmed than ever. In the early decades of the twentieth century, Jews who brought Christmas trees into their homes usually did so simply for fun. In 1971, however, when the UAHC completed a study of its movement, it found that although only less than ten percent of respondents had Christmas trees in their homes, it symbolized their "integration into a Predominantly Christian milieu." More disturbing, these people were younger, were much less likely to light Sabbath candles, and were somewhat less likely to light Hanukkah menorahs. While more than ninety percent of the families that did not have Christmas trees lighted menorahs, only fifty-two percent of those that did have Christmas trees did so.[66] Because the trend showed less interest in Hanukkah among younger adults, Reform Jewish organizations continued to combat the appeal of Christmas by increasing Hanukkah's fun factor without decorated trees. A Kansas City, Missouri, chapter of the NFTS submitted directions for a successful Hanukkah party that the national group printed in its monthly newsletter. Loaded with crafts, games, costumes, foods, sweets, and a bibliography listing seventeen Hanukkah books for adults and six for children, it updated the efforts of earlier generations of women who passed knowledge about children's parties among themselves through their national organizations.[67]

As in the past, many Jews strived to imbue home celebrations with greater meaning. By the 1970s, few rabbis felt the need to promote Hanukkah gift giving, as this practice had become so widely accepted that many rabbis felt uneasy about the degree to which gifts and goods had taken a central place in many families' holiday practices. More often, they refocused attention on the rite itself. "Only during the actual lighting of the candles is there a true feeling of holiness," counseled Rabbi Morrison Bial. His two-hundred-page *Liberal Judaism at Home* provided guidance and advice on domestic religious practices accepted as standard by the Reform movement. A congregational rabbi for many years who also taught modern Jewish thought at Reform's seminary, Bial authored a number of advice books to guide Reform Jews in raising their children. His Hanukkah discussion admitted, "In our desire to counteract the lure of Christmas we have added extensive gift-giving, decorations of the house, and a sense of . . . importan[ce]" to Hanukkah.[68] But those efforts may have distorted the holiday. Like the counterculture young Jews, this rabbi objected to the importance given to Hanukkah gifts, rather than to its rite. Now, he tried to rein in efforts to reshape Hanukkah that had been touted by rabbis in previous generations. His work signaled the attention to problems in Jewish home life that seemed to grow increasingly complex as the century drew to a close.

Jews also participated in a "domestic revolution" under way across the country in the late twentieth century as economic challenges pulled wives and mothers into the paid labor force. From the 1950s to the 1990s, "the fraction of women who work[ed] outside the home doubled from fewer than one in three to nearly two in three," writes sociologist Robert Putnam.[69] Although we do not have figures for the national rate of Jewish women's participation in the paid labor force in 1950, by 1990 they were slightly more likely than gentile women to be employed. Most Jewish women entered the labor force later than American women as a whole.[70]

Social trends away from extended family that marked postwar Jews' experience continued to hammer away at family life later in the century. Across America, "mobility, divorce and smaller families . . . reduced the relative importance of kinship ties, especially among the more educated" after 1970. Jews continued to have smaller families than non-Hispanic whites, and because both Jewish men and women customarily at least finished college and frequently completed graduate degrees, they tended to marry later. Jewish families underwent some of the same changes experienced by other Americans. The American divorce rate doubled from 1965 to a peak of fifty percent in the decade from 1975 to 1985. Yet the decline in the number of divorces after 1985 might be related to the larger number of cohabiting couples who never marry and so need not divorce when they part, rather than to any improvement in marriage stability rates.[71] Among Jews, in 1970, married couples constituted four-fifths of households: the divorce rate reached only five percent. But their divorce rate rose. By 2000, twenty-one percent of Jews had experienced a divorce.[72]

Those stresses on work and family life dramatically affected women's organizations. During the 1970s, the Women's League for Conservative Judaism saw its membership drop by fifty thousand. Early in the decade, it adapted the language of second-wave feminism—in which Jewish women played a prominent role—to claim that their seemingly old-fashioned commitments remained relevant. Like feminists, the WLCJ's president told members, "our challenge is consciousness-raising of our listeners to . . . needs of our time." WLCJ women freely chose their volunteer responsibilities, she said. Therefore, "Hanukkah . . . seems to have a special message for women today" because it celebrates "liberty." Yet, as Americans complained of always feeling too busy, "time" became a key term. The WLCJ gave its members a rhetoric by which to defend their sisterhood work. Merging feminist language with religious values, it said, "True freedom is . . . [the] right . . . to choose how we will spend our time. . . . We choose to use our time as volunteers to . . . strengthen . . . the Jewish family, . . . to fulfill its ancient functions with new meaning and strength." That way, the WLCJ hoped to "make the

As the Soviet Jewry movement struggled to obtain rights for Jews living in the Soviet Union, those who could obtain permission to travel became important emissaries. Here, Feige Shkolnik, whose husband, Isaak, had been imprisoned, was given the honor of lighting a large Hanukkah menorah at the Jewish Museum in New York City. (Courtesy American Jewish Historical Society)

world a better place."[73] Although it lost members, still, 150,000 women participated in seven hundred sisterhood chapters, and it remained a lively force among Conservative Jews.

What was a Jewish family? The changing family statistics confused some people, but not the WLCJ. It offered a "Credo": "The core is the husband-wife, father-mother relationship." Divorce can be prevented not only by psychological compatibility but also by compatibility in Judaism. A "family should look to Jewish sources for its guidance." Parents should be role models for their children in living Jewish lives. But communication among all family members is key, it insisted. Everyone "should be involved in determining how the family will live out its Jewish life."[74]

The Reform movement handled the changing Jewish demographic

differently. In 1983, the Central Conference of American Rabbis issued a "Resolution on Patrilineal Descent" stipulating that any child with a Jewish parent who is being actively raised Jewish would be considered a Jew in Reform synagogues. By the dawn of the new millennium, "about half of all marriages involving Jews [were] mixed marriages." As Jews constitute less than 2.4 percent of the U.S. population, this is really not very surprising. Yet, because Jewish life is so thoroughly embedded in family life, the numbers challenged Jews to think in novel ways. Noting that America's tolerant society encouraged "each partner to maintain his or her own distinctive, pre-marriage identity," Reform strived to bring all parties in a mixed marriage into synagogue life and extended its education outreach especially to them.[75]

Many American Jews looked to domestic holidays such as Hanukkah and Passover to enhance what seemed to be their increasingly complicated home lives. It is no surprise that guides to Jewish living especially proliferated in this era. Rabbis and women's groups already accustomed to publishing these items continued to produce them. Reform rabbis compiled both prayer books and guides—a "beloved" Passover Haggadah became their best seller. But a High Holiday book for young children also sold well. A Hanukkah guide included the candle-lighting liturgy and additional readings, along with musical selections, instructions for playing dreidel, and latke recipes. The WRJ (successor to the NFTS) assured its members that the guide would be "cherished" in their families for "years to come," becoming an object that marked both the holiday and their family's religious identity.[76]

In the mid 1980s, the Conservative movement's Federation of Jewish Men's Clubs responded to the increasing stresses on family life and joined the growing trend toward adult education that had begun in the postwar suburbs, by producing practical guides to Jewish life—texts, workbooks, and audio tapes—on many subjects. Its "Art of Jewish Living" series, which provided many examples of Jewish-themed family activities, proved especially popular. Following up its Shabbat seder guide with one for the Passover seder, in 1990 it published a volume on Hanukkah that filled nearly two hundred pages and carried the postwar innovation of Hanukkah manuals to new heights. Its compiler, Rabbi Ron Wolfson, an instructor and later vice president of the University of Judaism, described himself as a "family educator." He also led a national

A Christian grandfather joins his Jewish grandson in lighting Hanukkah candles during a visit in Presque Isle, Maine. (Courtesy Debra M. Faye)

effort to invigorate synagogues and to make them "spiritual centers." His Hanukkah volume displayed his commitment to addressing the needs of real Jewish families and helping them to build their own Jewish lives. Wolfson drew on his own experience as a *havurah* member and viewed Jewish religious life as a creative activity, rather than one which implemented practices and laws commanded by God. To help Jewish families infuse religion and spirituality into their Hanukkah creations, Wolfson, like the authors of most Hanukkah guides before him, included lengthy discussions of Antiochus's oppression, the cultural conflict with Hellenism, and the Maccabean revolt. Songs, especially "Maoz Tsur" and "Rock of Ages," as well as recipes and games, also filled many pages of his book. But his interviews with several families who recounted their own particular customs supported his volume's insistence that families need to "evolve [their] own answers to the December Dilemmas" that challenged Jews to make Hanukkah into an especially meaningful event. Wolfson also recalled his own personal experience as a Jewish child confronting Christmas. Upon reflection, he concluded that, ironically, "Christmas heightens the awareness of one's Jewishness almost as much as any single Jewish holiday." It provides the first awareness that as a Jew, one is not like "almost everyone else."[77]

The families Wolfson interviewed for his book included those in which one parent either practiced Christianity or converted from Christianity to Judaism. These families experienced a distinctive December dilemma. By 1990, only sixty-eight percent of all "currently married born Jews were married to someone also born Jewish," while another four percent were married to someone who converted to Judaism. Another twenty-eight percent had married gentiles. Intermarried couples "were twice as likely to divorce" as in-married couples. Even among gentile Americans, marriages between members of different religions are far more likely to end in divorce than are in-marriages.[78] And, for Jews who married between 1990 and 2001, fifty percent chose a non-Jewish spouse.[79] For them, holiday tensions challenged their ability to create a family identity.

Each family finds its own way forward. Most often it is the mother's religious commitments that have the greatest influence on determining the family's practices.[80] Although in 1990 more than seventy-five percent of North American Jews reported celebrating Hanukkah, what did those celebrations actually comprise? Families sometimes determined their own customs. Two families and their customs can illustrate some of the range of ways people accommodated Hanukkah to their own needs. A family in central New Jersey that participated in the Conservative movement lighted candles each night, selecting from their collection of ten menorahs amassed after they received two as wedding gifts. Their young daughter received a gift every night, though each year's array of gifts also included practical items such as socks—although especially pretty ones. Mom hoped her child would grow to love Judaism as much as she herself did. By contrast, a family that belonged to a Reform congregation in upstate New York did things differently. Shaping the holiday to fit busy schedules filled with schoolwork, dance and music classes, and chess matches, they designated one day of the holiday for Hanukkah. As they ate homemade latkes, lighted the entire menorah, and received all their gifts at once, their Hanukkah served to accomplish the larger purpose of ensuring a happy family experience. In some years, their Hanukkah celebrations enhanced the annual visit by cousins who lived hundreds of miles away. Mom hoped the children in both families would remain close all their lives despite the geographic distance between them. These very different families and their customs illustrate Wolfson's assertion that family dynamics play a key role for many Jews at Hanukkah.[81]

Families whose heritage includes other religions in addition to Judaism often are left to find their own, distinctive ways to celebrate Hanukkah. In one Cherry Hill, New Jersey, family, Mom's enthusiastic conversion to Judaism led her to active participation in her Reform synagogue's sisterhood, which she served as president. She also convinced her own parents to respect and maintain her nuclear family's religious integrity. When she brought her husband and children to visit her parents in Presque Isle, Maine, one December, her father donned a *kippah* (skullcap) to join his grandson in lighting the Hanukkah candles.[82] The Reform movement provides sophisticated educational programming to win the hearts and minds of the non-Jewish spouses of its intermarried congregants. For this family, it worked very well.

Conversionary families report that their children's gentile grandparents find it difficult to deprive their Jewish grandchildren of the Christmas trees that they believe symbolize family togetherness and the joy of childhood. The authors of *The Intermarriage Handbook* urged families to deal with the feelings of rejection that may arise among grandparents in July, not in December. Or hold family gatherings on December twenty-fifth, a day when most people are free of school and job demands.[83] Those families that blend or maintain the different religious backgrounds of each parent face a December that challenges their creativity, if they hope to give at least equal weight to Jewish tradition.

These families' homes seem to reflect American culture's own merging of religious ideas. The post–World War II era touted a Judeo-Christian tradition that provided the country's moral foundation. Political leaders claimed that its values enabled Americans to steer clear of a "godless," tyrannical, and dehumanizing Communism. By the 1970s, Americans had become accustomed to seeing decorated trees next to lighted menorahs in holiday displays, and many schoolchildren learned songs about dreidels as well as Santa. When the popular folk singing group Peter, Paul and Mary released *A Holiday Celebration* album in 1988, amid many Christmas tunes, it featured one for Hanukkah by Yarrow that urged listeners to "light one candle for the Maccabee children,

Cartoonist Skip Morrow's greeting card extends good wishes for the December holidays and urges easy camaraderie between them. (Courtesy Recycled Paper Products, Inc.; design by Skip Morrow)

give thanks that their light didn't die."[84] By the time the Soviet Union fell the next year, the U.S. Supreme Court's ruling that when trees and menorahs are placed together they convey a distinctive message about multicultural tolerance worked well for many intermarried families that strived to instill values of social tolerance and respect in their children. These families also could send greeting cards that expressed those same values. One of the earliest, by cartoonist Skip Morrow's (circa 1990), depicted both Santa and a Jewish man holding a menorah. Each smiles at the viewer, and together they convey the happy message that we can all get along.

Passover, the other popular Jewish domestic holiday about freedom and liberation, received similar treatment. Although no Passover-Easter cards appeared—probably because Easter's domestic practices have not received the elaboration that Christmas has—some Jews rewrite Passover Haggadahs to reflect other values, including Holocaust remembrance, feminism, the plight of Soviet Jewry, earth ecology, and vegetarianism, among others.[85] In 2010, Cokie and Steve Roberts published *Our Haggadah: Uniting Traditions for Interfaith Families*, based on the guide they developed for their own family. Because Jesus's Last Supper was likely a Passover seder, some believing Christians have developed an interest in experiencing it. For the Roberts family, who included the African American hymns "Go Down Moses" and "We Shall Overcome" in their seder (seders normally conclude with songs), Passover celebrated American ideas about freedom and the divine. Although the Robertses based their creation on the 1941 Haggadah compiled by Mordecai M. Kaplan, which, like his Sabbath prayer book, eliminated any reference to the Jews as a chosen people, they added many elements drawn from broader American culture.[86] Another 1990s family "augmented the Passover service by singing songs based upon Broadway melodies."[87] These families bring together Jewish holiday traditions with elements of American culture. They select and merge American and Jewish values, continuing a practice evident among American Jews since Revolutionary days, when Jews implemented the era's values in their religious lives by drawing up constitutions for their congregations. Generations of Jews comfortable in weaving together those two sources to create outcomes felt to be appropriate for their lives built Hanukkah into an occasion whose popularity matched that of one of Judaism's most significant holidays, Passover.

Yet one Orthodox rabbi and teacher felt particularly disturbed that this broad array of approaches to Jewish practice created factions that distrusted each other and inhibited communication among America's Jews. Intermarried families who celebrated tolerance appalled observant Jews who believed intermarriage sounded a death knell for the future. They pointed to statistics that showed that fifty percent of Jews raised in intermarried families also married non-Jews. Calling it "marrying-out," observant Jews felt sure neither those children nor their descendants would "return" to Judaism. Jewish Survivalists added to that fear by pointing to the "perilous erosion of any distinguishing boundaries that define 'Jewishness' in America."[88] Deploring the distrust growing between Jewish groups, this rabbi, Irving Greenberg, in 1974 formed the Jewish Center for Leadership and Learning to create an environment where Jews from many different backgrounds could read and discuss religious texts and issues together, creating a think tank on Jewish issues. Holding a Harvard Ph.D., Greenberg also served as an associate professor of history at Yeshiva University and later founded the Department of Jewish Studies at City College of the City University of New York. Instead of deploring the lack of unity among American Jews, as earlier twentieth-century rabbis did, Greenberg believed that the pluralism that marked American Jewish life could be a source of strength.

Greenberg, like a century and a half of rabbis before him, found in Hanukkah's story special meaning for contemporary American Jews. To him, more than ever, the American situation seemed to mirror the ancient divisions among Jews that foregrounded the events that led to Hanukkah. "Hanukkah is actually a case study of three Jewish strategies in response to a dynamic external culture: separation, acculturation, and assimilation," he explained.[89] But, whereas many earlier rabbis also had pointed to similarities between America's divisions and those of ancient Jewry, they commonly identified clear heroes and villains in both the ancient and modern situations. Their ideological opponents became identified as the Hellenists, while they claimed to be Maccabees. Greenberg, however, insisted that the historical record points to a more complex reality.

It seemed clear to him that no single approach could have ensured that Judaism would survive. "Each of the groups that pursued these policies alone proved inadequate to take charge of Jewish destiny," he said. The situation that gave rise to the Maccabean revolt simply presented too complex a challenge. Most importantly, the historical record shows how different strategies worked together to effect victory. "Many Hellenizing Jews," he said, "decided to stand by their fellow Jews rather than . . . the Greeks." In part because of that experience, "rabbis deepened Judaism to cope with a dynamic civilization"—the Hellenic culture. Contemporary American society, he said, presents an even greater challenge to Judaism. It "is more developed, magnetic, and challenging" to Jews than was the Hellenic world. Because "no one group can offer all the answers for all the life situations or cope with all the options in society," Jews need to form coalitions "to correct one another" and to provide Jewish people with "the strength and variety of numbers."[90]

Greenberg's approach owed much to his professional training in history, to the contemporary American culture that deemed diversity a positive good, and to the influence of Mordecai Kaplan, the earlier American rabbi and thinker who taught that Judaism is the expression of the dynamic civilization of the Jews. Moreover, Greenberg insisted, "the further lesson of Hanukkah is not to write off assimilating Jews" as some who used intermarriage statistics seemed to do. We need a "coalition" of "traditional . . . modernizing . . . and assimilating Jews" like the one which "pulled off the Maccabee miracle" to strengthen the current American Jewish community. "The battle of Hanukkah is being fought again," he said, this time "through creating family ties, competing educationally"—that is, by making Jewish schools academically rigorous—"communicating values and messages, and holding and deepening loyalties." In this process, Jews cannot "insist" on "human perfection" in their leaders "because no person can do so." Instead, Jews must accept that this modern version of the Hanukkah battle for the Jewish future "can only be won by partial solutions, visionary persistence, and realistic dreams." In other words, Jews across the broad spectrum of religious approaches and values should understand that each can offer something—but not the same things—to bring about a stronger, more vibrant future for American Jews. They need to accept that each brings a strength that the others lack. "The proper response . . . as Hanukkah teaches," Greenberg said, "is not to curse the darkness but to light a candle."[91] Greenberg's Hanukkah celebrated Jews finding strength through their diversity now and in the ancient past.

In the closing decades of the twentieth century, a divided Jewry elaborated on the various aspects of Hanukkah that held meaning for each group or individual. Feeling more confident as Americans than had Jews in past eras, they brought their celebrations into more public spaces. Jewish newspapers and some secular television stations covered the local Chabad menorah lightings. Yet, ironically, holiday marketing brought Hanukkah into many more public spaces, as special greeting cards appeared in supermarkets and shops. Each November, displays of Hanukkah paper goods in blue and white or silver took their place alongside the much larger assortment in red and green marketed for Christmas. Hallmark offered more than sixteen different Hanukkah greeting cards along with wrapping paper and dreidel kits, and dozens of Internet sites offer Hanukkah greeting cards.[92] Newspapers and television news programs reported on the holiday's arrival among their Jewish readers and viewers.

By 2000, Hanukkah had become a winter festival familiar to broad swaths of Americans. Non-Jews who conclude that Hanukkah must be the most important of Jewish holidays should not be faulted for their error. After all, it garners more public attention than any other Jewish holiday. Moreover, it occurs at the same time as their own significant festival and seems to consist of the same sorts of activities—family gatherings and gifts to children. The many Christians who judge Christmas to be the most important Christian holiday value its capacity to sanctify family bonds. If Hanukkah does the same for Jews, surely it must hold a parallel significance. Are they wrong? The widespread popularity of domestic holidays Hanukkah and Passover suggest that Jews also might, in fact, be celebrating their familial bonds—a centerpiece of their lives—despite Hanukkah's official ranking as a minor festival.

We have seen that in 1990 more than three-fourths of American Jews reported performing Hanukkah's central ritual, the lighting of special candles at home in a candelabra designed only for this use. As Jewish families withstood shocks from immigration, relocation, shrinking size, women's labor outside the home, and interreligious marriages, Hanukkah's value as a vehicle for enhancing family ties became ever more important.

The expanded array of Hanukkah activities and special Hanukkah goods available at the close of the twentieth century also indicated its significance. Children viewed Hanukkah cartoons in movie theaters and on television and video, and they played Hanukkah music from CDs purchased in their local music store or from websites. The U.S. Library of Congress owns more than eight hundred Hanukkah items, including song sheets and recorded music, cookbooks, holiday guide books and story books for children and adults, and original Hanukkah dramas to be performed by children in religious and Jewish cultural schools or by adults in religious and social clubs. Most items were written, composed, or created in the United States—reflecting American

Jews' own creativity and interest in the holiday—and were purchased to augment an occasion that grew increasingly important. Jews turned to these prayer books, published sermons, songs, stories, ritual manuals, and plays each December to find ancient reflections of their own experience in confronting a compelling contemporary non-Jewish culture. They looked to the ancient tale that explained Hanukkah for inspiration, reassurance, domestic joy, and new sources of fun to carry them through the annual Christmas frenzy in safety and in style.

Conclusion

As the twenty-first century opened, American Jews once again found in Hanukkah's story a way to apply the consoling language of faith while facing new threats to their existence. For more than a century and a half, Hanukkah's account of dangerous foreigners, assimilating traitors, loyal martyrs, and faithful heroes provided a way to talk about dangers to Jewish life that might lurk beneath a benign experience of life in the United States. Nineteenth-century rabbis who debated what Judaism needed to do in order to survive in America used that story to clarify and promote their own fitness for leading the country's Jewry. In the opening years of the twentieth century, Yiddish-speaking newspaper editor Abraham Cahan claimed Jewish socialists to be "humanity's Maccabees." Twentieth-century Zionists confidently promoted themselves as new Maccabees fighting to claim their land. Throughout that century, when denominational distinctions outlined different commitments to religious practices, each organization felt sure that its rivals who accommodated more of American cultural life behaved like the ancient Hellenists who assimilated to Greek culture and betrayed their people.

In each era's Hanukkah, Jews spoke of America's similarity to the ancient Hellenic world. Its sophisticated and welcoming society improved Jews' lives, they admitted, but the foreign religious beliefs at its heart, its secularism, and its impediments to the practice of Judaism posed threats to their religion. The ancient resolution to those difficulties that led to the creation of Hanukkah itself offered a promise that the new American challenges, like those of old, could be overcome. But as the millennium turned, a new threat led American Jews to revise those familiar stories.

Three months after the September 11, 2001, attacks on the World Trade Center, on the Pentagon and the attempted attack on the White House that killed almost three thousand Americans—including many Jews—Jewish newspapers pointed out that Hanukkah's special message of faith and commitment should be seen as especially applicable to the contemporary situation. "Another foe has risen up and targeted the core ideals, values, and practices not only of our people, but also of western society," wrote the *Jewish News of Greater Phoenix*. "Once again we are rising to the task."[1] The Jewish Telegraphic Agency, which provides copy to Jewish newspapers, claimed that Jews now needed both kinds of Hanukkah miracles—the oil, "which symbolizes our commitment to Judaism," along with military power, "to dispel the darkness that has fallen on our world."[2] Watching new political alliances blame Jews for the bombers' hatred of the West, one observer concluded, "anti-Semitism is the last acceptable prejudice."[3]

At the same time, however, in the first Hanukkah after the attacks, the differences between Jews and their American neighbors seemed to fade. Philadelphia's *Jewish Exponent* compared the heroism of "fire fighters, police officers, [and] emergency personnel who answered the call on September 11" to that of the Maccabees. Hanukkah "is particularly apt today," it told readers, because the bombings challenged the "will of the Jewish people to stay faithful to our traditions."[4] Were those traditions uniquely Jewish? The many gentiles in the paper's list of 9/11's "Maccabees" suggests not. The attackers, Arab Muslim extremists based in the Middle East, opposed Israel and Jews with as much fury as they opposed the United States. For many Americans, that made the differences between Jews—now only little more than two percent of the American population—and other Americans almost irrelevant. President George W. Bush echoed that sentiment at the Hanukkah menorah lighting at the White House residence held on December tenth of that year. "It's a symbol that . . . this house . . . belongs to people of all faiths," he began. Unlike previous presidents, Bush not only invited schoolchildren to watch him light a far more impressive and imposing menorah than President Clinton had used, but he also held annual Hanukkah parties that were completely kosher. Bush described himself as a deeply religious man, and he seemed to easily adapt his own Christian views to the Hanukkah ceremony. The holiday reminds us of "the ancient story of Israel's courage and of the power of faith to make the darkness bright," he said, and he wished Jews everywhere "many joyous Hanukkahs in the years ahead."[5] Both Jewish newspapers and the devout Christian president found meaning and purpose in this holiday.

Others echoed that sentiment. Daniel Brenner, a rabbi at the New York–based National Jewish Center for Learning and Leadership, joined the moment's seamless blend of American experience and Hanukkah values. He detailed a parallel between the holiday's origins and the contemporary challenge Americans faced in emotionally overcoming the attack's devastation. "When one of the Temple priests searched through the rubble of the vandalized sacred house . . . [and] pour[ed] the oil into the tarnished menorah, . . . relight[ing] it was an act of hope and renewal," he began. That act was "comparable" to the rescuer in Lower Manhattan who found an American flag in the rubble and "broke free from the collective sense of anguish to affirm life" by raising the flag. Both acts embodied "hope and renewal." Further linking Hanukkah to the contemporary situation, he urged Jews to use the holiday's eight nights to "dedicate ourselves to sustaining this renewed sense of public engagement and to continue the quiet acts that matter: caring, . . . appreciating, . . . loving." To remain inspired, Jews ought to "dedicate each night to a hero," Brenner said. His list drew on the specifics of the attack and responses to it. Dedicate the first night to "fire fighters, police officers and everyday citizens who gave their lives"; the second to "doctors, counselors, volunteers, red cross and others who assisted at the scene"; the third to "government and community leaders who transcended ideological differences to build national strength"; the fourth to "parents and teachers who help children cope"; the seventh, to "allies around the world who have condemned terrorism and, finally, to all of us who . . . valiantly move on and strengthen America's commitment to . . . religious and intellectual freedoms."[6] For Rabbi Brenner, too, American and Jewish values merged.

That autumn's somber mood affected the orgy of buying that ordinarily occurs in December. Chicago's *Jewish Press* suggested that "relentless" and "mindless consumerism" were "dimming the spiritual lights of Hanukkah" and posed a threat to freedom as great as terrorism did. The *Chicago Sun-Times* suggested donating money ordinarily spent on Hanukkah gifts instead to the Family Relief Fund assisting the families of those killed on September 11 and to New York City's meals on wheels.[7] A few decades earlier, few voices had urged restraint in holiday gift giving, but now, many others also urged behavior more appropriate to the country's sorrow.

But that discipline, if it ever existed, did not last long. Merchants sought holiday sales, and Jewish newspapers, as they had since the nineteenth century, continued to need the income provided by advertising. On the same page as the article that equated the dangers of consumerism with those of terrorism, the *Jewish Press* ran several inches of advertising for gift electronics. Parents felt the pressure to buy, despite the anticonsumer commentary. "Gift-giving is a seasonal reality," wrote columnist Jane Ulman. "That doesn't mean I have to like it." Besides, she said, "the real gift is the holiday itself. The opportunity to get together with family and friends, eat latkes and jelly donuts, play dreidel, perform the mitzvot, and . . . reinforce our Jewish identity in a positive and fun way."[8]

By the twenty-first century, Hanukkah had moved beyond the confines of Jewish homes and synagogues and into American culture. Special Hanukkah evenings might include listening to National Public Radio's annual program of short stories about Hanukkah or to any of many CDs of Hanukkah music that might be produced by both non-Jewish and Jewish companies.[9] Jews might turn to the web and share with family and friends rabbinic commentary on the holiday or recipes for Hanukkah foods, watch the performance of a new Hanukkah song on YouTube, or arrange a holiday visit with distant friends and family through Skype.[10] Yet gifts seemed essential. For most American Jewish households, Hanukkah's real importance lay in its capacity to create festive domestic occasions that renewed familial bonds, which holiday gifts reinforced.

Jewish-identified gift items could still be purchased through small synagogue gifts shops but also through a far larger outlet for Jewish goods, Hamakor Judaica. In the company's September 2003 catalog, for example, only twenty-seven of its seventy pages held no Hanukkah-identified items. Hanukkah menorahs could be art objects, nostalgic reproductions of nineteenth-century styles, or designed with sports themes. Candles, too, could be multicolored tapers or squat, simple items. Plastic or wooden dreidels were designed for play, whereas those with ornate metalwork or glass were best to display. Many parents gave their children items without Jewish markers. Ulman shopped the web for her sons' gifts—sports jerseys and snow boards; several mothers reported that, after the first night of the holiday and particularly for younger children, gifts were likely to include everyday items such as pajamas or socks, made special simply by being more colorful. But Hamakor offered items that might further Hanukkah's capacity to enhance Jewish identity.[11]

Hanukkah's ability to reaffirm Jewishness and strengthen family bonds continued to be important to American Jews. But a growing number of intermarried families forged novel adaptations of both Hanukkah and Christmas, hoping to elide the season's serious potential for religious conflict. Earlier generations of Jews noted that Christmas's impressive presence in the American December actually reinforced their Jewish identity because they became more aware of their difference from gentile Americans. Hanukkah's timing provided them an authentically Jewish and meaningful way to enact their Jewish identity during the season when they felt it most acutely. But the 2000 National Jewish Population Survey revealed the intermarriage rate climbing to forty-seven percent; forty-one percent of married Jews under age thirty-five claimed a non-Jewish spouse.[12] One such family in Kansas City whose children were "as familiar with the menorah as with a manger scene" were now sending hybrid holiday greeting cards like those that proclaim "Merry Chrismukkah," rather than the nonsectarian items with winter scenes they had used in the past. These new cards, which elide the differences between Judaism and Christianity, they

A New Jersey woman began this collection of Hanukkah menorahs with two she received as wedding gifts forty years ago. Each Hanukkah, she selects one to use that year. (Courtesy Fredda Sacharow and Steve Stern)

believe, are respectful to both holidays. Businesses market increasing varieties of these cards, which first emerged two decades earlier as the intermarriage rate began rising.[13] They serve a growing market. One 2001 study found that fifty percent of Jews agreed that "it is racist to oppose intermarriage."[14] A study of greater New York City's Jews done a decade later found that "one out of two marriages in which one partner was a non Orthodox Jew was to a person who was not Jewish and did not convert to Judaism."[15] Interfaith marriages linking Jews and gentiles reflect a larger American trend. In 2010, "roughly half of all married Americans . . . are married to someone who came originally from a different religious tradition."[16]

Sociologists have surmised that because "Americans have become increasingly likely to work with, live alongside, and marry people of other religions," interfaith relations generally have improved. "It is difficult to demonize the religion, or lack of religion, of people you know," argue Robert Putnam and David Campbell.[17] Familiarity with Jews and Judaism likely prompted some gentiles to challenge antisemitic acts that sometimes occurred at Hanukkah, especially when large, public menorahs provided easy targets. The Bella Vista United Civic Association in Philadelphia replaced the menorah that had stood lighted in a South Philly park but was destroyed by vandals. "This act of hate will not be tolerated," the group's director, Ben Anastasio, said. "Today in Bella Vista we are all Jews." The civic association in that largely Italian American neighborhood erected a new menorah the next day.[18] Similarly, in Billings, Montana, when a vandal shot at the lighted menorah that a Jewish family had placed in the front window of their home, locals protested. Photographer Frederic Brenner brought together dozens of local residents to create a photographic image of support for the targeted family. The participants wear clothing that expresses a wide range of American identities: they appear in Native American headdresses, clerical robes, police uniforms, cowboy hats, aprons, dresses, and on horseback, among others. Posed in the street next to the targeted house, standing before a huge American flag, each person carries a white cardboard Hanukkah menorah. Brenner shot the image through the window of the home, so that the bullet hole is plainly visible. His message is clear: for everyone who shoots a bullet at a Jewish home, many more support their Jewish neighbor. Editors of a 2007 collection of essays on American Jewish life found that the image captured their point so well, they placed it on their cover.[19] Perhaps more importantly, support for diverse religious celebrations in December became commonplace. Two years later, President Barack Obama hosted a kosher Hanukkah party at the White House, lighted a menorah, and, additionally, distributed two versions of a national Hanukkah message of cheer, one in English and another in Hebrew.[20] In South Orange, New Jersey, and in Queens, New York, Chinese American and Hispanic American mothers welcomed the delight their young children showed in the Hanukkah practices and dreidel games they had learned at public kindergarten, because it proved their school's embrace of diversity among its students.[21]

These citizens of Billings, Montana, joined in 1994 to protest a Hanukkah attack on a Jewish home in their town. Each carries an image of a Hanukkah menorah, while through their dress, they depict their town's diversity. *Citizens Protesting Anti-Semitic Acts, Billings, Montana*, by Frederic Brenner. (Courtesy Howard Greenberg Gallery, New York)

Pat Oliphant's 2005 cartoon for December 24 countered some Americans' dislike of any December greeting but "Merry Christmas" by pointing out that Jesus would have celebrated Hanukkah. (Oliphant 2005, Universal Uclick; reprinted with permission; all rights reserved)

Yet it also seemed that many Christian Americans who lived in areas with large Jewish populations did not feel comfortable sharing what they understood to be the Christmas season with Hanukkah. Less violent protests against Hanukkah's growing public presence could be heard in calls for merchants to instruct their staff to wish their customers "Merry Christmas," as they had decades earlier, instead of the increasingly customary, more encompassing phrase "Happy Holidays."[22] Cartoonist Pat Oliphant penned a humorous rebuttal to the protest, pointing out that if the infant Jesus, a Jew himself, could have spoken at that tender age, he would have likely wished the three wise men a Happy Hanukkah, rather than a Merry Christmas. As Hanukkah grew less strange to gentile Americans, Jews found more allies in national conversations about religious liberty.

A growing number of Hanukkah events in public venues welcomed all comers to enjoy a celebration while learning something about the holiday. Places such as Chicago's Spertus Museum and that city's Jewish Theater Company; New York's Yeshiva University Museum at the

Center for Jewish History; Phoenix, Arizona's Fiddlestick's Family Fun Park; and the Oxford Valley Mall near Philadelphia, just to name a few places, have all hosted Hanukkah activities.[23] One man in his twenties relished the array of choices. "I live in Philadelphia and there are several Jewish events to choose from on any given night (especially days like the last day of Passover or the first night of Chanukah) through several organizations. . . . These organizations make facebook [announcements] for all of their events, and many list things like drink specials or no cover from such-a-time to such-a-time, . . . which could be an enticement to pick one event over another."[24] Many institutions provided arts and craft activities in order to create an informal, welcoming atmosphere that can bring together Jews of diverse religious commitments, Jewish families, intermarried families, Jews who live alone who seek a lively holiday experience, and curious onlookers seeking cross-cultural fun. Like the Hanukkah concerts held in New York's music halls in the early twentieth century, these festivals a century later provided an open door to any interested visitor with the price of a ticket. They can bring together people of all backgrounds to share a common, entertaining Jewish experience. For intermarried families, these occasions might provide less stressful Hanukkah experiences free of negotiations or discussions about domestic religious standards. For Jews, they can affirm Jewish identity and religious commitments. Curious gentile visitors can find that a different religious culture is less strange than they suspected. In these festivals, Hanukkah, a holiday that grew out of religious dissension, can forge common bonds.

In the twenty-first century, in most American Jewish congregations, the tradition of Hanukkah children's festivals begun in the late nineteenth century remains customary. As early as 1971, a small synagogue in Buffalo noted with surprise that over three hundred parents and grandparents attended their Sunday-morning Hanukkah assembly, far more than turned out for any model seders (evening events) that the congregation had arranged at the more important holiday of Passover.[25] Sunday events took advantage of the fact that most parents and grandparents did not need to report to work that day and so easily built on Sunday's customary place in the religious-school calendar. By the 1990s, many synagogues added special family Hanukkah fun events that brought families and children together for hours of holiday activities,

As a brother and sister completed inflating a menorah decoration for
their front yard, their mother snapped this photo. In this New Jersey
neighborhood, large markers of Jewish identity do not challenge the
local religious status quo. (Courtesy Debra M. Faye)

and their popularity continued in the new century. These events are
often advertised in local newspapers, and synagogue membership committees hope that a welcoming holiday festival will entice newcomers
to join their congregations. Some congregations began to adapt other
holidays to this style of holiday-themed family fun. In early autumn,
Sukkot offers time for a similar synagogue-based festival, as does Purim
in midwinter: Congregation Beth Tikvah in New Jersey, for example,
hosts both a "Sukkahbration" and a "Purimpalooza." Those build on
older Hanukkah events.

Synagogue programming committees strive to create experiences that are familiar enough to feel appropriate to the holiday and welcoming enough to disarm newcomers and yet offer something new to pique interest. In the new century, synagogues around the country hosted a wide array of Sunday Hanukkah events that capitalized on and enhanced the tradition's popularity. One synagogue in Philadelphia hosted a "Recycled Menorah-Making Contest," while another joined with the local fire department for an arts-and-crafts, "family friendly fire safety program and free Chanukah party."[26] In Phoenix, a synagogue's senior-citizens group held a latke luncheon, while the larger congregation hosted a brisket and latke dinner for both members and nonmembers.[27] Several Chicago synagogues advertised holiday parties with hot dogs, latkes, children's choirs, klezmer (eastern European Jewish folk music) performances, bingo, and games.[28] In 2005, the Sisterhood Gift Shop at a Tampa, Florida, congregation held its first annual Children's Chanuka Bazaar, which attracted many parents and grandparents to its latke lunch.[29] These events encouraged Jews to turn to synagogues for pleasurable, identity-reinforcing activities that are also religiously appropriate. Yet their emphasis on forging and reinforcing communal and familial ties is a sharp contrast to the pageantry and spectacle staged by late nineteenth-century young men who hoped to impress American Jews with Hanukkah's importance. After more than a century in which the holiday's popularity steadily increased, congregations tapped Hanukkah's glamor for their own goals. Synagogues hoped these events would keep their members walking in their doors, rather than going to local Jewish community centers for sports or cultural activities.

Hanukkah events outside the home also help Jews avoid feeling "invisible" during the Christmas season. At holiday parties and festivals in synagogues, at special entertainments in other public venues, or in restaurants that offer Hanukkah dinner specials, the holiday moves into the public realm.[30] Jewish drivers might even see large lighted electric Hanukkah menorahs mounted on the roofs of cars driven by Chabad members who literally take the holiday to the streets on its dark winter evenings. Encountering the blue-and-white holiday paper goods in stores, the reports on national Hanukkah celebrations, and the advertising for local Hanukkah events in newspapers, Jews see their own holiday embedded in American life.

Cartoonists Terry and Patty LaBan found humor in the futility of getting Jewish children to see any meaning for Hanukkah besides presents, December 2005. (Terry & Patty LaBan; distributed by King Features syndicate)

For the ten percent of American Jews who are Orthodox, Hanukkah is celebrated because its particular ways to acknowledge the ancient miracle of the Maccabean revolt are required by Jewish law. For many other American Jews, it is all for the children. The measure of success for any Hanukkah celebration, whether at home, in a synagogue, or at a more public "family fun day," is that children learn about their faith and have a good time. Yet Orthodox Jews, too, make sure to create within their own homes and communities festive occasions that both instruct and delight their children.[31] The threats posed to Jewish life by the simple fact of being so small a minority, and by the divergent ways Jews craft religious lives that sometimes share little in common with

MRJ Latkes

It is time again to order delicious latkes made by the Beth-El Men of Reformed Judaism. Latkes are $7.00 per dozen, 3 dozen for $18.00. (Such a Deal!)

Choose from traditional flavor or the new Southwest latkes, mildly seasoned with cilantro, garlic, onion and pepper.

Please fill out the order form and return to the Temple before Dec 6, or email AdamSiegel@sbcglobal.net

Dozen	Flavor	Price
_____	*Traditional Latkes*	____
_____	Southwest Seasoned	____
_____	Totals	____

NAME_____

PHONE NUMBER_____

Men of a Fort Worth, Texas, synagogue expected latkes prepared with the flavors of southwestern cuisine to raise more funds than those made according to a traditional recipe. In 2010, customers could email their orders. (Courtesy Beth El Archives, Fort Worth, Texas)

each other, can, with Hanukkah, be reframed as an age-old problem that has been overcome before. Similarly, the catastrophic dangers such as those posed by Nazi conquests, by Soviet oppression, or by terrorist bombings can each be reconceptualized within Hanukkah's promise of rescue. American Jews regularly turn to Hanukkah's story to help them face contemporary challenges and to assuage their fears, just as they have for the past century and a half. Making a fun time for children allows adults to be childlike, too, to forget grown-up worries. In the second decade of the twenty-first century, Hanukkah allows Jews to be happy that divine rescue saved (or inspired) their ancestors and gives them light in the midst of winter darkness, courage in the midst of war, and encouragement that miracles (however they are defined) do happen—all this despite, or even because of, their diverse ways of practicing their traditions. After nearly two centuries of American Jews finding in Hanukkah's ancient tale the assurance that their own problems will be solved, they are likely to continue to make Hanukkah celebrations a significant part of their religious calendars.

American Jews who enhanced Hanukkah's importance told a Maccabean story about the appeal of foreign cultures and the oppression of foreign tyrants, the traitors who betrayed Judaism and the martyrs and loyalists who defended Judaism against them. Dramatic action and vivid imagery pervaded this story, and divine rescue capped it off. The story condensed historical events into a mythic structure that lent it a timeless quality. In that form, it became useful to American Jews seeking to understand the complexities of their own religious lives in an open society. By 1972, one rabbi called Hanukkah "one of the most relevant of Jewish holidays."[32]

As the story is told, it begins with Jewish contact with the attractive, powerful Hellenic empire whose ideas reshaped the ancient world. After many Judeans accustomed themselves to the Hellenic world, a new ruler demanded near-complete abandonment of their religio-national heritage. Loyalists emerged who defeated that ruler and his Jewish collaborators and restored the centerpiece of Jewish worship. It is a simple story with well-defined heroes and villains. It recounts a situation that changed from opportunity to danger to victory. In this form, it echoes the Passover Haggadah, which begins with the rise of a new king—this time in Egypt—who is hostile to his country's Jews. It links the minor festival Hanukkah to the far more important story of the Exodus. Thus, as Jews in America found themselves in historically new circumstances, they took an event that tradition had abstracted into a minor tale about God's power and made it a more complicated, robust story about challenges to humans motivated by faith.

Religion scholar Wendy Doniger O'Flaherty teaches us that myths can be tools for both thinking and feeling, making it possible to try on experiences far from ordinary life that nonetheless illuminate it. Although she surmises that "other people's myths" prove most useful,

Hanukkah's evolving retellings suggest that changing historical circumstances can open familiar myths to new readings and meanings.[33] Those changes can allow religious traditions to adapt to new circumstances and so remain alive and vital. The changes help explain how Judaism adapted to America. Jews, by using a story of their own past, reassured themselves that they deduced legitimate Jewish lessons from Hanukkah's events no matter how they reshaped their accounts of them.

Though the account of Hanukkah that American Jews told presumes Hellenism's great appeal, it always is seen as a threat to Judaism. Its intellectual power to reshape even biblical attitudes is seldom retold. Ancient Jews "Hellenized" in myriad choices about ideas, economic endeavors, sports, and fashion. The mythic story suggests a looming danger within that seemingly benign world. Among American Jews, that story tells them to be wary about their own integration into American society. The future may require them to make more difficult choices, it suggests, and they should approach their cultural adaptation to America with caution.

Hanukkah gave American Jews an annual occasion to ponder the demands of Jewish loyalty, the dangers of dissension among Jews, and the courage they would need to remain faithful Jews during the Christmas season, when their minority status became most vivid. At the same time, as we have seen, Hanukkah also provided a vehicle for reaching the social goals of enhancing familial bonds, educating children, and promoting communal ties. With so rich a capacity to improve and enlighten Jewish lives, Hanukkah achieved a new, more significant place in the American Jewish calendar than it had known in two thousand years of Jewish history.

ACKNOWLEDGMENTS

It is a great pleasure for me to publicly thank the many people and institutions who supported my research into Hanukkah's growth in America. From the very beginning, when I first began talking about this idea, I was heartened by the warm encouragement I received from two exceptional scholars of American Jewry, Hasia R. Diner and Jonathan D. Sarna. Through many years, they remained willing to discuss the project, to read too many rough drafts, and to evaluate the almost-final manuscript with great patience and insight. They are extraordinary people.

I am also grateful to the institutions that supported my research and writing by subsidizing some of the costs. These are the National Endowment for the Humanities, the Gilder Lehrman Institute for American History, the Hadassah Brandeis Institute, and the American Jewish Archives. I am deeply grateful to Rowan University for providing me many research grants and teaching reductions so that I could conduct research and begin to write, as well as a sabbatical leave in order to complete the book.

At New York University Press, Eric Zinner's consistent helpfulness and wisdom proved invaluable. Enormous assistance was provided by editor David Lobenstine. I learned so much from him. I relied on the prompt efficiency of Ciara McLaughlin, Alicia Nadkarni, and Andrew Katz to take care of many of the details involved in bringing out a book. I am also grateful to the anonymous readers who gave me careful and close critiques of the manuscript.

Students at Rowan helped me in many ways. Valerie Buickerood, Susan Minnick, Holly Friedman, and Sean Fischer provided research assistance while I was busy with administrative and teaching duties. For several semesters, I taught a seminar on holidays in American culture whose students regaled me with accounts of family customs I would not otherwise have learned. Perhaps more importantly, those seminars provided arenas in which we all could discuss and critique theories and ideas about American religion, rites, politics, and domesticity. Those students helped me more than they know.

Students at other schools assisted in locating materials. I relied on Michelle Warner at Hebrew Union College's Klau Library in Cincinnati and on Hila Rabinowitz, who culled items for me at both the Jewish Theological Seminary's Rare Book Room and the Women's League for Conservative Judaism Archives.

Jews in America produced documents in several languages, and I sometimes relied on the assistance of translators. Niv Hartman helped me with Hebrew, and Heide Thumlert provided German translations. I am especially grateful for Chana Pollock's enthusiastic and sharp translations of many articles from Yiddish newspapers. All translations from Yiddish, unless otherwise noted, are hers.

Archivists at several different institutions provided invaluable assistance. Don Davis at the Philadelphia Jewish Archives Center (now at Temple University) offered his usual high standard of meticulous and inventive help at an early stage of this work. The extraordinary Dan Sharon at the Asher Library, Spertus Institute of Jewish Studies in Chicago, sent me a surfeit of materials that evidenced his own amazing and wonderful diligence. Archivist and friend Kevin Proffitt, along with Devhra Bennett Jones, provided crucial help to me in locating items at the American Jewish Archives in Cincinnati, as did Katherine Goff at the American Jewish Periodical Center. Mary Karen Delmont at the Butler Library of SUNY College at Buffalo kindly made room for me to read papers that I had asked to see. Robin Waldman at the Jewish Museum of Maryland proved similarly helpful.

Librarian Hayim Sheynin and the entire library staff at Gratz College remained consistently cheerful, helpful, and instructive to me over many, many visits there. Gratz's Professor of Jewish Music, Marcia Bryan Edelman, helped me understand the outlines of the history of Jewish music and shared space in her offices where I could examine the rich holdings of Gratz's music library. Marilyn Krider at Klau Library and the American Jewish Periodical Center, Eleanor Yadin at the Dorot Jewish Division of the New York Public Library, and Peggy Pearlstein at the Library of Congress also provided valuable assistance. Throughout the research and writing process, I depended on the cheerful, helpful, and professional assistance of the staff at Rowan University's Campbell Library, particularly Dean Bruce Whitham and Librarian Cynthia Mullens. It has been a pleasure to work with them.

I am truly fortunate that some of my closest friends are talented scholars who have been supportive of my work. Four dear friends and inspirational colleagues deserve special thanks. I could always count on philosopher Stuart Charme to listen to my ideas carefully and then to challenge each one. His friendship, patience, and sharp intelligence have remained invaluable to me for many years. For more years than I care to admit, historian Colleen McDannell and I have shared countless long conversations about religions in America, many of which pushed the work on Hanukkah along in its early stages. She also read and offered helpful suggestions on early drafts. Similarly, I learned much from my Rowan colleague and friend sociologist Harriet Hartman, who asks questions and offers data that I always find fascinating. Conversations about the craft of writing with journalist Fredda Sacharow taught me a great deal while making me smile. I hope this book makes each of them smile in return.

Historians, friends, and colleagues Stephen Brumberg, Beth Wenger, Rachmiel Peltz, Sara R. Horowitz, Michael Zuckerman, Deborah Dash Moore, Riv-Ellen Prell, Melissa Klapper, Lila Corwin Berman, Warren Hoffman, Arthur Kiron, and Andrew Heinze were more helpful in their support and advice than they know. Malka Zeiger Simkovich and Gary Gans generously shared their time and expertise.

To the many people who filled out surveys and offered me their family photos and stories and to my friends and family who enthusiastically participated in this research while I posed queries about everything they did at various holidays, I hope each of you understands that I am in your debt. My brother and sister-in-law, Adam and Cindy Ashton, impressed me with the obvious point that domestic celebrations are fully under familial control and all that implies. The members of Havurah Shirim who cheerfully and quickly responded to my many emails asking about their practices, knowledge, and values—and connected me to their extended clans for further queries—have been a source of great support. Thank you.

My gratitude of another sort must go to my parents, now deceased, who made *such* a big deal out of Hanukkah. My father showed me the great importance of music and humor in Jewish American culture, while my mother and grandmother showed me endless instances of "this is what Jews do"—that unity of identity and action that was so much a part of eastern European Jewish understandings of Judaism. They, of course, made this book possible.

I am profoundly grateful to my husband, Richard Drucker. I have depended on his intriguing questions about American Jewry and, more importantly, on his unwavering love, for twenty-five years. I doubt that this book would have been written without his support.

Finally, I want to acknowledge a debt to Kibbutz Palmach Tsuba, Israel, my home for six months in 1971, where I noticed an electric Hanukkah menorah curiously perched atop a silo.

NOTES

ABBREVIATIONS

AJA   American Jewish Archives
AJHS   American Jewish Historical Society
AJYB   *American Jewish Year Book*
NFTS   National Federation of Temple Sisterhoods
WRJ   Women of Reform Judaism

NOTES TO THE INTRODUCTION

1. Hyman E. Goldin, *The Jew and His Duties: The Essence of the Kitzur Shulchan Aruch* (New York: Hebrew Publishing Company, 1953), 160.

2. There is an extensive literature on American religions. Among the best are Jonathan D. Sarna, *American Judaism: A History* (New Haven: Yale University Press, 2004); Colleen McDannell, *The Spirit of Vatican II: A History of Catholic Reform in America* (New York: Basic Books, 2011); McDannell, ed., *Religions of the United States in Practice,* 2 vols. (Princeton: Princeton University Press, 2001); Wade Clark Roof, *Spiritual Marketplace: Baby Boomers and the Remaking of American Religion* (Princeton: Princeton University Press, 1999); Mark Chaves, *Congregations in America* (Cambridge: Harvard University Press, 2004).

3. Albert I. Baumgarten and Marina Rustow, "Judaism and Tradition: Continuity, Change, and Innovation," in *Jewish Studies at the Crossroads of Anthropology and History: Authority, Diaspora, and Tradition,* ed. Ra'anan S. Boustan, Oren Kosansky, and Marina Rustow (Philadelphia: University of Pennsylvania Press, 2011), 209–210. They modify earlier work on invented traditions described by Eric Hobsbawm and, before him, Karl Marx. Hobsbawm and Marx deem such appeals to the past to legitimate current changes as symptomatic of "false consciousness." Baumgarten and Rustow, however, reject any falseness about it when looking at Jewish tradition. Instead, they differentiate between "weak" appeals to tradition that commonly occur in simply handing down a "corpus of knowledge or practices" versus "strong" appeals to tradition that occur when new rituals emerge to bring a sense of historical continuity to something utterly new. See Eric J. Hobsbawm, "Introduction: Inventing Traditions," in *The Invention of Tradition,* ed. Eric J. Hobsbawm and Terence O. Ranger (Cambridge: Cambridge University Press, 1993), 2–3.

4. Yehuda Kurtzer, *Shuva: The Future of the Jewish Past* (Lebanon, NH: Brandeis University Press / University Press of New England, 2012), 2

5. Yosef Hayim Yerushalmi, *Zakhor: Jewish History and Jewish Memory* (Seattle: University of Washington Press, 1996), 11.

6. Philip N. Steel, Jr., "Survey Questionnaire on Hanukkah Observance," compiled by the author, February 7, 2008.

7. David Cheal, *The Gift Economy* (New York: Routledge, 1988); William B. Waits, *The Modern Christmas in America: A Cultural History of Gift Giving* (New York: NYU Press, 1993), 13–15.

8. Carole Kur, "Noel Coward," in *Jewish Possibilities: The Best of Moment Magazine*, ed. Leonard Fein (Northvale, NJ: Jason Aronson, 1987), 13.

9. Anne Bayme, "Survey Questionnaire on Hanukkah Observance," compiled by author, February 14, 2008.

10. Hallmark website: http://www.hallmark.com (accessed November 10, 2007).

11. Marilyn Halter, *Shopping for Identity: The Marketing of Ethnic Identity* (New York: Schocken Books, 2000).

12. Hayim Donin, *To Raise a Jewish Child: A Guide for Parents* (New York: Basic Books, 1977), 124–125.

13. Rabbi Gary Gans, Congregation Beth Tikvah, Marlton, New Jersey, to the author, November 11, 2010.

14. Gertrude Braun Migler to the author, December 25, 2010.

15. Jennie Fine and Melissa Klapper to the author, October 28, 2010.

16. *Women's League Outlook* (Fall 1990): 35.

17. Steven M. Cohen and Arnold Eisen, *The Jew Within: Self, Family, and Community in America* (Bloomington: Indiana University Press, 2000), 87.

18. "Our Greatest Enemy," *Tageblatt* (December 15, 1907); Andrew R. Heinze, *Adapting to Abundance: Jewish Immigrants, Mass Consumption, and the Search for American Identity* (New York: Columbia University Press, 1990), 77.

19. "The Festivals," in *The Jewish Catalog*, ed. Richard Siegel, Michael Strassfeld, and Sharon Strassfeld (Philadelphia: Jewish Publication Society, 1973), 133; *The Source for Everything Jewish* (Chanukah, 2010); Morrison David Bial, *Liberal Judaism at Home* (New York: UAHC, 1971), 159–163; Mae Shafter Rockland, *The Hanukkah Book* (New York: Schocken Books, 1975), x; Kenneth White, "American Jewish Response to Christmas" (ordination thesis, Hebrew Union College, Cincinnati, 1982), 222.

20. Editorial Board [Ira Eisenstein], "Toward a Guide for Ritual Usage," *Reconstructionist* (October 31, 1941): foreword.

21. Barbara Meyerhoff, "Death in Due Time: Construction of Self and Culture in Ritual Drama," in *Readings in Ritual Studies*, ed. Ronald Grimes (Upper Saddle River, NJ: Prentice Hall, 1996), 395.

22. John Corrigan, Frederick M. Denny, Carlos M. N. Eire, and Martin S. Jaffee, *Jews, Christians, Muslims: A Comparative Introduction to Monotheistic Religions* (Upper Saddle River, NJ: Prentice Hall, 1998), xiv.

23. Israel Abrahams, *Festival Studies* (London: Edward Goldston, 1934), in

Hanukkah: The Feast of Lights, ed. Emily Solis-Cohen, Jr. (Philadelphia: Jewish Publication Society, 1955), 99–106.

24. Daniel Stauben, *Scenes of Jewish Life in Alsace* (originally published 1885–1890), trans. Rose Choron (Malibu, CA: Joseph Simon / Pangloss, 1992), 129.

25. Abraham W. Binder, "Hanukkah in Music," in Solis-Cohen, *Hanukkah*, 68–69.

26. Lev. 11:1–46. Unless otherwise specified, all citations of the Hebrew Bible are from *The Jewish Study Bible*, trans. Jewish Publication Society (1985; repr., New York: Oxford University Press, 1999).

27. Eliezer Segal, *Holidays, History, and Halakhah* (Northvale, NJ: Jason Aaronson, 2000), 88–89.

28. W. Weinberg, *How Do You Spell Chanukah? A General Purpose Romanization of Hebrew for Speakers of English* (New York: Behrman House, 1976); "A Jewish View of Christmas," *New York Times* (December 29, 1889).

NOTES TO CHAPTER 1

1. Moshe David Herr, "Hanukkah," in *Encyclopaedia Judaica*, ed. Michael Berenbaum and Fred Skolnik, 2nd ed., vol. 8 (Detroit: Macmillan Reference, 2007), 331.

2. 1 Macc. 4:51–60; 2 Macc. 10:6–9. All citations from First and Second Maccabees are from *Oxford Study Bible*, ed. M. Jack Suggs, Katherine Doob Sakenfeld, and James R. Mueller (New York: Oxford University Press, 1992).

3. Chron. 29:17; Lee I. Levine, *Jerusalem: Portrait of the City in the Second Temple Period (538 B.C.E.–70 C.E.)* (Philadelphia: Jewish Publication Society, 2002), 83.

4. Levine, *Jerusalem*, 36.

5. Martin Goodman, "Jews in the Second Temple Period," in *Oxford Handbook of Jewish Studies*, ed. Martin Goodman (New York: Oxford University Press, 2002), 38.

6. Chron. 3:1.

7. Elias J. Bickerman, *Jews in the Greek Age* (Cambridge: Harvard University Press, 1988), 27.

8. Ibid., 133–134.

9. Zech. 4:1–4, 10–14.

10. Ex. 20–21, 30:7–8.

11. Bickerman, *Jews in the Greek Age*, 134–135.

12. Ex. 29:38–39.

13. Ex. 62–63, 134–136; Lev. 1–9; Wilhelm Bacher and Jacob Zallel Lauterbach, "Tamid," *Jewish Encyclopedia*, http://www.jewishencyclopedia.com (accessed 2002).

14. Bickerman, *Jews in the Greek Age*, 140–141.

15. Seth Schwartz, *Imperialism and Jewish Society, 200 B.C.E. to 640 C.E.* (Princeton: Princeton University Press, 2001), 23; Eric M. Meyers, "Jewish Culture in Greco-Roman Palestine," in *Cultures of the Jews: A New History*, ed. David Biale (New York: Schocken Books, 2002), 145–146.

16. Schwartz, *Imperialism and Jewish Society*, 30–35; Jeffrey S. Gurock, *Judaism's Encounter with American Sports* (Bloomington: Indiana University Press, 2005), 16–18.
17. See for example Norbert Lohfink, *Qoheleth*, trans. Sean McEvenue (Minneapolis: Fortress, 2003).
18. Schwartz, *Imperialism and Jewish Society*, 26–27.
19. Bickerman, *Jews in the Greek Age*, 26–27.
20. "Seleucid Kingdom," *Encyclopedia Britannica Online* (2008), http://www.britannica.com/eb/article-9066667.
21. Levine, *Jerusalem*, 78.
22. Joseph Sievers, *The Hasmoneans and Their Supporters: From Mattathias to the Death of John Hyrcanus* (Atlanta: Scholars Press, 1990), 15.
23. First Book of the Maccabees is the chronicle, while the Second, Third, and Fourth Books of the Maccabees provide more heartrending descriptions of events.
24. Sievers, *Hasmoneans and Their Supporters*, 19; Levine, *Jerusalem*, 73–75.
25. 1 Macc. 1:20–24 says Antiochus himself entered the Temple and robbed it. 2 Macc. 5:15–17 says Antiochus entered the Temple guided by Menelaus, who had purchased the office of the High Priest. 2 Macc. 6:1–9 says Antiochus "sent an elderly Athenian to compel the Jews to give up their ancestral customs and to cease regulating their lives by the laws of God." It further explains the ways in which the Temple itself was polluted.
26. Steven L. Derfler, *The Hasmonean Revolt: Rebellion or Revolution?* (Lewiston, NY: Edwin Mellen, 1989), 17.
27. Lev. 23:42, 43; Shaye J. D. Cohen, *From the Maccabees to the Mishnah* (Philadelphia: Westminster, 1987); Lawrence Wills, review of *Heritage and Hellenism: The Reinvention of Jewish Tradition*, by Erich Gruen (Berkeley: University of California Press, 1998), *AJS Review* 26, no. 2 (November 2002): 354–356.
28. Sievers, *Hasmoneans and Their Supporters*, 20; sources disagree about who initiated these measures, but several attest to them. 1 Macc. 1:41–57; 2 Macc. 6:1; Dan. 11:31–33; Flavius Josephus, *The Jewish War*, 1.32–35; Flavius Josephus, *Antiquities of the Jews*, 12.248–256; Jubilees 23:16–23; See also E. J. Bickerman, *The God of the Maccabees: Studies on the Meaning and Origin of the Maccabean Revolt* (Leiden: Brill); for an overview, see John H. Tullock, *The Old Testament Story*, 4th ed. (Upper Saddle River, NJ: Prentice Hall, 1997), 329.
29. 1 Macc. 1:60–61; 2 Macc. 6:10.
30. Levine, *Jerusalem*, 69–75.
31. Sievers, *Hasmoneans and Their Supporters*, 24; 1 Macc. 1:60–63; 2 Macc. 6:10; Josephus, *Antiquities of the Jews*, 12.256.
32. 2 Macc. 2:10–11.
33. "First Maccabees," in *Oxford Study Bible*, 1197; Peter Kirby, "3 Maccabees," in *Early Christian Writings*, http://www.earlyjewishwritings.com/3maccabees.html (accessed June 8, 2007).

34. Seth Schwartz, *Imperialism and Jewish Society, 200 B.C.E. to 640 C.E.* (Princeton: Princeton University Press, 2001), 52–53.
35. Sievers, *Hasmoneans and Their Supporters*, 23–24.
36. 1 Macc. 2:12–13 (*Oxford Study Bible*), 1200.
37. 1 Macc. (*Oxford Study Bible*), 1197.
38. Sievers, *Hasmoneans and Their Supporters*, 26; Dan. 11:32–34; 1 Enoch 90:9; Menachem Stern, ed. and trans., *Greek and Latin Authors on Jews and Judaism*, 3 vols. (Jerusalem: Israel Academy of Sciences and Humanities, 1974–84), 2:46 R.
39. 1 Macc. (*Oxford Study Bible*), 1197.
40. 1 Macc. 1:19–21, 42–44; Schwartz, *Imperialism and Jewish Society*, 35.
41. 1 Macc. 1:49–69.
42. Jonathan A. Goldstein, *II Maccabees*, Anchor Bible (Garden City, NY: Doubleday, 1983); Sara Raup Johnson, *Historical Fictions and Hellenistic Identity: Third Maccabees in Its Cultural Context* (Berkeley: University of California Press, 2004), 39.
43. Johnson, *Historical Fictions*, 41.
44. Schwartz, *Imperialism and Jewish Society*, 33.
45. Ibid., 34; Levine, *Jerusalem*, 79–80.
46. 1 Macc. 4:57; 2 Macc. 10:6–7. But by conducting the dedication on the twenty-fifth day of Kislev, some days after retaking the Temple, Judah and his band also chose a date with ironic significance. On that date four years earlier, Antiochus IV first conducted his Hellenic sacrifices in the Temple. It was also Antiochus's own birthday, an occasion on which sacrifices in his honor would normally have been required. Instead of conducting honorific rites for Antiochus, Judah instructed Jews to reaffirm their dedication to their own religion.
47. James C. VanderKam, "Hanukkah: Its Timing and Significance According to 1 and 2 Maccabees," *Journal for the Study of the Pseudepigrapha* 1 (1987): 32–33; the Holy of Holies was conceptually and architecturally linked to the tabernacle in the wilderness dedicated by Moses and Aaron (Ex. 40:30–33).
48. Schwartz, *Imperialism and Jewish Society*, 60–61.
49. Michael Satlow, *Creating Judaism* (New York: Columbia University Press, 2006), 107–110.
50. Meyers, "Jewish Culture in Greco-Roman Palestine," 144.
51. Schwartz, *Imperialism and Jewish Society*, 175.
52. Josephus, *Antiquities of the Jews*, 12.7 (325); VanderKam, "Hanukkah," 23.
53. Nahum N. Glatzer, "Megillat Ta'anit," in *Encyclopaedia Judaica*, vol. 13, 769.
54. Joseph Heinemann, *Prayer in the Talmud: Forms and Patterns* (Berlin: Walter de Gruyter, 1977), 35.
55. 1 Macc. 3:19–20.
56. Ibid.
57. 2 Macc. 7; 4 Macc. 8:1–15; Gittin 57b; Lamentations Rabbah 1:16:50.
58. *Oxford Study Bible*, 1234n. 18; Theodor Herzl Gaster, *Purim and Hanukkah in Custom and Tradition* (New York: Schuman, 1950), 103–105.

59. Herr, "Hanukkah," 331; see also 2 Macc. 1:18–36, 2:8–12, 14, 10:3.

60. Herr, "Hanukkah," 331–333.

61. Sidney Greenberg and Jonathan D. Levine, eds., *Siddur Hadash* (Bridgeport, CT: Prayer Book Press of Media Judaica, 2000), 723.

62. Philip Kieval, "The Talmudic View of the Hasmonean and Early Herodian Periods in Jewish History" (Ph.D. diss., Brandeis University, 1970), 122.

63. Ibid.

64. Ben Zion Bokser and Baruch M. Bokser, introduction to *The Talmud: Selected Writings* (New York: Paulist, 1989), 10.

65. Daniel Boyarin, "Tricksters, Martyrs, and Collaborators: Diaspora and the Gendered Politics of Resistance," in *Powers of Diaspora: Two Essays on the Relevance of Jewish Culture*, by Jonathan Boyarin and Daniel Boyarin (Minneapolis: University of Minnesota Press, 2002), 53–55.

66. Yosef Hayim Yerushalmi, "Servants of Kings and Not Servants of Servants: Some Aspects of the Political History of the Jews" (unpublished paper, Emory University, 2005), 7.

67. Salo Wittmayer Baron, *A Social and Religious History of the Jews*, 2nd ed., 18 vols. (New York: Columbia University Press, 1952–1983), 4:36–43.

68. Paul Kriwaczek, *Yiddish Civilisation: The Rise and Fall of a Forgotten Nation* (New York: Knopf, 2005), 144.

69. Catherine Bell, *Ritual: Perspectives and Dimensions* (New York: Oxford University Press, 1997), 138–139.

70. Eliezer Segal, *In Those Days, at This Time: Holiness and History in the Jewish Calendar* (Calgary: University of Calgary Press, 2007), xiii.

71. Joseph Caro, *Shulchan Arukh*, Orach Chaim, 670:2.

72. Susan L. Braunstein, "Hanukkah Lamp," in *Encyclopaedia Judaica*, vol. 8., 333–336.

73. Benjamin Zvieli, "The Scroll of Antiochus," Bar Ilan University's Parashat Hashavua Study Center, Parashat MiKetz-Shabbat Hanukkah 5766/December 31, 2005, http://www.biu.ac.il/JH/Parasha/eng/miketz/zev.html (accessed February 2, 2007); Louis Ginzberg, "Scroll of Antiochus," *Jewish Encyclopedia*, http://jewishencyclopedia.com (accessed February 5, 2007); Leon Nemoy, "The Yiddish Yossipon of 1546 in the Alexander Kohut Memorial Collection of Judaica," *Yale University Library Gazette* 4 (1930): 36–39.

74. Avodat Yisrael's introduction to the scroll in this prayer book says that it was translated into German and published in Venice in 1548. Rabbi Behr Frank of Pressburg translated it into Hebrew in 1806. Zvieli, "Scroll of Antiochus"; *Ha-Siddur Ha-Shalem, Daily Prayer Book*, translated and annotated with an introduction by Philip Birnbaum (New York: Hebrew Publishing Company, 1949), 714.

75. Eliyahu Touger, trans., *Mishneh Torah: Hilchot Ta'aniot and Hilchot Megillah VaChanukah*, by Maimonides (New York: Moznaim, 1991), 142–144.

76. "Moses ben Israel Isserles," *Encyclopedia Britannica Online*, http://britannica.

com/eb/article-9042992 (accessed March 9, 2008); Solomon B. Freehof, "Ceremonial Creativity among the Ashkenazim," *Jewish Quarterly Review*, 75th anniversary vol. (1967): 210.

77. Robert Bruce Mullin, *Miracles and the Modern Religious Imagination* (New Haven: Yale University Press, 1996), 31–50.

78. Abraham W. Binder, "Hanukkah in Music," in *Studies in Jewish Music: Collected Writings of A. W. Binder*, ed. Irene Heskes (New York: Bloch, 1971), 67.

79. Arnold Van Gennep, *Rites of Passage* (1909; trans., Chicago: University of Chicago Press, 1960); Victor Turner, ed., *Celebration: Studies in Festivity and Ritual* (Washington, DC: Smithsonian Institution Press, 1982); Victor Turner, *Dramas, Fields, and Metaphors: Symbolic Action in Human Society* (Ithaca: Cornell University Press, 1974).

80. Jerome R. Mintz, *Hasidic People: A Place in the New World* (Cambridge: Harvard University Press, 1992), 9; see also Max L. Margolis and Alexander Marx, *A History of the Jewish People* (Philadelphia: Jewish Publication Society, 1975), 580–581.

81. Jacob Katz, *Out of the Ghetto: The Social Background of Jewish Emancipation, 1770–1870* (New York: Schocken Books, 1978), 17–19.

82. Ibid., 20–25.

83. Daniel Stauben, *Scenes of Jewish Life in Alsace* (originally published 1885–1890), trans. Rose Choron (Malibu, CA: Joseph Simon / Pangloss, 1992), 129.

84. William R. Hutchison, *The Modernist Impulse in American Protestantism* (Durham: Duke University Press, 1992), 102; Lance J. Sussman, "The Myth of the Trefa Banquet: American Culinary Culture and the Radicalization of Food Policy in American Reform Judaism," *American Jewish Archives Journal* 57. nos. 1–2 (2005): 42.

85. Henry Ward Beecher, "The Advance of a Century," *New York Tribune*, extra no. 33, Independence Day Orations (July 4, 1876): 37–44, reprinted in *Democratic Vistas, 1860–1880*, ed. Alan Trachtenberg (New York: George Braziller, 1970), 70; T. J. Jackson Lears, *No Place of Grace: Antimodernism and the Transformation of American Culture, 1880–1920* (1981; repr., Chicago: University of Chicago Press, 1994), 7.

86. Lears, *No Place of Grace*, 17.

87. Sir Roger L'Estrange, *Works of Josephus*, 6 vols. (Philadelphia: W. & T. Bradford, 1773–1775).

88. Stephen A. Cummins, *Paul and the Crucified Christ: Maccabean Martyrdom and Galatians 1 and 2* (Cambridge: Cambridge University Press, 2001); Jan Willem Van Henten, *The Maccabean Martyrs as Saviors of the Jewish People: A Study of 2 and 4 Maccabees* (Leiden: Brill, 1997).

89. Van Henten, *Maccabean Martyrs*.

90. Abraham Geiger, *Judaism and Its History: Lectures Given in Frankfurt, 1863–1864*, trans. Maurice Mayer (New York: M. Thalmessinger, 1865).

91. Abraham Geiger, *Abraham Geiger and Liberal Judaism: The Challenge of the*

Nineteenth Century, comp. Max Wiener, trans. Ernst J. Schloshauer (Philadelphia: Jewish Publication Society, 1962).

92. Michael A, Meyer, *Response to Modernity: A History of the Reform Movement in Judaism* (Oxford: Oxford University Press, 1988), 190.

93. Heinrich Graetz, *Geschichte der Juden*, 11 vols. (1853–1875); Graetz, *Volkstümliche Geschichte der Juden*, 3 vols. (Leipzig: O. Leiner, 1888); Graetz, *History of the Jews*, trans. Bela Lowry (Philadelphia: Jewish Publication Society, 1891–1898).

94. Stephen J. Whitfield, "Declaration of Independence: American Jewish Culture in the Twentieth Century," in *Cultures of the Jews: A New History*, ed. David Biale (New York: Schocken Books, 2002), 1100.

95. Allen S. Maller, "Hanukkah: Its Rise and Fall," *Jewish Heritage* (Fall–Winter 1972): 24; see also Kenneth White, "American Jewish Response to Christmas" (ordination thesis, Hebrew Union College, Cincinnati, 1982), 220.

NOTES TO CHAPTER 2

A version of this chapter appeared in *New Essays in American Jewish History*, ed. Pamela S. Nadell, Jonathan D. Sarna, and Lance J. Sussman (New York: KTAV, 2010), 197–228.

1. One of the best descriptions of the nineteenth-century American Jewish crisis of religious leadership is in Bruce L. Ruben, *Max Lilienthal: The Making of the American Rabbinate* (Detroit: Wayne State University Press, 2011), 85–94.

2. Dianne Ashton, *Rebecca Gratz: Women and Judaism in Antebellum America* (Detroit: Wayne State University Press, 1997), 32, 35, 115, 124, 132, 222; Jonathan D. Sarna, *American Judaism: A History* (New Haven: Yale University Press, 2004), 49; David Philipson, *Letters of Rebecca Gratz* (Philadelphia: Jewish Publication Society, 1929), 75–76.

3. Naomi Cohen, "Pioneers of American Jewish Defense," *American Jewish Archives* 29 (November 1977): 134.

4. Dena Wilansky, *Sinai to Cincinnati: Lay Views on the Writings of Isaac M. Wise* (New York: Renaissance, 1937), 261–265. Jacob J. Petuchowski suggested that the Enlightenment and ensuing political revolutions made Hanukkah's miracles seem implausible. Petuchowski, "The Magnification of Chanukah," *Commentary* 29 (January 1960): 38–40.

5. Jonathan D. Sarna, "The Democratization of American Judaism," in *New Essays in American Jewish History*, ed. Pamela S. Nadell, Jonathan D. Sarna, and Lance J. Sussman (Cincinnati: American Jewish Archives, 2010), 99; see also Sydney M. Fish, "The Problem of Intermarriage in Early America," *Gratz College Annual of Jewish Studies* 4 (1975): 85–95; Edwin Wolf II and Maxwell Whiteman, *The History of the Jews of Philadelphia from Colonial Times to the Age of Jackson* (Philadelphia: Jewish Publication Society, 1956), 128–131.

6. Sarna, "Democratization of American Judaism," 97–98.

7. Sarna, *American Judaism*, 59–60.

8. Sarna *American Judaism*, 24–25, 74, 135; Ashton, *Rebecca Gratz*, 134–140.

9. The new, more reform worship in turn offended traditionalist members, who left to form their own congregation, Sheareth Israel. Gary Philip Zola, *Isaac Harby of Charleston* (Tuscaloosa: University of Alabama Press, 1994), 112–150; Gary P. Zola, "The First Reform Prayer Book in America: The Liturgy of the Reformed Society of Israelites," in *Platforms and Prayer Books: Theological and Liturgical Perspectives on Reform Judaism*, ed. Dana Kaplan (Lanham, MD: Rowman and Littlefield, 2002), 20; Robert Rosen, *Pocket Guide to Kahal Kadosh Beth Elohim and Charleston Jewish History* (Kahal Kadosh Beth Elohim, June 2005), 4; Penina Moise, *Fancy's Sketch Book* (Charleston, SC: J. S. Burges, 1833). The Moise volume was the first book of verse published by an American Jewish woman.

10. Jonathan D. Sarna, "The Question of Music in American Judaism: Reflections at 350 Years," *American Jewish History* 91 (June 2003): 201.

11. Psalm 30, in *The Jewish Study Bible*, trans. Jewish Publication Society (1985; repr., New York: Oxford University Press, 1999), 1430.

12. David de Sola Pool and Tamar de Sola Pool, *An Old Faith in the New World: Portrait of Sheareth Israel, 1654–1954* (New York: Columbia University Press, 1955), 99; see also Sarna, "Question of Music," 196.

13. Christine Leigh Heyrman, *Southern Cross: The Beginnings of the Bible Belt* (New York: Knopf, 1997).

14. Rebecca Samuel (Petersburg, VA, 1790), in *The Jews in America: A Treasury of Art and Literature*, ed. Abraham Karp (Southport, CT: Hugh Lauter Levin, 1994), 48–50; Hasia R. Diner and Beryl Leiff Benderly, *Her Works Praise Her: A History of Jewish Women in America from Colonial Times to the Present* (New York: Basic Books, 2002), 15–16.

15. Sarna, *American Judaism*, 62–135; Hasia R. Diner, *The Jews of the United States* (Berkeley: University of California Press, 2004), 128–131.

16. Shaye Cohen, *From the Maccabees to the Mishnah* (Louisville, KY: Westminster John Knox Press, 1987), 37–38.

17. Isaac Leeser, "The Demands of the Times," *Occident and American Jewish Advocate* 1, no. 12 (March 1844), http://www.jewish-history.com/occident/volume 1/ jan1844/demands.html (accessed June 8, 2007).

18. Ashton, *Rebecca Gratz*, 121–169.

19. Isaac Leeser, "Festival Observance," *Occident* 48 (1861): 285. See Kenneth Libo and Irving Howe, *We Lived There Too* (New York: St. Mark's, 1984), 172, for a Hanukkah menorah made by San Francisco hardware merchant Charles Brown in 1865.

20. Lance J. Sussman, *Isaac Leeser and the Making of American Judaism* (Detroit: Wayne State University Press, 1995).

21. See for example H. A. Henry, "Festival Observance: Sermon Delivered at Shearith Israel Synagogue, San Francisco, on Feast of Hanukkah 5627," *Occident* 25 (1867): 290.

22. Samuel Isaacs, *Jewish Messenger* (December 18, 1857): 100.

23. Sussman, *Isaac Leeser*, 80–104; Arthur Kiron, "Golden Ages, Promised Lands: The Victorian Rabbinic Humanism of Sabato Morais" (Ph.D. diss., Columbia University, 1999), 275–318; Sarna, *American Judaism*, 80–81.

24. Kiron, "Golden Ages, Promised Lands," 108.

25. Ibid., 282; Benjamin Rabinowitz, "The Young Men's Hebrew Assoc., 1854–1913," *Publications in American Jewish History* 37 (1947): 221–326.

26. Samuel Isaacs, *Jewish Messenger* (December 4, 1863): 21.

27. Cyrus Adler and Louis H. Levin, "Szold, Benjamin," *Encyclopedia Judaica*, ed. Michael Berenbaum and Fred Skolnik (Jerusalem: Keter, 2007), 409.

28. Sarna, *American Judaism*, 78; Sussman, *Isaac Leeser*, 162.

29. Sussman, *Isaac Leeser*, 175.

30. Sarna, *American Judaism*, 95.

31. Michael A. Meyer, *Response to Modernity: A History of the Reform Movement in Judaism* (New York: Oxford University Press, 1988), 248; Alan Silverstein, *Alternatives to Assimilation: The Response of Reform Judaism to American Culture, 1840–1930* (Hanover, NH: Brandeis University Press / University Press of New England, 1994), 10; Sarna, *American Judaism*, 43–44.

32. Marc Lee Raphael, *Profiles in American Judaism* (San Francisco: Harper and Row, 1984), 197;. Others count a greater number of Reform congregations. Note by contrast that Hasia Diner counts, by 1880, "only twelve synagogues—out of two hundred—had not affiliated" with the Union of American Hebrew Congregations. Diner, *Jews of the United States*, 122. Gerald Sorin also claims that most of the country's "well over 200 congregations" were Reform. Sorin, *Tradition Transformed: The Jewish Experience in America* (Baltimore: Johns Hopkins University Press, 1997), 29. Sarna and Sorin both agree that no one paid much attention to the "small number of newly formed congregations established by arriving Eastern Europeans." Sorin, *Tradition Transformed*, 29; Sarna, *American Judaism*, 101–102.

33. Hasia R. Diner, *A Time for Gathering: The Second Migration, 1820–1880* (Baltimore: Johns Hopkins University Press, 1992), 44–48; Lee Shai Weissbach, *Jewish Life in Small-Town America* (New Haven: Yale University Press, 2005).

34. Edith Gelles, introduction to *The Letters of Abigaill Levy Franks, 1733–1748*, ed. Edith Gelles (New Haven: Yale University Press, 2004), xviii; Sarna, *American Judaism*, 45.

35. Sarna, *American Judaism*, 75.

36. Jonathan D. Sarna, "The Cult of Synthesis in American Jewish Life," *Jewish Social Studies*, n.s., 5 (Fall–Winter 1999): 52–79.

37. Max Lilienthal, "The Festival of Chanuckah," *Occident* 4, no. 12 (March 1847); "The Jews in China," *Occident* 1, no. 4 (July 1843); "The Cincinnati Hebrew Benevolent Society," *Occident* 4, no. 11 (February 1847); "The New York Hebrew Benevolent Society," *Occident* 3, no. 9 (December 1845); "Manifesto of German Rabbis," translated from the Hebrew by Mr. Neumegen, *Occident* (July 1845).

38. Isaac M. Wise, *Israelite* (July 28, 1865): 29; and Wise, *Israelite* (December 23,

1887): 4; James Gutheim Heller, *Isaac M. Wise: His Life, Work, and Thought* (New York: Union of American Hebrew Congregations, 1965), 534–564; Eric Friedland, *Were Our Mouths Filled with Song: Studies in Liberal Jewish Liturgy* (Cincinnati: Hebrew Union College Press, 1997). As Sefton D. Temkin explains about *Minhag America*, in *Isaac Mayer Wise: Shaping American Judaism* (New York: Oxford University Press, 1992), 276, "The 17th benediction, in which traditional form petitions for restoration of the Temple service, . . . reads *veheshev shechinatcha lidvir betecha*—let the glory of thy majesty return to the hall of thy house; . . . The penultimate benediction has the narrative part of the insertions for Hanukkah and Purim, but not the introductory prayer *Al Hanissim*—Wise did not believe in miracles." Isaac M. Wise, *The History of the Israelitish Nation from Abraham to the Present Time* (Albany, NY: J. Munsell, 1854).

39. Isaac M. Wise, "Hanucah: the Dedication Feast," *Israelite* (December 18, 1857): 18. Moshe Davis noted Wise's belief in Judaism's universalist message that is echoed here. Davis, *The Emergence of Conservative Judaism: The Historical School in 19th Century America* (Philadelphia: Jewish Publication Society, 1963), 153–154.

40. Isaac M. Wise, "Thoughts from Denver, Colorado," *American Israelite* (January 2, 1885): 2.

41. Abraham Geiger, *Judaism and Its History*, trans. Charles Newburgh (New York: Bloch, 1911). Originally published in 1865, the manuscript was reprinted in New York that same year.

42. Joseph Caro, *Shulchan Arukh*, Orach Chaim, 670:2.

43. New RSV *Oxford Annotated Bible*, AP 341; Peter Kirby, "4 Maccabees," *Early Christian Writings*, http://www.earlyjewishwritings.com/4maccabees.html (accessed June 8, 2007); Paul Halsall, "The Death of the Maccabees from the Fourth Book of Maccabees," Internet Medieval Source Book, May 1997, http://www.fordham.edu/halsall/source/macc4.html.

44. Advertisement, *The Israelite* 7, no. 22 (November 23, 1860): 166.

45. R. Glanz, "Where the Jewish Press Was Distributed in Pre–Civil War America," *Western States Jewish Historical Quarterly* 5 (1972): 1–14.

46. Isaac M. Wise, *The World of My Books*, trans. Albert H. Friedlander (Cincinnati: American Jewish Archives, 1954), 21.

47. Wise, *History of the Israelitish Nation*.

48. Jonathan M. Hess, "Beyond Subversion: German Jewry and the Poetics of Middlebrow Culture," *German Quarterly* 82, no. 3 (Summer 2009): 317–318.

49. Virginia Larkin Redway, "Handel in Colonial and Post-Colonial America (to 1820)," *Musical Quarterly* 21, no. 2 (1935): 192.

50. Alexander L. Ringer, "Handel and the Jews," *Music & Letters* 42, no. 1 (January 1961): 22.

51. Ibid., 27.

52. "Handelian FAQs," GFHandel.org, http://gfhandel.org/faqs.html (accessed February 3, 2007).

53. Georg Friedrich Handel, *Judas Maccabaeus: A Sacred Drama* (1747), words by Thomas Morell, Act One, available at http://opera.stanford.edu/iu/libretti/judas .htm (accessed June 30, 2007); Ringer, "Handel and the Jews," 17–29.

54. "Handelian FAQs," GFHandel.org, http://gfhandel.org/faqs.html (accessed June 30, 2007).

55. E. Hayter, "Music in America," *Musical Times and Singing Class Circular* (May 1888): 303–304.

56. Loring B. Barnes, "Musical Progress in the United States," *Musical Times* (February 1, 1887): 110.

57. Ludwig Philippson, "Literarischer Wochenbericht," *Allegemeine Zeitung des Judemthums* 46 (1882): 750–751. For a comparison of that genre with ghetto tales, see Jonathan M. Hess, "Leopold Kompert and the Work of Nostalgia: The Cultural Capital of German Jewish Ghetto Fiction," *Jewish Quarterly Review* 97, no. 4 (Fall 2007); on Jewish historical fiction, see Jonathan S. Skolnik, "Writing Jewish History between Gutzkow and Goethe," *Prooftexts* 19 (1999): 101–125; Skolnik, "Writing Jewish History at the Margins of the Weimer Classics: Minority Culture and National Identity in Germany, 1837–1873," in *Searching for Common Ground: Diskurse zur deutschen Identitat, 1750–1871,* ed. Nicholas Vaszonyi (Cologne: Böhlau, 2000), 227–238; and Skolnik, " 'Who Learns History from Heine?': The German-Jewish Historical Novel as Cultural Memory and Minority Culture, 1824–1933" (Ph.D. diss., Columbia University, 1999).

58. I am grateful to Jonathan M. Hess for pointing this out to me. Hess, "Leopold Kompert," 577; Emil Lehmann, "Zum Weihefeste," *Der Orient* 9 (1848): 412.

59. "Hanucah: The Feast of Dedication," *The Israelite* 10, no. 24 (December 11, 1863): 188.

60. Isaac M. Wise, "The First of the Maccabees," *The Israelite* (1860). An advertisement for the novel in book form ran in *The Israelite* (November 23, 1860): 166.

61. Michael Satlow, *Creating Judaism* (New York: Columbia University Press, 2006), 115–187.

62. Kiron, "Golden Ages, Promised Lands," 284.

63. Jonathan D. Sarna, *A Great Awakening: The Transformation That Shaped Twentieth Century Judaism and Its Implications for Today* (New York: Council for Initiatives in Jewish Education, 1995), 15.

64. Ibid., 4.

65. Ibid., 16–17.

66. Ibid., 16.

67. "Chanucka," *American Hebrew* 9, no. 3 (December 16, 1881): 50.

68. David Glassberg, *American Historical Pageantry: The Uses of Tradition in the Early Twentieth Century* (Chapel Hill: University of North Carolina Press, 1990), 9–15.

69. David Kaufman, *Shul with a Pool: The "Synagogue-Center" in American Jewish History* (Hanover, NH: Brandeis University Press / University Press of New England, 1999), 69.

70. Mark C. Carnes, *Secret Ritual and Manhood in Victorian America* (New Haven: Yale University Press, 1989).

71. Clifford Putney, *Muscular Christianity: Manhood and Sports in Protestant America, 1880–1930* (Princeton: Princeton University Press, 1995).

72. Young Men's Hebrew Association, *Libretto of the Chanucka Entertainment Given at Lexington Ave. Opera House, December 28, 1878*, text by Julius Frank (New York: Young Men's Hebrew Association, 1878); includes sections from Handel's oratorio *Judas Maccabaeus*.

73. See front page and "Our Philadelphia Letter," *American Hebrew* 5, no. 4 (December 10, 1880): 39.

74. Glassberg, *American Historical Pageantry*, 39.

75. "Grand Chanukah Celebration," *American Hebrew* (December 19, 1879): 56.

76. "The Festival of Chanucka," *Frank Leslie's Illustrated Newspaper* (January 3, 1880): 317.

77. John B. Jentz, review of *Beyond the Lines: Pictorial Reporting, Everyday Life, and the Crisis of the Gilded Age*, by Joshua Brown (Berkeley: University of California Press, 2003), *Journal of American History* 90, no. 3 (December 2003): 68, 80.

78. Alan Silverstein, *Alternatives to Assimilation: The Response of Reform Judaism to American Culture, 1840–1930* (Hanover, NH: Brandeis University Press / University Press of New England, 1994), 82.

79. Paula Hyman, *Gender and Assimilation in Modern Jewish History* (Seattle: University of Washington Press, 1995), 139–140.

80. E. Anthony Rotundo, *American Manhood: Transformations in American Manhood from the Revolution to the Modern Era* (New York: Basic Books, 1993), 246.

81. Some evidence suggests that Longfellow composed his poem after seeing a full performance of Handel's *Judas Maccabaeus* in Europe. Wilbert Snow, "Review of *The Diary of Clara Crowninshield: A European Tour with Longfellow 1835–1836*, by Andrew Hilen," *Modern Language Notes* 73, no. 5 (May 1958): 367–368.

82. "Christmas," *Philadelphia Inquirer* (December 26, 1879): front page.

83. *Frank Leslie's Illustrated Weekly* (December 27, 1879): 293, and Supplement (January 3, 1880): 338.

84. Ellen M. Litwicki, *American's Public Holidays, 1865–1920* (Washington, DC: Smithsonian Institution Press, 2000), 9–10.

85. Harley Erdman, *Staging the Jew: The Performance of an American Ethnicity, 1860–1920* (New Brunswick: Rutgers University Press, 1997), 42–79; Stephen J. Whitfield, "The Politics of Pageantry, 1936–1946," *American Jewish History* 84 (September 1996): 221–252.

86. *American Hebrew* (December 10, 1880): 39.

87. Erdman, *Staging the Jew*, 40–62.

88. Max Cohen to Solomon Solis-Cohen, October 14, 1879, Solomon Solis-Cohen Collection, National Museum of American Jewish History.

89. Solomon Solis-Cohen, "Chanuka," *American Hebrew* 37, no. 4 (November 30,

1888): 34; Jonathan Boyarin and Daniel Boyarin, *Powers of Diaspora* (Minneapolis: University of Minnesota Press, 2002), 4.

90. Max Cohen to Solomon Solis-Cohen, December 22, 1879, Solis-Cohen Papers, National Museum of American Jewish History; see also Sarna, *American Judaism*, 136; Sarna, "The Making of an American Jewish Culture," in *When Philadelphia Was the Capital of Jewish America*, ed. Murray Friedman (Philadelphia: Balch Institute for Ethnic Studies, 1993), 149.

91. Philip Cowen, *American Hebrew* 37, no. 3 (November 23, 1888): front page.

92. Rachel Oliveri, "Guide to the Collection of the Purim Association of New York City" (1862–1902), I-20, American Jewish Historical Society Papers, 1865–1906, AJHS.

93. Jonathan D. Sarna, "The Cult of Synthesis in American Jewish Culture," *Jewish Social Studies*, n.s., 5, nos. 1–2 (Autumn 1998–Winter 1999): 52–79; Sorin, *Tradition Transformed*, 3. Several scholars have made this point. See for example Marshall Sklare, *Conservative Judaism: An American Religious Movement*, 2nd ed. (New York: Irvington, 1972); Leon Jick, *The Americanization of the Synagogue, 1820–1870* (1976; repr., Hanover, NH: Brandeis University Press / University Press of New England, 1992); Sarna, *American Judaism*.

94. Sarna, *American Judaism*.

95. Litwicki, *America's Public Holidays*.

96. Leigh Eric Schmidt, *Consumer Rites: The Buying and Selling of American Holidays* (Princeton: Princeton University Press, 1995), 105–191; Karal Ann Marling, *Merry Christmas: Celebrating America's Greatest Holiday* (Cambridge: Harvard University Press, 2000); Penne Restad, *Christmas in America: A History* (New York: Oxford University Press, 1995).

97. Joshua Eli Plaut, *A Kosher Christmas: 'Tis the Season to Be Jewish* (New Brunswick: Rutgers University Press, 2012), 10–35.

98. *The Jews of Boston: Essays on the Occasion of the Centenary*, ed. Jonathan D. Sarna and Ellen Smith (Boston: Combined Jewish Philanthropies of Greater Boston, 1995), 252.

99. Leo Kaul, "Hanukkah or Christmas," *Reform Advocate* (December 26, 1903): 428.

100. Theodor Herzl, "The Menorah," *Menorah Journal* 1, no. 5 (December 1915): 261 (translated by Bessie London Pouzzner); Warren Boronson and Rebecca Boronson, "Coping with Santa Claus," *Jewish Living* (November–December 1979): 31–32; Kenneth White, "American Jewish Response to Christmas" (ordination thesis, Hebrew Union College, Cincinnati, 1982), 252–253.

101. Jonathan M. Hess, *Germans, Jews, and the Claims of Modernity* (New Haven: Yale University Press, 2002), 2–27.

102. For more on this trend, see Beth S. Wenger, "Rites of Citizenship: Jewish Celebrations of the Nation," in *The Columbia History of Jews and Judaism in America*, ed. Marc Lee Raphael (New York: Columbia University Press, 2008), 366–383.

103. Sarna, "Cult of Synthesis," 52–79.

104. Anonymous, "Jews in the Union Army: Sketches from the Seat of War, by a Jewish Soldier," *Jewish Messenger* 11, no. 5 (February 7, 1867): 41.

105. Litwicki, *America's Public Holidays*, 241.

106. Emanuel Schreiber, "Thoughts from Denver Colorado," *American Israelite* 31 (January 2, 1885): 2.

107. "Schreiber, Emanuel," in *American Jewish Biography*, ed. Jacob Raider Marcus, vol. 2 (Brooklyn, NY: Carlson, 1994), 569.

108. "The Pittsburgh Liberal Religious Platform, November 16–19, 1885," in *The Jew in the American World: A Source Book*, ed. Jacob Rader Marcus (Detroit: Wayne State University Press, 1996), 241–243.

109. Michael A. Meyer, *Response to Modernity: A History of the Reform Movement in Judaism* (New York: Oxford University Press, 1998), 3.

110. Benny Kraut, in "Jewish Survival in Protestant America," in *Minority Faiths and the American Protestant Mainstream*, ed. Jonathan D. Sarna (Urbana: University of Illinois Press, 1998), 16, describes 1865–1915 as a "period of most intense creativity and wrestling over issues of group continuity."

111. W. Gunther Plaut, *Mount Zion, 1856–1956, the First Hundred Years* (St. Paul, MN: North Central, 1956), 48.

112. Gustav Gottheil, "What Christians Owe the Maccabees," *Jewish Messenger* (January 4, 1884): 6; Jenna Weissman Joselit, *The Wonders of America: Reinventing Jewish Culture, 1880–1950* (New York: Hill and Wang, 1994), 230.

113. Nathan H. Lemowitz, "Jewish Pupils in Public Schools," *American Jewish Chronicle* (September 1, 1916): 521; Joselit, *Wonders of America*, 230.

114. Joselit, *Wonders of America*, 230.

115. "Correspondence," *American Hebrew* (November 28, 1879): 4.

NOTES TO CHAPTER 3

1. Karen Halttunen, *Confidence Men and Painted Women: A Study of Middle-Class Culture in America, 1830–1870* (New Haven: Yale University Press, 1982), 56–68.

2. Anne C. Rose, *Victorian America and the Civil War* (Cambridge: Cambridge University Press, 1992), 162–163.

3. Penne L. Restad, *Christmas in America: A History* (New York: Oxford University Press, 1995), 102–104.

4. Sylvia Barack Fishman, *The Way into the Varieties of Jewishness* (Woodstock, VT: Jewish Lights, 2007), 198.

5. Uriel Rappoport, "Hadrian, Publius Aelius," in *Encyclopaedia Judaica*, ed. Michael Berenbaum and Fred Skolnik, 2nd ed., vol. 8 (Detroit: Macmillan Reference, 2007), 193; Alan Richard Schulman, "Antoninus Pius," in *Encyclopaedia Judaica*, vol. 2, 248; Bernhard Blumenkranz, "Hadrian (Adrian)," in *Encyclopaedia Judaica*, vol. 8, 193. When Pope Hadrian (772–795) called the Second Council of Nicea in 787, he condemned as too Jewish those attendees

who argued for an iconoclastic Christianity. He erected boundaries between Christians and Jews by forbidding Christians from celebrating the Passover and Sabbath "in the Jewish fashion" and discouraged his flocks from socializing that involved eating in Jews' homes.

6. Fishman, *Way into the Varieties of Jewishness*, 199–200; Shaye J. D. Cohen, *The Beginnings of Jewishness: Boundaries, Varieties, Uncertainties* (Berkeley: University of California Press, 1999), 110–111, 211–233.

7. Cyrus Adler and Herbert Friedenwald, "Warder Cresson," *Jewish Encyclopedia*, http://www.jewishencyclopedia.com (accessed March 20, 2011).

8. "The McGuffey Readers—1836 Version," *McGuffey's Readers World*, http://www.mcguffeyreaders.com/1836_original.htm (accessed June 12, 2008).

9. Isaac M. Wise, editorial, *American Israelite* (December 1870): 9; Kenneth White, "American Jewish Response to Christmas" (ordination thesis, Hebrew Union College, Cincinnati, 1982), 185.

10. Max Lilienthal, "War of the Maccabees," *Sabbath Visitor* (November 23, 1876): 365.

11. *Sabbath Visitor* (November 26, 1880): front page.

12. Lee Eric Schmidt, *Consumer Rites: The Buying and Selling of American Holidays* (Princeton: Princeton University Press, 1995), 20–23; Elizabeth Pleck, *Celebrating the Family: Ethnicity, Consumer Culture, and Family Rituals* (Cambridge: Harvard University Press, 2000), 20–35.

13. Restad, *Christmas in America*, 92–95.

14. Marion A. Kaplan, "Women and Tradition in the German-Jewish Family," in *The Jewish Family: Myths and Reality*, ed. Steven M. Cohen and Paula E. Hyman (New York: Holmes and Meier, 1986), 69; "Immigration: German," Learning Page, American Memory, Library of Congress, http://memory.loc.gov/features/immig/german3.htm (accessed May 8, 2008).

15. Schmidt, *Consumer Rites*, 105–175; Karal Ann Marling, *Merry Christmas: Celebrating America's Greatest Holiday* (Cambridge: Harvard University Press, 2000); Pleck, *Celebrating the Family*; Jeffrey Shandler, *Jews, God, and Videotape: Religion and Media in America* (New York: NYU Press, 2009), 185–190.

16. James Gutheim Heller, *Isaac M. Wise: His Life, Work, and Thought* (New York: Union of American Hebrew Congregations, 1965), 242.

17. Sefton D. Temkin, "Isaac Mayer Wise and the Civil War," *American Jewish Archives* 15 (November 1963): 121.

18. See for example "Christmas," *Jewish Messenger* (December 31, 1864): 4; "A Christmas Story," *Israelite* (December 22 and December 29, 1864): front pages; "Hannucah and Christmas," *Occident* (1867): 510–511; Max Lilienthal, "The Chanukah Festival!," *Sabbath Visitor* (December 15, 1876): 388; Lilienthal, "Origin of Chanukah," *Sabbath Visitor* (December 5, 1879): 388; "Chanukah," *American Hebrew* (December 12, 1879): 38.

19. Jonathan D. Sarna, "Max Lilienthal," in *American National Biography*, vol. 13 (New York: Oxford University Press, 1999), 653–654.

20. Max Lilienthal, "Let's Have a Chanukah Festival!," *Sabbath Visitor* (December 15, 1876): 388.

21. Max Lilienthal, "The Chanukah Festival," *Sabbath Visitor* (December 1874): 194.

22. Editorial, *Sabbath Visitor* (December 1874): front page.

23. Sally Moore and Barbara Meyerhoff, "Introduction: Secular Ritual: Forms and Meanings," in *Secular Ritual*, ed. Sally Moore and Barbara Meyerhoff (Assen, Netherlands: Van Gorcum, 1977), 24; Pleck, *Celebrating the Family*, 23.

24. "Chanukah," *American Israelite* (December 30, 1870): 9; Karla Goldman, "Public Religious Lives of Cincinnati's Jewish Women," in *Women and American Judaism: Historical Perspectives*, ed. Pamela S. Nadell and Jonathan D. Sarna (Hanover, NH: Brandeis University Press / University Press of New England, 2001), 115; Herman Rosenthal, "Lilienthal, Max," *Jewish Encyclopedia*, http:// www.jewishencyclopedia.com (accessed October 10, 2007).

25. Yaffa Eliach, *There Once Was a World: A 900-Year Chronicle of the Shtetl of Eishyshok* (Boston: Little, Brown, 1998), 125, 287; Hasia R. Diner, *A Time for Gathering: The Second Migration, 1820–1880* (Baltimore: Johns Hopkins University Press, 1992), 9.

26. Naomi W. Cohen, *What the Rabbis Said: The Public Discourse of Nineteenth-Century American Rabbis* (New York: NYU Press, 2008), 76. Born in Munich in 1815 and educated at the university there, Lilienthal became the first principal of a newly established Jewish school in Riga in 1840. Convinced that the rising generation of Jews needed a modernized Jewish education, he also established innovative Jewish schools after immigrating to the United States a few years later. In 1844, he established a day school that served children of three New York congregations that he served as rabbi. He became known for the warmth of his manner and the personal attention he gave to his students, and he often spoke about Jews' parental duties. While still living in New York, he penned a Hanukkah sermon for his congregants, which, translated from German into English by his brother, also reached the small Jewish community in Augusta, Georgia, where fewer than 240 Jews lived. The "useful lesson" that Lilienthal drew for them from "the miraculous deeds of our forefathers" asked Jews to devote themselves to their children. "Mothers," he said, by assuring their children's religious education, would join centuries of "pious mothers in Israel." Fathers should teach by example how their Jewish faith "ennobles" them. Max Lilienthal, "Sermon," 1846, translated from the German by S. Lilienthal, collection P-363, AJHS. Wise encouraged Lilienthal, a frequent contributor to Wise's magazine, to come to Cincinnati to lead a congregation. In 1854, Lilienthal relocated with his family westward, where he remained until his death in 1882.

27. "The Chanukah Festival," *Sabbath Visitor* (December 1874): 194.

28. Editorial, *American Israelite* (January 2, 1876): 2; White, "American Jewish Response to Christmas," 192.

29. Michael A. Meyer, *Response to Modernity: A History of the Reform Movement in Judaism* (New York: Oxford University Press, 1998), 42.

30. "Correspondence: Cincinnati," *Sabbath Visitor* (December 14, 1877): 899.

31. Irving I. Katz, *The Beth El Story, with a History of the Jews of Michigan before 1850* (Detroit: Wayne State University Press, 1955), 88; W. Gunther Plaut, *Mount Zion, 1856–1956, the First Hundred Years* (St. Paul, MN: North Central, 1956), 48, 64. Courtesy Cynthia Gensheimer.

32. "Baltimore Correspondent Shulamith" (Henrietta Szold), *Jewish Messenger* (January 17, 1879): 20.

33. Editorial, *American Hebrew* (November 12, 1880): front page.

34. "A Sensation at Saratoga: New Rules for the Grand Union," *New York Times* (June 19, 1877): 1

35. Walter T. K. Nugent's *The Tolerant Populists: Kansas, Populism, and Nativism* (Chicago: University of Chicago Press, 1963) describes both religious and ethnic tolerance and intolerance among rural midwesterners; see also Hasia R. Diner, *The Jews of the United States* (Berkeley: University of California Press, 2004), 170.

36. Editorial, *American Hebrew* (November 12, 1880): front page.

37. "Sneak Thieves among Jews," *American Hebrew* (November 12, 1880): 146.

38. "Dr. Sonneschein's Statement" (St. Louis, MO, June 29, 1886), Klau Library, Hebrew Union College, Cincinnati.

39. Editorial, *American Hebrew* (December 3, 1884): front page.

40. Selma Berrol, "Julia Richman's Work in New York," *American Jewish History* 70 (September 1980): 35–51; Judah Pilch, ed., *A History of Jewish Education in America* (New York: National Curriculum Research Institute of the American Association for Jewish Education, 1969).

41. "Correspondence," *American Hebrew* (November 28, 1879): 43.

42. "Correspondence: Philadelphia," *American Hebrew* (December 19, 1879): front page.

43. "Correspondence" columns in *American Israelite* (December 17, 1884): 194; *American Israelite* (December 26, 1884): 191; *American Israelite* (December 3, 1881): 33; *American Israelite* (December 18, 1885): 3; *American Israelite* (January 2, 1890): 7; *American Hebrew* (December 23, 1898): 290.

44. "Correspondence," *American Israelite* (December 11, 1885): 2.

45. White, "American Jewish Response to Christmas," 187.

46. *American Israelite* (December 6, 1900): 3; "Women's League," *American Israelite* (December 13, 1900): 2; "Correspondence: Richmond, VA," *American Israelite* (December 20, 1900): 2.

47. "Editorial Notes," *American Hebrew* (December 8, 1899): front page.

48. "Correspondence: San Francisco," *American Israelite* (January 11, 1884): 5.

49. Ella Jacobs, *Children's Prayers for Use in the School and Home*, 3rd ed. (Philadelphia, 1893), n.p.

50. Henry Iliowizi, *Chag Haneroth / The Feast of Lights* (Philadelphia, 1894), dedication, PJAC; see also Isaac S. Moses, *Hanukkah Festival: A Song Service for the Feast of Lights* (Chicago: American Hebrew Publishing House, 1893);

Irene Heskes, *Yiddish American Popular Songs, 1895–1950* (Washington, DC: Library of Congress, 1992), 3; Henry Iliowizi, *Chag Haneroth, "Feast of Lights,"* in Hebrew and English (Philadelphia, 1894), n.p.; Herman Bien, *The Feast of Lights, or Chanukoh: Three Character Poems and Grand Tableau Finale; Containing the Story of the Book of the Maccabees and Designed for Representation by Sabbath Schools and YMHA* (Vicksburg, MS: Vicksburg Printing and Publishing Company, 1885).

51. Bill Briggs, "Music as Medicine: Docs Use Tunes as Treatment," *MSNBC*, http://www.msnbc.com/id/30990170 (accessed June 1, 2009); Sandra E. Trehub, Judy Plantinga, and Jelena Brcic, "Infants Detect Cross-Modal Cues to Identity in Speech and Singing," in *Neurosciences and Music III—Disorders and Plasticity*, Annals of the New York Academy of Sciences 1169, ed. Simone Dalla Bella, Nina Kraus, Katie Overy, Christo Pantev, Joel S. Snyder, Mari Tervanieri, Barbara Tillam, and Gottfired Schlag (New York: New York Academy of Sciences, 2009). Although nineteenth-century Hanukkah celebrants did not know the science behind their love of singing, they knew it made them feel good. Hearing music provides a natural mood elevation by releasing endorphins and by lowering heart rates and levels of the stress hormone cortisol.

52. "The Meaning of Words: Marcus Jastrow and the Making of Rabbinic Dictionaries," Judaica Online Exhibitions, Penn Libraries, http://www.library.upenn.edu/exhibits/cajs/jastrow/01.html (accessed May 6, 2008).

53. Marcus Jastrow and Gustav Gottheil, "Rock of Ages," in *Union Hymnal for Jewish Worship*, ed. Gustav Gottheil (1896; repr., New York: Central Conference of American Rabbis, 1914), hymn 189.

54. "Hanuka," *American Hebrew* (November 21, 1890), 106.

55. Jeffrey A. Summit, *The Lord's Song in a Strange Land* (New York: Oxford University Press, 2000), 33.

56. "Is Chanuka a Minor Festival?," *American Hebrew* (December 13, 1895): 168.

57. Edward Said, *Culture and Imperialism* (New York: Knopf, 1993), xii–xiii.

58. Julia Richman, "Report of National Committee on Religious School Work, National Council of Jewish Women," in *Four Centuries of Jewish Women's Spirituality*, rev. ed., ed. Ellen M. Umansky and Dianne Ashton (Lebanon, NH: Brandeis University Press / University Press of New England, 2008), 149.

59. Karla Goldman, *Beyond the Synagogue Gallery: Finding a Place for Women in American Judaism* (Cambridge: Harvard University Press, 2000), 180.

60. Henry A. Henry, "Festival Observance Sermon Delivered at Sheareth Israel Synagogue, San Francisco, on Feast of Hanukkah 5627," *Occident* (1867): 290.

61. Marion Kaplan, *The Making of the Jewish Middle Class: Women, Family, and Identity in Imperial Germany* (New York: Oxford University Press, 1991), 65.

62. Max Lilienthal, "Our Chanukah," *Sabbath Visitor* (December 1874): 194.

63. *Shulchan Aruch*, Orach Chaim, 670:2, in Aryeh Kaplan, *The Laws of Chanukah* (New York: Moznaim, 1977), 4.

64. Ibid.

65. Benjamin Zvieli, "The Scroll of Antiochus," Bar-Ilan University Parashat Hasha-vua Study Center, Parashat MiKetz-Shabbat Hanukkah 5766/December 31, 2005, http://www.biu.ac.il/JH/Parasha/eng/miketz/zev.html (accessed February 2, 2007).

66. Those accounts of Judith's exploits, from rabbinic discussions in the Middle Ages, drew on the older Book of Judith, which scholars judge to have been written shortly after the Maccabean revolt. It describes Judith only as "a beautiful widow" and places her three hundred years earlier in the fictional town of Bethulia, during Judea's conquest by the Babylonian king Nebuchadnezzar, who destroyed the First Temple in Jerusalem. See Sara Raup Johnson, *Historical Fictions and Hellenistic Jewish Identity: Third Maccabees in Its Cultural Context* (Berkeley: University of California Press, 2004), xii; "Judith," *Oxford Study Bible* (New York: Oxford University Press, 1992), 1071–1079; A. J. Levine, ed., *Women Like This: New Perspectives on Jewish Women in the Greco-Roman World* (Atlanta: Scholars, 1991); Moshe David Herr, "Midrash," in *Encyclopaedia Judaica*, vol. 14, 182–185. The stories about defending the Jerusalem Temple amplify each other and underscore their image of widespread Jewish devotion.

67. *Shulchan Aruch*, Orach Chaim, 670:2, in Kaplan, *Laws of Chanukah*, 6.

68. Dianne Ashton, *Rebecca Gratz: Women and Judaism in Antebellum America* (Detroit: Wayne State University Press, 1997), 121–146.

69. *Sabbath Visitor* (December 24, 1880): 415.

70. "News from Lancaster," *Jewish Exponent* (December 23, 1887), n.p., scrap, Solomon Solis-Cohen Collection, National Museum of American Jewish History.

71. Reform leaders hoped their streamlined approach to Judaism would be able to keep busy American Jews within the fold. A fictional short story in the reformist *Hebrew Sabbath School Visitor* portrayed one such family whose "stern" father had renounced home festivals and insisted his wife and older daughter join him in devoting themselves to wage labor. Those rituals, properly executed with decorum and appropriate material items, marked a middle-class American home with time and opulence too luxurious for the working poor. In the story, when the family's eldest daughter is invited to a Hanukkah ball by the wife of a Reform rabbi, her experience transforms the family's religious life. The daughter's face is "lit with joy" as she recounts her pleasant holiday evening to her parents. That night, the father dreams of his dead sister, who, like Marley's ghost in Dickens's *A Christmas Carol*, insists that he reassess his life and reclaim Judaism. The next evening he brings home a Hanukkah menorah and candles, finds the Bible his father had given him, and vows to be a better husband, father, and Jew. The Reform rabbi's wife, a Hanukkah ball, and his daughter's delight renew the family's domestic religion. The story portrays Reform women and the new American festivals they helped to orchestrate, paving the way for a renewed religious life among eastern European immigrants who knew little about Reform. Cousin Cynthius, "Mrs. Halvick's Chanukah Ball and Its Results," *Sabbath Visitor* (December 9, 1892): 250.

72. Deborah Dwork, "Immigrant Jewish Life on the Lower East Side, 1880–1914," in *The American Jewish Experience*, ed. Jonathan D. Sarna (New York: Holmes and Meier, 1986), 117.

73. Moses Rischin, "Germans versus Russians," in Sarna, *American Jewish Experience*, 124–126.

74. *American Hebrew* (December 28, 1898): 211; *American Hebrew* (November 17, 1899): 86.

75. Edwin Wolf and Maxwell Whiteman, *History of the Jews of Philadelphia* (Philadelphia: Jewish Publication Society, 1975), 141; Goldman, *Beyond the Synagogue Gallery*, 72–74; Jenna Weissman Joselit, *Wonders of America: Reinventing Jewish Culture, 1880–1950* (New York: Hill and Wang, 1994), 230.

76. Gustav Gottheil, "The Jewish Reformation," *Journal of Theology* 6 (1902): 2.

77. "Religion's Best Place," *American Hebrew* (December 29, 1899): 264.

78. Sabato Morais, "Tribute to Ephraim Lederer," *Jewish Exponent* (November 19, 1897): 7. Thanks to Dr. Arthur Kiron for alerting me to this source.

79. Restad, *Christmas in America*, 20–22.

80. Goldman, *Beyond the Synagogue Gallery*, 170–171.

81. Melissa R. Klapper, *Jewish Girls Coming of Age in America, 1860–1920* (New York: NYU Press, 2005), 173.

82. Kaufman Kohler, "Chanukah and Christmas," *The Menorah* (December 1890): 306; Joselit, *Wonders of America*, 230.

83. "Correspondent," *American Israelite* (January 7, 1887): 4.

84. Sara Hart, *The Pleasure Is Mine* (Chicago: Valentine-Newman, 1947), 20.

85. "For the Elders," *American Hebrew* (December 13, 1895): 175.

86. Max Lilienthal, "The Trenderle," *Sabbath Visitor* (December 22, 1876): 396.

87. "For the Elders," *American Hebrew* (November 29, 1895): 103.

88. Marling, *Merry Christmas*, 176.

89. Cover, *Harper's Weekly* (December 29, 1860).

90. *Frank Leslie's Illustrated Newspaper* (January 13, 1877): 312; "Christmas Eve— Getting Ready for Santa Claus," *Harper's Weekly* 30 (December 1876): 1052; "A Fruitful Tree," *Sunday School Advocate* (December 28, 1872): 24. For discussion, see Marling, *Merry Christmas*; Schmidt, *Consumer Rites*, 105–175.

91. Schmidt, *Consumer Rites*, 34.

92. Ibid., 160–162.

93. Restad, *Christmas in America*, 111.

94. Ibid., 143–153.

95. Schmidt, *Consumer Rites*, 141.

96. Joseph Krauskopf, "Hanucca and Christmas," *Jewish Exponent* (December 15, 1899): 4; "Editorial: Response to Dr. Sonneschein," *American Hebrew* (December 14, 1883): front page.

97. Lilienthal, "The Trenderle," 396.

98. Max Lilienthal, "The Maccabean War," *Sabbath Visitor* (December 9, 1879): 388.

99. Editorial, *American Hebrew* (December 9, 1881): front page.

100. Anonymous, *Sabbath Visitor* (December 21, 1883): 893.

101. Kaufman Kohler, "Chanukah and Christmas," *Sabbath Visitor* (December 19, 1884).

102. Sarah Hirsch Guggenheim, "Proselyten," *Der Israelit* (1876–1877): 478–479; Jonathan M. Hess, "Beyond Subversion: German Jewry and the Poetics of Middlebrow Culture," *German Quarterly* 82, no. 3 (Summer 2009): 322.

103. Editorial, *American Hebrew* (December 23, 1881): front page.

104. Anti-Humbug, "Christmas among the Jews," *American Hebrew* (December 30, 1887): 2–3.

105. Emma Lazarus, "In the Name of Jesus of Nazareth," *American Hebrew* (December 12, 1890): 170.

106. "Correspondents: Buffalo," *American Israelite* (January 1, 1881): 222.

107. See for example "Chicago," *Die Deborah* (January 11, 1878): 2 (trans. Ellen Gezork); *American Hebrew* (January 21, 1886): 123.

108. Jacob Voorsanger, editorial, *Sabbath Visitor* (December 21, 1883); see also Dianne Ashton, "Grace Aguilar and the Matriarchal Theme in Jewish Women's Spirituality," in *Active Voices: Women in Jewish Culture*, ed. Maurie Sacks (Urbana: University of Illinois Press, 1995), 79–83; Grace Aguilar, *Grace Aguilar: Selected Writings*, ed. Michael Galchinsky (Peterborough, ON: Broadview, 2003).

109. "Books in the Home," *American Hebrew* (November 21, 1890): 46.

110. Sabato Morais, "Education," sermon given at Kahal Kadosh Mickve Israel, Philadelphia, Pennsylvania, n.d. Thanks to Dr. Arthur Kiron for providing me with this source.

111. Schmidt, *Consumer Rites*, 148–153.

112. Jacob Vorsanger, "Our Mothers," *Sabbath Visitor* (December 28, 1883): front page.

113. See for example Emma Lazarus, "Feast of Lights," *Sabbath Visitor* (December 1, 1890): 427, and (December 9, 1892): front page.

114. Max Lilienthal, "Chanuka Is Coming!," *Sabbath Visitor* (December 13, 1878): 396.

115. Melissa R. Klapper, "The History of Jewish Education in America," in *The Columbia History of Jews and Judaism in America*, ed. Marc Lee Raphael (New York: Columbia University Press, 2008), 196.

116. Alan Silverstein, *Alternatives to Assimilation: The Response of Reform Judaism to American Culture, 1840–1930* (Hanover, NH: Brandeis University Press / University Press of New England, 1994).

117. Editorial, *American Hebrew* (December 21, 1894): front page.

118. David Kaufman, *Shul with a Pool: The "Synagogue-Center" in American Jewish History* (Hanover, NH: Brandeis University Press / University Press of New England, 1999).

NOTES TO CHAPTER 4

1. Israel Bartol, *The Jews of Eastern Europe, 1772–1881* (Philadelphia: University of Pennsylvania Press, 2010), 15, 40–66 (translated by Chaya Naor).

2. Ibid., 15, 40–66.

3. A. D. Aguz, "A Monologue by a Khanike Dreydl," *Morgen Zhurnal* (December 13, 1909): 4. All Yiddish translations are by Chana Pollock unless otherwise noted.

4. D. M. Hermalin, "Yude Maccabee," *Idisher Zhurnal* (December 13, 1901): front page.

5. Stuart Ewen and Elizabeth Ewen, *Channels of Desire: Mass Images and the Shaping of American Consciousness* (Minneapolis: University of Minnesota Press, 1992), 47–50.

6. Dianne Ashton, *Rebecca Gratz: Women and Judaism in Antebellum America* (Detroit: Wayne State University Press, 1997), 40; Stanley M. Fish, *Barnard and Michael Gratz: Their Lives and Times* (Boston: University Press of America, 1994), 30; Jacob Rader Marcus, *The Colonial American Jew, 1492–1776*, vol. 3 (Detroit: Wayne State University Press, 1970).

7. Aviva Ben-Ur, *Sephardic Jews in America: A Diasporic History* (New York: NYU Press, 2009), 35, 88–90.

8. Deborah R. Weiner, *Coalfield Jews: An Appalachian History* (Urbana: University of Illinois Press, 2006), 13.

9. Irving Ashton (born Ascanazy, Jacob's son) to the author.

10. Ronald Richards, Pinchas Keller's great-grandson, to the author.

11. Tillie Kaminker Keller, Deenah's daughter, to the author.

12. Gerald Sorin, *Tradition Transformed: The Jewish Experience in America* (Baltimore: Johns Hopkins University Press, 1997), 12.

13. Yuri Slezkine, *The Jewish Century* (Princeton: Princeton University Press, 2004), 117.

14. Andrew Godley, *Jewish Immigrant Entrepreneurship in New York and London, 1880–1914: Enterprise and Culture* (New York: Palgrave, 2001), 71–72; Slezkine, *Jewish Century*, 117.

15. Gerald Sorin, *A Time for Building: The Third Migration: 1880–1920* (Baltimore: Johns Hopkins University Press, 1992), 47.

16. Lee Shai Weissbach, *Jewish Life in Small-Town America: A History* (New Haven: Yale University Press, 2005), 54.

17. Sorin, *A Time for Building*, 71.

18. Steven Mintz, *Huck's Raft: A History of American Childhood* (Cambridge: Belknap Press of Harvard University Press, 2004), 202.

19. Hasia R. Diner, *Lower East Side Memories: A Jewish Place in America* (Princeton: Princeton University Press, 2000), 35–49.

20. Ibid.

21. Tony Michels, *A Fire in Their Hearts* (Cambridge: Harvard University Press, 2005), 8.

22. Steven J. Diner, *A Very Different Age: Americans of the Progressive Era* (New York: Hill and Wang, 1998), 66.

23. Moses Rischin, *The Promised City: New York's Jews, 1870–1914* (Cambridge: Harvard University Press, 1962), 146–147.

24. Moshe D. Sherman, *Orthodox Judaism in America* (Westport, CT: Greenwood, 1996), 6.

25. Kimmy Caplan, "The Ever Dying Denomination: American Jewish Orthodoxy, 1824–1965," in *The Columbia History of Jews and Judaism in America*, ed. Marc Lee Raphael (New York: Columbia University Press, 2008), 172, 177.

26. This is discussed in a broad literature. Among the best are Jonathan D. Sarna, *American Judaism: A History* (New Haven: Yale University Press, 2004); Lance J. Sussman, *Isaac Leeser and the Making of American Judaism* (Detroit: Wayne State University Press, 1995); Marc Lee Raphael, *Judaism in America* (New York: Columbia University Press, 2003); Hasia R. Diner, *The Jews of the United States, 1654–2000* (Berkeley: University of California Press, 2003); Riv-Ellen Prell, ed., *Women Remaking American Judaism* (Detroit: Wayne State University Press, 2007); and Jonathan D. Sarna, *People Walk on Their Heads: Moses Weinberger's Jews and Judaism in America* (New York: Holmes and Meier, 1982).

27. Andrew R. Heinze, *Adapting to Abundance: Jewish Immigrants, Mass Consumption, and the Search for American Identity* (New York: Columbia University Press, 1990), 2; see also David M. Potter, *People of Plenty: Economic Abundance and the American Character* (Chicago: University of Chicago Press, 1966), first appearing 1954; Frederick Jackson Turner, *The Frontier in American History* (New York: Holt, 1920); Daniel J. Boorstin, *The Americans: The Democratic Experience* (New York: Random House, 1973); Daniel Miller, *Material Culture and Mass Consumption* (Oxford, UK: Blackwell, 1987).

28. Heinze, *Adapting to Abundance*, 4, 3.

29. "K. Rez's Tea and Coffee Stores, Khanike Presents to Purchase," *Forverts* (December 15, 1906): 8.

30. Heinze, *Adapting to Abundance*, 77.

31. Abraham Cahan, "New Season, New Hats," *Forverts* (September 7, 1905), quoted in Marilyn Halter, *Shopping for Identity: The Marketing of Ethnicity* (New York: Schocken Books, 2000), 25.

32. Heinze, *Adapting to Abundance*, 77.

33. "Don't Miss the Opportunity for Khanike," *Forverts* (December 11, 1920): 5; *Forverts* (December 9, 1912): 7, 2; advertisement for Ridley's Department Store, *Tageblatt* (December 19, 1897); Heinze, *Adapting to Abundance*, 78.

34. *Forverts* (December 7, 1912): 4, 5.

35. "Our Greatest Enemy," *Tageblatt* (December 15, 1907), quoted in Heinze, *Adapting to Abundance*, 77.

36. Heinze, *Adapting to Abundance*, 51–88.

37. *Tageblatt* (December 19, 1900), quoted in ibid., 73.

38. Marc Shapiro, "Torah Study on Christmas Eve," *Journal of Jewish Thought and Philosophy* 8 (1959): 319–321.

39. Quoted in Hasia R. Diner and Beryl Lief Benderly, *Her Works Praise Her: A History of Jewish Women in America from Colonial Times to the Present* (New York: Basic Books, 2002), 235.

40. "Frum zaynen zeym nor fun krismes halten zay oykh" (They're pious [Jews], but they also celebrate Christmas), *Forverts* (December 25, 1904), 4 (translated by Jeffrey Shandler), quoted in Jeffrey Shandler, *Jews, God, and Videotape: Religion and Media in America* (New York: NYU Press, 2009), 190–194.

41. Heinze, *Adapting to Abundance*, 74.

42. Ellen M. Litwicki, *America's Public Holidays, 1865–1920* (Washington, DC: Smithsonian Institution Press, 2000), 193–221; Matthew Dennis, *Red, White, and Blue Letter Days: An American Calendar* (Ithaca: Cornell University Press, 2002), 84–160; Stephan F. Brumberg, *Going to America, Going to School: The Jewish Immigrant Public School Experience in Turn-of-the-Century New York City America* (New York: Praeger, 1986), 8–10, 126 (quote).

43. Gil Ribak, "'They Are Slitting the Throats of Jewish Children': The 1906 New York School Riots and Contending Images of Gentiles," *American Jewish History* 94 (September 2008): 183–193.

44. Leonard Bloom, "A Successful Jewish Boycott of the New York Public Schools —Christmas 1906," *American Jewish History* 70 (December 1980): 184–189; Kenneth White, "American Jewish Response to Christmas" (ordination thesis, Hebrew Union College, Cincinnati, 1982), 146–147.

45. [Victor Harris?], editorial, *B'nai B'rith Messenger* (Los Angeles) (December 28, 1906): front page.

46. Jeanetta, "El Centro Grammar School," *B'nai B'rith Messenger* (Los Angeles) (December 22, 1911): n.p.

47. Selecting particular foods to consume can be a declaration of identity and a way to literally incorporate items with strong cultural associations. Sidney W. Mintz, *Tasting Food, Tasting Freedom: Excursions into Eating, Culture, and the Past* (Boston: Beacon, 1996), 13.

48. *Aunt Babette's Cook Book* (Cincinnati: Bloch, 1889).

49. Abraham Cahan, "Feast of Chanukah" (December 20, 1897), in *Grandma Never Lived in America: The New Journalism of Abraham Cahan*, ed. Moses Rischin (Bloomington: Indiana University Press, 1985), 79–82.

50. "Crisco for Latkes," *Forverts* (December 9, 1920): 9; "End Your Slavery to a Cup of Shmalts," *Forverts* (December 7, 1920): 8.

51. *Forverts* (December 11, 1920): 12.

52. Heinze, *Adapting to Abundance*, 23; Hasia R. Diner, *Hungering for America: Italian, Irish, and Jewish Foodways in the Age of Migration* (Cambridge: Harvard University Press, 2001), 13–20.

53. See for example *Forverts* (December 16, 1900): 6; *Forverts* (December 12, 1903): 6; *Forverts* (December 12, 1903): 6; *Forverts* (December 13, 1903): 2.

54. Halter, *Shopping for Identity*.

55. H. Diner, *Hungering for America*, 195–202; Jenna Weissman Joselit, *Wonders of America: Reinventing Jewish Culture, 1880–1950* (New York: Hill and Wang, 1994), 171–219.

56. *Morgen Zhurnal* (December 9, 1906), 5.

57. "A Deluxe Khanike Turkey Dinner," *Forverts* (December 3, 1920): 2.

58. H. Diner, *Hungering for America*, 200–201.

59. David G. Roskies, *The Jewish Search for a Useable Past* (Bloomington: Indiana University Press, 1999), 3.

60. Mathilde S. Schechter and Lewis M. Isaacs, preface to *Kol Rina: Hebrew Hymnal for School and Home*, ed. Lewis M. Isaacs and Mathilde S. Schechter (New York: Bloch, 1910), 3.

61. Morris Rosenfeld, "The Hanukkah Candles," *American Hebrew and Jewish Messenger* (December 4, 1903), 175 (translated by Rebecca Altman), and in *Anthology of Yiddish Folksongs*, vol. 2, ed. Aharon Vinkovetzky, Abba Kovner, and Sinai Leichter (Jerusalem: Mount Scopus publications / Magnes Press, 1984), 195–205.

62. Daniel Soyer, *Jewish Immigrant Associations and American Identity in New York, 1880–1930* (Cambridge: Harvard University Press, 1997); Michels, *A Fire in Their Hearts*; Irving Howe, *The World of Our Fathers* (New York: Touchstone, 1976); Michael R. Weisser, *A Brotherhood of Memory: Jewish Landsmanshaftn in the New World* (New York: Basic Books, 1985).

63. Chane Mlotek and Malke Gottlieb, eds., *Yontefdike Teg: Song Book for the Jewish Holidays* (New York: Workmen's Circle and Jewish Education Press, 1984), 24–36.

64. Mark Slobin, *Tenement Songs: The Popular Music of the Jewish Immigrants* (Urbana: University of Illinois Press, 1982), 25–45.

65. Quoted in ibid., 67–68.

66. Judah M. Cohen, *The Making of a Reform Jewish Cantor: Musical Authority, Cultural Investment* (Bloomington: Indiana University Press, 2009), 131, 161.

67. Compare Shandler, *Jews, God, and Videotape*, 14, and Cohen, *Making of a Reform Jewish Cantor*, 24–28.

68. Shandler, *Jews, God, and Videotape*, 14.

69. Ibid., 23.

70. Irene Heskes, *Yiddish American Popular Songs, 1895–1950: A Catalog Based on the Lawrence Marwick Roster of Copyright Entries* (Washington, DC: Library of Congress, 1992).

71. Aaron Lansky, *Outwitting History: The Amazing Adventures of a Man Who Rescued a Million Yiddish Books* (Chapel Hill, NC: Algonquin Books, 2005), 215.

72. S. Zeemachson, "Chanukas Habajis" (self-published, 1915), Gratz College Music Library.

73. Heskes, *Yiddish American Popular Songs*, 12.

74. See for example E. Kartschmaroff, *Ten Choice Hebrew Song Classics*, for voice and pianoforte (New York: Globe Music, 1915); and Israel Goldfarb and Samuel E. Goldfarb, *The Jewish Songster* (Brooklyn: Religious Schools of Congregation Beth Israel, 1919), Gratz College Music Library.

75. Jeanette Bicknell, "Just a Song? Exploring the Aesthetics of Popular Song Performance," *Journal of Aesthetics and Art Criticism* 63, no. 3 (Summer 2005).

76. Slobin, *Tenement Songs*, 93–144, 170.

77. Sherman, *Orthodox Judaism in America*, 4; Slobin, *Tenement Songs*, 19.

78. Slobin, *Tenement Songs*, 19–21.

79. G. Zelikovits, "Khanike Concert, or, The Ancient Musical Instrument String Lost," *Idischer Zhurnal* (December 21, 1900), front page.

80. Getsl Zelikovitsch, "Khanike Concert or the Ancient Musical String Lost," *Idisher Zhurnal* (December 21, 1900): front page; Roskies, *Jewish Search*, 91.

81. Getsl Zelikovitsch, "Khanike Concert or the Ancient Musical String Lost," front page.

82. C. Major (may be a pseudonym for Abraham Cahan), "It's Khanike and the Annual Fair of Khanike Concerts Has Begun," *Forverts* (December 21, 1927): 3.

83. "Today's Celebration of the New Taletoyre" and "Khanike Concert at the Brooklyn Schools," *Morgen Zhurnal* (December 8, 1912): 2.

84. See for example "Khanike Concert and Festival," "Wonderful Khanike Concert in Boro Park," "Khanike Concert," and "Biggest Surprise for Bronx Jews!," *Morgen Zhurnal* (December 1, 1918): 8; and "Khanike Concert," same issue, 3.

85. "Khanike Celebration Today for Immigrants," *Morgen Zhurnal* (December 1, 1915): 8 ; S. Diner, *A Very Different Age*, 91–93.

86. "Khanike Concert and Festival," *Morgen Zhurnal* (December 1, 1918): 8.

87. Hutchins Hapgood, *The Spirit of the Ghetto* (Cambridge: Harvard University Press, 1967), 74–75.

88. "An Open Letter from Odessa Cantoress Madame Sofia Kurtser," *Morgen Zhurnal* (December 7, 1920): 10.

89. C. Major, "It's Khanike."

90. "Today! In Brooklyn Today! A Khanike Evening of the Paoli Tsion," *Forverts* (December 3, 1915): 3; and "Today! Today! Khanike Fest of the Yiddish Radical School," *Forverts* (December 4, 1915): 10.

91. Slobin, *Tenement Songs*, 68.

92. Donald Weber, *Haunted in the New World: Jewish American Culture from Cahan to the Goldbergs* (Bloomington: Indiana University Press, 2005), 43–44, 47.

93. Ben-Ur, *Sephardic Jews in America*, 141.

94. "Khanike Concert in Sing Sing," *Morgen Zhurnal* (December 9, 1915): 4.

95. Litwicki, *America's Public Holidays*, 113–116.

96. Jonathan M. Hess, "Beyond Subversion: German Jewry and the Poetics of Middlebrow Culture," *German Quarterly* 82, no. 3 (Summer 2009): 318.

97. Sorin, *A Time for Building*, 100–104

98. Michels, *A Fire in Their Hearts*, 142–145.

99. Evening schools in New York City attracted one hundred thousand students at the turn of the century, the majority of whom were Jews, and almost forty percent of those Jewish students were women. Sorin, *A Time for Building*, 105.

100. In the same way, the Ladino newspaper *La America*, also published in New York City, served the Sephardi immigrants. When several Yiddish newspapers

reported on it, the Ashkenazim learned about these Jews who had remained unnoticed by most of them. News about Sephardi Jews eased their access to social services which expected to serve only Yiddish-speaking individuals. Sephardi business owners also publicized their stores in Yiddish papers. Ben-Ur, *Sephardic Jews in America*, 141–142.

101. Efroyem Kaplan, "The Khanike Lights," *Morgen Zhurnal* (December 4, 1912): 4.

102. Judah David Eisenstein, *Otsar Drashot: Anthology of Jewish Sermons*, trans. Niv Hartman (New York, 1919).

103. *Tageblatt* (December 19, 1900), quoted in Heinze, *Adapting to Abundance*, 73; Bella Chagall, *Burning Lights* (New York: Schocken Books, 1946), 125.

104. Morris Rosenfeld, "Feast of Lights" and "Chanukah Thoughts," in *Songs of Labor and Other Poems* [1917?], 34–35.

105. Ephraim Kaplan, "Khanike Lights and Electric Lights," *Morgen Zhurnal* (December 8, 1909): 4.

106. Stanley Lebergott, *Pursuing Happiness: American Consumers in the Twentieth Century* (Princeton: Princeton University Press, 1993), 120.

107. Michael Higger, "The Interpretation of Jewish Law: Its Relevance to Our Life Today," in *Proceedings of the Rabbinical Assembly*, vol. 5 (New York: Rabbinical Assembly, 1927–1989); "May Electric Lights Be Used Instead of Candles?," in *An Index of Conservative Responsa and Practical Halakhic Studies: 1917–1990*, ed. Rabbi David Golinkin (New York: Rabbinical Assembly, 1992), 38.

108. Abraham Cahan, "Khanike and the Gershunis," editorial, *Forverts* (December 12, 1906): 4.

109. Marc Lee Raphael, *Profiles in American Judaism* (New York: Harper and Row, 1985), 138. By 1924, in New York alone, Orthodox Jews raised one million dollars to establish their flagship educational institution, Yeshiva College, which offered both a secular undergraduate program and traditional rabbinic training.

110. Cahan, "Khanike and the Gershunis," 4.

111. Abraham Cahan, "Khanike," editorial, *Forverts* (December 14, 1903): 4.

112. "Khanike," *Idisher Zhurnal* (December 29, 1905): front page.

113. Cahan, "Khanike and the Gershunis."

114. Cahan, "Khanike."

115. Abraham Liesen, "The Classes and the Masses," *Forverts* (December 22, 1900): 4–5.

116. Abraham Liesen, "Khanike Thoughts," *Forverts* (December 22, 1900): 4; Michels, *A Fire in Their Hearts*, 9.

117. Abraham Liesen, "The Hasmoneans—The Heroes of Khanike," *Forverts* (December 12, 1909): 4.

118. Cahan, "Khanike and the Gershunis," 4; Sholem Aleichem, "Vos Is Khanike / What Is Khanike," *Forverts*, serialized: part 1 (December 17, 1901): 4; part 2 (December 18, 1901): 4; part 3 (December 19, 1901): 4; Chagall, *Burning Lights*, 136–152.

119. Riv-Ellen Prell, *Fighting to Become Americans* (Boston: Beacon, 1999), 58–59.

120. Sorin, *A Time for Building*, 21.

121. Howe, *World of Our Fathers*, 120.

122. Sorin, *Tradition Transformed*, 113.

123. Alfred Kazin, *Starting Out in the Thirties* (1965; repr., Ithaca: Cornell University Press, 1989), 4.

124. Cahan, "Khanike."

125. Alexander Harkavy, *The Jewish Revolution Two Thousand Years Ago; or, The History of the Maccabees* (New York: Kruger and Lipshitz, 1892), 15.

126. Ibid., 16.

127. Sarna, *People Walk on Their Heads*.

NOTES TO CHAPTER 5

1. "Talmud Torah Sefaradi de Siatli," *La Vara* (New York) (January 1, 1932). Sephardi Jews in Los Angeles also turned Hanukkah into an educational event with important social benefits. Each Hanukkah, their Talmud Torahs conducted public student examinations followed by an appeal for donations. Their students received tickets to the movies and enjoyed a Hanukkah party featuring Hebrew Hanukkah songs. Music and dancing "Turkish style" continued late into the night. "Los Egzamenes de los Elevos del Talmud Torah," *El Mesajero* (Los Angeles) (December 21, 1934): 5

2. Charles H. Lippy, *Being Religious American Style: A History of Popular Religiosity in the United States* (Westport, CT: Greenwood, 1994), 168–169.

3. Hasia R. Diner, *Jews of the United States, 1654–2000* (Berkeley: University of California Press, 2003), 246; author's own family.

4. Michael R. Weisser, *A Brotherhood of Memory: Jewish Landsmanschaftn in the New World* (New York: Basic Books, 1985), 259–267.

5. Deborah Dash Moore, *At Home in America: Second Generation New York Jews* (New York: Columbia University Press, 1981), 34–38.

6. Irving Cutler, *The Jews of Chicago* (Urbana: University of Illinois Press, 1996), 119.

7. Paula S. Fass, "Creating New Identities: Youth and Ethnicity in New York City High Schools in the 1930s and 1940s," in *Generations of Youth: Youth Cultures and History in Twentieth-Century America*, ed. Joe Austin and Michael Nevin Willard (New York: NYU Press, 1998), 104–105.

8. Henry Feingold, *A Time for Searching: Entering the Mainstream, 1920–1945* (Baltimore: Johns Hopkins University Press, 1992), 69.

9. Ellen M. Litwicki, *America's Public Holidays, 1860–1920* (Washington, DC: Smithsonian Institution Press, 2000), 205.

10. Hyman E. Goldin, *The Jewish Woman and Her Home* (New York: Hebrew Publishing Company, 1941), 231.

11. Marsha Bryan Edelman, *Discovering Jewish Music* (Philadelphia: Jewish Publication Society, 2003), 97.

12. David G. Roskies, *The Jewish Search for a Useable Past* (Bloomington: Indiana

University Press, 1999), 93; Khrone Shmeruk, *Mahazot mik-rai'im beyidish, 1697–1750* (Yiddish Biblical Plays, 1697–1750) (Jerusalem: Israel Academy of Sciences and Humanities, 1979).

13. Jonathan B. Krasner, "A Recipe for American Jewish Integration: The Adventures of K'tonton and Hillel's Happy Holidays," *The Lion and the Unicorn* 27 (September 2003): 344–361.

14. Rose Zaltsman, comp., "100 Plays for Hanukah: An Annotated Bibliography" (New York: National Jewish Welfare Board, 1950), n.p.

15. Goodman Lipkind, *What Happened on Chanukah: A Play for Adults* (New York: Bloch, 1924), Monographs Collection, AJHS. All quotations from the play are from this version.

16. William Toll, "Creating Cultural Space: Jews and Judaism at a Public University in the 1920s," in *New Essays in American Jewish History: Commemorating the Sixtieth Anniversary of the Founding of the American Jewish Archives*, ed. Pamela Susan Nadell, Jonathan D. Sarna, and Lance J. Sussman (Cincinnati: American Jewish Archives, 2010), 250.

17. Marcia Graham Synnott, *The Half-Opened Door: Discrimination in Admissions at Harvard, Yale, and Princeton, 1900–1970* (Westport, CT: Greenwood, 1979), 35; Daniel Greene, *The Jewish Origins of Cultural Pluralism* (Bloomington: Indiana University Press, 2011), 53; Feingold, *A Time for Searching*, 14.

18. Synnott, *Half-Opened Door*, 35.

19. Feingold, *A Time for Searching*, 15; Toll, "Creating Cultural Space," 248.

20. Feingold, *A Time for Searching*, 23.

21. K. Kohler and Jacob Z. Lauterbach, "Forfeiture of Congregational Membership by Intermarriage," in *American Reform Responsa: Jewish Questions, Rabbinic Answers*, ed. Walter Jacob (New York: Central Conference of American Rabbis, 1983), 49.

22. Elma Ehrlich Levinger, *The Unlighted Menorah: A Chanukah Fantasy of the Time of Felix Mendelssohn in One Act* (New York: Hebrew Publishing Company, 1923), published for the Department of Synagogue and School Extension, UAHC, 1923, box 6, Isaac Klein Papers, Butler Library, Buffalo State College. All quotations from the play are from this version.

23. Annette Kohn, "Letter," *American Israelite* (December 22, 1921): 4, quoted in Kenneth White, "American Jewish Response to Christmas" (ordination thesis, Hebrew Union College, Cincinnati, 1982), 109.

24. Joshua Eli Plaut, *A Kosher Christmas: 'Tis the Season to Be Jewish* (New Brunswick: Rutgers University Press, 2012), 20–25.

25. Moise Soulam, "Postemas de Mujer," *La Vara* (New York) (December 27, 1929): 10 (trans. Aviva Ben-Ur).

26. Samuel M. Segal, *Scientific Chanukah* (New York: Behrman's Jewish Book House, 1932), 22, Monographs Collection, AJHS.

27. Sidney Hook, "The Plural Sources for American Life" (paper prepared for the fortieth annual conference of the American Jewish Committee, January 25,

1947), Sidney Hook Papers, Stanford University; Edward S. Shapiro, *A Time for Healing: American Jewry after World War II* (Baltimore: Johns Hopkins University Press, 1992), 62.

28. Lynn Dumenil, "The Rise of a Consumer Society," in *The Roaring Twenties*, ed. Philip Margulies (New York: Greenhaven, 2004), 46–47.

29. Deborah Melamed, *The Three Pillars: Thought, Worship, and Practice* (New York: Women's League for Conservative Judaism, 1927), 120–125.

30. "Survey," in *AJYB* 32 (1928): 29.

31. Samuel M. Segal, *Treasure Chanukah: A Fantasy* (New York: Hebrew Publishing Company, 1923), Monographs Collection, AJHS.

32. Ann Douglas, *Terrible Honesty: Mongrel Manhattan in the 1920s* (New York: Farrar, Straus & Giroux, 1995); Leonard S. Marcus, *Minders of Make-Believe: Idealists, Centrists, Entrepreneurs, and the Shaping of American Children's Literature* (Boston: Houghton Mifflin, 2008), 110.

33. Henry Woolf, *The Dreambook: A Story of Hanukkah in One Act* (New York: UAHC, Department of Synagogue and School Extension, 1928). All quotations from the play are from this version.

34. Fanny Evelyn Freehof, *Forever And—A Chanukah Play* (New York: Bloch, 1929).

35. Joan S. Friedman, "The Making of a Reform Rabbi: Solomon B. Freehof from Childhood to HUC," *American Jewish Archives Journal* 58, no. 1 (2006): 1–49.

36. Victor Turner, *The Anthropology of Performance* (New York: PAJ, 1986), 81, 142.

37. "Make Yours a Real Chanukkoh at Home and in School," UAHC, Series E, box 32, folder 3, MS-73, NFTS/WRJ, AJA.

38. Karla Goldman, "Women in Reform Judaism," in *Women Remaking American Judaism*, ed. Riv-Ellen Prell (Detroit: Wayne State University Press, 2007), 116; Goldman, *Beyond the Synagogue Gallery: Finding a Place for Women in American Judaism* (Cambridge: Harvard University Press, 2000), 210–211.

39. Mrs. Henry Nathan, letter, November 19, 1923, box 26, folder 1, MS-73, NFTS/WRJ, AJA.

40. Mrs. Leon Goodman, letter, December 6, 1921, box 23, folder 1, MS-73, NFTS/WRJ, AJA.

41. Ibid.

42. Mrs. Henry Nathan, letter, November 19, 1923.

43. Ibid.

44. Melanie Archer, "Xmas Excess," in *The Business of Holidays*, ed. Maud Lavin (New York: Monacelli, 2004), 237.

45. NFTS Policies, 1923–24, Series K, box 70, folder 1, MS-73, NFTS/WRJ, AJA.

46. Howard P. Chudacoff, *Children at Play: An American History* (New York: NYU Press, 2007), 106.

47. Peter N. Stearns, *Anxious Parents: A History of Modern Childrearing in America* (New York: NYU Press, 2003), 36–61.

48. David Philipson, "Chanukah Lights or Christmas Candles," *Rockdale Bulletin* (December 15, 1927): n.p., series F, box 24, MS-42, AJA.

49. Ibid.
50. Editorial, *American Israelite* (December 24, 1925), 4.
51. "Finds Jewish Feast Like Christmas," *New York Times* (December 6, 1926), ProQuest Historical Newspapers, NYT, 26.
52. Philipson, "Chanukah Lights or Christmas Candles."
53. Mrs. Leon Goodman, letter, NFTS Committee on Religion (September 2, 1925), Series E, box 26, folder 1, MS-73, NFTS/WRJ, AJA.
54. Mrs. Leon Goodman, letter, NFTS Committee on Religion (October, 1925), Series E, box 26, folder 1, MS-73, NFTS/WRJ, AJA.
55. Mrs. Leon Goodman, letter, NFTS Committee on Religion (October 19, 1927), Series E, box 26, folder 1, MS-73, NFTS/WRJ, AJA.
56. Mrs. Leon Goodman, NFTS Committee on Religion (November 8, 1927), Series E, box 26, folder 1, MS-73, NFTS/WRJ, AJA.
57. Jacob Mann and Committee, "Less than a Minyan of Ten at Services," in *American Reform Responsa*, 5.
58. Jacob Z. Lauterbach, "Ordination of Women," in ibid., 25–31.
59. Deborah Melamed, "Women's Opportunity in the Synagogue," *United Synagogue Recorder* 1, no. 2 (1921): 12; for discussion, see Jack Wertheimer, "The Conservative Synagogue," in *The American Synagogue: A Sanctuary Transformed*, ed. Jack Wertheimer (Hanover, NH: Brandeis University Press / University Press of New England, 1987), 121–153.
60. Marjorie Lehman, "Melamed, Deborah Marcus," in *Jewish Women in America: An Historical Encyclopedia*, vol. 2, ed. Paula Hyman and Deborah Dash Moore (New York: Routledge, 1998), 909.
61. Ibid., 909–910; Shuly Rubin Schwartz, "Women's League for Conservative Judaism," in Hyman and Moore, *Jewish Women in America*, vol. 2, 1493; Deborah Melamed, *The Three Pillars: Thought, Worship, and Practice* (New York: Women's League for Conservative Judaism, 1927), 13–14.
62. Shuly Rubin Schwartz, *The Rabbi's Wife* (New York: NYU Press, 2006), 68.
63. Melamed, *Three Pillars*, 15; Erich S. Gruen, "Hebraism and Hellenism," in *Oxford Handbook of Hellenic Studies*, ed. George Boys-Stones, Barbara Graziosi, and Phiroze Vasunia (Oxford: Oxford University Press, 2009), 128–139.
64. Melamed, *Three Pillars*, 15.
65. Jenna Weissman Joselit, *New York's Jewish Jews: The Orthodox Community in the Interwar Years* (Bloomington: Indiana University Press, 1990), 97–110.
66. Betty Greenberg and Althea O. Silverman, *The Jewish Home Beautiful* (New York: Women's League of the United Synagogue of America, 1941), 4, quoted in Jenna Weissman Joselit, *Wonders of America: Reinventing Jewish Culture, 1880–1950* (New York: Hill and Wang, 1994), 238.
67. Solomon Ganzfried, *Code of Jewish Law* (*Kitzur Shulchan Aruch*): *A Compilation of Jewish Laws and Customs by Rabbi Solomon Ganzfried*, trans. Hyman E. Goldin (New York: Hebrew Publishing Company, 1927), 108–109.

68. A. Z. Idelsohn, *The Ceremonies of Judaism*, vol. 4, xvi, series E, box 3, folder 2, MS-73, NFTS/WRJ, AJA.

69. "Survey," *AJYB* 32 (1928): 29.

70. Sarah Kussy, "The Maccabean Spirit," *Women's League Outlook* 1, no. 2 (December 1930): 11.

71. S. Greenberg, "Chanukah as Evidence of the Reality of the Spirit," *Har Zion Record* (January 8, 1928), Series 2, box 1, Har Zion Records, Ratner Center, Jewish Theological Seminary, New York.

72. Andrew Heinze, *Jews and the American Soul* (Princeton: Princeton University Press, 2004), 87–100, 110.

73. Greenberg, "Chanukah as Evidence"; Alfred Gottschalk, "From Nachman Krochmal to Ahad Ha-Am," in Nadell, Sarna, and Sussman, *New Essays in American Jewish History*, 232–234.

74. Mordecai M. Kaplan, *Communings of the Spirit: The Journals of Mordecai M. Kaplan*, vol. 1, *1913–1934*, ed. Mel Scult (Detroit: Wayne State University Press, 2001), 286–287.

75. Mordecai M. Kaplan, *Judaism as a Civilization* (New York: Schocken Books, 1967), 451. First published 1934 by Macmillan.

76. Betty D. Greenberg, "Chanukah Ramblings and Reflections," *Women's League Outlook* 7, no. 2 (December 1936): front page.

77. Diner, *Jews of the United States*, 233; Beth S. Wenger, *New York Jews and the Great Depression* (Syracuse: Syracuse University Press, 1999), 169.

78. Cecile Alexander, *The Night of the Eighth Candle* (New York: Hebrew Publishing Company, 1935).

79. Shelly Tenenbaum, *A Credit to Their Community: Jewish Loan Societies in the United States, 1880–1945* (Detroit: Wayne State University Press, 1993), 64.

80. David M. Kennedy, *Freedom from Fear: The American People in Depression and War* (New York: Oxford University Press, 1999), 229–232. Violence sometimes erupted. In Newark, New Jersey, where sixty-five thousand Jews and forty-seven thousand gentiles of German descent lived amid a larger mixed gentile population, pro-Nazi rallies in 1933 sparked confrontations. In September, a group of Jewish men, including a former lightweight boxer, tossed stink bombs (supplied by a sympathetic pharmacist) through a window where a rally was held, then attacked the Nazis as they ran outside. The same Jewish gang attacked a second Nazi rally a month later. There, on October 16, the self-proclaimed "American Fuhrer," Hans Spanknoebel, stood before a huge swastika to speak to a crowd of eight hundred, many of whom also dressed in Nazi regalia. For this attack, recruits from the local Young Men's Hebrew Association and members of the Jewish War Veterans joined the Jewish gang. Now numbering about fifty fighters, the group repeated their stink-bomb method. They later attacked Nazis at rallies in Irvington, Union City, and Elizabeth, New Jersey. The Jewish fighters felt that the "American Nazis . . . were out to destroy Jews" and that they were in

a "battle for survival." Ron Nessen, "Newark's Other Riots," *New Jersey Monthly*, July 2005, http://www.njmonthly.com/issues/July05/riots.html (accessed July 6, 2005).

81. Deborah Dash Moore, *B'nai B'rith and the Challenge of Ethnic Leadership* (Albany: SUNY Press, 1981), 120.

82. Nat Hentoff, *Boston Boy* (Philadelphia: Paul Dry Books 1986), 18–22; see also Fass, "Creating New Identities," 109; similar experience reported to the author by Irving Ashton (Ascanazy).

83. *Topics & Trends* (March–April 1936): 2, Series K, MS-73, NFTS/WRJ, AJA.

84. Kurt Lewin, "Bringing Up a Jewish Child," *Menorah Journal* 28 (1940): 29–45; see also Lewin, "Self-Hatred among Jews," *Contemporary Jewish Record* 4 (1941): 219–232; Diner, *Jews of the United States*, 229.

85. Enrico Glicenstein and Alexander M. Dushkin, *The Tree of Life: Sketches from Jewish Life of Yesterday and Today in Drawing, Prose and Verse* (Chicago: L. M. Stein, 1933), 37.

86. Samuel S. Cohon, "The Jew and Christmas," *Union Tidings* (January 1930): 12.

87. "Lehman Bids Jews Hold to Tradition," *New York Times* (December 6, 1937).

88. Kennedy, *Freedom from Fear*, 229.

89. "Month by Month Programs," *Hadassah Newsletter* (December 1936): n.p., Hadassah Archives, R615/program department, AJHS.

90. Hayyim Schauss, *The Jewish Festivals* (New York: UAHC, 1938), 216–217.

91. Editors, "Review of the Year," *AJYB* 30 (1931).

92. Paul Vincent, "Assembly Syllabus for Jewish Schools," *Bulletin of Associated Talmud Torahs* (Philadelphia) 38 (1934): front page; "Jewish Arts and Crafts," *Bulletin of Associated Talmud Torahs* (Philadelphia) 57 (1935): 7.

93. Elsie Chomsky, "Experience with a Holiday Program as a Center of Interest in the Curriculum," *Jewish Educator* 5 (April–June 1933): 95–100; Adeline R. Rosewater, "Primary Songs and Games for Children in the Jewish Religious School," *Jewish Teacher* 6 (November 1937); 3–7; Ben M. Edidin, "Teaching Holidays and Customs," *Jewish Teacher* 5 (March 1937): 1–24; Samuel Silver and Alvin Fine, "Chanukko Marches On," *Jewish Teacher* 7 (1939): 8.

94. Ben M. Edidin, *Projects about Religious Ideas and Customs* (Cincinnati: UAHC, 1938).

95. Fass, "Creating New Identities," 97–100.

96. Shalom Altman, *Judean Songbook, for Young Judea Clubs* (1934), n.p.

97. Moshe Nathanson, *Maginoth Shiraynu, Hebrew Melodies Old and New, Religious and Secular* (New York: Hebrew Publishing Company, 1939); Judith Kaplan Eisenstein, *Gateway to Jewish Song*, illustrations by Temima Nimtzowitz (New York: Beherman House, 1939), 61.

98. "The Maccabean Spirit Today," in *Sabbath Prayer Book* (New York: Jewish Reconstructionist Foundation, 1979), 516. Originally published 1945.

99. "Hanukkah and Its Modern Analogues," *Reconstructionist* (December 1940): front page. Editorial could have been written by one of nine contributing editors.

100. Kennedy, *Freedom from Fear*, 435–441, 453 (quote).

101. "Religion and Morale," editorial, *Reconstructionist* (February 20, 1942): 9.

102. Mordecai M. Kaplan, "In Reply to Dr. Gordis," *Reconstructionist* (November 27, 1942): 15.

103. "A Word from the Y," *Jewish Ledger* (New Orleans) (December 15, 1939): n.p.

104. Isaac Klein, "Friends of the Radio Audience" [1940–44?], box 6, Isaac Klein Papers, Butler Library, Buffalo State College.

105. Emily Solis-Cohen, Jr., *Hanukkah: The Feast of Lights* (Philadelphia: Jewish Publication Society, 1937).

106. M. David Hoffman, "*Hanukkah: The Feast of Lights* by Emily Solis-Cohen, Jr.," *Jewish Quarterly Review* (July 1938): 80.

107. Ben M. Edidin, *Jewish Holidays and Festivals*, illustrated by Kyra Markham (New York: Hebrew Publishing Company, 1940), 102.

108. Jane Bearman, *Happy Chanuko* (New York: Union of American Hebrew Congregations, 1943); Judith Kaplan Eisenstein, *Festival Songs* (New York: Bloch, 1943); Ben M. Edidin, *Jewish Customs and Ceremonies* (New York: Hebrew Publishing Company, 1941); Harry Coopersmith, *Hanukkah Songster for Choral Groups* (New York: Jewish Education Committee, 1940); Lydia Caplan, *Chanuko in Song and Dance, a Festival for Chanuko for Children* (Cincinnati: UAHC, 1940); Aharon Kessler, *Hanukkah: A Manual for Junior Clubs* (New York: Young Judea, 1942); see also Jacob Golub, "Chanuko Projects," *Jewish Teacher* 12 (November 1943): 17–26; Libbie Braverman, "Chanuko and Our Neighbors," *Jewish Teacher* 11 (April 1943): 13–17 .

109. "Use Sisterhood Chanuko Accessories," *Topics & Trends* (1940), Series K, box 69, folder 2, MS-73, NFTS/WRJ, AJA.

110. Norman Kiell, *Phonograph Recordings of Jewish Interest* (Washington, DC: B'nai B'rith Foundation, 1941), 1–19.

111. *Meet Me in St. Louis* (MGM, 1944); *Since You Went Away* (United Artists, 1944).

112. Theodore H. Gordon, "A Challenge to Jewish Parents," *Reconstructionist* 7 (December 26, 1941): 12; Kenneth White, "American Jewish Response to Christmas" (ordination thesis, Hebrew Union College, Cincinnati, 1982), 114.

113. "Hanukkah Candles and Christmas Trees," *Women's League Outlook* (December 1940): n.p.

114. Eric Caplan, "What Does It Imply? How Does It Apply? Holiday Editorials in *The Reconstructionist*, 1935–1955," *Shofar* 24 (Spring 2006): 47–48; see also "Hanukah and Its Modern Analogues," *Reconstructionist* (December 27, 1940): 3, 4.

115. Caplan, "What Does It Imply?," 47.

116. Letty Cottin Pogrebin, personal account in *Transforming the Faiths of Our Fathers: Women Who Changed American Religion*, ed. Ann Braude (New York: Palgrave Macmillan, 2004), 35.

117. "Jews in Uniform: Chanukah in Honolulu," *Jewish Ledger* (New Orleans) (January 30, 1942): n.p.

118. Bryan Edward Stone, *The Chosen Folks: Jews on the Frontiers of Texas* (Austin: University of Texas Press, 2010), 180.

119. "Bright Ideas," *Topics & Trends* (September–October 1942): 3, series E, box 36, folder 3, MS-73, WRJ, AJA.

120. Editorial, "Our Modern Hellenists," *Reconstructionist* (December 24, 1943): 1, 4.

121. David I. Cedarblum, *Beware of Hellenism in the Ranks: A Set of Holiday Sermons* (Cincinnati: Commission on Information about Judaism, UAHC and CCAR, 1944), 37; White, "American Jewish Response to Christmas," 115.

122. Photos, *Sentinel* (Chicago) (December 21, 1944): photo page.

123. Ganzfried, *Code of Jewish Law*; Ganzfried condensed the first four parts of the *Shulchan Aruch* dealing with practical life and added other sections on charity, marriage, business, and mourning. Material on ethics was drawn from Maimonides's *Mishneh Torah*. Nahum N. Glatzer, *The Judaic Tradition*, rev. ed. (New York: Behrman House, 1969), 62.

124. Goldin, *Jewish Woman and Her Home*, 7.

NOTES TO CHAPTER 6

1. Robert Putnam, *Bowling Alone: The Collapse and Revival of American Community* (New York: Simon and Schuster, 2001), 1–20.

2. Hasia R. Diner and Beryl Leif Benderly, *Her Works Praise Her: A History of Jewish Women in America from Colonial Times to the Present* (New York: Perseus Books, 2002), 305; Jewish Women's Archive, "Jewish Women and World War II," online exhibit, http://jwa.org/exhibits/ww2 (accessed December 1, 2010); Jewish Women's Archive, "We Remember—Hannah Bloch, 1913–2009," http://jwa.org/weremember/block-hannah (accessed December 1, 2010); Jewish Women's Archive, "Air Force: Selma Cronan," http://jwa.org/discover/infocus/military/airforce/cronan.html (accessed December 1, 2010); Jewish Women's Archive, "Army: Matilda and Bernice Blaustein," http://jwa.org/discover/infocus/military/army/blaustein.html (accessed December 1, 2010); Jewish Women's Archive, "Jewish Women in the Military: Navy," http://jwa.org/discover/infocus/military/navy/index.html (accessed December 1, 2010).

3. "Sarah Kopelman," in *They Dare to Dream: A History of National Women's League* (New York: National Women's League of the United Synagogue of America, 1967), 16–17.

4. Louis Kraft, "Jews in the Armed Forces," *AJYB* 47 (1946): 264.

5. Marc Dollinger, *Quest for Inclusion: Jews and Liberalism in Modern America* (Princeton: Princeton University Press, 2000), 82; Joshua Trachtenberg et al., "Review of the Year," *AJYB* 44 (1943): 96, 97, 137.

6. Editors, "Review of the Year 5705," *AJYB* 47 (1945–1946): 210; Howard Fast, *My Glorious Brothers* (Boston: Little, Brown, 1948).

7. Sarah L. Kopelman, "President's Page," *Women's League Outlook* 17, no. 2 (1946): n.p.

8. Jakob J. Petuchowski, "The Magnification of Chanukah: Afterthoughts on a Festival," *Commentary* 29 (January 1960): 38–60.

9. Peter N. Stearns, *Anxious Parents: A History of Modern Childrearing in America* (New York: NYU Press, 2003), 44–45.

10. "The American Jew: Some Demographic Features," *AJYB* 51 (1950): 9.

11. Erich Rosenthal, "Jewish Fertility in the United States," *AJYB* 62 (1961): 9–12.

12. Deborah Dash Moore, *To the Golden Cities: Pursuing the American Dream in Miami and L.A.* (New York: Free Press, 1994); Alvin Chenkin, "Jewish Population in the United States, 1959," *AJYB* 61 (1960): 3–10.

13. Sylvia Barack Fishman, *The Way into the Varieties of Jewishness* (Woodstock, VT: Jewish Lights, 2007), 118.

14. Elaine Tyler May, *Homeward Bound: American Families in the Cold War Era*, rev. ed. (New York: Basic Books, 1999), 65.

15. James T. Patterson, *Grand Expectations: The United States, 1945–1974* (New York: Oxford University Press, 1996), 328–329; Steven Whitfield, *The Culture of the Cold War* (Baltimore: Johns Hopkins University Press, 1991), 88.

16. Julius Draschler, *Intermarriage in New York City: A Statistical Study of the Amalgamation of European People* (New York, 1921), 17–18; Ruby Jo Reeves Kennedy, "Single or Triple Melting Pot? Intermarriage Trends in New Haven, 1870–1940," *American Journal of Sociology* 49, no. 4 (January 1944): 331–339, and 38, no. 1 (July 1952): 56–59; Lila Corwin Berman, "Sociology, Jews and Intermarriage in Twentieth-Century America," *Jewish Social Studies* 14 (Winter 2008): 37; see also Milton M. Gordon, *Religion in American Life: The Role of Race, Religion and National Origins* (Oxford: Oxford University Press, 1964), 122–123, 181.

17. Berman, "Sociology, Jews and Intermarriage," 44.

18. Shuly Rubin Schwartz, "Women's League for Conservative Judaism," *Jewish Women in America: An Historical Encyclopedia*, vol. 2, ed. Paula Hyman and Deborah Dash Moore (New York: Routledge, 1998), 1495; Dean W. Roberts, "Highlights of the Midcentury White House Conference on Children and Youth," *American Journal of Public Health* 41, no. 1 (January 1951): 96–99, available at http://www.ncbi.nlm.nih.gov/pmc/articles/PMC1525921/?.

19. Erik Erikson, *Childhood and Society* (New York: Norton, 1950).

20. David Reisman, *The Lonely Crowd: A Study in the Changing American Character* (New Haven: Yale University Press, 1950).

21. Andrew Heinze, *Jews and the American Soul: Human Nature in the 20th Century* (Princeton: Princeton University Press, 2004), 271.

22. Joshua Trachtenberg, "Religious Activities," *AJYB* 47 (1946): 217.

23. Uriah Z. Engelman, "Jewish Education," *AJYB* 51 (1950): 160.

24. Ruth Zalman, "Parents' Corner: Telling the Hanuka Story," *Jewish Currents* (December 14–21, 1960): 15.

25. Henry Feingold, *A Time for Searching: Entering the Mainstream, 1920–1945* (Baltimore: Johns Hopkins University Press, 1992), 110.

26. Hasia R. Diner, *The Jews of the United States, 1654–2000* (Berkeley: University of California Press, 2003), 257; Jeffrey S. Gurock, *American Jewish Orthodoxy in Historical Perspective* (New York: KTAV, 1996), 308–311.

27. *Chabad* is an acronym for the Hebrew words for wisdom, understanding, and knowledge, coined by the movement's founder, Rabbi Shneur Zalman of Liadi (1745–1813), in the town of Lubavitch in White Russia. These also are the guiding principles of Orthodoxy, and Hasidic Jews are fully observant. Lubavitchers are one variety of the larger Hasidic movement that began in eastern Poland-Lithuania in the mid-eighteenth century and that rapidly spread throughout eastern Europe. Insisting that joyful worship pleased God as much as did Talmudic erudition and organized around charismatic leaders called *rebbes* who guided their followers' lives, Hasidism offered ordinary Jews both assurance of divine attention and practical assistance in everyday life. Jerome R. Mintz, *Hasidic People: A Place in the New World* (Cambridge: Harvard University Press, 1992), 9–50.

28. Jeffrey S. Gurock, *Orthodox Jews in America* (Bloomington: Indiana University Press, 2009), 216.

29. Robert Gordis, *Judaism for the Modern Age* (New York: Farrar, Straus & Cuddihy, 1955), 30, 111.

30. Abba Hillel Silver, *Where Judaism Differed: An Inquiry into the Distinctiveness of Judaism* (New York: Macmillan, 1956), 88–89.

31. Theodor Herzl Gaster, *Purim and Hanukkah in Custom and Tradition* (New York: Henry Schuman, 1950); Morris N. Kertzer, *What Is a Jew?*, rev. ed. (New York: Macmillan, 1960), 143.

32. Joachim Prinz, *The Dilemma of the Modern Jew* (Boston: Little, Brown, 1962), 179, 217–218.

33. Daniel J. Elazar and Rela Mintz Geffen, *The Conservative Movement in Judaism: Dilemmas and Opportunities* (Albany: SUNY Press, 2000), 85.

34. Ibid.; Stearns, *Anxious Parents*, 75–78.

35. Albert I. Gordon, *How to Celebrate Hanukkah at Home* (New York: United Synagogue of America, 1947), 1, 5.

36. Schwartz, "Women's League for Conservative Judaism," 1494.

37. "The American Jew: Some Demographic Features," *AJYB* 51 (1950): 35; Abraham Mayer Heller, *The Vocabulary of Jewish Life* (New York: Hebrew Publishing Company, 1942), vii; Betty Davis Greenberg and Althea O. Silverman, *The Jewish Home Beautiful*, 7th printing (New York: National Women's League of the United Synagogue of America, 1953), Marjorie Lehman, "Deborah Marcus Melamed," *Jewish Women: A Comprehensive Historical Encyclopedia*, March 1, 2009, http://www.jwa.org/encyclopedia/article/melamed-deborah-marcus.

38. Joshua Trachtenberg, "Religious Activities," *AJYB* 47 (1945–1946): 215.

39. Morris Adler, "The Seminary as Interpreter of Judaism to Modern Jews" (paper presented at the Conference on the Role of Judaism in the Modern World,

Chicago, April 19, 1942), 91, Ratner Center, Jewish Theological Seminary, New York; Zachary Silver, "The Excommunication of Mordecai Kaplan," *American Jewish Archives Journal* 62, no. 1 (2010): 36.

40. Hyman E. Goldin, *A Treasury of Jewish Holidays: History, Legends, Traditions* (New York: Twayne, 1952), 53.

41. Hyman E. Goldin, *The Jew and His Duties* (New York: Hebrew Publishing Company, 1953), 158–159.

42. Hyman E. Goldin, *The Jewish Woman and Her Home* (New York: Hebrew Publishing Company, 1941), 224.

43. Albert I. Gordon, *How to Celebrate Hanukkah at Home* (Whitefish, MT: Kessinger, 2007).

44. Albert I. Gordon, *How to Celebrate Hanukah at Home* (New York: United Synagogue of America, 1947), Brandies quote inside front cover, Gordon quote on p. 1; on the Holocaust's challenge to Jewish faith, see for example Richard J. Rubenstein, *After Auschwitz: Radical Theology and Contemporary Judaism* (Indianapolis: Bobbs-Merrill, 1966).

45. Dore Schary, *Al Hanissim: Special Service for Hanukkah Meal Times* (New York: United Synagogue of America, 1950), Communications 11c-33-41, Holidays: Chanuka 1930–1960s, folder 41, Ratner Center.

46. Gordon, *How to Celebrate Hanukah at Home*, 5.

47. Eliza Rosen, "Merry Hanukah," in *The Business of Holidays*, ed. Maud Lavin (New York: Monacelli, 2004), 222.

48. Joellyn Wallen Zellman, "The Gifts of the Jews: Ideology and Material Culture in the American Synagogue Gift Shop," *American Jewish Archives Journal* 58, no. 1 (2006): 51.

49. Catalog of Model Judaica Shop, 1961, Series E, box 4, folder 3, MS-73, NFTS/WRJ, AJA; see also Rosen, "Merry Hanukah," 222; Jenna Weissman Joselit, *Wonders of America: Reinventing Jewish Culture, 1880–1950* (New York: Hill and Wang, 1994), 239; "The House of Zion for the Ideal Chanukah Gift," *New York Post* (December 2, 1942).

50. "Let's Talk Shop: Your Sisterhood Judaica Shop," *Topics & Trends* (1960), series K, box 70, folder 2, MS-73, AJA; Catalog of a Model Judaica Shop (1961), series E, box 4, folder 3, MS-73, NFTS, AJA; "Do Your Hanukkah Shopping Here," *Women's League Outlook* (October 1967): advertisement page; "Do Your Hanukkah Shopping Here," *Women's League Outlook* (Winter 1967), 14; "Chanukah Fund Raising Ideas!," *Women's League Outlook* (Fall 1966): 25.

51. Kenneth White, "American Jewish Response to Christmas" (ordination thesis, Hebrew Union College, Cincinnati, 1982), 211.

52. Jeffrey S. Gurock, *American Jewish Orthodoxy in Historical Perspective* (New York: KTAV, 1996), 308–310.

53. Kenneth T. Jackson, *Crabgrass Frontier: The Suburbanization of the United States* (New York: Oxford University Press, 1985), 233.

54. Jack Wertheimer, "The Conservative Synagogue," in *The American Synagogue: A Sanctuary Transformed*, ed. Jack Wertheimer (Hanover, NH: Brandeis University Press / University Press of New England, 1987), 123–126.

55. Leon A. Jick, "The Reform Synagogue," in Wertheimer, *American Synagogue*, 102.

56. Marshall Sklare, *America's Jews* (New York: Random House, 1971), 114; Raphael Patai, *The Jewish Mind* (New York: Scribner, 1977), 401; Sidney Goldstein and Calvin Goldscheider, *Jewish Americans: Three Generations in a Jewish Community* (Englewood Cliffs, NJ: Prentice-Hall, 1968), 201

57. Daniel J. Elazar, "Developments in Jewish Community Organization in the Second Postwar Generation," in *American Pluralism and the Jewish Community*, ed. Seymour Martin Lipset (New Brunswick, NJ: Transaction, 1990), 181.

58. Sarah Kussy, *Women's League Handbook and Guide* (New York: United Synagogue of America, 1947), 49.

59. Ibid.; for the Ashkenazi custom, see Albert I . Gordon, *Jews in Transition* (Minneapolis: University of Minnesota Press, 1949), 117; Goldin, *Jew and His Duties*, 158–159.

60. Kussy, *Women's League Handbook and Guide*, 49.

61. Alvin Chenkin, "Jewish Population of the United States, 1954," *AJYB* 56 (1955): 176; Patterson, *Grand Expectations*, 348; Erik Barnouw, *Tube of Plenty: The Evolution of American Television* (New York: Oxford University Press, 1982); Karal Ann Marling, *As Seen on TV: The Visual Culture of Everyday Life in the 1950s* (Cambridge: Harvard University Press, 1994); Steven Whitfield, *The Culture of the Cold War* (Baltimore: Johns Hopkins University Press, 1991).

62. Israel Chipkin, "Twenty Years of Jewish Education in the United States," *AJYB* 38 (1937): 27–36; Uriah Zevi Engelman, "Educational and Cultural Activities," *AJYB* 47 (1945–1946): 228–229.

63. Ilana Gerard Singer, "Red-Diaper Daughter," *Lilith* 17 (Summer 1992): 7.

64. Moore, *To the Golden Cities*, 102.

65. Kussy, *Women's League Handbook and Guide*, 49.

66. Ibid., 50.

67. See for example *The Neziner* (December 1, 1933), Philadelphia Jewish Archives Center; *Har Zion Bulletin* (December 13, 1933) and (November 28, 1934), series 2, box 1 and box 2, Har Zion Records, Ratner Center; Carmel Finkelstein, "The War for Peace," *Women's League Outlook* (December 1933): front page; "Hanukkah Plans," *Topics & Trends* (September–October 1936): 4; "Bright Ideas," *Topics & Trends* (November–December 1938): 2, series K, box 69, folder 2, MS-73, AJA; Ben M. Edidin, *Projects about Religious Ideas and Customs* (Cincinnati: UAHC, 1938); "Home Observance for Hanukkah," *Park Avenue Synagogue Bulletin* (December 9, 1946), Communications, 11c-33–41, Holidays: Chanuka 1930–1960s, folder 41, Ratner Center.

68. Kinneret Chiel, *The Complete Book of Hanukkah* (New York: KTAV, 1959).

69. Barbara Schwartz, "One Mother Offers Her Ideas as to How She Makes the

Chanukah Festival Exciting for the Children," *Sentinel* (Chicago) (December 22, 1951).

70. Howard Chudacoff, *Children at Play: An American History* (New York: NYU Press, 2007), 164.

71. Grace Goldin, "Christmas-Chanukah: December Is the Cruelest Month," *Commentary* (November 1950): 416–125.

72. Albert I. Gordon, *Jews in Transition* (Minneapolis: University of Minnesota Press, 1949).

73. Nathan Brilliant and Libbie L. Braverman, *Activities in the Religious School* (New York: Union of American Hebrew Congregations, 1951), 59. These included cut-outs, instructional games, and food.

74. White, "American Jewish Response to Christmas," 26, 207, 28.

75. Gordon, *Jews in Transition*, 117; White, "American Jewish Response to Christmas," 26.

76. Diary of Lois Greene, December 17, 1946, and December 25, 1946, AJHS; see also Riv-Ellen Prell, *Fighting to Become Americans* (Boston: Beacon, 1999), 167.

77. Morton Cohn, "Hanukkah Isn't for Cowards," sermon listing, and "Shall It Be Hanukkah or . . . ?," both in *Temple Tidings* (Temple Beth Israel, San Diego) (December 15, 1949), 4.

78. Riv Ellen Prell, "Triumph, Accommodation, and Resistance: American Jewish Life from the End of World War II to the Six Day War," in *The Columbia History of Jews and Judaism in America*, ed. Marc Lee Raphael (New York: Columbia University Press, 2008), 123; Jack Wertheimer, "Jewish Education in the United States: Recent Trends and Issues," *AJYB* 99 (1999).

79. Melissa Klapper, "The History of Jewish Education in America," in Raphael, *Columbia History of Jews and Judaism*, 211; Judah Pilch, ed., *A History of Jewish Education in America* (New York: National Curriculum Research Institute of the American Association for Jewish Education, 1969), 153–157, 173.

80. Eugene B. Borowitz, "Problems Facing Jewish Educational Philosophy in the Sixties," *AJYB* 62 (1961): 149; Daniel Isaacman, "Jewish Education in America —1971: An Analysis," *Gratz College 75th Anniversary Volume* (1972): 147–163.

81. Uriah Z. Engelman, "Jewish Education," *AJYB* 61 (1960): 128, 147.

82. Harry Coopersmith, *Favorite Songs of the Jewish People* (New York: United Synagogue Commission on Jewish Education, 1939); Coopersmith, *The Songs We Sing* and *Companion to the Songs We Sing* (New York: United Synagogue Commission on Jewish Education, 1950); and Coopersmith, *More of the Songs We Sing* (New York: United Synagogue Commission on Jewish Education, 1971).

83. *Union Songster, Shiru Ladonoy* (New York: Central Conference of American Rabbis, 1954), 2.

84. "Report of the Committee on Synagog Music," 1955, XY1, Fc39r, Klau Library, Hebrew Union College.

85. Jerry Goodman, *P'tsah B'Zemer* (New York: United Synagogue of America, 1964), 1.

86. John Blacking, "Expressing Human Experience through Music," in *Selected Papers of John Blacking*, ed. Reginald Byron (Chicago: University of Chicago Press, 1995), 35–52; A. W. Binder, *Songs Israel Sings* (New York: Metro Music, 1951); Coopersmith, *Songs We Sing*; "Report of the Committee on Synagog Music"; Ruth Rubin, ed., *A Treasury of Jewish Folksong* (New York: Schocken Books, 1950); *Songs and Stories of the Jewish Holidays* (Decca Records, early 1960s); *Holiday Sing Along* (New York: Collectors Guild, 1962); *Shiron Habonim* (London: Education Department, Habonim, 1971), 22; Kinneret Chiel, *The Complete Book of Hanukkah* (New York: KTAV, 1959).

87. Irving White, "This Year Chanukah Brings Deep Meaning and Bright Hope," *Sentinel* (December 23, 1948): 34.

88. Kurt List, "Music," *AJYB* 52 (1951): 184.

89. "Z.O.C. Re-Lives Festival of Hanukkah at Opera House," *Sentinel* (December 23, 1948), front page; program, *The Hanukah Festival* (December 23, 1951), and *Ninth Annual Hanukkah Festival* (Chicago: Civic Opera House, 1954), Chicago Jewish Archives Collection.

90. Ruth Rubin, *Voices of a People: The Story of Yiddish Folksong* (New York: McGraw-Hill, 1963), 9.

91. Ben Aronin, *Latke Ditties* (Chicago: Board of Jewish Education, 1951).

92. Samuel H. Markowitz, *Adjusting the Jewish Child to His World*, rev. ed. (New York: NFTS, 1961), 63.

93. See for example Rubin, *Treasury of Jewish Folksong*; Seymour Silbermintz, ed., *Songs of Israel* (New York: Young Zionist Action Committee, 1949); Emily Solis-Cohen, Jr., ed., *Hanukkah: The Feast of Light* (Philadelphia: Jewish Publication Society, 1940), 68–81; Coopersmith, *Companion to the Songs We Sing*.

94. Betty A. Bailey and Jane W. Davidson, "Effects of Group Singing and Performance for Marginalized and Middle-Class Singers," *Psychology of Music* 33, no. 3 (2005): 271.

95. "In his veins flows [the] gift of song," promised the album cover. *Moyshe Oysher Chanukah Party* (Rozanna Records, 1950).

96. *Chanukah Music Box*, written and sung by Shirley R. Cohen (Kinor Records, n.d. [circa 1950s]).

97. *Shalom Sings: Jewish Holiday Songs for Children* (Friends of Jewish Music, 1960); *Sholom Secunda's Family Chanukah* (Twentieth Century Fox Records, 1964).

98. Judith K. Eisenstein, "On the Record," *Hadassah Magazine* (November 1961): 18–19.

99. Cary Hillebrand to the author, November 5, 2010.

100. Deborah Dash Moore, *G.I. Jews: How World War II Changed a Generation* (Cambridge: Belknap Press of Harvard University Press, 2004), 263–264.

101. "Jewish Population in the United States," *AJYB* 62 (1961), 54; A. Herbert Fedder to Arthur J. S. Rosenbaum, Monthly Report (January 11, 1950), Brooklyn Jewish Community Council, box 4, folder 8, MS-164, AJA.

102. *Temple Tidings* (Temple Beth Israel, San Diego) (December 23, 1948): 3.

103. Editorial, *Women's League Outlook* 21, no. 2 (1950): 2.

104. "The Menorah or the Tree," *Rodeph Sholom Bulletin* (December 14, 1959): 3, Rodeph Sholom Collection, Philadelphia Jewish Archives Center.

105. Abraham Karp, *Our December Dilemma: Your Child and You* (New York: United Synagogue Commission on Jewish Education, 1958), 1–8; White, "American Jewish Response to Christmas," 123–124.

106. Edward Cohen, *The Peddler's Grandson: Growing Up Jewish in Mississippi* (New York: Dell, 1999), 47–49.

107. Gordon, *Jews in Transition*, 117.

108. Author's observation, 1963; Peter S. Lemish, "Hanukkah Bush: The Jewish Experience in America," *Theory into Practice* 20, no. 1 (2001): 26–30; Peter Lemish to the author, February 11, 2011.

109. Melanie Archer, "Xmas Excess," in *The Business of Holidays*, ed. Maud Lavin (New York: Monacelli, 2004), 237.

110. Grace Goldin, "Succahs Open to the American Skies: A Commentary on the Feast of Tabernacles," *Commentary* (October 1954).

111. Irving Ashton to the author; Philip Shabecoff, "Greeting Card Manufacturers in Holiday Mood," *New York Times* (November 30, 1962).

112. Herbert Gans, "The Future of American Jewry," part 2, *Commentary* (June 1956): 555–563; Deborah Dash Moore, *At Home in America: Second Generation New York Jews* (New York: Columbia University Press, 1981), 233–234.

113. Benjamin Ringer, *The Edge of Friendliness: A Study of Jewish-Gentile Relations* (New York: Basic Books, 1967), 131; White, "American Jewish Response to Christmas," 83.

114. *Women's League Outlook* (December 1963); Nancy L. Waldman, "Hanukkah Doors," *Women's League Outlook* (Fall 1978): 11.

115. Marc Dollinger, *Quest for Inclusion: Jews and Liberalism in Modern America* (Princeton: Princeton University Press, 2000), 156.

116. Cohen, *Peddler's Grandson*, 49.

117. Jules Cohen, "Some Non-legal Arguments against Chanukah Programs in Public Schools," *Jewish Life* (December 1958): 18; White, "American Jewish Response to Christmas," 159.

118. Dollinger, *Quest for Inclusion*, 156.

119. Arthur Gilbert, "The Season of Good Will and Interreligious Tension," *Reconstructionist* (November 14, 1958): 13–18; White, "American Jewish Response to Christmas," 160.

120. Colleen McDannell to the author, October 1994.

121. Irving J. Rosenbaum, *Your Neighbor Celebrates: The Jewish Holidays* (Chicago: Department of Interreligious Cooperation, Anti-Defamation League of B'nai B'rith, 1947).

122. Arthur Gilbert and Oscar Tarcov, *Your Neighbor Celebrates* (New York: Friendly House, 1957).

123. Literature Committee of the Association for Childhood Education, *Told under the Christmas Tree: An Umbrella Book* (New York: Macmillan, 1948), vii–viii.

124. "Christmas and Hanukkah Lights Go On at City Hall," *New York Times* (December 12, 1968).

125. Kinneret Chiel, *The Complete Book of Hanukkah* (New York: KTAV, 1959), 24, 50.

126. Shuly Rubin Schwartz, *The Rabbi's Wife: The Rebbetzin in American Jewish Life* (New York: NYU Press, 2006), 2–5.

127. Leon Spitz, "A Hanukkah Night in Old Philadelphia," in Chiel, *Complete Book of Hanukkah*, 51–54.

128. Emily Solis Cohen, Jr., "Hanukkah at Valley Forge," in *Hanukkah: The Feast of Lights* (Philadelphia: Jewish Publication Society, 1955), 329–337.

129. Phillip Moses Russell (1747–1830), Mikveh Israel Spruce Street Cemetery. Lou Kessler to the author, December 5, 2005.

130. Sylvia Barack Fishman, *Double or Nothing? Jewish Families and Mixed Marriage* (Lebanon, NH: Brandeis University Press / University Press of New England, 2004), 131–132.

131. Beth S. Wenger, *History Lessons: The Creation of American Jewish Heritage* (Princeton: Princeton University Press, 2010), 145–161.

132. Harold D. Kastle, *658 Stories* (New York: Jewish Education Committee of New York, 1956), 3–7.

133. Bulletin of Temple B'nai Abraham, Newark, New Jersey (December 1960), series A, box 1, folder 3, MS-742, AJA.

134. *World Over: A Magazine for Jewish Youth* (November 20, 1964): 8–9, Klau Library, Hebrew Union College, Cincinnati.

135. Editorial, *Women's League Outlook* (December 1965): 14.

136. Gladys D. Kauffman, *The Secret Chanukah* (New York: UAHC, 1965).

137. Gal Beckerman, *When They Come for Us We'll Be Gone: The Epic Struggle to Save Soviet Jewry* (New York: Houghton Mifflin, 2010), 71–75, 131; Irving Spiegel, "Soviet Curbs on Jews Protested," *New York Times* (December 12, 1966).

138. Beckerman, *When They Come*, 131; "The Soviet Jewry Protest: Student Struggle for Soviet Jewry," *Hadassah Magazine* (December 1965).

139. Mordecai M. Kaplan, *The Purpose and Meaning of Jewish Existence: A People in the Image of God* (Philadelphia: Jewish Publication Society, 1964), 287, 300.

140. Engelman, "Jewish Education," 142.

141. Cantor study quoted in Jeffrey Shandler, *Jews, God, and Videotape: Religion and Media in America* (New York: NYU Press, 2009), 203–206; Sylvia Jacobs to the author, November 14, 2010.

142. Milton Matz, "The Meaning of the Christmas Tree to the American Jew," *Jewish Journal of Sociology* 3 (June 1961): 13; White, "American Jewish Response to Christmas," 125; Marcus L. Hansen, "The Problem of the Third Generation Immigrant," Augustana Historical Society, Rock Island, Illinois, 1938, reprinted with a foreword by Oscar Handlin in *Commentary* (November 1952): 492–500.

143. Marshall Sklare, "The Changing Profile of the American Jew: A Preliminary Report in a Study of a Midwestern Jewish Community Sponsored by the American Jewish Committee" (June 1959), http://www.ajcarchives.org/ajcarchive/Digital/Archive.aspx; Ringer, *Edge of Friendliness*, 124.

144. Cited in Jonathan D. Sarna, *American Judaism: A History* (New Haven: Yale University Press, 2004), 278.

NOTES TO CHAPTER 7

1. James T. Patterson, *Restless Giant: The United States from Watergate to "Bush v. Gore"* (New York: Oxford University Press, 2005), 294–295.

2. Sylvia Barack Fishman, *The Way into the Varieties of Jewishness* (Woodstock, VT: Jewish Lights, 2007), 171; Steven M. Cohen, "Change in a Very Conservative Movement," *Sh'ma* 36 (February 2006): 6.

3. Patterson, *Restless Giant*; Robert D. Putnam, *Bowling Alone: The Collapse and Revival of American Community* (New York: Simon and Schuster, 2000), 152; Jack Wertheimer, *A People Divided: Judaism in Contemporary America* (New York: Basic Books, 1999); Fishman, *Way into the Varieties*.

4. Deborah Dash Moore, *To the Golden Cities: Pursuing the American Jewish Dream in Miami and L.A.* (Cambridge: Harvard University Press, 1994), 4.

5. Gerald Sorin, *Tradition Transformed: The Jewish Experience in America* (Baltimore: Johns Hopkins University Press, 1997), 64, 235.

6. Penni Crabtree, "Judaism on Decline in Towns: Exodus of Young Alters Way of Life," box 9, Temple Israel Sisterhood Yearbooks 1990–1991, MS-713, AJA.

7. Wertheimer, *A People Divided*.

8. Michael Oppenheimer, foreword to *Let's Celebrate Chanukah*, comp. Mrs. Nelson (Jeanne) Friedman (Beachwood, OH, c. 1985), 2. Thank you, Jane Rothstein.

9. "The Festivals," in *The Jewish Catalog*, ed. Richard Siegel, Michael Strassfeld, and Sharon Strassfeld (Philadelphia: Jewish Publication Society, 1973), 133.

10. Richard Siegel, Michael Strassfeld, and Sharon Strassfeld, introduction to *Jewish Catalog*, 9.

11. Hasia R. Diner, *Lower East Side Memories: A Jewish Place in America* (Princeton: Princeton University Press, 2000), 96–97; Riv-Ellen Prell, *Prayer and Community: The Havurah Movement in American Judaism* (Detroit: Wayne State University Press, 1989), 39.

12. Prell, *Prayer and Community*, 75–97; David Glanz, "An Interpretation of the Jewish Counterculture," *Jewish Social Studies* 39 (Winter–Spring 1977): 112–128.

13. Everett Gendler, "On the Judaism of Nature," in *The New Jews*, ed. James A. Sleeper and Alan Mintz (New York: Vintage Books, 1971), 239.

14. "The Festivals," 134.

15. Sorin, *Tradition Transformed*, 234.

16. Arnold M. Eisen, *Taking Hold of Torah: Jewish Commitment and Community in America* (Bloomington: Indiana University Press, 1997), 15–16.

17. Mark Silk, "Notes on the Judaic-Christian Tradition," *American Quarterly* 36 (Spring 1984): 83.
18. Wertheimer, *A People Divided*, 85.
19. Edward Shapiro, *A Time for Healing* (Baltimore: Johns Hopkins University Press, 1992), 86; Irving Greenberg, "Jewish Survival and the College Campus," *Judaism* 17 (Summer 1968): 260–281.
20. Shapiro, *A Time for Healing*, 81; Robert Alter, "What Jewish Studies Can Do," *Commentary* (October 1974): 73.
21. Letters page, *University Jewish Voice* (January 23, 1972), reprinted in *Jewish Student Press* (Fall 1972): 32.
22. Steven M. Cohen and Arnold Eisen, *The Jew Within: Self, Family, and Community in America* (Bloomington: Indiana University Press, 2000), 53.
23. Glanz, "Interpretation of the Jewish Counterculture."
24. David King, "The Ultimate Food Fight," *Time Out Chicago* (November 17–24, 2005), in HF: Hillel-Faculty, Campus Jewish Views (November 21, 2005); Ruth Friedman Cernea, ed., *The Great Latke-Hamantash Debate* (Chicago: University of Chicago Press, 2006). The University of Minnesota holds its debate at Purim, rather than Hanukkah. Riv-Ellen Prell to the author, November 21, 2005.
25. Marsha Bryan Edelman, *Discovering Jewish Music* (Philadelphia: Jewish Publication Society, 2003), 141; Ari Goldman, "Schlomo Carlebach," obituary, *New York Times* (October 22, 1994).
26. Velvel Pasternak, *Songs of the Chassidim II* (New York: Bloch, 1971), 1.
27. *Festival of Light* (Six Degrees Records, 1996); *Festival of Light 2* (Six Degrees Records, 1999).
28. Richard J. Rubenstein, *After Auschwitz: Radical Theology and Contemporary Judaism* (Indianapolis: Bobbs-Merrill, 1966), 89, 114; Søren Aabye Kierkegaard, *Concluding Unscientific Postscript*, trans. David F. Swenson (Princeton: Princeton University Press, 1941), 188.
29. Rubenstein, *After Auschwitz*, 5.
30. Irving Greenberg, "Cloud of Smoke, Pillar of Fire: Judaism, Christianity, and Modernity after the Holocaust," in *Auschwitz: Beginning of a New Era?*, ed. Eva Fleischner (New York: KTAV, 1977), 9–13; Rubenstein, *After Auschwitz*, 159.
31. Martin Buber, *I and Thou*, trans. Ronald Gregor (New York: Scribner, 1958), and as a new translation by Walter Kaufmann (New York: Scribner, 1970); Norman L. Friedman, "Social Movement Legacies: The American Jewish Counterculture, 1973–1988," *Jewish Social Studies* 50, nos. 3–4 (1988): 127, available at http://www.jstor.org/stable/4467421 (accessed August 2, 2011).
32. Mark Oppenheimer, *Knocking on Heaven's Door: American Religion in the Age of Counterculture* (New Haven: Yale University Press, 2003), 100–101; Chava Weissler, "Bar Mitzvah in the Havurah Family," in *The Jewish Family: Myths and Reality*, ed. Steven M. Cohen and Paula E. Hyman (New York: Holmes and Meier, 1986), 202, 204–205.
33. Jody Myers, "The Midrashic Enterprise of Contemporary Jewish Women," in

Jews and Gender: The Challenge to Hierarchy, Studies in Contemporary Jewry 16, ed. Jonathan Frankel (Jerusalem: Hebrew University, 2000), 136. See also Prell, *Prayer and Community*; and Riv-Ellen Prell, *Women Remaking American Judaism* (Detroit: Wayne State University Press, 2007).

34. Havurah Shir Hadash, "Zalman Schachter-Shalomi," http://www.havurah shirhadash.org/rebzalman.html (accessed February 9, 2011).

35. Gershom Scholem, *Kabbalah* (Jerusalem: Keter, 1974; New York: New American Library, 1974), 138–142.

36. Chava Weissler, "Meanings of Shekhinah in the 'Jewish Renewal Movement,'" *Nashim: A Journal of Jewish Women's Studies & Gender Issues* 10 (Fall 2005): 53–83; Arthur Waskow, "Dear Friends," *New Menorah: The Journal of ALEPH: Alliance for Jewish Renewal* (Winter 1994): 1, 5, 14.

37. Jerome R. Mintz, *Hasidic People: A Place in the New World* (Cambridge: Harvard University Press, 1992), 43.

38. Ibid., 6; Ira Robinson, "The First Hasidic Rabbis in North America," *American Jewish Archives* 44 (1992): 501–506; Jonathan Sarna, "How Matza Became Square: Manischewitz and the Development of Machine-Made Matzah in the United States," *Sixth Annual Lecture of the Victor J. Selmanowitz Chair of Jewish History*, Graduate School of Jewish Studies, Touro College, 2005; Kehillah (Jewish Community) of New York City, *Jewish Communal Register of New York City, 1917–1918* (New York: Kehillah, 1918), 431–446.

39. Mintz, *Hasidic People*, 93.

40. "Hasidim," in *Encyclopaedia Judaica*, ed. Michael Berenbaum and Fred Skolnik, 2nd ed., vol. 8 (Detroit: Macmillan Reference, 2007), 394–395.

41. "Radical Jews and Jewish Radicals: A Look at Jewish Student Revolutionaries," *Congregation Beth Israel Tidings* (San Diego) (November–December 1973): 4.

42. Ibid.

43. Maya Balakirsky Katz, "Trademarks of Faith: Chabad and Chanukah in America," *Modern Judaism* 29 (May 2009): 243–244; *B'nai B'rith Messenger* 18 (1981): 1; Kenneth White, "American Jewish Response to Christmas" (ordination thesis, Hebrew Union College, Cincinnati, 1982), 226.

44. Stephanie Wellen Levine, *Mystics, Mavericks, and Merrymakers: An Intimate Journey among Hasidic Girls* (New York: NYU Press, 2003), 180–181.

45. *Laws and Customs of Chanukah According to the Traditions of Chabad*, comp. Rabbi Shmuel Hurwitz, trans. Rabbi Daniel Goldberg (Brooklyn: Empire, 1983), 45–47.

46. Bernard A. Poupko, "Sharing the Oil," in *Sermon Manual*, ed. Joseph I. Singer, Joseph H. Lookstein, Manuel Laderman, and Bernard A. Poupko (New York: Rabbinical Council of America and Rabbinical Council Press, 1974), 95.

47. Jeffrey S. Gurock, *Orthodox Jews in America* (Bloomington: Indiana University Press, 2009), 216.

48. Myers, "Midrashic Enterprise," 136.

49. Poupko, "Sharing the Oil," 96–99; Abraham Scheinberg, *What Is the Halacha?*

Encyclopedia of Halacha/Otzar Hat'shuvos, Bibliography of Responsa, Book II (New York: Shulsinger, 1974), 121; Gurock, *Orthodox Jews in America*, 200–219. Poupko may have been related to the stepfather of Yisrael Meir Kagan (the Chofetz Chaim).

50. Menachem M. Schneerson, "A Chanukah Message from Rabbi Menachem M. Schneerson," in *Laws and Customs of Chanukah According to the Traditions of Chabad*, comp. Shmuel Hurwitz, trans. Rabbi Daniel Goldberg. (Brooklyn, NY: Empress, 1983), 11–12.

51. Menachem M. Schneerson, "The Street Lamp Lighter," in *Let There Be Light: Thirty Days in the Lives of the Chabad-Lubavitch Lamplighters*, comp. Simcha Gottlieb (Brooklyn, NY: Merkos L'inyonei Chinuch, 1986), n.p., Monographs Collection, AJHS.

52. See for example UPI, "Menorah Permit Is Revoked," *New York Times* (December 27, 1986); Lisa Foderaro, "White Plains Council Blocks Electric Menorah for Park," *New York Times* (December 3, 1991); "Travel Advisory: Hanukkah Events on Two Coasts," *New York Times* (November 28, 1993); Alejandro Alvarez, "Hanukkah Menorah," *Philadelphia Daily News* (November 28, 1994); Ron Goldwyn, "Park's a Place Where Religion Has a Place," *Philadelphia Daily News* (December 15, 1997); Editorial Opinion, "The Liberty Bell Is Symbol Enough," *Philadelphia Daily News* (December 16, 1997).

53. Schneerson, "Street Lamp Lighter."

54. "Giant Menorah on Daley Plaza," *Chabad Journal*, Chanukah issue (Skokie: Lubavitch Chabad of Illinois, 1985), n.p.

55. Mintz, *Hasidic People*, 194; Linda Greenhouse, "Court Decisions on Religious Displays," *New York Times* (July 4, 1989); "Supreme Court Rejects Pittsburgh Appeal against Menorah," *New York Times* (December 30, 1989).

56. Mintz, *Hasidic People*, 196; Libby Olar, "Off the Record," *Sentinel* (December 31, 1987), 5; "1988–1989: New York, Jan. 3. American Jewish Organizations Are Getting Involved . . . ," *Chicago Jewish Star* (December 19, 2008–2009).

57. Joseph B. Glaser to Menachem M. Schneerson, April 25, 1978; May 31, 1978; and August 14, 1978, in *Religion and State in the American Jewish Experience*, ed. Jonathan D. Sarna and David G. Dalin (Notre Dame: University of Notre Dame Press, 1997), 288–291.

58. Steven J. Whitfield, "Why America Has Not Seemed Like Exile," in *Jewish in America*, ed. Sara Blair and Jonathan Freedman (Ann Arbor: University of Michigan Press, 2007), 248; Charles S. Liebman and Steven M. Cohen, *Two Worlds of Judaism: The Israeli and American Experiences* (New Haven: Yale University Press, 1990), 107; Alan M. Dershowitz, *Vanishing American Jew: In Search of Jewish Identity for the Next Century* (Boston: Little, Brown, 1997), 350n. 41.

59. M. Herbert Danziger, *Returning to Tradition: The Contemporary Revival of Orthodox Judaism* (New Haven: Yale University Press, 1989); Lynn Davidman, *Tradition in a Rootless World: Women Turn to Orthodox Judaism* (Berkeley: University of California Press, 1991).

60. Jonathan D. Sarna, "How Hanukkah Came to the White House," *Forward* (December 2, 2009).

61. "Christmas in Public Schools," *Congregation Beth Israel Tidings* (December 1, 1972): 3.

62. Jeffrey Sinensky, Kara Stein, Danielle Samulon, and Jillian Perlberger, *Religion in the Public Schools: A Primer for Students, Parents, Teachers, and School Administrators* (New York: American Jewish Committee, August 1972); Ray Ruppert, "Guide for Schools Helps Ease a Special Christmas Problem," *Seattle Times* (December 9, 1972); White, "American Jewish Response to Christmas," 163.

63. Deborah Dash Moore, *American Jews and the Separationist Faith: The New Debate on Religion in Public Life*, ed. David G. Dalin (Washington, DC: Ethics and Public Policy Center, 1993), 84–85; Fred Bilofsky to the author, December 19, 2010.

64. Arnold M. Eisen, *Taking Hold of Torah: Jewish Commitment and Community in America* (Bloomington: Indiana University Press, 1997), 16: "I liked the Christmas carols we sang in school, except for the 'Christ the Lord' part at the end of 'O Come All Ye Faithful,' when I looked around nervously to see if the other Jewish kids were saying the words, or if the Gentile kids were noticing I wasn't. That too was a not unwelcome boundary marker, though it caused me some anxiety. It reinforced my pride in who I was and pointed to the fact that I could sing the rest of the song, even being who I was, without any hesitation."

65. As a student in the Sweet Home High School chorus, I sang Handel's "Hallelujah Chorus" under the musical direction of teacher Vera Green—a member of my synagogue.

66. Leonard J. Fein, *UAHC Long Range Planning Committee Report* (New York: UAHC, 1971); White, "American Jewish Response to Christmas," 84–85.

67. "A Chanukah Party," *NFTS* (1972), series K, box 70, folder 1, MS-73, WRJ, AJA.

68. Morrison David Bial, *Liberal Judaism at Home: The Practices of Modern Reform Judaism* (New York: Union of American Hebrew Congregations, 1971), 159–160.

69. Steven Mintz and Susan Kellogg, *Domestic Revolutions: A Social History of American Family Life* (New York: Free Press, 1988), 203–250; Putnam, *Bowling Alone*, 194.

70. Moshe Hartman and Harriet Hartman, *Gender Equality and American Jews* (Albany: SUNY Press, 1996), 61–71.

71. Patterson, *Restless Giant*, 50.

72. Tom W. Smith, *Jewish Distinctiveness in America: A Statistical Portrait* (New York: American Jewish Committee, April 2006), 34.

73. "Our President Speaks," *Women's League Outlook* (Fall 1971): 4.

74. "Our President Speaks," *Women's League Outlook* (Fall 1977): 30.

75. Sylvia Barack Fishman, *Double or Nothing? Jewish Families and Mixed Marriage* (Hanover, NH: Brandeis University Press / University Press of New England, 2004), 4–5.

76. "Notes for Now: Home for Hanukkah," *Women of Reform Judaism* (November 1992): 3.

77. Ron Wolfson, *The Art of Jewish Living: Hanukkah* (New York: Federation of Jewish Men's Clubs and University of Judaism, 1990), 155, 14.

78. Fishman, *Double or Nothing?*, 44; see also "The Changing American Jewish Family Faces the 1990s," in *Jews in America: A Contemporary Reader*, ed. Roberta Rosenberg Farber and Chaim Isaac Waxman (Hanover, NH: Brandeis University Press / University Press of New England, 1999), 51–88; Fishman, *Double or Nothing?*; Barry A. Kosmin, Sidney Goldstein, Joseph Waksberg, Nava Lerer, Ariella Keysar, and Jeffrey Scheckner, *Highlights of the Council of Jewish Federations National Jewish Population Survey* (New York: Council of Jewish Federations, 1991), 13.

79. Egon Mayer, Barry Kosmin, and Ariela Keysar, *American Jewish Identity Survey* (New York: Center for Cultural Judaism, 2001), 10.

80. Keren McGinity, *Still Jewish: A History of Women and Intermarriage in America* (New York: NYU Press, 2009).

81. Fredda Sacharow to the author, November 14, 2010; Adam Ashton to the author, December 16, 2004; Wolfson, *Art of Jewish Living*, 22–23.

82. Janet Moss to the author, January 10, 2011.

83. Judy Personk and Jim Remson, *The Intermarriage Handbook: A Guide for Jews and Christians* (New York: Quill, 1988), cited in Wolfson, *Art of Jewish Living*, 182–183; Elizabeth Pleck, *Celebrating the Family: Ethnicity, Consumer Culture, and Family Rituals* (Cambridge: Harvard University Press, 2000).

84. Peter, Paul and Mary, "Light One Candle," on *A Holiday Celebration* (Gold Castle, 1988), lyrics available at http://www.peterpaulandmary.com/music/f-15 .htm.

85. See for example E. M. Broner with Naomi Nimrod, *The Women's Haggadah* (San Francisco: HarperSanFrancisco, 1994); Michael Kagan with Zalman Schachter-Shalomi, *The Holistic Haggadah: How Will You Be Different This Passover Night?* (Jerusalem: Urim, 2004); Gershon Weiss, *The Holocaust Haggadah: Foundations of Our Faith* (Southfield, MI: Targum, 2000); David Geffen, *American Heritage Haggadah* (Jerusalem: Gefen, 1992); Roberta Kalechofsky, *The Haggadah for the Liberated Lamb* (Marblehead, MA: Micah, 1988).

86. Cokie Roberts and Steve Roberts, *Our Haggadah: Uniting Traditions for Interfaith Families* (New York: HarperCollins, 2011); Vanessa L. Ochs, "Passover on the Potomac," *Jewish Review of Books* 5 (Spring 2011): 10–12.

87. Leanne Italie, "Mainstay at Passover Seder Gets a Makeover," *NorthJersey.com* (April 14, 2011), http://www.northjersey.com/news/119824834_Mainstay_at_ Passover_Seder_gets_a_makeover.html.

88. Sorin, *Tradition Transformed*, 235

89. Irving Greenberg, *The Jewish Way: Living the Holidays* (New York: Summit Books, 1988), 29.

90. Ibid., 29, 280.

91. Ibid., 280–282.

92. See for example Hallmark's selection at http://www.hallmark.com/search/products/?context=chmkvucvsencontent%23%23-1%23.

NOTES TO THE CONCLUSION

1. "Hanukkah Illumines Darkness," *Jewish News of Greater Phoenix* (December 7, 2001).

2. Jane Ulman, "In a Dark Time, a Holiday of Light: What Is Chanukah? The Talmud Wonders," Jewish Telegraphic Agency, *Chicago Jewish Star* (December 7–20, 2001): 17.

3. Phyllis Chesler, *The New Anti-Semitism: The Current Crisis and What We Must Do about It* (San Francisco: Jossey-Bass, 2003), 40.

4. Brian Mono, "Chanukah in Wartime," *Philadelphia Jewish Exponent* (December 6, 2001): 7; and editorial, "The Essence of Chanukah," same issue, 56.

5. George W. Bush, "Remarks by the President on Lighting the Menorah," December 10, 2011, http://www.georgewbush-whitehouse.archives.gov/news/releases/2001/12/20011210-7.html.

6. Daniel S. Brenner, "Hope, Heroes, and Chanukah: In the Wake of Sept. 11 the Holiday Takes on New Meaning," *Jewish Exponent* (November 29, 2001): 36.

7. Steven K. Walz, "Making the Miracle of Chanuka More Meaningful," *Jewish Press* (Chicago) (November 30, 2001): 8.

8. Jane Ulman, "When It Comes to Chanukah, It's Hard Not to Give In to Gift-Giving," *Chicago Jewish News* (December 19–25, 2003): 23.

9. Lisa Stein, "Hanukkah Spreads Light through the Holidays," *Chicago Tribune* (December 2, 2005).

10. There are many, many websites. See for example http://www.beingjewish.com; http://www.akhlah.com; http://www.jewish.com/Chanukah; http://www.kidsdomain.com/holidays; http://learn.jtsa.edu/hanukkah; http://www.ou.org/chagim/chanukah; http://www.neohasid.org.

11. Riv-Ellen Prell, Shuly Rubin Schwartz, Michelle Blask, Myra Hirschorn, Donna Snyder, Janet Davidson, and Rona Sheramy to the author, July 4, 2012.

12. Rona Sheramy, Ellen Umansky, Harriet Hartman, Fredda Sacharow, Zara Myers, Myra Hirschorn, Gertrude Migler, Sylvia Jacobs, and Meira Itzkowitz to the author; Joe Berkofsky, "Jews by the Numbers," Jewish Telegraphic Agency, *Chicago Jewish News* (September 12–18, 2003): 25.

13. Matt Sedensky, "Chrismukkah Cards Merge Both Holidays," *Detroit Business News* (December 1, 2004).

14. Marianne Sanua, "AJC and Intermarriage: The Complexities of Jewish Continuity 1960–2006," *AJYB* 107 (2007): 1–30.

15. Joseph Berger, "With Orthodox Growth, City's Jewish Population Climbing Again," *New York Times* (June 12, 2012): A18.

16. Robert D. Putnam and David E. Campbell, *American Grace: How Religion Divides and Unites Us* (New York: Simon and Schuster, 2010), 148.

17. Ibid., 6.

18. Barbara Boyer, "Vandals Destroy a Menorah in South Philadelphia Park," *Philadelphia Inquirer* (December 21, 2005): B1.

19. Frederic Brenner, *Citizens Protesting Anti-Semitic Acts, Billings, Montana* (1994): a view through the window of a Jewish family's home damaged by bullet fire (Howard Greenberg Gallery, New York City). The photo appears on the cover of Sara Blair and Jonathan Freedman, eds., *Jewish in America* (Ann Arbor: University of Michigan Press, 2007).

20. Joshua Eli Plaut, *A Kosher Christmas: 'Tis the Season to Be Jewish* (New Brunswick: Rutgers University Press, 2012), 41.

21. Lisa Keys, "Who's Got Hanukkah Envy?," *Tablet* (December 6, 2012), http://www.tabletmag.com/jewish-life-and-religion/118178/whos-got-hanukkah-envy.

22. Rabbi Daniel Cotzin Burg, "When a Rabbi Can Appreciate Christmas Music," *Chicago Sun Times* (December 25, 2008).

23. "Festivities for the Festival of Dedication," *Chicago Jewish Star* (November 29–December 12, 2002): 13; "A Chanukah Cabaret & Holiday Celebration," flyer (December 5, 2010), Center for Jewish History, New York; "Valley Hanukkah Celebrations," *Jewish News of Greater Phoenix* (December 7, 2001); "Community Calendar," *Jewish Exponent* (December 6, 2001): 17.

24. David R. Harris, "Facebook: It's Not Just Social Networking Anymore: Best Practices for Jewish Organizations" (M.A. thesis, Hebrew Union College, April 2009), 45.

25. Temple Sinai Religious School Education Committee, "Principal's Report" (December 22, 1971), box 23, Selig Adler Collection, Butler Library, Buffalo State College.

26. "Community Calendar," *Philadelphia Jewish Exponent* (December 6, 2001): 17;

27. "Valley Hanukkah Celebrations."

28. "Eight Days of Chanukah Festivities," *Chicago Jewish Star* (November 23–December 6, 2001).

29. Judy Van Dir Stelt, "Educationally Speaking," *Congregation Rodeph Sholom Menorah* (January 2006): 7.

30. See for example "The Original What's Cooking? Restaurant," *Chicago Jewish Star* (December 23, 2005): 12.

31. Author's interview with a Maryland family, July 7, 2012.

32. Allen S. Maller, "Hanukkah: Its Rise and Fall," *Jewish Heritage* (Fall–Winter 1972): 24; Kenneth White, "American Jewish Response to Christmas" (ordination thesis, Hebrew Union College, Cincinnati, 1982), 220.

33. Wendy Doniger O'Flaherty, *Other People's Myths* (New York: Macmillan, 1988), 15.

INDEX

THE GOLDSTEIN-GOREN SERIES
IN AMERICAN JEWISH HISTORY

General editor: Hasia R. Diner

We Remember with Reverence and Love: American Jews and the Myth of Silence after the Holocaust, 1945–1962
Hasia R. Diner

Is Diss a System? A Milt Gross Comic Reader
Edited by Ari Y. Kelman

All Together Different: Yiddish Socialists, Garment Workers, and the Labor Roots of Multiculturalism
Daniel Katz

Jews and Booze: Becoming American in the Age of Prohibition
Marni Davis

Jewish Radicals: A Documentary History
Tony Michels

1929: Mapping the Jewish World
Edited by Hasia R. Diner and Gennady Estraikh

An Unusual Relationship: Evangelical Christians and Jews
Yaakov Ariel

Unclean Lips: Obscenity, Jews, and American Literature
Josh Lambert

Hanukkah in America: A History
Dianne Ashton

ABOUT THE AUTHOR

Dianne Ashton is Professor of Religion Studies and former director of the American Studies program at Rowan University. She is the author of four previous books, including the first modern biography of the American Jewish education trailblazer Rebecca Gratz (1997) and, with Ellen M. Umansky, the widely read *Four Centuries of Jewish Women's Spirituality: A Sourcebook* (1992). A newly revised edition of *Four Centuries* appeared in 2009. Her many articles on American Judaism appear in leading collections in the field. She is currently editor of the scholarly journal *American Jewish History*.